In the Name of Hawaiians

In the Name of Hawaiians

NATIVE IDENTITIES
AND
CULTURAL POLITICS

Rona Tamiko Halualani

University of Minnesota Press
Minneapolis / London

Published by the University of Minnesota Press
111 Third Avenue South, Suite 290
Minneapolis, MN 55401-2520
http://www.upress.umn.edu

Library of Congress Cataloging-in-Publication Data

Halualani, Rona Tamiko.
    In the name of Hawaiians : native identities and cultural politics / Rona Tamiko Halualani.
        p.   cm.
    Includes bibliographical references and index.
    ISBN 0-8166-3726-1 (hardback : alk. paper) — ISBN 0-8166-3727-X (pbk. : alk. paper)
        1. Hawaiians—Ethnic identity.   2. Hawaiians—Government relations.
    3. Hawaiians—Migrations.   I. Title.
    DU624.65 .H345 2002
    305.89942—dc21
                                                                                    2002005311

Printed in the United States of America on acid-free paper

The University of Minnesota is an equal-opportunity educator and employer.

12 11 10 09 08 07 06 05 04 03 02   10 9 8 7 6 5 4 3 2 1

Contents

Acknowledgments

I have been thinking through and composing this project ever since I was young and actively seeking out my Hawaiian identity. As a diasporic Hawaiian, the questions about my identity are never easy: I am Hawaiian but not a former resident of Hawai'i, my ancestral homeland. I have been enculturated into my Hawaiianness by way of a differently assembled historical memory, as constituted by popular tourist sites and texts, official history books, Hawaiian summer camps, and photographs and stories of family I have never met. This different relation should not be deemed inferior, as it usually is by society's many efforts to reauthenticate the original homeland site; rather, my positionality has provided me with a unique view and perspective on Hawaiian cultural politics. Blood quantum stands as "proof" of my Hawaiianness while my positionality as an "off-island" Hawaiian threatens any claim of native authenticity that I make (let alone my claims in writing a book about Hawaiian identity). I have always been interested in the linkages, disconnections, oppositions, and contradictions in identifying Hawaiians over time and in identifying who I am. My lifelong journey can be traced through each page of this book as I write with my family and my Hawaiian private memory in mind, heart, and spirit.

This project would not have been possible without the loving support and critical insights of my parents, Ronald Alohikea Halualani and

Jennie Halualani, and my brothers, Michael and Roger Halualani. My father provided a much-needed critical focus to the book and pushed me to examine the historical context surrounding the Hawaiians and the social injustices done to them. His life experiences as a Hawaiian born and raised on a Hawaiian homestead became an invaluable and rare source of knowledge. I have embarked on this project with my family in mind, those in the mainland and Hawaiʻi and those who lived before me and are no longer with us (namely the remembered "faces" featured in this book: my great grandmother Eva Kahula Alohikea Halualani Kahauolopua, my grandmother Hattie Kuʻulei Namahoe Halualani, and my grandfather John Ululani Halualani).

This book, originally my doctoral dissertation from the Department of Communication at Arizona State University, made it to press because of the strong encouragement and advice from David Theo Goldberg, my dissertation chair and mentor. His insights and critiques, and his confidence in my work, inspired me to further develop the book. I owe a great debt of gratitude to Thomas Nakayama, Kent Ono, and Leah VandeBerg for their ongoing advice, interest, and mentorship in my academic career. Angela Tretheway and Lisa Flores provided valuable feedback and support for this project. I have been fortunate to have worked with a wonderfully supportive editor, Carrie Mullen, who always believed in this project. The comments and suggestions by Wendy Ho and Davianna Pōmaikaʻi McGregor were key in strengthening my analysis. I have also gained important insights from my conversations about cultural politics and identity with my graduate school contemporaries: Lily Mendoza, Jolanta Drzewiecka, Anu Chitgopekar, and Tim Kuhn, all of whom have always supported and helped to fill the theoretical gaps in my work.

This book project was supported by the Faculty Career Development Grant and the California State University Research Grant from San José State University. My "home," the Department of Communication Studies at San José State University, and my chair, Dennis Jaehne, greatly encouraged the completion of this book and provided much-needed institutional and collegial support. I also thank Wendy Ho, Kent Ono, and the Asian American Studies Department at the University of California at Davis for the invitation to present my book chapters to the Asian Pacific American Cultural Politics Research Group in spring 2000.

I appreciate the expedient assistance from and reprint permission provided by Gary Fitzpatrick at Editions Limited Publishing; DeSoto Brown; and Kevin Leamon and the Dixson Galleries, State Library of New South Wales Mitchell Library, Sydney, Australia. Special thanks go to my Aunty Haleloke and Uncle Allen Goo for their cooperation and for providing the Halualani photo album. I also extend thanks to Kunio Sato for the beautiful reprints of my family photographs. *Mahalo a nui loa!*

Finally, my partner in life, Kung Chiao, inspired me to continue on an extremely long, hard road. You always accompanied me on the many research trips required for this book. I value the loving support you always give me and I thank you for pushing me to take up new challenges.

Glossary of Hawaiian Words

Translations from Mary Kawena Pukui and S. H. Elbert, *Hawaiian Dictionary* (1986).

ahupuaʻa	land division usually extending from the uplands to the sea
ʻāina	land, earth
akua	god, goddess, spirit
aliʻi	chief, ruler, monarch, nobility
Aliʻi Nui	high chief
haole	formerly, foreigner; now, White person, American, Englishman, Caucasian
kanaka	human being; Hawaiian (plural is *kānaka*)
kapu	taboo; prohibition

koko	blood
konohiki	supervisor or the head of an *ahupua'a* land division under the chief
Kū	ancient Hawaiian god of war
kūpuna	grandparent, ancestor, relative, or close friend of the grandparent's generation
lāhui	nation, race, tribe, or people
Lono	one of the four major gods brought from Kahiki; god of fertility and agriculture
māhele	portion, division, section; *Ka Mahele* denotes the land division of 1848
maka'āinana	commoner; people in general
mana	supernatural or divine power; power
mō'ī	king, sovereign, monarch, ruler
'ohana	family, relative, kin group
pi'ikoi	to claim to be of higher rank than one is; to claim honors not rightfully due

Introduction
The Legacy of Identity

Deep within the historical imagination, there lies the image of a Western explorer surrounded by dark and strange natives. A gold-embossed frame presents the intricately painted figure of Captain James Cook, rifle in hand, who faces the "native" from the ever-famous Pacific story of Western contact. The naked "natives," each indistinguishable from another, sneak up behind an unsuspecting Cook, with spears in hand, ready to strike at any moment.[1]

Across from this image (in the intersecting space between historical memory and tourist fantasy), one can move toward the native's hut *(hale),* made of *pili* grass and *ti* leaves, absorbing literally hundreds of ancient ("primitive") artifacts (e.g., spears, adzes, pieces of *kapa, ipu* gourds, or containers from precontact Hawai'i). Through a rear opening in the *hale,* you can see him preparing food; he sits on a floor scraping two objects together. Around him, there is nothing—no adornments, no *'ohana,* no other counterparts. He is the sole spectacle and memory of nativism and Hawaiianness: dark, premodern, and male.

In the modern and postmodern spaces of tourism, images of an antiquated nativism that is already dead are quickly consumed. Visitors rush to witness former native living sites, artifacts, and material traces of "what used to be the cultural past." Most, however, are exposed to widely imagined reflections of Hawaiians splashed over travel posters, advertisements, T-shirts, and souvenirs around the globe: the requisite hula girl and her sexualized body, the native male surfer, the happy, *'ukulele*-playing Hawaiian who greets you as you walk by, and the famed *Aloha* spirit (the notion that Hawai'i and Hawaiians are naturally benevolent, generous, and willing to share everything Hawaiian: native residency, experience, artifacts, and identity).

In cooperation, the State of Hawaii codifies the *Aloha* spirit into the civil discourse and ideology of multiculturalism. For instance, the state defines the Hawai'i Multiculturalism Model as "a shared tradition of tolerance and peaceful coexistence . . . which can be traced to the traditional Hawaiian value of 'Aloha.'"[2] The most powerful form of unifying magic—one that would not only mitigate the struggle over the meaning of Hawaiianness but name the very struggle an antisocial threat to civil life and everything Hawaiian—lies within the local Hawaii State discourse of multiculturalism. From such a tradition, there emerges "harmonious race and ethnic relations . . . evident in 'cordial' and 'low keyed' social relationships and in relatively high rates of intermarriage compared to the continental United States"[3] and "'equalization of opportunity and status' in the ethnic stratification order."[4] Indeed, multiculturalism is a spirit that creates a shared "'local' culture and identity evident in 'multicultural lifestyles' and based on points of commonality."[5] Multiculturalism in Hawai'i thus seems to stand as both an exemplar of productive, positive social relations and, on a closer level, an illustration of Hawaiianness itself. Peaceful relations and equalized citizenry—not activist challenge or dueling claims over the indigenous—are hailed and identified as *aloha kanaka* (love for people) or the "Native Hawaiian legacy of tolerance."[6] More specifically, Hawai'i's multiculturalism is hailed precisely because it has taken on the semblance of a Hawaiian origin or an interiority that seems native. The proclaimed multicultural unity and racial equality in the name of Hawaiians also confuse and defuse the protest practices of Hawaiian sovereignty and land activists as largely "un-Hawaiian," "racist," and "antisocial."

As every aspect of the State of Hawaii and its citizen-subjects are deemed Hawaiian, the specific cultural and racialized group of Hawaiians is denied any claim of being so. As a result of the 1921 Hawaiian Homes Commission Act (HHCA), a Native Hawaiian means "any descendant of not less than one-half part of the blood of the races inhabiting the Hawaiian Islands previous to 1778."[7] In order to claim Hawaiianness and homestead leases and benefits in the name of Hawaiians, individuals must formally substantiate their 50 percent blood quantum in a process of identification administered and enforced by the State Department of Hawaiian Home Lands (DHHL), a process that requires the presentation of official and formal records of their Hawaiian ancestors: birth, marriage, and death certificates, and census records. Many Hawaiians to this day, however, cannot formally prove their Hawaiianness.

Hawaiian sovereignty movement activists are featured in the popular press, with their stance of self-determination and independent rule for a Hawaiian nation.[8] These images of challenge present the most extreme picture of a culture and place of *Aloha*. At a recent event commemorating the illegal overthrow of the Hawaiian monarchy in 1893, one sovereignty activist shouted, "We are the true people of Hawai'i, an independent nation that has long been established." Yet, on the continental U.S. mainland, settled diasporic Hawaiian communities are moving into their first and second generations of mainland Hawaiians born and raised away from Hawai'i. In fact, about one third of the total number of Hawaiians live on the continental U.S. mainland.[9] According to Jon, an eighteen-year-old Hawaiian male, born and raised in Las Vegas, Nevada, who has never been to Hawai'i, "In community practice, my teacher told of our past. How for centuries we lived in an ordered society, ruled by *ali'i* and then it changed as more and more outsiders came. The sovereign period had ended with the 1893 overthrow of the kingdom. Which is how I am here today. The Hawaiian people left home when their home changed . . . to Oregon, Washington, California, New York, and Nevada." In the diaspora, Hawaiians therefore frame themselves as culturally authentic natives with a strong tie to their culture.

Identities are legacies in the making. In critical, cultural, and postcolonial studies, we have retheorized identity as a formation greater than personal affirmation, self-recognition, natural essence, or mere invented rhetorical tradition. Instead, identity stands as a larger social arena in which specific meanings of "who we are" are connected to and combined with certain practices, subject positions, and power interests. At an unseen level, these meanings of identity are organized in line with historically specific conditions, structural interests, and colonial periods of occupation. Identity articulations created in specific historical moments and by powerful structures (national powers, the legal and economic state, and government agencies) are hegemonically embedded

into social belief and some of these articulations are continually reproduced by structural-dominant power interests. Moreover, articulations
of identity shaped by excised or overwritten groups remain held and
understood within the dominant terms of already established discourses.
It is through these conditions of historical dominance, signifying power,
and political interest that constitute identity over time that a legacy of
meaning is born.

The aforementioned instances, spanning a range of historical and
political moments and contexts, are linked together in what I theorize as
a *legacy of identity.* Each instance reveals a specific, vested articulation of
Hawaiian or "native" identity. Identity constructions are never neutral
or equivalent to one another but rather are advanced by differently located power interests such as colonial forces, the nation-state, missionaries, state citizens and residents, and the indigenous native group. I use
the term *legacy,* then, to refer to the historicized fixities and reproduced
meanings of identity over time. That is, while poststructuralist theories
emphasize that the signifier-signified relation is inherently unnecessary,
the authoritative history of particular social forces can indeed produce
necessary relations of identity. For example, certain images and signified
meanings of Hawaiian identity—Hawaiians as prehuman natives, as a
naturally benevolent people of *Aloha,* and as a race determined by blood
amount—have been naturalized over time through the historical establishment, endurance, and gained power of structured interests (colonial/
neocolonial forces, the federal and local states, and the capitalist marketplace). Historical texts have identified Hawaiians as both primitive savages and a generous people defined in contradistinction from Native
Americans. Tourist venues continue to represent Hawaiians as a people
never meant to exist into modernity and as "dead" in tours of empty,
archaeologically framed cultural sites and homes of past *ali'i.* U.S. federal and local state mandates define Hawaiian identity as derivative of a
specific blood amount. Hawaiianness, therefore, has become inexorably bound to "prehumanity," "native," and "blood" images because
of the historically extensive presence of Western power and U.S. neocolonialism. It is clear then that Hawaiian identity cannot be separated
from dominant identifications of "prehumanity" and "nativism." Historically, these significations have articulated and framed the conditions
through which Hawaiian identity is constituted, theorized, challenged,
and remade.

In this book, I trace the legacy of Hawaiian identity that I have un-covered in my deeply personal journey through contextually specific identity encodings and theories about identity and the social subject. More specifically, I analyze the significations of Hawaiian identity across several interrelated contexts: representations and narratives of the his-torical imaginary (museum culture, explorer journals, and maps), law and governance (U.S. census technology, blood quantum mandates, government commissions, and the neocolonial administration), tourism (sites, tours, discourses, and performances; and "Hawaiiana" curios, col-lectibles, and representations), and lived community practice (diasporic mainland Hawaiian community remakings of identity via private memo-ry histories and narrative performances in terms of civic clubs and pri-vate families). These contexts—the historical imaginary, law and gover-nance, tourism, and diasporic community practice—are highlighted because they represent larger forces from different historical moments that significantly changed the social relations surrounding Hawaiians, the ways in which they have been identified, and how they make sense of "who they are." For instance, through constructions of prehumanity, settlement patterns, and the Captain Cook tale, explorer and anthropo-logical accounts have historicized the Hawaiian (male) out of moderni-ty, civility, and indigenous claims. Western law and governance fused re-ligious ideology and economic incentive via "capitalist virtue," thereby excising the Hawaiian indigenous subject and producing a new hier-archy of identities: the raced Hawaiians as "prehuman, soon-to-be-extinct" aborigines strange to modernity; the sovereign white resident (the *haole* or foreigner who claims supreme authority, rights, and privi-leges as a "native" to Hawai'i), an identity position politically endorsed and recognized by national governance at home (the empire) and in Hawai'i; and the supposedly "raceless" citizen-subject created through incorporated Western and U.S. legal practices such as the "equal" land-application process, due process and procedure, and individual protec-tion by law. Throughout the 1900s, as U.S. nation building and Western capitalism merged, the tourist industry, local government, and popular culture re-created a "native"/Hawaiian so fantastical and spectacled that consumption became both an escape and class privilege (a "native" you could experience through the reenactment of "his" demise at tour sites). Global capitalism intensified and naturalized the traveling of the Ha-waiian and its geographic placement, ultimately reconstructing a "new native" with the meaningfulness of moral character and a civilizing Western ideology of love. Resulting from global capitalism's depressing impact on the local economy and survival of Hawaiians, the migration of Hawaiians to the mainland has forever changed the ways in which Hawaiian identity is experienced and performed. This has led to the reworkings of Hawaiian identity (as in, for example, the redefinitions of Hawaiianness that are based on historical/collective memory as opposed to geographic residency and the redeployment of tourist spectacles to speak to mainland Hawaiians).

THEORETICAL FRAMEWORK: IDENTITY, CULTURAL
STUDIES, AND ARTICULATION

This project grew out of my experiences as a diasporic Hawaiian woman who was born and raised in the mainland (suburban California). Most people have presumed that I am a "rooted islander," falsely believing that to be Hawaiian, you must have been born and raised there, remaining only a temporary migrant in the mainland. Yet, my identification as a Hawaiian has been much different and "disorganized" from that of my father, a Hawaiian man born on the Hawaiian homestead of Keaukaha, Hawaiʻi. While we both strongly identify with the Hawaiian culture, we each experienced different ways of invoking and relating to our culture, remembering our histories, and practicing our Hawaiianness. My father was surrounded by the language and practices of Hawaiian culture; I first encountered and identified with my culture via popularized television discourses and tourist spectacles about Hawaiʻi and its people.

Over the years, while trying to understand both my cultural history and my experience as a Hawaiian in the diaspora, I confronted several questions: Who are the Hawaiians? What does it mean to be a Hawaiian? What are the boundaries of authentic Hawaiian membership (especially with regard to the notion that Hawaiians live on ʻāina)? But I noticed many colliding versions and accounts of Hawaiian identity that circulated in historical and popular discourse when I looked at examples of what constitutes being Hawaiian or native to Hawaiʻi. Thus, my questions merged into a larger one: What are the different identity positions created *in the name of Hawaiians* by larger structural interests (federal and state law and governance, official history discourses, tourist and commercial sites), various resident groups of Hawaiʻi (Locals, or those groups that immigrated to Hawaiʻi in the mid- to late 1800s), and Hawaiians themselves (those who can claim Hawaiian descendancy and reside in Hawai'i or on the continental mainland)?[10] I grew curious as to how identity constructions "in the name of Hawaiians" emanated from a wide-ranging field of differently vested interests (e.g., indigenous local and diasporic Hawaiians, colonial forces, state structures, and resident groups of Hawai'i), each one articulating the terms that constitute the cultural character of Hawaiians and specifically who is entitled to native rights and belonging, with some interests gaining more signifying power and political and economic benefit than others.

I have always been drawn to identity constructions that I have seen play out in my own life, topics that are rarely discussed in current academic literature: the historical encoding of Hawaiians as benevolent, the abstraction of Hawaiianness into citizenship, tourist spectacles as forms of identification for Hawaiians, the racialization of Hawaiians through blood quantum and its impact on the lives of everyday Hawaiians, and the growing interregional network of diasporic Hawaiian communities in the continental United States and the unique subjectivity of diasporic Hawaiians. Thus, I contribute a larger analysis of Hawaiian identity and the neglected aspects above to the extant scholarly research on Hawaiians, most of which is either historical-anthropological analyses of ancient Hawai'i, sovereignty movement works, or legal analyses of past legislative acts and trials affecting Hawaiians.[11]

Identity and the Social Subject

In the Name of Hawaiians: Native Identities and Cultural Politics stands as a retheorizing of the relationship between identity, social agency, and power. My theoretical detour represents not a more truthful or verifiable path but one that labors to recognize and trace the historically specific developments and practices of identity affecting and shaping a particular social group. It is a space where I explore—for the moment—the productions of culture, identity, and lived experience through social formations in the context of Hawaiians. It is also a theoretical moment through which I recognize their struggle over subjectivity as starkly difficult and creatively lived.

An analysis of identity and the social subject reveals pressure points between poststructuralism and cultural studies. From the realm of poststructuralist studies, the social subject is trapped within its imagined extremes: at one end, shaped through and contained underneath structural law, authority, and power, its movements are always known and never free; at the other, unshackled from structural determinations, it moves freely without consequence.[12] In the infamous divide between structuralism-culturalism and poststructuralism, there would either be a doomed struggle over freedom *or* the luxury of freedom without struggle.[13] Here the subject, firmly held hostage by formalizing theory, is wholly undervalued and engaged as mere abstraction.

Cultural studies lives precisely within the tensions between a guaranteed sociality (via ideological determinations and a chain of equivalences) and celebratory individuated pluralism without social structures. Stuart Hall addresses the debate over the nature of society and the origin and operations of the social subject.[14] In so doing, Hall, with specific contexts in mind, theorizes the neglected space overlapping the culturalist and poststructuralist positions. Culturalism lays claim to a totality of social "givens" or guarantees; "the coherence and totality of a particular social structure (and the nature of the power relations within it) are already given, defined as a series of correspondences between different levels of social experiences, cultural practices, economic and political relations."[15] From this perspective, each identity, cultural practice, and representation belongs to some fixed structural origin, particularly having to do with the economic. Identities naturally correspond with particular experiences and power relations in the first or last instance or from a stable place. Through its structural formation, the social subject is known at all times, thus codifying an abstract principle of necessary correspondence regarding social life, identity, and politics. Social action and resistance are narrowly foreseen in "simple unity."[16]

The poststructuralist turn unleashes the individuated subject from a network of fixities to one of pluralistic differences and subject positions where anything is possible. "There are no necessary relations, no correspondences; that is guaranteed outside of any concrete struggle."[17] Power is therefore without structure or organization; it is individually brought out through micropractices, or the sole actions of the undetermined and socially unaffected subject. The subject, placed into and yet detached from a positionality, can roam the free world of signification, fragmentation, and contradiction, this being the nature of an individual and decentered agency severed from a field of forces. As a theory of necessary noncorrespondence, this theoretical turn plays on our social hopes of optimal agency, tormenting us all the while with promises often placed outside of any real sense of power.

Cultural studies therefore moves within the theoretical divide between culturalism and poststructuralism. Projects from this vein underscore the sociohistorical production of society and its subjects by way of historical specificity, social struggle (through which community and individual acts of challenge are possible), and a "structure in dominance," or a concrete assemblage of relatively autonomous "social relations, practices, and experiences."[18] Thus, from context to context, moment to moment, structural forms (governmental authority, the nation-state, the apparatus of citizenship, education, media, and community) are recognized as formatively shaping the nature of the subject. Society is understood through its specific placement in an organized yet varied arrangement of power relations, social hierarchies, and everyday experiences and also through its unspoken spaces. Indeed, while a field of forces requires a mapping, so too must a critical eye seek out possible spaces open for resignifying and remaking the already-spoken conditions in which social subjects live. This is less an attempt to theorize as abstraction the fixity of resistance; it is more characteristic of a commitment to optimistically uphold social agency but within historically limited and produced conditions. This notion requires a strong belief in social freedom within the depths of often overdetermined and suppressive structural forces. With such a spirit, to understand the relational points, near or far, between the different and relatively autonomous levels of society (the governmental, legal, economic, and everyday), power, and meaning is to do the work of cultural studies. Cultural studies scholars remember and explore the complexity of Marx's notion that subjects "make history in conditions not of their own making."[19] It is a remembrance often too difficult to translate into concrete interrogations, with historical specificity, contextual engagement, and compassion for community its most tragic costs.

In the spirit of Stuart Hall and Lisa Lowe, then, culture is the site of struggle over meanings and practices implicated in a hierarchy of locationalities.[20] Identity represents the specific nexus of such a struggle. Hall eloquently frames this as a point of suture; the pressure point of the "discourses and practices which attempt to 'interpellate,' speak to us or hail us into place as the social subjects of particular discourses" in relation to "the processes which produce subjectivities, which construct us as subjects which can be 'spoken.'"[21] Identities are "points of temporary attachment to the subject positions which discursive practices construct for us."[22] Thus, identity names an uneven and shaky dialectic among several hierarchies of meaning and significance.

But, as in any political struggle, we are not forever doomed to ideological operations of subject formation as fully determined products.[23] Rather, we are socially and historically constituted subjects who undergo processes of change, transformation, and resignification. During these processes, social subjects encounter a dynamic struggle of meaning in which their "willing consent" to social structures and identity positions is never fully guaranteed but continually solicited through ideological and hegemonic practices.[24] In this way, social experience and positionality enable subjects to pivot between different kinds of consciousness, using the historicity of experience and oppression to challenge particular identity (mis)recognitions and subjections.[25]

The *unfixed yet marked* social subject is constituted, therefore, by many overlapping structures and determinations: the institutional arenas of law, governance, and regulation; state or official memory; and global capitalism. While seemingly autonomous, these different structures work in line and in conjunction with one another, powerfully establishing overdetermining conditions for particular subject positions. Consequently, resistance and change call for an in-depth analysis of identity constructions through multiple axes of power and, then, ferreting out identity challenges and resignifications at uncovered pressure points. For example, in the case of indigenous groups seeking official status as sovereign nations such as Hawai'i, the power to fully resignify one's self or group requires not only a politically resistive consciousness among social members but formal recognition from structural forms of power (e.g., the law, governmental status, state agency certification). Identity thus becomes an ongoing contest between competing subject positions and the political interests bringing those positions into being.

Articulation

With a cultural studies framework of identity, I embrace the theoretical and methodological practice of articulation as my central guide. According to the key works of Ernesto Laclau and Chantal Mouffe and the reconceptualizations of Stuart Hall, articulation names a powerfully engaging practice of tracing how ideological forces, structured meanings, and identified social groups cohere and are necessarily linked through various relational significations: difference, opposition, conflict, likeness/

sameness, and paradox.[26] They encourage us to rethink circulated discourses, symbols, meanings, and identifications not as being naturally there but as requiring cultural work (the constant interplay of discursive and signified rearticulations) to appear so necessary in nature. These discussions speak to the complex arena of identity as more than self-recognitions, natural essences, or invented traditions and constructed "nostalgia." Hall adds that indeed identity cannot be conceptualized in this old way nor can it ignore the core issues of power in social life.[27] That is, how are we, as social-historical subjects, related to power in terms of the structural forces that invisibly inscribe how we see and enact "who we are"? And what are the ways in which we can actively move through framed conditions? These questions mark the cornerstones of identity.

Meanings in or against correspondence, according to Hall, are historically produced much in the same way a "structure in dominance" historically comes into being. Over time, these meanings are naturalized into particular relations, structures of power and signification, and correspondences. Correspondences establish and seem to guarantee specific practices and identities. But, with no such guarantee, Hall urges us to ask how these correspondences and relations are articulated.[28] How are these meanings and significations connected to and combined with certain practices, subject positions, and experiences? How are they organized in line with structural interests? This type of inquiry compels a powerful theory of articulation, or the critical insight into the specific struggles over meaning and the varied, unexpected yet historically lingering ways in which meaning is produced, reproduced, and reassembled via relations of "essence," "similarity," "difference," "paradox," and "contradiction," among others. Through Hall's influence, articulation brings us closer to understanding the difficult yet hopeful positioning of the subject within historical formations and structural conditions of power.

Lawrence Grossberg further emphasizes that articulation is "the production of identity on top of differences, of unities, of fragments, of structures across practices. Articulation links this practice to that effect, this text to that meaning to that reality, these experiences to those politics. And these links are themselves articulated into larger structures."[29] Articulation enables cultural studies scholars to examine a context deeply and to unveil *how* meanings constituting subject positions are aligned with and against one another into unpredictable, unimaginable articulated combinations and the political operations of such relations. The practice of articulation problematizes and, at the same time, reinvigorates the theoretical purview of cultural studies by enabling a deeper analysis into how subject positions, meanings, and social relations are bound together through connotative or signifying marks and how these create certain political effects.

History, context, and power all shed light on how some structures of meaning may, in fact, become normatively established as necessarily corresponding. For example, since the passage of the 1921 HHCA, Hawaiian identity and factual parentage of 50 percent blood quantum are continually signified as necessarily equivalent; thus, it is this articulation of a *necessarily corresponding structure* between meanings—tying together "blood relations" and Hawaiianness—that needs to be analyzed in the context of Hawaiians. How did this articulation historically come into being? What were/are its operations of identification? How do Hawaiian communities practice this articulation?

In analyzing articulated structures, we revisit signified meanings as seductively enclosing and yet unguaranteed, shifting, and in relation to power interests and historical moments.[30] We can no longer presume that meanings are guaranteed or remain stable over time (or even that such meanings are necessarily unguaranteed or in dynamic political motion) or that identity is homogeneously constituted or uniformly invoked.

Through articulation, I explore the interrelationships among subject positions in the name of Hawaiians in different spheres and among different political interests. More specifically, articulation lends insight into how particular subject positions have been articulated as essentially and naturally Hawaiian throughout history and also how opposing subject positions have confined the material options of Hawaiians. For example, how is it that a "Hawaiianness at heart" (the popular notion that any person, regardless of ethnicity, descendancy, or residency, can become a member of the Hawaiian culture) has been articulated at the same time and in opposition to the 50 percent factual parentage definition of Hawaiianness (the official statute that defines Hawaiians in terms of scientific and verifiable criteria that must be met in order to claim benefits, loans, and land leases delimited specifically for Hawaiians)? How is the opposition of these two subject positions necessary for the disidentification of Hawaiians? How does the construct of "Hawaiianness at heart" privilege a position of dislocation for tourists, residents, and Locals in

Hawai'i? How does this articulated combination of "Hawaiianness at heart" and "pure or 50 percent blood Hawaiian" operate and what are its political consequences? This book uncovers these questions about unforeseen relations of meaning and identity positions that lie deep within the context.

For Hawaiians, identity significations are articulated through historically specific shifts (e.g., colonizing "initial contact," the structural dissolution of a system based on *'āina* to one of capitalist virtue, population decimation) and the imperialist project by European (the British, French, Spanish, and Russian governments) and U.S. interests; the varied distribution of power (e.g., political conquest, missionary cleansing, economic trade and business, military occupation, tourist commodification); legal (mis)recognitions; government agencies created to "be Native" as in the case of the state-affiliated Office of Hawaiian Affairs (OHA); seemingly unitary narrative constructions of "who we once were" by Hawaiian sovereignty groups; and material claims to land, territory, and self-determination. All of these layers, interrelated and contradictory at times, underscore how identity construction/reconstruction among different indigenous cultures entails *much more* than a reactionary debate about who gets to be truly "Native," at the exclusion of others. These layers illustrate that Hawaiianness comes into being in social relation to other categories—nativism, foreignness, race, gender, nationalism, and citizenship—and other spheres—the historical imagination, law and governance, the boundaries of modernity, tourist discourses and the postmodern fantasy of travel, and private community practice and sovereignty discourses—if in uneven and contradictory ways. Across these modes of power and configured relations, subject positions in the name of Hawaiians are produced in specific historical and institutional sites and carry different political implications. Through these spheres, we are articulated and chained into particular subject positions and summoned—by way of ideological forces, sociopolitical conditions, and social classifications—to partially, temporarily, or completely invoke structured forms of Hawaiianness.

Through cultural studies ethnography and the theoretical concept of articulation, I trace the formations of identity *in the name of* Hawaiians and how these identity positions operate in terms of specific power interests and cultural and speaking practices. I use this marker—*in the name of*—to signify the different political interests and positions that construct, shape, and benefit from identity constructions of Hawaiian-ness. I recognize that this marker can indicate different power interests from moment to moment and refer to subject positions of Hawaiian-ness created and practiced by Hawaiians themselves (or those who are genealogically linked and connected through historical memory) as well as dominant and structural interests (e.g., history proper by explorers, academics, and military-appointed historians, tourist industries, federal acts and legislative mandates, nation-state administrations and discourses, everyday speech acts and vernacular discourses). Sometimes, the identity discourses in the name of Hawaiians issued by communities and the state appear to be uniform but may, in fact, be understood, practiced, and located quite differently in terms of the political histories, interests, and benefits surrounding the subject positions that are articulated. Thus, each identity articulation's form, positionality, and surrounding legacy of significations need to be closely traced in dynamic fashion so as to truly engage the contextually embedded cultural politics surrounding Hawaiian identity.

Throughout this book, I firmly hold Hawaiians as a lived group filled with members who are genealogically linked and connected through performed social relations and a historical memory of cultural beginnings, meanings, and practices, as well as crises, upheavals, and unjust subjections as a dispossessed and (mis)recognized people. This conceptualization has been informed by my situated position as a Hawaiian and my lived practice of a differently constituted nativism: that of a diasporic mainland Hawaiian who grew up away from *ʻāina* and yet is still bound to a historical memory of Hawaiianness.

In the Name of Hawaiians speaks to the challenge of theorizing identity as posed by Frantz Fanon, Ernesto Laclau, Chantal Mouffe, and Stuart Hall and presents new theoretical insights informed by the historical specificity of the struggle over Hawaiian identity. There are three major conclusions in this analysis. First, as I analyze the historical imaginary in the name of Hawaiians in relation to Western law and governance and tourism, I confront the structured encodings of the prehuman native, the blooded legal subject, and the "neonative," all powerfully inviting and spoken with force even in its disembodiment (or failed "full" hailing). As I wrote this book, I questioned my fixation on these identity positions and their political effectivity for Hawaiians. I constantly asked, Why is it that my project always leads back to analyzing these dominant

forms of Hawaiian identity? I realized later that my penchant for preferred meanings unveiled precisely the tricky nature of articulated
Hawaiianness.

I was in the midst of Hawaiian identity at its most extreme operation: its naturalized linkage in both identifying Hawaiianness *and* in-
terrogating the work of identity. Thus, the fantastical contact between
Cook and the "before-time native" who is settled and mapped through
the racializing iconography of the geographic; the native who is "soft
and savage," or "naturally" benevolent yet still primitive; the "native"
who is blooded as a primordialist vestige of a time never meant to exist
in modernity; he and she, the "gone" Hawaiian in Waimea Falls Park,
the tragically misplaced queen, and the spectacled hula girl. All of these
structured identifications of Hawaiianness reveal how meanings can be
reproduced and rearticulated so persistently that, in Mouffe's words,
"over time [they] become so inbred that they are assumed to have been
linked since the beginning of language."[31] The ideal positionings of
Hawaiianness for the historical reader, tourist, and through the deemed
authority of history, anthropology, museums, the supposedly neutral
state, and the commodification of travel are naturalized into place. So it
is no longer enough to theorize that such meanings are articulated by
the structural forces of the historical, the legal, and the economic. At
this moment, it is imperative that we acknowledge these significations as
lingering legacies constituted precisely through the historical establishment, endurance, and gained reproductive power of structured interests
(Western and U.S. colonialism and neocolonialism, the state, and the
marketplace) over time. While the signifier-signified relation is inherently unnecessary, the authoritative history of particular social forces can
produce necessary relations of identity. Hawaiianness, therefore, has become inexorably bound to "prehumanity" and "native" images because
of the historically extensive presence of Western (namely, U.S.) colonial
power, and as such Hawaiian identity cannot be severed from these
dominant identifications. Historically, these significations have articulated and framed the conditions through which Hawaiian identity is constituted, theorized, and challenged. In acknowledging this, I recognize
both the colonialist dispossession of Hawaiians and their imaginative re-
organizations of imposed meanings. Specifically, in chapter 5, Hawaiian
community members practice differently their cast images of "prehumanity" and "nativism"—through blooded speech and hierarchies and

tourist faces—thereby illustrating the power these forms exert on Hawaiian subjectivity and the necessity with which these form and outline Hawaiianness.

My drawn-out lingering over dominant images reflects then their seeming naturalness—their deep imbrication into the political situation affecting Hawaiians. I could not ignore or deny their necessity to Hawaiian identity. Their historicized weight and seamlessness hold me, eventually leading me to encodings that identify Hawaiians and larger insights about the politics of identity. Identity can become necessary given the time and space of enforced and dispersed dominant power. Such a claim powerfully resonates in the face of deadlocked abstract debates between theoretical positions that either affirm the predominance of social structural spheres or shun the necessity of any meaning or structure. My project locates contextually and historically a reproduced assemblage of meanings—"prehumanity," "normative benevolence," "new natives," and primordialist blooded subjects—made necessary and endemic to the identity and lived conditions of Hawaiians. Could it be that eventually our theoretical detours would reveal a moment when necessary correspondence and the historical limits of meaning become more stabilized points of identity signification? That is, in the long divide between culturalism and poststructuralism, essentialism and antiessentialism, we still would have to figure out what to do with historicized fixities and accumulating traditions of meanings. Would the point of fixities historically brought into being lock my position into that of romantic essentialism or make a theorizing of resistance grim? In the Hawaiian context, analyzing the articulations of Hawaiianness has resurrected history as an assemblage of meanings, structured in dominance over time, eventually becoming established, somewhat stable, and double-sided. Thus, as anthropology, discovery, and the colonial nation intermingled, images of the "native" and their inherent cultural nature were shaped and naturalized so intensely that societal common sense has inherited, invoked, and reproduced museum-like significations of Hawaiians (and made it so that anything geographic to Hawai'i is naturally Hawaiian—people, goods, practices, and politics). This has forever shaped the relation between Hawaiians and history, place, and origins; it provided the raw material for how they would protest their historical condition of colonialism and the contemporary politics of sovereignty. So too, tourism magnifies the Hawaiian exotic primarily through reliving its archaic nature, its demise in the modern world. Tourism's commodified historical fantasies have also become confused with and a part of Hawaiian cultural practice. The state administration and blood technology have forever changed the terms through which Hawaiians are identified and how they see themselves in relation to others. These meanings represent traditions brought to life through historicization and the reproduction of dominant power interests.

And with such lingering legacies, the promise of the conjunctural and social agency seems that much more difficult to locate, unless you explore the seemingly locked-in edges of dominant identifications. In Stuart Hall's notion of suturing, social agency can be located deeply within and at the edge of necessary meanings: at its overdetermined limits. Overdetermination describes the overlaid activity of structural meanings, the overloaded network of relations, from a variety of forces (e.g., capitalism, patriarchy, nationalism, and colonial power, to name a few) and social practices of agents; forces that variously grate against each other, open up fissures, and remain temporarily in process. The interests collide and at some point implode, illustrating the multiplicity or doubleness of signifying power within a network of Hawaiian overdeterminations—that any point in the assemblage can be used against itself.

For example, in the case of Hawaiians, the very structures of suppressive meaning—blood and "prehumanity nativism"—become the most promising points of identity challenge. At the edges and through the framing of a preferred encoding meanings can be performatively rearranged and possibly reconstituted (via a remembrance of identity). For instance, blood identifications as empirical truths are reformed by the diasporic Hawaiian community members as still authoritative but from a localized standpoint of cultural practice. Within the very practice of "Hawaiianness at heart" and the image of "soft and savage" Hawaiianness, early Hawaiians performatively mocked and mimicked Western trade relations to increase their own indigenous power. In the confines of commercialized tourism where the Hawaiian sacred is domesticated out of its political agency, Hawaiian tour guides and community members re-create an invisible cultural world of the spectral (ghosts and spirits) so as to infuse a contesting historical narration of their lives (angry spirits of since-passed kings, queens, and deities who have been historically situated and informed to "take" any threat to them). Tourist spectacles also become performative means to integrate differently situated

Hawaiian mainlanders into privatized practice and gain public recognition as "real" away from authenticating *'āina*. Through *pi'ikoi* (or the speaking practice of claiming to be of higher rank than one is; to claim to be related to Hawaiian royalty), diasporic Hawaiians work hard to re-establish relationships with historical moments when Hawaiian self-determination and sovereignty were articulated more forcefully. Diasporic Hawaiians practice "Hawaiianness at heart" as a sincere social relation that enables "non-Hawaiian" members to become a part of their community, not as cultural equals but as adaptations to differently situated political moments (e.g., the rise of intermarriage as foreigners reside in Hawai'i and mainlanders leave in response to identity enclosures).

Throughout the chapters, I have highlighted how Hawaiians practice identity forms structured for them and it is somewhere within this performative locus, the doubling over of significations, that the cultural subject can reassemble and resignify their identifications. Identifications hold resignifiable material, but the particular ways in which meaning is rearranged and practiced becomes key. Namely, the political moment and interest from which a signification is approached and used greatly matters here. The Aloha Club uses tourist images to gain dominant recognition as a Hawaiian community in the mainland and integrate mainland youth into privatized practice. The degree to which tourist images are reused and in what political space makes a difference in that the same image used, perhaps, in a popularized *lū'au* might reproduce a public historical fantasy about Hawaiianness. At the same time, social power and meaning move in such complexity that any one space or moment may hold varied politicalities. A Waikiki *lū'au* can infuse resistive images of Hawaiianness (war dances, mockery of explorers and tourists) and speak to mainland Hawaiian members visiting the islands, while also being fastened to a legacy of colonialist fantasy, an appropriation of *Aloha,* and normative benevolence. Thus, how one practices and makes use of identity enclosures in relation to the political interests of where she or he stands as well as the legacies of meaning framing social existence determines the nature of social agency and resistance.

In this project, I theorize resistance to be located in relational moments: between a range of historical articulations and the practicing of identity that dialectically grates and challenges the signified identifications or the overdetermined moments. There is no pure space of resistance. Instead, given the contextual specificity of meaning, resistance represents those acts and practices that disorder structures of identity. This type of practice will look different depending on the nature of social power and the form of its challenge. For instance, in the portrait entitled *The Death of Cook* by George Carter, which hangs in the Bishop Museum, Carter turns Captain James Cook to face the natives. In this context, the Cook tale represents a resistive resignification more so today because it grates against the larger mythic structure of his deification. In the same way, the decision by some Hawaiian summer camps to take campers to see only the Hawaiian royalty displays of the museum represents a practice in response to a cultural articulation of Hawaiians as "savage prehumanity" and "dead forms." For these camps, Hawaiian royalty exemplifies the lived spirit of Hawaiian sovereignty and pride. Purchasing tourist souvenir statues of Kū (the god of war) demonstrates the important relationship between social resistance, cultural articulations, structured identifications, and identity practices. A couple purchasing the statue as a generalized token of nativism is positioned much differently than a Hawaiian youth buying the same statue, plastic and all, as a collectible of cultural sovereign distinction within his community and historical memory. Symbols and their constitutive cultural capital are borne out in the political and relational moment of practice. It just so happened in this context that such relational moments were collapsed within the seemingly confined structured identifications of Hawaiianness—through "nativism" and blood. I almost missed them, not realizing until later that relational moments of resistance in particular contexts, with lingering legacies of identifications, are folded over in overdetermined spaces. So, as we are called to inhabit particular subject positions, it is our performative and practiced relation between our historicized self and the politics surrounding the subject position that can make a world of difference.

Within the seemingly enclosed boundaries of Hawaiianness lie the few openings left for identity resignification (as the State of Hawaii pushes for an organized and state-directed form of Hawaiian sovereignty and self-determination, and grassroots Hawaiian sovereignty demands are continually rejected by the nation-state): the overdetermined and thus implosive limits of a (mis)recognizing legacy. The conjectures of identity are therefore also historically specific and politically formed. While larger structures cannot be completely brought down, Hawaiians could practice and perform them in challenge.

This analysis of Hawaiian identity also urges us as cultural critics to closely examine the contextualized forms and practices of identity: the textual, discursive, performative, legal mandates, and the produced flow of capital. Textuality—the visual forms and signified relations in narrative form—greatly unpacks historical memory, museums, and tourist representations, only to reveal, as I cover in chapters 2 and 3, that "native" representations when backed by military coercion and the authority of law and governance can intensify the struggle over identity to a different level. Both textual and institutional forms of power frame the lives of Hawaiians and cultural subjects, but the institutionalized and more immediate material spheres such as law and governance demand specific forms of agency and challenge. These are agencies that require the traversing of dominant paths and procedures (practicing the delimited state procedures, participating as employees and tour guides at tourist sites, and staging media protests on land) so as to avoid policed action, state violence, and material destitution. Also, the flow of both material/economic and cultural capital reflects the reconstruction of Hawaiianness and the production of new social relations between tourists, consumers, Hawaiians, and varied positionalities.

We must expect different forms of agencies for different kinds of power and identifications. Such forms might exist primarily through the performative jouissance of a structured encoding—the practicing itself (signification and meaning through its processual performativity): through the performances of certifying blood, through the enactment of tourist-created dances, and the strategic display of "benevolence." How Hawaiians live and practice identity in relation to different social powers brings to bear the surprising and creative acts of social agency.

The larger question engaged throughout this book is, What is Hawaiianness, or does a real Hawaiian identity exist? My firm belief in a real, lived Hawaiian community has compelled this project. The most interesting questions that compelled me to this larger question were, Where is Hawaiianness located? How is it located? Within which terms, conditions, and risks? By repeatedly emphasizing historical specificity, I take this to heart, knowing that a real group of Hawaiians whose real situations and remakings of power cannot be denied. In making this claim, I recognize a Hawaiianness that resonates more powerfully to a group of Hawaiians, but one that historically and politically changes to some degree and in relation to varied locationalities within the community and in terms of specific political moments. My phrases—*resignification, remakings*—refer to the practices in response and challenge to the historically stabilized identifications and lingering legacies created for Hawaiians. This designation practice therefore acknowledges the power dynamic embedded within the existence of Hawaiians. Hawaiianness, its terms and debates of authenticity or falsity, shift in terms of the specific context you are addressing and the interest/person with whom you are speaking. So, when speaking to those who are located outside of a Hawaiian historical memory, Hawaiianness is firmly held as a real lived group bound by historical practice, pains, and triumphs. When speaking to other Hawaiian community members, the identity terms for an internal sense of authenticity and history become more complicated, as the Aloha Club demonstrated with "pure-bloods" deemed the authorities and "mixed-bloods" the modern-day results of the Hawaiian overthrow. In this context, then, I reemphasize the point that Hawaiians represent a real, lived cultural group by way of historical memory. If, as this project shows, our identities are formalized, structured, and denied (as many, even in academe, reimpose externally structured identifications back onto us, challenging the existence of an indigenous Hawaiianness), Hawaiians will have to continue to relationally reshape their identity through historical memory and by way of reperforming within the overdetermined limits of who they are. Our identity practices and performances through authenticating functions serve to distinguish and politically determine the nature of Hawaiian social agency and cultural politics. But these, housed within the structures that have framed us in glass cases, sold admission tickets to our *heiau* (Hawaiian place of worship), and administered blood quantum might slip by unnoticed, unappreciated, and untheorized. Only contextually specific cultural studies projects such as this one reveal how our theorizing of identity has entered the moving scene of identity and memory too late and become too comfortable with the politics of the past. That we would keep coming back to Marx yet still hold him at bay, not fully understanding how we might approach the complexity of sociality.

Each chapter of *In the Name of Hawaiians* analyzes a particular identity arena. The first half of the book (chapters 1 and 2) analyzes the structured identifications created in the name of Hawaiians by larger forces such as public historical discourse and law and governance. The second part of the book (chapters 3, 4, and 5) explores the ways in which

Hawaiians rearticulate and refashion the structured identifications and live within overdetermined meanings as new forms of agency and social challenge.

In chapter 1, I examine the identity encodings of Hawaiianness in the historical imagination (as represented by explorer journals, maps, and official narratives). I discuss how signified ambivalence and several discursive moves abstract and liberalize nativism out of its ethnic distinction and into sovereign residency and state citizenship while also racially identifying Hawaiians as "prehistoric" migrants and later, as "potential" citizens.

Chapter 2 traces the "prehumanity" construction of Hawaiians from chapter 1 as a racializing vehicle via modern law and governmentality. In a new era and the emergence of the modern nation-state, I frame how an indigenous subjectivity is dissolved through the incorporation of modern law and governance. As *haoles* become sovereign residents in Hawai'i (meaning their naturalized right of possession and residency is granted before and outside of indigenous rule and by way of their sovereign governments at home), Hawaiians are racialized through land commissions and blood quantum technology. I analyze the identity positions created for Hawaiians in the transcripts of the 1920 Congressional Hearings before the Committee on Territories, United States Senate, and the construction of Hawaiians (namely the part Hawaiians) as either potential (white) citizens or as a racially exclusive and pure group in terms of a prehuman, extinct, and gone pure Hawaiian race. In this way, Hawaiianness and indigenous rights are economized, regulated, and surveilled while citizenship remains white. Tragically, the speaking authority of Hawaiians is determined in line with blood quantum. "Mixed-bloods" are not truly Hawaiian and thus have no identity right or claim to things Hawaiian (sovereignty, sacred lands and artifacts, and cultural practices like hula and chanting); and the authentic Hawaiian—the "pure-blood"—is deemed, according to the population counts and certified records, "gone"/extinct and since passed.

In chapter 3, I present the identity challenges of everyday Hawaiians against the state. For example, many Hawaiians participate in the DHHL in order to attain a homestead lease granted to Hawaiians through the 1921 HHCA. In order to secure such a lease, each Hawaiian applicant must present official documents that verify her or his 50 percent Hawaiian blood quantum. Through ethnographic interviews and oral histories,

I feature narrative performances by Hawaiians who cannot formally prove their Hawaiianness. In their performances, they follow the state requirements of identity to their most logical endpoint and unveil the historical and political exclusions and subjective perceptions used in the identity surveillance and documentation of Hawaiians. The private performances of Hawaiians in this chapter represent a critical locus from which everyday Hawaiians (or those not involved in explicit sovereignty movement groups) can challenge and contest the racial state and its blood quantum restrictions.

Chapter 4 reframes Hawaiianness in its most well-known context: tourism. I analyze how travel and tourism construct and shape Hawaiian identity; traveling itself signifies movement throughout the native body politic. Using the historical construction of nativism as prehuman, tourist sites such as the Waimea Falls Park and Iolani Palace relationally construct an articulation of Hawaiians as "gone" or "this once was" to one of "this would never be." Cultural parks and sites therefore inscribe a position of witnessing the death of nativism and its ill fit with modernity. Yet, a new form of tourism emerges in the postmodern era, one that no longer needs the faces of natives. Instead, there are tours of the first Waikiki hotel, the famous tourist shipliners, and of the history of tourism itself. Here tourism becomes nativized and incorporated into the history of Hawai'i as "Hawaiiana," which reproduces the class-specific distinctions of travel from yesterday. Thus, nativism becomes essential for the articulation of a white elite class and the privilege, not plasticity, of travel. Hawaiian tour guides, however, subtly challenge these global capitalist structures of tourism through stories and unofficial tours of the cultural ghosts and spirits. By sharing stories of angry and restless Hawaiian spirits who roam tourist sites at night, Hawaiians circulate subtle social critique of tourist structures that exploit and commodify Hawaiianness.

Chapter 5 engages lived diasporic Hawaiian communities on the mainland and their identities. Through ethnographic fieldwork and interviews, I highlight the creative ways in which Hawaiians positioned in the diaspora practice identity differently. I share the most significant performances, oral histories, private memories, and speech acts illustrating how the Hawaiians reorganize their identifications and subjections in everyday life. In the diaspora, historical memory calls for a reimagining of our relations to one another as Hawaiians. For example, through a speaking practice known as *pi'ikoi,* community members aspire to be the Hawaiians they once were: sovereign, proud, and authentic. They revel in re-creating their identity connections to royal figures and their resignified historical moments of Hawaiian glory. In this practice, they momentarily shatter state and public suspicion of their indigenous, sovereign selves. Hawaiians—whose identity is concealed in the blood and exalted through *pi'ikoi*—also rework blood classifications and definitions in their speaking practices to address their felt needs for cultural authority and voice. The scientized image of blood and its rhetorical potency as already real offer a powerful practice. Repracticing blood speech reauthorizes Hawaiians as the true cultural subjects. These Hawaiians use what they can, when they can, and with a strong mindful sense of the collective spirit of the *Kanaka Maoli* (indigenous Hawaiians). They are incredibly creative in that they have more distant connections to a cultural agency historically centered on *'āina* or Hawai'i and thus have more to lose. Their unique Hawaiian practices store identity possibilities for an impending future in which the U.S. nation-state and local state regirds more power and Hawaiians are continually denied homesteads, benefits, legal agency, and the right to claim themselves as indigenous. We can look to Hawaiian community both in Hawai'i and the diaspora for contextualized practices through which we can strongly emerge in a postcapitalist world and reimagine our self-determination as Hawaiians.

This project locates, names, and reveals Hawaiianness as a multifaceted struggle over identity claims to subjectivity, movement, cultural nature, and sovereignty. Essentialism never looked shakier or more interesting in its complexity. Historically established structures of identification have framed how Hawaiian identity is practiced and analyzed, while Hawaiians, in the cracks and the hidden corners of these structures, repractice assembled meanings in relation to their memory of who they are, what they have become for others, and where social freedom and cultural spirit lie for them. It is a memory that has and will continue to pave our way.

1

Abstract Nativism
and the Historical Imagination

Cultural groups are often identified and understood by expressions, images, and myths of the past. Indigenous groups in particular are remembered through constructions of the past such as representations of the
first mystical meeting between natives and Western explorers, and images of naked, "exotic savages," tribal dance spectacles, and native kings
and queens. Enunciations of the past, which invoke a sense of authentic
realness and empirical truth in the process of representation, powerfully
constitute and frame the nature of a specific group, its origins and collective experiences. These enunciations, whether in a museum display, a
historical portrait, or popularized cultural legend, derive from the historical imagination, a force too seductive and powerful to reside as merely a physical structure or a matter of interpretation. Instead, the historical imagination stands as a visual and narrative dialectic of selectively
shaping, "remembering, and forgetting the past" and in this specific context, historically identifying Hawaiianness.[1] The historical imaginary is a
multivocal, multivested collection of flashes of memory that call forth
particular myths, fantasies, and hegemonic beliefs over others. Such a
force is just as much spoken as it is ideologically engrained into popular
thought and is made up of several colliding forms: dominant memory
(official histories by the colonial, nation-state, and local governments),
popular memory (public representations of history in museum displays,

1

tourist discourses and kitsch, consumer culture, widely reproduced legends and social histories), private memory (the practices and performances of the past—historical retellings, dances, celebrations, and traditions—within a lived indigenous community), and counter- or oppositional memory (politically resistive narratives and rhetoric by activist movement groups and everyday social actors).[2]

Indeed, the power of the historical imagination lies in its invisible semblance as the undisputed historical past while at the same time continually activating images and discourses that shape and manage contemporary cultural politics of identity. In Hawai'i, for example, the debate over the question of who is truly a "native" of Hawai'i has been outlined and restrained by discourses of the historical imagination. In this debate, identity claims of nativism and Hawaiianness collide against one another in the context of Hawai'i and its constitutive cultural politics.

For example, nativism has been defined in many different ways from different positionalities:

> We have lived here for twenty years. Like the Hawaiians, we are from here. They opened up this place to us and I have grown to love and respect their culture.
>
> —Ray from Manoa, Oahu

> I hear the sovereignty stuff and I question the objective. If it is [about] being native to Hawai'i, then all the groups who came and made a life here are native too.
>
> —Betty from Kona, Hawai'i

> The native Hawaiians have no legitimate claim to ownership of any public lands in Hawaii and the federal government is not going to turn land over to them or allow them to secede.
>
> —John Goemans, a Honolulu lawyer who issued a suit against Governor Benjamin Cayetano that challenged the constitutionality of the 1996 Hawaiian vote[3]

These clashing claims over nativism call into question the notion of native belonging with respect to either shared group membership and identification, common historical experience, the formal/legal recognition of such indigenous belonging via sovereignty *or* state citizenship/geographic residency. The first quote, for example, is from a *haole* male resident who migrated to and settled in Honolulu in the 1960s.[4] He considers himself a "native" via residency and shared place. With a solid link to the communities of Hawai'i, Ray locates his belonging in an empathic identification with a culture ethnically different from his own, its boundaries permeable.

Betty, unlike Ray, speaks from a "Local" position, one that acknowledges the historical migration and settlement of ethnic laborers to Hawai'i from China, Japan, Portugal, Philippines, Korea, and other lands in the mid-1800s (as Hawai'i rapidly became an emerging capitalist space).[5] These people became necessary, exploitable, and legally unrecognized labor for the burgeoning sugar plantations—that is, labor in contention with a dying race of Hawaiians who clung to the traditional land-communal system. Here "Locals" are differentiated from *haoles*. Far from being mere geographic residents of Hawai'i, *Locals* refers to descendants of those groups who took part in the working-class plantation experience, endured difficult and enforced travels to Hawai'i (many pushed out by economic pressures at home, threats to their nation, and the gendered roles of marriage, family, and labor) and were not part of dominant society (i.e., *haole* business/governmental interests and residents). Sociological and ethnic studies scholars also describe Local culture as polycultural or one that blends many different ethnic groups into a larger community.[6] Such a community has defined itself primarily against encroaching outsiders to the interests of Hawai'i like *haole*/mainland business interests and foreign investment parties from other countries (e.g., Japan, Korea). A Local identity, then, mostly speaks to while also eliding race and class divisions among Chinese, Japanese, Portuguese, Filipino/as, Koreans, Puerto Ricans, and many other groups, some of whom have emerged as the middle classes in Hawai'i.[7] Yet, a Local signifies an important and complex identity position, as Candace Fujikane explains, that too often obscures all Asian Pacific identities in Hawai'i as being Native Hawaiian, an obscuring reflective of tensions between the two.[8] "Localities" and "Nativism" relate to a matrix of historicized identity politics in Hawai'i, as described by Asian American literary scholar Stephen Sumida: "In Hawai'i, 'Hawaiian' is commonly taken to mean 'native Hawaiian' and is usually reserved for that use in order to avoid ambiguity among those who speak these terms—that is, among locals. A Hawaiian is quintessentially a local, but a local is not necessarily a Hawaiian."[9]

All the while, a Local identity, particularly in naming itself "indigenous," or "native to the islands," risks the erasing and reinscription of the colonial histories of and U.S. imperialism over Pacific Islanders. In fact, many Local groups have benefited from the dispossession of Hawaiians via economic gains, private land ownership, and middle-class opportunities.[10]

Conflicting visions of nationalism and belonging thus arise between the notion of a Local Hawai'i and a Hawaiian Sovereign Nation. In 1999, for example, a controversy erupted over "who" should have access to tuition waivers at the University of Hawaii.[11] Under pressure from the Office of Hawaiian Affairs (OHA) and Hawaiian communities, state Senator Norman Mizuguchi proposed a bill that would "direct the university to give 500 more waivers to native Hawaiians."[12] The University of Hawaii at Manoa campus sits on ceded land, or royal land illegally seized upon U.S. annexation of Hawai'i. In partial recognition of this historical injustice, the state is beholden to furnish 20 percent of the revenue made off of the land to the OHA for disbursement to Hawaiians. Tuition waivers for Hawaiians would be considered due compensation for the ceded native land. The bill was challenged by Local students who opposed the use of university or state funds to distribute more waivers to Hawaiians because other students deserved such an entitlement as state residents with equal rights.[13] Hawaiians challenged these claims by arguing for their special status as indigenous peoples of Hawai'i and the need to be "compensated" for the illegal use of native land. Haunani Kay Trask, professor of Hawaiian Studies at the University of Hawaii at Manoa campus, charged, "The university sits on our stolen land."[14] Once again, the terrain of native entitlement is contested by Locals, indigenous Hawaiians, and state politicians. A Local position, spoken by Betty, therefore complicates a nativism in its calling attention to the struggling, legally disenfranchised laborers who settled in Hawai'i as their new "home" and experienced hardship underneath *haole* business interests, and this Local position exists in tension with the cultural politics surrounding indigenous Hawaiians who were displaced via land occupation and the immigrant labor of Locals.

Such nativist sentiment also transitions into a discourse on civil rights and state citizenry. The third quote, from legal counsel John Goemans, represents a deeply felt nativism based on the invocation of colorless or "raceless" equal rights as a state and U.S. citizen.[15] He speaks

[handwritten margin note: but don't native people deserve more rights]

to the issue of the Hawaiian vote. Amid the continuing sovereignty struggle in Hawai'i, in 1996 the Hawaiian Elections Sovereignty Council and the State of Hawaii sponsored a "Hawaiian Vote" plebiscite in which all Hawaiians were asked the question: Shall the Hawaiian people elect delegates to propose a native Hawaiian government? The vote raised heated debate in Hawai'i and on the mainland.[16] Many self-defined "native" residents (*haoles,* business interests, and Locals) challenged the state-sponsored referendum, claiming they were also "native" to the islands and were illegally excluded from the process. One *haole* rancher Harold Rice brought suit against the State of Hawaii, arguing that all state residents were not included in the vote and thus the vote stands as a form of unconstitutional race-based discrimination.[17] Rice also issued the same suit against the OHA for excluding him from the voting process for OHA trustees, a practice reserved solely for Hawaiians. In an unprecedented move, Rice took the case to the United States Supreme Court, which ruled in his favor, thereby jeopardizing the future of special "Hawaiians only" designated programs.[18] U.S. citizenry and state residency are thus conflated with the identity claim of Hawaiianness and native/sovereign belonging.

Many non-Hawaiian residents and tourists in Hawai'i, or those not genealogically linked to a Hawaiian private memory, argue that they are, in fact, "Hawaiians," or from Hawai'i, with the same rights and access to Native Hawaiian culture, music, dance, and material land claims. Since the early 1970s, in the public sphere, resistive demands by Hawaiian sovereignty groups were and still are contested by many state residents who argue that their identities as Local and as inhabitants of the islands, are equally significant to those of the Hawaiian protesters.[19] The dangerous logic being, Why should their native identities be devalued in a multicultural haven? (this is Hawai'i, after all) and, Why should they have to give up ceded land areas that Hawaiians want restored? (it is state property and they are citizens).

In the extended struggle over sovereign rights, land, and benefits, *haoles,* Locals, and Native Hawaiians fight over the claim to being truly Hawaiian and native to the islands. But, how did such a multivested discourse of nativism historically come into being? How did nativism and specifically Hawaiian identity become liberalized and abstract so that it could be hailed by several different groups? One approach to this problematic lies in tracing those moments and discourses of the historical imagination when Hawaiian identity, originally rooted in a traditional, rigid class hierarchy between *mōʻī* (king), *aliʻi* (chiefs), *konohiki* (land supervisor), and *makaʻāinana* (commoners) is liberalized out of its sovereign status and ethnic distinction.[20] In this chapter, I argue that the discourses of "open" nativism and Hawaiianness emanate in part from a larger inscription of the geographic and the historical. The cultural signification of geography articulates Hawaiian identity via a representational ambivalence in the mid-1700s through the 1900s via the scientific technology of mapping and the circulation of the geographic in explorer journals, historical narratives, and popular discourses. For example, the first explorer maps and journals feature an *unpeopled* Hawaiʻi *and at the same time* as a place with seemingly indigenous settlers. Hawaiʻi is, therefore, (re)discovered by Captain James Cook and others in the face of already being "settled" by Native Hawaiians. The native settlers are surprisingly inviting and generous *and,* as expected, dangerously savage and violent, as signified through the famous "killing" of Captain Cook. These forms in effect racialize Hawaiians out of modern time and into *anachronistic space,* distinguishing Hawaiians from colonial explorers through the construction of a temporal difference of prehumanity. Hawaiians are framed as residing within a since-past static present, one in complete distance from modern, moving European time. *Kānaka* become, then, vestiges of a cultural past, their presence and discovery/ origination of Hawaiʻi unrecognized and thus their claims of sovereignty devalued.

Signified ambivalence operates through the representation of Hawaiian inhabitants as not only being *there* in Hawaiʻi but also being naturally open, inviting, and benevolent. Explorers' narrative accounts of Hawaiians reveal a fascination with the Hawaiian cultural value of *Aloha,* the spirit of reciprocal giving and exchange between Hawaiians. Cook himself encounters such an *Aloha* spirit, deeming the "natives" an inviting and generous people. Based on examples from explorer journals, I contend that from these first intercultural encounters, the indigenous cultural value of *Aloha* is misread and distorted to not only include *haole* foreigners into often unequal trade exchanges (nails from a ship's deck for large feasts and sacred artifacts) but to nativize foreigners among Hawaiʻi and Hawaiians. Ultimately, these dominant misreadings establish a *normative* benevolence (a naturalized condition presuming that all Hawaiians are naturally open and generous) and a reconfigured *Aloha* spirit without its cultural sense, and work to nativize in particular European and American foreigners.

Temporal space and geographic representation in maps "naturally place" foreigners in Hawai'i, as Hawaiian identity is rehauled. A heavily impacting subject position of Hawaiianness as "naturally placed" is created through signifying and representational processes within maps that Denis Wood deems as the "culturalization of the natural" and the "naturalization of the cultural."[21] Hawaiians, thus, are to be understood through the "natural" elements of what is already *out there,* which are themselves sociopolitical constructions; through the kind, calming oceans, the pleasant tradewinds and breezes, and the abundance, the lushness, of food and land (they are indeed inherently calm, pleasant, and rich in generosity of what they have). By iconically inscribing the "natural" and the "geographic" via maps and charts, Western imperialism imagined and brought into being national modern space and its communities, "races," and "genders."[22] Inscribed through "nature" was a continually reifying image of "realness" and a set of social relations for how subjects would be read into such representational space. The cultural and political production of geography serves then to naturalize the colonial occupation and newly established nativism of Hawai'i and its people by the British and later U.S. forces.

Colonization's Impact

However, such ambivalence is sublated, for once Hawaiians are recognized within the boundaries of modern time—the 1900s and the U.S. territorialization of Hawai'i—their racialization kicks in. Hawaiians, formerly deemed prehuman and excluded from colonial law and governance, are reinserted into the temporal space and social hierarchy of the territory through a nation-ward set of relations (U.S. government as the trustee and Hawaiians as the wards of the nation-state). The result: they are surveilled by blood quantum technology and policies and articulated as "strange," nonadaptive, unproductive, unfit, and in need of rehabilitation, thereby maintaining the whiteness of the territory. Racially distinguished through time and geography, the reincorporation of Hawaiians into modern time and structure further displaces Hawaiians whose "development" is simultaneously overseen and denied by the colonial state.

In this chapter, I trace only a few of the discursive moves within the historical imagination that abstracted and liberalized nativism into sovereign residency and gradually into state citizenship and racially identified Hawaiians as "prehistoric" migrants and "potential" citizens. My goal here is to initiate a critique through which we can historically contextualize the power differentials in the contemporary discourses of nativism and identity in Hawai'i.

Reminded by the practice of articulation, I focus on how identity positions are constituted and produced not only historically but through the "historical" itself: through the images of the "past," through the representation of "history," "nostalgia," and "the geographic." Specifically, how might Hawaiianness and nativism be articulated through historical images, narratives, and displays, or the seemingly objective lines of a map? How do history and objective science à la geography signify the Hawaiian and the "native" and how might Hawaiianness function and work for the "historical"? How in this context did sovereign nativism become fused with a discourse of white citizenship? I initially analyzed a multitude of historical narratives related to Hawaiians: texts from official history books, traditional empiricist accounts, explorer journals, missionary diaries, visual representations, indigenous versions, and museum exhibits in well-attended sites and in popular tourist areas of Waikiki and Kona. After analyzing the different articulations, I distinguished between those identity positions created by dominant and structural interests and by Hawaiians themselves over time. In this chapter, I analyze mostly the meanings that are historically persistent and positioned as the *preferred readings* in popular memory. I trace through the geographic in colonial maps and explorer journals the restructuring of nativism and Hawaiian identity in the period from 1778 to the 1930s. In relation to other theoretical concepts from Johannes Fabian, David Theo Goldberg, Anne McClintock, and Denis Wood among others, I examine several historically specific conditions through which various native and Hawaiian subject positions are framed and constructed as well as signifying relations between and among them (or relations that meaningfully render and constitute these identity positions).[23]

I make the central claim that the cultural representation of the geographic is a racialized discourse, producing subjects through the power-vested reproduction of logics, expressions, and exclusions differentiating and racializing groups from one another.[24] As racialized articulations, social and "natural" differences are organized within a hierarchy of identities and identifications and take on various forms (between the indigenous peoples, new settlers/colonizers, and other laterally positioned groups): moral and religious conflicts, large differentials in rationality and "development," differing perceptions of economic and political progress, modernity as superior over premodern times as marked by pre-existing cultural groups, and differences in land systems. Specifically, in the case of Hawaiians, land and space become critical to articulating racial differences between Hawaiian and *haole* residents/interests. With a strategically located space in the Pacific, the Hawaiians are conceptually redefined. Their subjectivity is reconfigured and racialized through a discourse of the geographic and "nature" (aided by its formal authority in Europe and the West) and time, which transforms native belonging into sovereign residency, or the presumption of nativism on the part of many *haole* residents from Britain, France, Russia, and the United States over any formal institution of Hawaiian law and through sovereign ideologies back at home. One could argue that this discourse is no different from that surrounding Native American Indians and African peoples and while the parallels exist (the signification of unruliness and pre-human characteristics among the "natives"), the articulations are not uniform.[25] I argue that an ambivalent grammar threads within this discourse, constructing Hawaiians as equally benevolent and savage (often in the same turn) and Hawai'i as both empty and opportune for settlement and yet also inhabited and already discovered. These cooperating articulations suggest that Hawai'i was not conceptualized in the exact same vein as the lands occupied by Native Americans; its land expanse was modest in comparison to the colonial empire and its people were not viewed as savage as the Native Americans and yet not as foreign as the "Orientals." An exotic reconstruction of Hawaiians as naturally kind and generous, while still being marked by an underdeveloped prehuman state, emerges with a strange particularity. What appears to be a contradiction in defining the cultural nature of Hawaiians—the conflict between an inherent goodness and a savageness that resulted in the "killing" of Captain James Cook—promises an open and long-lasting nativism for foreign interests in addition to necessitating external governance and development by those very interests.

exotic representation is stereotypical

A POLITICS OF AMBIVALENT IDENTIFICATIONS

Rediscovering the Natives

Upon its sight, the land of Hawai'i is fresh, uncharted, and relatively unpeopled (see Figure 1).[26] In this first printed map of Hawai'i by British Lieutenant Henry Roberts, the lines of explorer movement from island

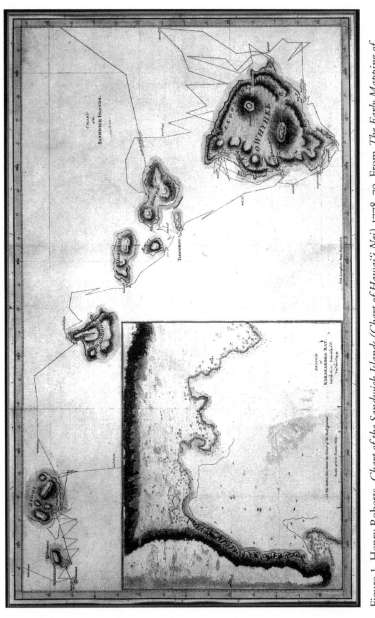

Figure 1. Henry Roberts, *Chart of the Sandwich Islands* (*Chart of Hawai'i Nei*), 1778–79. From *The Early Mapping of Hawaii*, by Gary Fitzpatrick. Image courtesy of Gary Fitzpatrick.

site to site seem traversed for the first time. Each island name is spelled in exotic difference—Owhyee, Mowee, Ranai, Morotoi, and Woahoo. In the bottom left, a close-up inset sketch features "Karakakooa Bay," a seemingly unoccupied region from ocean to land strip, which is where the tragic confrontation between Cook and the Hawaiians would take place on February 14, 1779. Only barren strips of land are depicted; no trace of "native" presence is suggested, other than a few thatched houses. However, in explorer journal accounts and subsequent maps, there are references to and drawings of Hawaiian native "settlers." Cook did detail many encounters with Hawaiians, commenting on their friendly, generous nature: "They [the Hawaiians] seem to be blest with a frank, cheerful disposition; and, were I to draw any comparisons, should say, that they are equally free from the fickle levity which distinguishes the natives of Taheite, and the sedate case observable amongst many of the Tongabatoo."[27]

In addition, Cook's ship artist John Webber painted a detailed view of Karakakooa Bay (see Figure 2), the bay in the inset on Figure 1. Roberts, Cook's colleague, created his map during Cook's third voyage, the same period when Webber sketched his detailed view in which he represents the intercultural meeting of the British and Hawaiians. Groups of Hawaiians can be seen all along the bay region and in canoes brushing out toward Cook's arriving ship. In contradiction, this view documents the existence of Hawaiians and their long-established cultural system (canoes, tools, and whole villages in sight). Multiple references

Figure 2. John Webber, *A View of Karakakooa Bay, in Owhyee*, 1779. Printed in Cook 1784. Courtesy of the Dixson Galleries, State Library of New South Wales Mitchell Library, Sydney.

in public documents (maps, journals, and historical retellings) to the presence of natives in Hawai'i problematizes the colonial mapping of open and empty "virgin" lands and the designation of Hawai'i's discovery as not occurring until much later in 1778, the period in which Cook arrived.[28] Why do these conflicting images exist—Hawai'i as simultaneously empty and peopled and Hawai'i as already discovered and then "rediscovered" by Cook—in the same historical moment? How did this discourse operate and for which particular interests? What were the larger effects of this discourse on the reconfiguration of nativism and Hawaiian identity?

The notion that Hawai'i is both empty and peopled and discovered and rediscovered reflects a larger representational scheme operating through ambivalence. Within a discursive field, signified ambivalence names those meanings recombined and fused together in contradiction and conflict. These linkages seem curious because of their oppositional (double-edged) meanings and more specifically, the necessity of the opposition for a political project. Figures 1 and 2 stem from a colonial project in which the map served as a technology of possession: a vehicle of control, identification, and formal ownership.[29] The finding of new territories by European (namely British) explorers was not recognized until it was documented via a map. Once recorded, although often according to imprecise and inaccurate scales, the mapping was publicized as an official account in the British empire. As Mary Louise Pratt explains, "It only gets 'made' for real after the traveler returns home and brings it into being through texts: a name, a map, a report to the Royal Geographical Society, the Foreign Office, the London Mission Society, a diary, a lecture, a travel book."[30] The colonial map (that of Roberts and the later explorers La Perouse, Vancouver, and their map sketchers Bernizet and Baker, respectively) thus legitimizes, formalizes, and makes real the discovery of Hawai'i.[31] It is a device that preceded and formally invented the conquest of the Hawaiian islands.

In one sense then the early mapping of Hawai'i, like other colonial maps (as with the "dark and unknown lands" known as Africa), conceptually emptied Hawai'i of its people, culture, and sovereign nativism, reorganizing and reordering these according to a displacement of time.[32] This partially explains why Hawai'i is deemed empty and "discovery" is attributed to European exploration (while Cook's arrival is not explicitly labeled as a late discovery or a rediscovery in light of the prior settlement of Hawaiians on the islands). Rather, European exploration occupies a privileged position to formal discovery and existence via *anachronistic space* and *anterior time*.[33] Through these modes, Hawai'i and Hawaiian culture are continually placed outside of the boundaries of the modern empire and relegated to a prehistoric zone of racial difference.[34]

This can be seen in map discourses, settlement and migration theories, and historical narratives, which are read through a linear narration of time, a time without substance, or a timelessness.[35] In Honolulu's highly visited Bishop Museum, an impressive private collection of Pacific cultural artifacts (a place established by Princess Bernice Pauahi Bishop in order "to preserve Hawai'i's cultural heritage"), there sits a display of "The Origins of the Hawaiians," which retells the theory of "beginnings" and "origins" both of place and culture. It reads:

> The first people to settle in the Hawaiian Islands were Polynesians who arrived about A.D. 600. These ancient mariners sailed across thousands of miles of open ocean, bringing with them the various plants and animals they would need to survive in a new land. According to current theory, the first settlers came from the Marquesas Islands, some 2,400 miles south of Hawai'i. Evidence suggests that a second group of Polynesian immigrants came to the islands about 500 years later from the Society Islands. By the time Westerners discovered Hawai'i in 1778, the Polynesians had already been living in the islands for well over 1,000 years.[36]

As an impressive sequence is narrated for visitors and the historical reader is intrigued about native origins—"Where do they really come from?"—the documentation, as girded by the legitimizing mechanisms of scientific theory and empirical data, works through an acontextual, acultural mimetic representation. The sequence explains that the first "Polynesians" actually came from the Marquesas Islands and made their way to the chain of islands. The "Polynesian Triangle" diagram featured in the display is understood point to point, from finger-following arrow to arrow. It is a cultural straightaway abstracted from the structures and time of culture.

In his outlining of the "Polynesian Triangle," Donald Kilolani Mitchell details the probable order of settlements and emphasizes how this order has been verified through examination of radio carbon dating and archaeological artifacts and records.[37] Settling and migration thus constitute a larger discourse of "Science," one that seems to retrace, to reflect the "movement" of a culture on its way toward becoming inhabitants.

1. Indo-Malay or Island Asian people arrived in Tonga from the west about 1,500 B.C. or possibly earlier.

2. Some of these settlers, now to be called Polynesians, migrated from Tonga to nearby Samoa.

3. Some left Samoa, western Polynesia, about the first century A.D. and settled in the Marquesas Islands.

4. Islands in the Society Group were settled a little later from the Marquesas.

5. Marquesas islanders sailed to Easter Island, Rapa Nui, and settled there about 500 A.D.

6. Marquesan voyagers sailed to Hawai'i, probably between 500 and 750 A.D. In Hawai'i as well as the previous landings, we believe that the settlers found the islands uninhabited.

7. Emigrants from Tahiti sailed to New Zealand, perhaps after 750 A.D., and became the Maori people.

8. Society islanders from Raiatea (Hava'iki) came to Hawai'i, probably between 1,000 and 1,250 A.D. By this time all of the larger islands in Polynesia had been discovered and colonized. Some of the smaller islands supported settlements, others were used as "stepping stone" islands which provided places for rest and refreshment on the long voyages to and from the large island groups.[38]

Historical narratives operate in this same vein. Territorial historian Ralph Kuykendall offers us a "Glimpse of Ancient Hawaii," describing how Hawaiian life once was: religion as nature worship, everyday rituals like *kapa* making and fishing, the social structural divisions of *ali'i*, *kahuna*, and *maka'āinana*.[39] From an "objective" distance, he explains that "so far as Hawaii is concerned, it is quite generally believed that there were successive arrivals of settlers extending over some hundreds of years."[40] From Tahiti and the Society Islands, Hawaiians are positioned as the earliest settlers, with two waves of "immigration," the latter one being six or eight hundred years ago. (The implication of "immigration" and what this means today has affected the selective deployment, or lack thereof, of this discourse for Hawaiians.) Temporally and spatially separating out Hawai'i and Hawaiians from the rest, from what lies beyond, Kuykendall tells us that "at the end of this period of the 'long voyages,' communication ceased between Hawaii and central Polynesia, and the Hawaiians lived in nearly complete isolation from the rest of the world until the year 1778."[41]

Likewise, historians Gavan Daws and A. Grove Day make brief mention of the settling moves of the first Polynesians, primarily representing the beginnings of Hawaiian society as exactly the moment Cook landed on the islands.[42] In Daws's account, the name of Cook is continually fused with "discovery," "discoverer," and "exploration" and the natives/Polynesians/Hawaiians with "settlement," "migration," and "immigration."

> Evidently, Hawaii was settled from the Marquesas and the Society Islands, probably as early as the eighth century A.D., possibly earlier still; and there was another wave of migration in the twelfth and thirteenth centuries, this time from Tahiti. After that, apparently, there were no more voyages back and forth to the South Pacific, and the Hawaiians lived in isolation until the arrival of Cook. The discovery of new islands was not part of Cook's official task on his third voyage.[43]

Day introduces the history of Hawai'i with a focus on Cook as the captain "of three voyages in the next ten years—a decade in which he became the foremost man of his time in Pacific discovery."[44] It is particularly interesting that these representations distinguish Hawai'i/Hawaiians from Cook/Europeans in a temporal way. These settlements and migrations form, according to Johannes Fabian, an "allochronic" sense (a static ethnographic present); "they" (externally categorized as Polynesians) found, settled, and lived in their own mode, away from the rest of the world, until 1778.[45] Changes in cultural structure and motivations for moving are effaced. "Spatialized time," in this sense, racializes a subject position for Hawaiians by marking them as primitive, isolated, and beyond Europe. They represent "Before Europe," or the pre-European condition.[46] In this way, an evolutionary system of classification—a taxonomy—is embedded in what looks to be an innocent, technical distinction between Polynesian settlement and European discovery. However, the categorical term *Polynesian,* an externally created identification that subdivides branches of a larger Pacific family, which includes the Maori of New Zealand, Samoans, Tongans, Tahitians, Marquesans, and Hawaiians among others, is sealed through a delineation of a type of "geographic movement." Classifying race via movement enables a narrative sequence about progress, rationality, and development. This representational mode inscribes a cultural nostalgia for Polynesians who were always coming from elsewhere (thus, never native) and whose origins are never consistently verifiable.[47] The settlers are therefore *stuck* in a frozen, pre-European time in which nothing is developed and civilized.[48] They move only within a premature form of development and are located in an all-defining anachronistic space. This is prehistory, which has been barely recorded, were it not for the salvage of scientific inquiry.

Cook's discovery is designated as the crystallizing juncture of historical recognition, the delimiting modern figure that triggers the historical memory for Hawaiians. His discovery is signified as the kick-start of moving time. There is pre-European/Western contact (before Cook time) and European/Western contact (Cook's time, or history proper of the written). And Cook brings with him the "Discovery" (both ship and recognition) and "origins," ushering in "contact," temporality, and activity. He completes the formative development of the Polynesian on a "virgin land," although Polynesians were surely its first "inhabitants" or residents of the islands, but, according to this representation, *not its natives or indigenous people*. This is a significantly consequential dominant encoding for the representation of a Polynesian inhabitant who merely settles, occupies, and holds a land, clears the way for the ongoing articulation of residency and citizenship in Hawai'i as *naturally native* identities; that *all* who inhabit Hawai'i are indeed Hawaiian settlers. It is the authority of "Science" that strongly encourages us to invoke this racialization of Hawaiians in terms of "origins" and "migrations" and not racialized articulations. Its theories and estimations seem to reflect the empirical reality of "pre-Hawaiians" in relation to the "naturalness" of Western movement.

As visiting inhabitants from somewhere else, their identities are configured as preexisting the conditions of modernity: agency, time, Europe, and movement. By becoming invisibly racialized through the geographic, Hawai'i and Hawaiians are distinguished and separated out from the British explorers and the subsequent *haole* residents who flocked to the islands in the late 1700s and throughout the 1800s. In effect, the temporal distinction casts Hawaiians as historically outdated, or not being of this world and not meant to survive into modernity. Such an image becomes historically persistent as Native Hawaiian culture is deemed dead, archaic, and thus, historically fascinating (an image that is deployed and reproduced in legal and tourist contexts). Hawaiian society, while acknowledged by explorers and missionaries is relegated to a separate category of society that *came before* and thus does not include formal law and governance and official sovereignty. It seems that representationally, "formal" is designated as being uniquely derivative of Western modern societies. With this set of meanings, control and governance over Hawai'i is *naturally* determined then by its first formal modern discovery, and colonial explorers, residents, and missionaries therefore become unmarked as *abstract natives* who are free to assume native belonging and control. I name these interests "abstract natives" because through the natural right of discovery, colonial explorers exercised an unconditional, liberalized (almost ethnic-less) form of sovereignty over existing indigenous structures and subjectivities. Through the historical imagination, Hawaiians become perpetually historical; they are represented as natives from a fading cultural past, thus making them unfit for citizenship and modern life. The cultural particulars of indigenous nativism are loosened out of existence through temporal difference (premodern and modern) and nativism both becomes liberalized to incorporate non-Hawaiian identities and interests by way of residency/travel, and speaks specifically for dominant *haole* interests. (Meaning, Local immigrants in the mid-1800s were not considered abstract natives in the same way as the *haole* business interests in the islands. These laborers were not considered citizens who had individual rights of freedom, equality, and the formal writ of law.) This marks the beginning stages of the inscription of whiteness through the remaking of nativism in Hawai'i.

Although the geographic stems from a widely reproduced colonial discourse, it carries a very specific effect for claims of nativism in Hawai'i.[49] While this settler/migration/inhabitant discourse racially separates Hawaiians from explorers and *haole* residents and (mis)recognizes their native origins (rather, Hawaiians themselves are outsiders coming in), it also excises the sovereign status from indigenous Hawaiians, which specifically denies them the authority to formally establish their own society and name their settlements sovereign "origins." Indigenous nativism is abstracted while native society is framed as nearing extinction and in need of development. Through signified ambivalence, sovereign nativism ultimately loses its ethnic distinction, as *haole* explorers and missionaries become abstract natives.

The contemporary consequences of these historical articulations have been harsh. From the 1960s to the present, many sovereignty movement groups have faced acrimonious opposition from politicians, business interests, and *haole* and Local residents. These opposing interests contend that Hawaiians have no privileged claim to Hawaiʻi over those of other resident groups. Often, there are references from the above geographic discourses and settlement theories to how even Hawaiians have come from somewhere else to "settle" on the islands.[50] As such, why should one group be highlighted as more native than another? B/c they are actually NATIVE.HAWAIIANS

Invocations of the discourse of settlement and migrations and the abstract native position are reflected in addresses by former state officials, former Governor of Hawaiʻi John Waihee, and Clayton Hee, former chair of the OHA, a state agency created to "aid in the process of Hawaiian sovereignty," during the 1993 Centennial Remembrance of the 1893 U.S. overthrow of the Hawaiian Kingdom. They both appealed to a vision of sovereignty that embraced the presence of the diverse residents who have emigrated to the islands. Waihee explains, "Our challenge is to redefine sovereignty for the 21st century and explore what it will mean for the pluralistic society in which we live today" and to feel a sense of pride in letting "our diversity . . . define who we are."[51] According to Hee, "Sovereignty must avoid racial prejudice, or the inscription of social divisions between Native Hawaiians and non-Hawaiian residents."[52] It becomes interesting how appeals to "race" and "multiculturalism" are explicitly called forth *only* when the identity privilege secured by non-Hawaiian geographic residents is threatened. Dangerously, everyone—at the expense of the Hawaiian—is deemed "natural" to Hawaiʻi.

I also cannot ignore how the identifier *immigrant,* used to describe the traveling shifts of Hawaiians, is deployed to signify equally positioned newcomers who called Hawaiʻi their home, "beginning with the English under Captain Cook, and then Americans who came as explorers, adventurers, businessmen, and missionaries." Joseph Mullins describes other waves of newcomers:

> Newcomers of European ancestry were only the first in a series of population waves bringing in people from many countries who would eventually far outnumber the native Hawaiian population. Next to come in large numbers were the Chinese, then the Japanese, Portuguese, Fili-

pinos, Koreans, Puerto Ricans, Samoans as well as a liberal sprinkling of people from other parts of the world. And, once here, they seldom kept exclusively to themselves, but mixed together in a potpourri of some of the most interesting racial mixtures to be found anywhere. Hawaii's multi-racial nature starts with the arrival of Cook's expedition and continues to this day.[53]

Articulations of selective racialization again cast *kānaka* as foreign inhabitants of their own *'āina* (land) while making all others unmarked natives (which has led to a pressure-filled hierarchy of identities between Locals who were forced travelers from their homes and indigenous Hawaiians who were historically and legally excised out of Hawai'i).[54] Since the 1970s, however, the middle-class Local groups such as the Chinese and Japanese have emerged as *native citizens,* or state residents and U.S. citizens who have become native to Hawai'i through the gradual granting of citizenship and civil rights of belonging. As demonstrated in the tuition waiver controversy at the University of Hawaii, these Locals seem to speak for the interests of the state (e.g., equal rights, the ideology of multicultural harmony), which undermines the claims made by Hawaiians about indigenous belonging and historical dispossession.

Settlement, migration, and origins suggest different power interests and construct particular subject positions: one racially marked for Hawaiians as presociety/prehumanity and the other unmarked as the "discoverer" or the major formal presence for establishing a society, mapping its territorial boundaries and economic relations, and providing workable forms of governance. To originate a place, a landscape, is to invent what has never been invented before. Here any distinction that the origin was externally induced or forced is glossed. The idea of an origin, as geographically and historically mapped, is strictly reserved for the true authorities on newly found societies, the (foreign) European explorers. Indeed *Captain Cook can discover the origins of Hawai'i while natives can merely settle and migrate.*[55]

HAWAIIANS AS SOFT (NORMATIVELY BENEVOLENT) AND SAVAGE (PREHUMAN)

The power of this geographic discourse lies not only in the ambivalent grammar but also in the map form in which it appears. Typically, maps are read as visually enabling views of landscapes, settings, oceans, and continents, views that would otherwise be out of sight. Maps, thus, become essential for knowing what already exists and what we unconsciously assume is beyond our world. This is, perhaps, the very beauty of map knowledges and practices of geographic representation.[56] They are simply invisible through the promise of the visible. What looks to be a panoramic view of the Hawaiian islands in the Pacific Ocean is a selective representation that masks its inscribed power interests through the guise of nature.[57] After all, maps just record what is there.

This particular logic emerges from the Enlightenment embracing of topography as a "Science" that is all at once technical, objective, rational, and reflective. James Duncan and David Ley argue that topography and cartography are practices embedded with power that themselves construct boundaries as they mark and outline them, form territories as they divide them, and historically remember, as in the remembering of Cook's discovery and his "murder."[58] According to J. B. Harley, maps indeed do great cultural work because their authority is unconditionally accepted and their operations taken for granted.

> Both in the selectivity of their content and in their signs and styles of representation, maps are a way of conceiving, articulating, and structuring the human world, which is biased towards, prompted by, and exerts influence upon particular sets of social relations.[59]

As "ceaseless reproduction(s) of culture," maps speak through the reader's expectation of the natural, its surety, and oddly, a demand for something *beyond* the natural—that is, for materially impossible views. So, we take what a map can give us, invoking its constitutive signs, myths, legends, and icons as the totality of a landscape. This is a cartographic consciousness, which subtly requires us to know first and then to learn how to read vested signs (e.g., empty lands, tracking lines, discovery terms, the memorialization of Cook's "murder"). Each sign and mapped point is always articulated in relation to another, to invisible entities, and histories. On its face, the map reader merely translates a mimetic legend. More deeply, we are practicing maps, calling forth naturalized symbols, signs, and hidden historical representations and imaginings, and bringing into being cultural relations, all at once.

In an interesting counterpoint, as sovereign nativism loses its ethnic distinction in the historical imagination, ethnic identity would be hailed for and in the name of *haole* and Local residents. This is achieved through the ambivalent articulation of Hawaiians as being both soft and savage. They would welcome you, open their hearts to you, shower you with gifts, and in the next moment, they would kill you.

Aloha *and Normative Benevolence*

In terms of the construction of Hawaiians as soft and inviting, explorer journal accounts and historical narratives depict a naturalized and unchangeable condition of benevolence. As maps reveal a "natural" remoteness and written histories geographically describe Hawai'i's landscape as pleasant, beguiling, and visually seductive, they are constitutively representing the imaginary ideal of the native via "fresh" and open lands. The represented locational attributes are mindful of its people, as the nature of the physical Hawai'i is read through the cultural nature of its people (the Hawaiians), but framed in such a way that the geographic naturalness is always a priori. Place thus seems derivative of Hawaiianness.

Meanwhile, just when the lines of history seem plainly obvious from those of geography, a formidable alliance surfaces. History and geography work through each other to establish a tight-locked signifying relation of place, nature, cultural values/condition, and identity. For example, most historical summaries of Hawai'i begin with a detailing of the geographic scenery and the highly advantageous climate of Hawai'i.[60] Territorial historian Ralph Kuykendall also maps the following:

> While sunshine is one of the distinctive features of Hawaiian climate, clouds are always to be seen; they drift across the sky and rest like a benediction on the mountain summits; within the space of a few minutes they can appear as if by magic out of the heavens and send down gentle showers or pelting rain . . . and the islands are sometimes spoken of as a "rainbow land."[61]

Kuykendall then identifies and cements together the geographic setting of Hawai'i and the inborn character of Hawaiians. In fact, a Hawaiian disposition fundamentally stems from the representation of nature. They become fused.

> It is a pleasant land in which to live, and hence it is no matter of surprise that the Hawaiian people, who dwelt close to nature in this "paradise of the Pacific" were a healthy, robust, intelligent, and good tempered folk.[62]

They emerged from a kindly nature in that "without hampering themselves with superfluous clothing, they lived a natural life, working as
much as was necessary and by means of their recreations giving the air,
sunshine, and sea water full opportunity to exert a beneficent influence
upon their bodies and spirits. The result was that they were strong in
body and cheerful in disposition."[63]
Clearly, Hawaiians were seen as essentially "cheerful," "pleasant,"
"friendly," and ultimately "benevolent." Even the earliest ship log accounts by Captain Cook and Captain James King described the implicit
connection of "Hawaiianness" to its natural surroundings. They state,

> The civilities of this society were not, however, confined to mere cere-
> mony and parade. Our party on shore received from them, every day, a
> constant supply of hogs and vegetables, . . . and several canoes loaded
> with provisions were sent to the ships with the same punctuality. No re-
> turn was ever demanded; or even hinted at in the most distant manner.
> Their presents were made with a regularity, more like the discharge of a
> religious duty than the effect of mere liberality.
> Three things made them our fast friends. Their own good Natured
> and benevolence disposition, gentle treatment on our part, and the
> dread of our Fire arms.[64]

taken advantage of?

Abundant is Hawai'i, peaceful, mild in temperature, and prosperous,
as are its good-natured, benevolent people. Geography inconspicuously
becomes so through an imagined historical fantasy of an unfeigned
world in the Pacific. Glances of Hawai'i as alone and unfettered, for instance in Kuykendall's map, in relation to historical descriptions of the
geographic nature of Hawai'i implant the first inklings of "Hawaiianness at heart," a necessary Hawaiian cultural value of generosity and
munificence.[65] Denis Wood names such an intricate process "the culturalization of the natural," to be actualized through "the naturalization of
the cultural."[66] He explains that what appears to be a "natural" landscape or indigenous people is the cultural product of meaning and historical and mythic significations, or a set of images and visualities that
bring into being the geographic and its empirical truth.[67] Wood adds
that "it is precisely to the extent that the map culturalizes the natural
that the cultural production the map is must be naturalized in turn, this
to make it easier to accept—as natural—the historically contingent landscape the society that wields the map has brought into being." According

to Wood, in this complicated process, maps "culturalize the natural into existence and naturalize the cultural out of existence."[68]

The sky, land, water, and sea have a "beneficent influence" on the inhabitants of Hawai'i who live close to nature. Cultural values and relations are read through and become conflated with the natural. Thus, Denis Wood's "culturalization of the natural" and "naturalization of the cultural" are tightly united. The natural is the origin of place and Hawaiian subjectivities; untraceable, it is *as is,* inanimate yet solidly real. It is invisibly the beginning (it comes from "Nature") and end (it is Hawaiian nature), both narrative content and outcome; its cultural production, ideally, is never questioned and fully ensured. Also, within such a construction, a feminized, virgin land shapes her people, rewriting an originally ignoble people into one of good cheer and manner. This, in turn, reveals how the openness of the geographic nature becomes partially a source of civilizing and domesticating a deemed "prehuman" race.

[margin note: good natured + beautiful land = conflicted values?]

The natural is created through a colonial encoding for open and free exploration, a primitive nostalgia for the way life was, and a drinking in of the splendor of "nature" (of what was to be racially found). Such a colonial discourse is drawn out and manifested in the naturalness and scientific authority of geography. The geographic provides license to claim its own predominance, without calling attention to its constructedness. You presume the naturalness of gazing at and landing on Hawai'i and engaging what is already there: the purity of the Pacific and the Hawaiians' inner cultural character of benevolence.

In this sense, then, "Hawaiianness at heart" is what I call "normative benevolence," a cultural value that is externally determined yet naturally and internally inscribed to a native subjectivity through "nature." The notion that "Hawaiians are inherently generous" is a vested rereading and (mis)recognition of the philosophical concepts of *aloha 'āina* (love and respect for the land), *Aloha* (sharing, exchange in reciprocity), and *'ohana* (family, kinship, and interdependence). These are reinscribings that mimic a native being and stand as distortions tightly guaranteeing a one-way line of compassion and charity. Thus "(mis)recognition" refers to the politicized appropriation and distortion of cultural practices and identity from a place of dominance. That such a normative value was created at a time period when Hawaiian warfare was at its height, during King Kamehameha's rise to power (when Hawaiian political power was never taken for granted) suggests that "friendly" social relations were

[margin note: but they are taken for granted? So before the text?]

ideologically motivated and articulated into a natural ensemble of relations during the developmental phase of Western colonialism in the Pacific.[69]

While my discussion may suggest that the demarcations between indigenous and reconfigured values are clear, I emphasize that such an encoding is slippery because Hawaiian culture does indeed invoke values based on caring, unity, collectivity, and giving. These values, which echo those naturalized through the "natural" and a fantasy about cultural nostalgia, seem to summon Hawaiians themselves, who easily invoke such a placed "Hawaiianness at heart" identity. How could they not? The values seem to resonate with the cultural practices circulating within their Hawaiian community and memory. For example, in terms of cultural values and modes for social protest, many Hawaiians dismiss sovereignty activists (like the Trasks of Ka Lāhui Hawai'i) for their un-Hawaiian ways; one Hawaiian woman explained, in an interview, that "when I see angry words by Hawaiians, that shows me they are un-Hawaiian. We are naturally peaceful and kind."[70] Another Hawaiian shared her views that sovereignty movements are un-Hawaiian: "We don't handle things that way."[71] Hawaiians do indeed attest to the peaceful nature and built-in reciprocity of their social relations, which are understood through private memory and cultural experience. And these relations make social protest and public challenge by local and diasporic Hawaiians and Hawaiian sovereignty activists especially difficult.

The political stance and subject position from which to interpret cultural values is certainly tricky. For what seems to be a truly indigenous set of cultural values and subjectivities must be understood within its own system of philosophies, languages, historical memories, and terms, and then reconnected to outer, intermingling systems, not to mention the momentary nature of politics. As argued earlier, the "geographic and historical" constitute a signifying process that helps to create a so-called Hawaiian cultural value of openness and generosity, which works in line with a racialized/feminized encoding of native lands. Geography, history, and normative benevolence dovetail into a deep-seated encoding of a subject position created for and in the name of Hawaiians, which is "naturally native."

However, this dominant construction laden throughout popular hegemonic discourse is also deeply resisted by Hawaiians. For example, the *Aloha* spirit or constructed normative benevolence of Hawaiians

("Hawaiianness at heart") that is structured through the culturalization and naturalization of the geographic via maps is rearticulated by Hawaiian scholars and community members as a distorted cultural practice.[72] Hawaiian studies scholar and historian Lilikala Kameʻelehiwa describes *Aloha* as indigenously being a relation of reciprocity between status-similar Hawaiians who would exchange what they received from each other. This was to *Aloha* your neighbor.[73]

However, in my legal-historical analysis of blood, identity, and Western law and governance in the next chapter, I emphasize early Hawaiʻi as not being a definitive social utopia. It was a harshly lived social hegemony sanctified through religion.[74] As such, *Aloha* represented a different social relation between Hawaiians of different status and positionality titles. Between *aliʻi* and commoners, *Aloha* captured the nature of an assumed political relationship. The *makaʻāinana* would gaze upon and love their chief, and herein *Aloha* symbolized their social obligations and loyalties to royalty while also reflecting their beholden social positions. The chief, the "privileged object" of affection, would have *Aloha* for his people, a compassion and duty, though in the reaffirmation of his supremacy.[75] I contend that discursively, this political economy of *Aloha* or love was appropriated by Western outsiders as an ideological structure that blurs the latter function through its former; the colonizing translation of Hawaiian giving (once a practice of exchange between social equals) as natural and willing for the benefit of a new "privileged object of affection," the colonial explorer, American business and government interests, visitor, and tourist, who extends *Aloha* for Hawaiians through a compassion mediated by formal, external law and governance, annexation, federal rehabilitation, capital investment, and consumer exchange. Thus, *Aloha* as the distorted *Aloha* spirit stems from a hegemonic political relationship of power rather than a cultural essence of Hawaiianness.

Moreover, David Malo, one of our earliest Hawaiian historians, who lived in the 1800s, provides us with more resignifications of an *Aloha* value.[76] He explains that Hawaiians often resisted their chiefs and used *Aloha* as a guise for challenging behavior, especially against oppressive ones. They would *Aloha* their chiefs while neglecting their daily duties (tending the land, collecting sandalwood) paid to *aliʻi*. Here *Aloha* or "Hawaiianness at heart" suddenly looks different. It once represented a strategic means of mimicry or performance for *makaʻāinana* to deceive and resist Hawaiian hegemony as well as to gain more goods through trade relations. Leia, a mainland community member, speaks in this vein: "Early days it [Hawai'i] was not about peace. It had wars, struggles. Kamehameha, ehh. To conquer the other chief. *Aloha* came later. Around Cook's time."[77]

The localized historical reader here alludes to the foreign insertion of *Aloha* as the essence of Hawaiianness as opposed to the theme of conquest that pervades narrations of wars between chiefs and kings, and she links it to a particular historical moment: Cook's time (again a signifier of devastating change to Hawaiian life). King Kamehameha I (the leader who unified the islands into a kingdom) therefore is known for his political might or his warrior image; a leader who like other *ali'i* continually engaged in both internal and external political conquest. "Hawaiianness at heart" and *Aloha* therefore form a complex ensemble of politicized constructions at different moments.

A representation of Hawaiians as naturally benevolent and willing to share everything (culture, land, and native sovereignty) further opens and liberalizes native belonging and cultural residents for non-Hawaiians or *haole* and Local residents. What becomes key, though, is that the reconstruction of Hawaiian benevolence in the colonial discourse of the geographic *naturalizes* the unquestioned sharing of everything Hawaiian: ethnic traditions, cultural membership, and claims to sovereignty, land, and artifacts, and as discussed earlier in this chapter, frames speaking practices, rhetorical acts, and modes of social protest as necessarily conciliatory. Once again, native identity and agency are delimited within confining parameters.

The Savage Side

In spite of normative benevolence, the Hawaiian is essentially "native" in the prehuman sense. The *kanaka* is imagined and remembered as ready to strike and pounce in a frenzy. Hawaiians are constructed as normatively benevolent subjects and savage masses, all at once. Historical narratives capture them as generous and friendly in one moment and deceitful and violent in the next. Such a construction speaks to the articulation of Hawaiian identity through complex structures and different linkages that seemingly present two different images: the pure goodness of nativism and its vile impulses. However, the opposition of two identities is precisely the articulatory work of identity; each subject image is needed for the other. Both work in conjunction to signify a Hawaiianness that would enable Western economic/political privilege (via normative benevolence and the friendly nature of natives) *and yet* necessitate a civilizing governance from formal Western religion and law and policy.

For instance, early ship logs and travel accounts by explorers represent a Hawaiian mass that is anxious to greet the newly arriving Westerners. They are remembered and inscribed as somewhat open, hospitable, and inviting. Kuykendall describes such a reflection:

> The appearance of these great ships, the like of which the Hawaiians of that day had never seen before, was a source of amazement and intense excitement among the natives. On both sides the first approaches were made in a friendly if somewhat cautious manner.[78]

But, upon Western arrival, Hawaiians are also constructed as having a dangerous and violent propensity for Western economic goods; *they would kill* just to have the new, shiny trinkets. Hawaiians are historically described as the epitome of foreign desire, raiding, ravaging, and stealing all Western goods from ships and traders. Such foreign desire, in historical fact, is recognized as inciting the large struggle that killed Captain Cook.

> The Hawaiians learned that the strangers had iron in abundance which they were willing to give in exchange for foodstuffs. The natives had only a few small bits of iron and were eager to get more of that precious metal.[79]

In his travel journal, Cook inscribed a Hawaiian savage impulse for Western goods, an irresistible urge the "natives" could not control.

> About noon, Mr. Williamson came back, and reported, that . . . he had attempted to land in another place, but was prevented by the natives, who, coming down to the boats in great numbers, attempted to take away the oars, muskets, and in short, everything that they could lay hold of; and pressed so thick upon him, that he was obliged to fire; by which one man was killed. . . . It did not appear to Mr. Williamson, that the natives had any design to kill, or even to hurt, any of his party; but they seemed excited by mere curiosity, to get from them what they had, being, at the same time, ready to give, in return, anything of their own.[80]

Historian Gavan Daws also naturalizes into being Hawaiian thievery:

> One thing more than most gave Cook trouble with Polynesians—they
> were thieves, and in this the Hawaiians of Kauai were like the rest. As
> soon as they came aboard the Resolution, even before the strangeness of
> the encounter died away, they began to pick things up with the idea of
> keeping them.[81]

Hawaiians, according to historians, could be "satisfied with an iron nail or two," but they always wanted more, never satisfied with just enough foreign objects such as metal, iron, and mirrors. They would want it all. Taken together, the historicized soft and savage identity for and in the name of Hawaiians invokes both their normative benevolence and their violent foreign desire. Cook narrates the cultural character of Hawaiians in the following way: "They seem to live very sociably in their intercourse with one another; and except for the propensity to thieving, which seems innate in most of the people we have visited in this ocean, they were exceedingly friendly to us."[82] He continues hailing their *Aloha* nature and yet their undeniable irrational selves.

> Three things made them our fast friends. Their own good Natured and
> benevolence disposition, gentle treatment on our part, and the dread of
> our Fire arms; by our ceasing to observe the Second the first would have
> wore of[f] of Course, and the too frequent use of the latter would have
> excited a spirit of revenge and perhaps have taught them that fire Arms
> were not such terrible things as they had imagined, they are very sensi-
> ble of the superiority they have over us in numbers and no one knows
> what an enraged multitude might do.[83]

Cook's description of the kindness yet naturalized savageness among Hawaiians takes a more dramatic turn in the discourses of the geographic. For example, in a world map by Samuel Dunn from 1781 (see Figure 3), the Hawaiian islands are marked by a reference to the site "where Captain Cook was killed."[84] Such a reference is reproduced over time in other maps. One example is found in ship artist Giovanni Cassini's map reproduction of Hawai'i (see Figure 4). Here you recognize the mapped tracking lines of explorers but the difference lies in the bottom left-hand corner. There is a visual rendition of a violent encounter between Cook and the "natives." As Cook seems to confront the natives, he is struck

[handwritten margin note: Why are they only examining Cook's account]

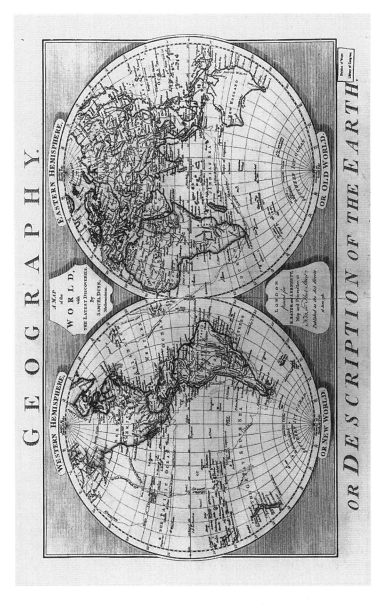

Figure 3. Samuel Dunn, *A Map of the World with the Latest Discoveries*, 1781. Courtesy of the Library of Congress, Washington, D.C.

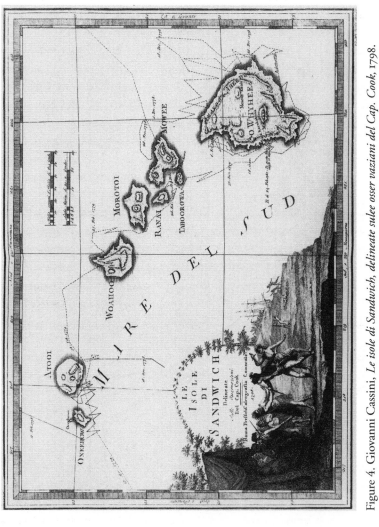

Figure 4. Giovanni Cassini, *Le isole di Sandwich, delineate sulee osser vaziani del Cap. Cook*, 1798.
Courtesy of the Library of Congress, Washington, D.C.

from behind. In addition to Cook's original discovery, Hawai'i therefore becomes a place known for the native killing of Cook, which memorializes the latent savagery of Hawaiians—that uncontrollable native essence.

Again, in map artist George Cruchley's version of the Western hemisphere (see Figure 5), Hawai'i is remembered and racialized via a now-dominant phrase in public memory: "Hawai'i, (Karakakooa Bay), Where Captain Cook was killed by the natives." It becomes interesting how a tragic confrontation between Hawaiians and Cook and his men (as debated by anthropologists Marshall Sahlins and Gannath Obeyesekere), one rumored to be the result of mass fighting and Cook finally drowning within the skirmish, is remembered through a *native* murder of the embraced Cook. The final effect is that Hawaiian identity becomes racialized and marked through the signification of anterior time, anachronistic space, and latent savagery (the thought being,

Hawaiian identity marked by this one historical event

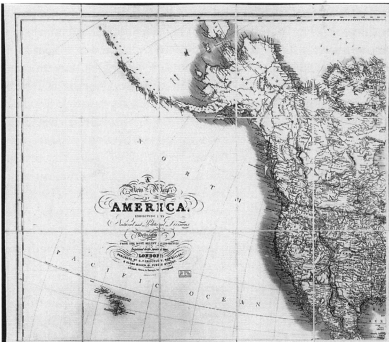

Figure 5. From George F. Cruchley, *A New Map of America, Exhibiting Its Natural and Political Divisions*, 1855. Courtesy of the Library of Congress, Washington, D.C.

Hawaiians would naturally kill, for it is in their nature) via Cook's mapped memorialization.[85]

Indeed, the seemingly contradictory articulation of Hawaiianness as both soft and savage becomes a seamless unity as Daws illustrates:

> They were a handsome race, fortunate enough to live on beautiful islands. Nature had been kind to them and they ought to have responded by developing a perfect humanity, but they had not.
>
> Sometimes Cook found them the most attractive of people, impulsively warm, welcoming, open, hospitable, and frank—a philosopher's delight. Just as often they were deceitful, even treacherous, and occasionally one set of attitudes cloaked the other.[86]

It is clear that Hawaiians are depicted as not only killing, but doing so for the express purposes of gaining Western goods. Anne McClintock argues that the represented native fetishism for Western goods was a colonial product.[87] It represented a construction that hailed the superiority of Western modern objects, their capital and commerce, the "modern" way of living, thus bemoaning the inadequacy of "prehuman" indigenous worlds. To want and lust for Western items was to want to be like *them*; to illustrate the natural human tendency for Western rationality and commodification. Thus, identity constructions of Hawaiianness and their social relations become economically vested in the circulation of commerce and capital; their *Aloha* nature surely opened the way for free trade, capitalism, and occupation (securing residency and travel through Hawai'i forever) while their "violent" ways not only implied the superiority of the Western capitalist system but indicated the need to control, govern, and develop the "ready-to-pounce" Hawaiians. Economic fetishes therefore performed a great deal of cultural work. They invisibly framed intercultural relations through Western economic gains and opened up a path for new ideological agents: Christianity and Western law and governance. Fetishes also gendered Hawaiians. Their *Aloha* nature was a feminized construction, or a signification that domesticated a once warring *lāhui* onto the Hawaiian female body ("she," with her swaying hips and graceful arms, would symbolize the openness—in every way—of the Hawaiian people). Their violence, by contrast, was visualized through the native male body, a masculinity that would be overdetermined and punished under Western patriarchal authority. In this preferred positioning Hawaiians therefore needed to be both, for Western colonialism had too much to lose (and gain). A Hawaiian who is welcoming and threatening reflects—either way and powerfully through both—the natural superiority and necessity of the modern Western world. This is how official memory would rearticulate Hawaiians: as both "soft and savage."

However, again there are openings to reread this construction. According to anthropologist Marshall Sahlins, in archival notes, Hawaiians are represented as engaging in resistive mimicry by not giving in to Western fetishes or laughing and throwing away Western items.[88] He describes ship accounts in which some of Cook's officers complain about the insulting nature of Hawaiians who refused to trade their local goods for modern technology (firearms, gun powder) or traded goods (agricultural foods) perceived to be unequivalent to the "high value" of Western objects (yet another insult to a colonialist ego). While such encodings of Hawaiian resistance remain only within private Hawaiian memory or a few academic accounts, they reverberate against the inviting identifications placed by the historical and popular reproduction of maps. Here a Hawaiian subjectivity is resignified as suspicious and unimpressed with Western arrivals, and *tactical* in attaining Western goods so as to increase social power in relation, not to Western hierarchies of significance, but to a still-felt Hawaiian hegemonic social structure. Such identity challenges become important for Hawaiians as they dialogically confront the dominant discourses of history proper and tourism.

Threaded through the soft and savage ambivalence is a contradistinction between Hawaiians and other savage peoples such as African and Native American peoples. Anthropologists John and Jean Comaroff remind us that not all indigenous peoples were deemed equally savage.[89] While these groups were regarded as generally unruly and savagelike in one way or another, there were critical differences in the articulations between groups. Hawaiians were represented as less savage or violent than the Indians and yet not as "foreign" as the Asian laborers. The contradiction in identifying Hawaiians as both naturally kind and generous and at the same time, strangely violent, constitutes the point of distinction. The discursive operations are complicated. An inherent cultural benevolence on the part of Hawaiians, their warring nature less emphasized, subdues and domesticates an indigenous people and ensures an open nativism and guaranteed sharing of all things to non-Hawaiians and *haole* residents. On the flip side, though, for Hawaiians, their natural predisposition toward fits of native prehumanity (and savagery), calls for and necessitates external "development" and civilizing on the part of foreign interests and British and U.S. law and governance. The people of Hawai'i are reconfigured as potentially adaptive to conditions of modernity but still located in that prehuman space and time. With dominant interests in check, through the oppositional construction of normative benevolence and essential savageness, the imperative to occupy and govern over Hawai'i by colonial forces takes on a morally superior tone. This suggests that such ambivalence extends from a deeper racialized ideology of British and American colonial interests; and the notion that Hawaiians could be "saved" by more civilized nations.

I dare not rationalize colonial sense-making. I only posit that—in terms of discourse and its operations—the geographic and signified ambivalence not only reconfigures indigenous peoples according to differentiating and racializing dimensions of time and space, it also employs oppositional linkages of meaning to empty ethnic distinctions from a traditional Hawaiian hegemony (à la normative benevolence), liberalizes and extends nativism to outside interests (via Cook time and rediscovery), and ensures the long-standing presence of British and U.S. forces within the islands (via the image of the soft and savage native). Throughout the nineteenth and twentieth centuries, Hawaiian benevolence would be popularized and even demanded while an indigenous native position is further stamped out by a modern discourse of citizenship and civil rights of equality.

CONCLUSION

My argument here serves as only a starting point of analysis into the historical discourses surrounding nativism and Hawaiian identity. I have attempted to present the cultural representations of the geographic and its signified ambivalence via maps, explorer accounts, historical narratives, popular texts, and "modern" discourse in reconfiguring sovereign belonging and Hawaiian identity in relation to contemporary debates over indigenous nativism and native entitlements in the cultural politics of Hawai'i.

As anterior time and anachronistic space racialized Hawaiians as premodern, the discovery and sovereign origins of Hawai'i are (mis)recognized in the name of colonial movement and authority. The discursive

[handwritten note:] → marked mischaracterization of identity of a whole group of people

results are long lasting; nativism and sovereignty are redefined along modern terms of racialized difference and extended to *haole* interests. Contemporary debates over who can claim sovereign status to Hawai'i continually resurface; many point to the settlement and migration theories documenting Hawaiians as coming from somewhere else. So the question becomes, At which point and through which means is sovereignty determined? The formalization of a map. The first landing. The presence of formal law and governance. Confounding these possibilities is that all can be favorably argued for both groups (Hawaiians and colonial explorers), though appearing in different forms. The critical difference lies in the privileged discourse and positioning of outside interests and the discursive vehicles of time and space, which in effect racialize Hawaiians.

I do firmly believe that the colonial state, no matter how powerful, proves to be ineffectual even in what appears to be the most overdetermined situations.[90] Hawaiian activists have continually resisted the discursive claims of the geographic by referring to an enduring historical memory and a cultural world and subjectivity in existence centuries before that of other nations. The sticky issue is that rhetorically Hawaiians' resistive claims are always contained within the very discourse that privileges linear time, progressive space, and formal, written language. Other strategic approaches by Hawaiian sovereignty and land movement groups have included appeals to modern edicts of law and governance (especially under the definition of "illegal seizures of land") or redefinitions of the terms of discourse as those systems of meaning that do not necessarily include colonial maps or a linear time vocabulary. And while negative consequences follow from each tactic, the persistent compounding of sovereign nativism with colonial discovery and the resulting *haole* residency in the islands today is troubling in light of my analysis. The key could be to locate contradictions and severe violations within U.S. law (as many activists have been doing) and use "contradiction" and "incoherency" against the nation-state.[91]

The challenge ahead of us is the continual interrogation of the struggle over nativism and sovereign belonging along a complex of varied interests. I argue that *haole* and U.S. interests occupy a different position from that of Locals, who have endured racial injustices as "foreign immigrants," though I am also quick to distinguish Local interests from that of indigenous Hawaiians (not one over the other) in terms of historical specificity, power interests, and racial articulations. They do not occupy the same position or interest. Once we map out these interests and better understand the consequences, pressures, and effected gains in relation to each other historically and politically, it is my hope that we can begin to reenvision indigenous claims of identity and sovereignty—in Hawai'i and across the Pacific and Native America—as significantly different from being just reverse-racist discriminations and exclusions.

The reconfiguration of Hawaiian subjectivity as normatively benevolent and naturally savage brings to light the colonial distortion and disintegration of indigenous context and specificity. By emptying the ethnic distinction of Hawaiian cultural membership and bounded sovereignty, *haole* interests are made native to everything Hawaiian: identity, land, belonging, and artifacts. Their acceptance and generosity is not just granted but made certain, stable, and normalized. This, however, would seem to impart a sense of equality between Hawaiian interests and foreign parties (explorers from Britain, France, Russia, and the United States, missionaries, and business interests). But, the articulated savagery of Hawaiians negates such a possibility, ensuring both liberalized nativism, open cultural belonging, and needed development and guidance by civilized others. Signified ambivalence here recuperates itself, achieving a balancing act and promising a forever-external presence in Hawai'i.

Over time, normative benevolence takes precedence over savagery. Through the golden age of tourism, travel, and global capitalism, Hawai'i and Hawaiians are identified through a requisite *Aloha* spirit— a gaping invocation of all into Hawaiian community and space. As a result, and with the immigration of many Asian Pacific laborers, now the Locals, to Hawai'i, the dangerous discourses of a pluralistic multiculturalism plagues the debates over nativism and sovereignty. State politicians, Locals, and even Hawaiians bemoan Hawaiian sovereignty claims; referencing the Hawaiian value of *Aloha* and benevolence, they argue that Hawai'i has always been open, inviting, and inclusive. Locals claim that they are settlers (just like Hawaiians) to Hawai'i (who have suffered legal and economic [racialized] disenfranchisement) and it has been their "home" for years, in addition to highlighting how Hawai'i has been built on multicultural traditions. Not surprisingly, modes of social protest for Hawaiian activists (in the name of more land or independence as a Hawaiian nation) are immediately devalued in the face of the hailed benevolence and naturalized multiculturalism. Could it be that an effective articulation is one that endures, muting and devaluing most challenges to its own vested production? When an indigenous value, documented in many texts by Hawaiian historians, is reproduced but slightly distorted and mimicked to work for expanded interests, one must consider the historical and political moment in which it is reconfigured, which, in line with the sublation of the warring nature of the early Hawaiians (and its remade symbolism through the popular commodification of Hawaiian warriors and helmets on T-shirts and souvenir tops), is curious. Ultimately, Hawaiians are remembered through a necessary goodness because of the imperative to domesticate and civilize native peoples in the colonial era. In addition, it is this subject position that fuses neatly with the formation of modern citizenship.

In the 1900s, with the incorporation of U.S. law and governance, the signified ambivalence of Hawaiians is recalled at points and reconciled at others. Through a federal "rehabilitation" program, which distributes land portions to qualified natives, Hawaiians are displaced through their incorporation into modern time and space. Their application for land claims, status for producing and tending land, and ability to function within the modern world are questioned. Hawaiians are judged based on modern criteria strange to them (and new in the sense that they for the earlier centuries had not been recognized in relation to them). The U.S. nation-state enacts a dallying dance, recognizing the individual status of Hawaiians, then denying it as they fall short of modern criteria, and overseeing their development. Hawaiians are recognized as potential citizens but only through federal aid and governance.

Perhaps this last discourse seems at this moment the most consequential in the debate over nativism. Business interests and Locals challenge Hawaiian claims to land, tuition waivers, and historical artifacts and sites by drawing on a state citizen discourse based on equal rights and individual freedom. Surely Hawaiians are not entitled to these because they are state properties and thus cannot be denied to any citizen on the basis of race. Race, the construction long denied even to this day in the colonial discourses of the geographic and the law and government commissions of the 1900s, now becomes the "trump card" for safeguarding all non-Hawaiian interests (*haole*, state, and Local interests). This is due to the formation of racialized citizenship, equal rights, and a neutral state through legal and state constructions of Hawaiianness.

but businesses (unless (locals) dont deserve same rights

2

Racialized Natives and White Citizenship

While historical memory shapes the images, expressions, and contemporary claims used to remember particular groups, contexts such as formal law and governance are also deeply imbricated in the cultural processes of modern identification. Federal definitions of indigenous groups (e.g., Pacific Islanders, Native Americans), census categories, legal mandates, the standing to sue, and court cases revolving around issues of native and cultural entitlements all reveal how identities are formally developed for and in the name of groups by dominant and state interests. Indeed, the legal and governmental spheres hold great power in defining, legislating, and enforcing structured identifications that circulate in everyday life and popular society. Critical and legal scholars such as Anne McClintock, Eric Yamamoto, and Mari Matsuda frame law and governance as violent technologies of struggle and identification that exceed the textuality of identity representations.[1] Legal definitions of identity, for instance, are activated and supported by militarization, courts of law, and state administrations and result in material consequences like the denial of indigenous identification for cultural rights and entitlements (land, benefits) and racial (mis)recognition as a means to negate one's formal claim of indigeneity. Moreover, state structures and legal (mis)recognitions shape us as social/cultural subjects and delimit our communicative positionalities and speaking authority within framed identities, thereby defining who is authorized to speak as a true member and who is not. Seen in this light, a social identity analysis should examine how identities are normatively formed by the state, how these are articulated and endorsed by both federal and state tenets through law and commerce, and how particular groups both negotiate and actively reconstitute the framed elements.

In the case of Hawaiians, such encoded identity practices are structurally determined through a blood reference that reifies into existence the primordialist "savage" of the historical imagination. Legal signifiers thus add an intense, violent dimension to Hawaiian identity positionings of prehumanity and savagery (discussed in chapter 1 in the context of historical imagination). These forces—modern law and policy—mystified through a moral spirit, capitalist virtue, and the ideal of (white) citizenship, powerfully (mis)recognize and write over a dynamic, cultural world and an indigenously performed subjectivity.

In this chapter, I trace the racialization of Hawaiians through blood quantum and the inscription of normative white citizenship from its official inception: through the historically situated logic, rhetorical claims, communicative expressions, and identity significations found within the transcripts of the 1920 Congressional Hearings before the Committee on Territories, United States Senate.[2] From these hearings, the Hawaiian Homes Commission Act (HHCA) was officially approved and activated, which ultimately formalized and legislated 50 percent blood quantum as the legal definition of Hawaiianness.[3] In the 1920s, as a result of the HHCA, government homesteading programs were created and designed to "rehabilitate a population-in-need" and place Hawaiians on land parcels. Programs such as these, however, intensely racialized the Hawaiians as "pre-dated savages," in line with the structured discourses of discovery and geography by legislatively inscribing a preformative Hawaiian identity of 50 percent blood quantum. In the HHCA, Native Hawaiians are simultaneously identified and designated a right to land:

> The Congress of the United States and the State of Hawaii declare that the policy of this Act is to enable Native Hawaiians to return to their lands in order to fully support self-sufficiency of Native Hawaiians in the administration of this Act. . . .
>
> "Native Hawaiian" means any descendant of not less than one-half

part of the blood of the races inhabiting the Hawaiian Islands previous to 1778.[4]

Drawing on David Theo Goldberg's (1993) field of racialized discourse and Stuart Hall's (1979) theory of articulation with regard to racial structures and economic relations, I unveil how a governmental-discursive mechanism of race via blood economizes identity for Hawaiians.[5] The spheres of federal and state governance and law (mis)recognize and further racialize Hawaiian identity through the blood discourse of the HHCA, intertwined with historically contingent material and economic demands. These forces write over and (mis)recognize indigenous forms of subjectivity, wholly misreading an indigenous blood metaphor.

Consequently, a hierarchy of subject positions for Hawaiians and *haole* sovereign residents is continually reproduced. Hawaiians become explicitly racialized while the position of citizenship is naturalized, in an unspoken and invisible manner, as white. The HHCA constructs a Native Hawaiian identity position that functions as a form of racial exclusivity or racial purity; that is, Native Hawaiians are designated as being of at least 50 percent Hawaiian blood *sixty years after* the birth of mixed Hawaiians. Despite this lapse of time, the construction of Hawaiianness as the equivalent of 50 percent blood quantum in 1921 is both structurally impossible to substantiate in later years and unreasonable as it excludes Hawaiians from formally claiming their own identity.[6] Part Hawaiians, on the other hand, are framed in terms of degrees of whiteness and white citizenship as opposed to Hawaiian blood, for part Hawaiians are signified as non-Hawaiian and measured against the historically antiquated image of the pure, before-time, and prehistoric native. Through quantum technology, the nation-state (U.S. federal power) determines Hawaiian agency and who is allowed to speak as a Hawaiian, all the while reviving the Western moral project. With the church at an arm's reach, the nation-state frames itself as the preeminent legal-moral authority. Its new promise: "homesteading" would offset the natural inferiority of *Hawaiians* and assimilate them into American citizenship and its dominant capitalist system. In this arena, Hawaiian identity is historically excised, scientifically and legally blooded, and stripped of legal voice and self-representation while also being framed as either a racial exclusivity or a modern identity of citizenship and whiteness.

How was the contemporary formal and legal identification of Hawaiianness in terms of blood quantum and identity expressions—"purebloods" and "mixed-bloods"—articulated and structured by the contexts of law and governance? Such identification of Hawaiians through blood first involved the disintegration of a Hawaiian reality and subjectivity and its replacement by modern law and governance. As such, I present a brief genealogy of Hawaiian reality before and after colonialist contact and, in so doing, examine how blood shifted from an indigenous Hawaiian self-definition to a colonialist technology legislated as policy by the HHCA. I critically engage the Western (British and U.S.) representation of land as a natural right and capitalist duty for all of "humanity," a humanity that conveniently writes out *kānaka* as pureblooded "abject aborigines," or a near-extinct population proven to be "unenterprising, apathetic, thriftless" and "indigent." They, the Hawaiians, historically would be located outside of, before, and incompatible with humanity. This way, the moral vision of Western imperialism could be magically reconciled with driving economic incentive, piercing contradictions concealed; dominant societies would push Christ, progress, and justice to the selectively natural few. The late 1800s would be the dawning of formal Western policy and law, its installed authority swift and merciless for Hawaiians. The natural rights logic of the time later aided the transition into its next historical step: If you couldn't take the blood out of the Hawaiians, surely you could *homestead* them. Land, that pure manifestation of tradition and civilization, would morally proselytize the "wretched." It would make them over. It would build a nation.

In analyzing the structural formations shaping formal-legal identity in the name of Hawaiians, I refer to the "nation-state" or "colonial administration" as the larger national bodies (e.g., Britain, the United States) that historically colonized and imposed their sovereignty over Hawai'i and its people in the mid 1700s. The designation—the "state"—refers to the power of the State of Hawaii, a consolidated localized force exerting control over Hawai'i and Hawaiians, as enabled by U.S. federal power.[7] The state, through administrative bodies, localized state-issued policy mandates, and normative rules, undoubtedly has inherited the authority of the colonial administration established through historical conditions, thus exacting a tight hold over Hawaiians.

Law and governance, therefore, names the historically specific moments and practices—from the late 1700s to early 1900s—through which British and then U.S. policy confronts and disintegrates an indigenous Hawaiian system and subjectivity. This becomes a pressured confrontation that writes out the *kanaka* through the structural exclusion of "prehumanity," a signification embedded in the historical imagination. Hawaiians are constructed as a soon-to-be-blooded group existing outside of Western moral/political jurisdiction through several discursive tools of excision: the doctrine of discovery, the sovereign resident position, the legal principles of ultimate land use and alienation, the incorporation of land commissions, the myth of pure Hawaiian extinction, and blood amount as a reflection of cultural character and authenticity. Tools such as these, normalize "rightful" *haole* citizenry and install a legacy of (mis)recognized identity positions for Hawaiians. While surely there is more than one way to recognize Hawaiianness within and outside of Hawaiian community, there are identity forms that more closely resonate with and serve a lived Hawaiian collective memory and its political interests. To be (mis)recognized is to externally mimic and speak for and in the name of one's subjectivity, inscribing it as native and natural. Understanding the historicization of the legal (mis)recognition of Hawaiians—the shift from an indigenous Hawaiian metaphor of blood to a contrasting Western technology of blood, and from a particular Hawaiian social structure grounded in land use *('āina)* to Western formal policy and governance based on land ownership/ citizenship—reveals the complicated nature of the legal (mis)recognition of Hawaiians and the encoded stakes in current political struggles. Our analytical movements should be to note the dominant framings of Hawaiian identity and uncover the cultural material useful for identity remakings.

MODERNIZATION, RACE, AND THE FORMATION OF CITIZENSHIP

Historically identified through a signified ambivalence in colonial discourse, Hawaiians are reinserted into modernity and its social order in the 1900s and only then recognized by U.S. law and governance in a very specific way. The ambivalent discourse that is discussed in chapter 1 is sublated and employed as the "prehuman" Hawaiians are incorporated into the already moving structure and conditions of modern governance and capitalism. This results in the further displacement of Hawaiians as "unfit," "unproductive," and "in need of rehabilitation" within a modern world, time, and space.

Throughout the HHCA Congressional Hearings, the internal differentiation of Hawaiianness based on blood percentage morally situated U.S. policy and law while also redrawing the race lines around abstract citizenship. Most crucially here, Hawaiians became racialized and judged in terms of individual productivity and citizenship while citizenship remains white. My historical genealogy of Hawaiian identity and land unveils how land already articulated one kind of subject (sovereign resident) over another *(kanaka)*. As U.S. law and policy entered the picture in the 1900s, the land that had been historically collected needed to be preserved in its name. Homesteading emerged as this act of preservation, framing the nation as the saving grace of a dying race, thus rehabilitating and reforming the Hawaiian race as its necessary moral duty.

The signified ambivalence of the 1700s and 1800s was invoked and sublated at the same time, deeming Hawaiians either as doomed to prehuman extinction and failure or as potential citizens who fall short of individual productivity and ideal (white) citizenship. Throughout the 1900s, Hawaiians were judged against modern notions of difference, possessive individualism, and citizenship. It is no wonder then that they fall short at every turn; formerly deemed prehuman and yet benevolent, Hawaiians were inserted, misrecognized, and disadvantaged within modern conditions. They differed in their means of tending land from Western ways and capitalist models of land production; as official citizens, Hawaiians were recognized as largely inferior. They were also seen as dying out. So the articulation of Hawaiian "prehumanity" still operates underneath a larger discourse of modern citizenship; the determining structure is based on modern conditions while Hawaiian subjectivity is based on colonial articulations of the geographic, again making necessary U.S. governance and development. Yet, those of mixed Hawaiian blood (part Hawaiian and part *haole*/Portuguese/Chinese) were characterized as possessing the potential for U.S. citizenship. A potential citizen position for these mixed-bloods was held at bay, which ultimately exempted the nation-state from furnishing valuable land and resources and ushered in an impending civil rights and equality discourse after statehood. Nativism in this way would be more about individual citizenship, ownership, and residency underneath a uniting U.S. nation-state.

The Historicized Race-ing of Hawaiians: A Genealogy of Identity

The dramatic restructuring of Hawaiian identity can be traced from the time of early Hawaiian society until the 1900s, a period in which the modern colonial state had already overwritten indigenous forms and inscribed new identities. Several excellent historical and legal analyses of Hawaiian land by historical/legal scholars Lilikalā Kameʻeleihiwa, Melodie MacKenzie, and Linda Parker ground my genealogy.[8]

Raced identities, specific to time and space, are created through articulated structures, namely the "fits between different instances, different periods and epochs, indeed different periodicities, e.g., times, histories" "and different moments within/out a structure."[9] By analyzing the combination of elements within a historically specific structure, we play with the possibility of temporarily witnessing the processes of power and identity construction, in all their moving forms. Lisa Lowe opens up the past in this way; she exposes the invisible race-ing of Asian American immigrants and links it to present strategies of Asian Pacific American movements and actors.[10] In the same spirit, the race-ing of Hawaiians—as an inferior race "in the blood" and in contradistinction from sovereign residents of Hawaiʻi (as national subjects of somewhere else), American citizens, "Oriental" labor, and Indian "aliens"—can be seen, though just for a moment, through several historical/political collisions and cataclysmic formation shifts. These include a uniquely noncapitalist Hawaiian social formation unified and stratified through religious ideology; the formal structures of governance, law, and commerce directed by Great Britain, France, and the United States; and unrelenting U.S. moral, political, and economic aggression.

Hawaiian subjectivity begins well *before* Captain Cook's arrival and the written word. It is captured in Hawaiian oral memory and genealogy as a moving world centered on *ʻāina* (life through land).[11] *ʻĀina* was not a mere physical space; it translates in Hawaiian as the act of living through land. *ʻĀina* was a way of life revolving around a spiritual understanding of land as the natural, deified force of Lono, the god of fertility and love, or Kāne, the god of agricultural growth. Land was therefore the physical manifestation of a greater nonmaterial power. You couldn't own it. You were blessed to have its sacred presence in your life.[12] Through the land, these *akua,* among others, watched over and cared for Hawaiians, bestowing rich soil and conditions for the bountiful production of food for a thriving population. The population, estimated by David Stannard to have been at least 800,000 to 1,000,000 at the time of contact, dropped to less than 40,000 by 1890.[13]

Collectively, within their own inherited social positions, Hawaiians were culturally summoned both to live through and work the land in specialized labor. Assigned different duties, the overall goal was to carefully tend the land so that it would bear enough food for all people.[14] The *akua* ruled over and emanated from the land, which explains why Hawaiians culturally never understood or expressed the principle of ownership. In their language, you could not commercially own or hold title to a greater religious being. You could temporarily possess land, but never truly materialize a larger structure of *mana* (spiritual power). The *mōʻī*, a supreme chief, held the land in their honor as a God-appointed trustee.[15] Trustees were those deemed to be of divine blood kinship, meaning that particular relations were honored and elevated because they were closer to the gods in birthright and thus held great *mana*. They were our *Aliʻi Nui* (Hawaiian leaders/royalty).

From an indigenous Hawaiian perspective, then, blood was understood in terms of performative kinship relations. Blood symbolized divine status as destined leaders of the Hawaiian *lāhui* and the relative closeness to the *akua*. Through the practice of blood via *Niʻaupiʻo* matings, or incestuous relations among the higher social classes, a higher social class of Hawaiians could increase and preserve their *mana*. To engage in incestuous relations was also performatively to be of Hawaiian divinity, such as with half-sibling matings and uncle-niece and aunt-nephew matings, which "bridged the generation gap."[16] Traditional Hawaiian genealogies, in this context, demonstrated the rightfulness of certain *Aliʻi Nui* to care for the Hawaiian people. Higher, close-to-*akua* status was established through a lived blood metaphor. Different from signifying a biological substance and percentage amount in the indigenous context, blood instead served as a performative indicator and producer of the collective honor and *mana* of a family, thereby marking a difference between an indigenous practice of blood and an imposed state policy of blood.[17]

While claims to the purity of a family line appear in traditional Hawaiian texts, genealogies serve a *cultural function*.[18] They bring into being an identity of "who one is" through those before and after her or him. We typically think of genealogies as family maps proving predetermined descendancy; but Hawaiian genealogies articulate from whom someone descends (top-down, in response to a question, Where are you from?) as well as how one's line ascended relations (how certain members could rise up).[19] As a metaphor, blood is double-sided, seemingly positioning genealogies as purely factual and indisputable tables of parentage, while symbolically encoding them as to-be-performed relations via *Niʻaupiʻo* matings and chantings. Genealogies were not guaranteed or even valued for their accuracy as fixed truths. They were to be, within a certain social class, re-created and reconstituted time and time again. Genealogies would move. If you were *aliʻi*, you could move through them. Genealogical practices ritually served to create and preserve a variety of Hawaiian epic stories and make real certain social relations, some of which were historically privileged.[20] For Hawaiians, these rich stories—their stories and crafted life-tales—represent sense-making models for everyday experiences and social relations.

With a genealogically divine status, the *mōʻī* was granted responsibility for a *moku,* a large land division equivalent to the size of an island, which typically was an independent kingdom.[21] The *mōʻī* and *aliʻi* politically protected those within their designated area in times of war, while religious priests made certain that all *akua* were respected with the appropriate ceremonies and sacrifices. To do so was to demonstrate their *mana* and secure more of the same. A leader who provided for his people was considered a favorite of the *akua.*

Lower in the social hierarchy were the *makaʻāinana* who worked and cultivated *ahupuaʻa,* which were land units that extended from mountaintop to coast, encompassing terrains for wet- and dryland farming and inshore fishing. On these land units, the commoners were entitled to use all food and water resources of the land. Use was a privilege granted by the *akua.* The *konohiki,* a type of land supervisor, managed the *makaʻāinana* labor in order to ensure organized and timely cultivation. Hawaiians religiously made sense of this status hierarchy; they believed that each Hawaiian, in different social roles, worked and lived in interdependence. Although the social hierarchy structurally formed disproportionate power relations between the chiefs and *makaʻāinana,* there was a perpetual give and take. If the *mōʻī* or *aliʻi* failed to care for the *makaʻāinana* or abused their power, the *makaʻāinana* could move their labor and loyalty to another chief's lands, a considerable loss to the *mō'ī.*[22] If the Hawaiians neglected their work or the *konohiki* abused their power, the *ali'i* could banish them from the land.[23]

In a cultural frame different from a market-driven society, *'āina* was *not* a capitalist-centered system with commercially valued land. Instead, productivity was always a spiritually infused offering by the *akua*. Land productivity therefore meant the amount of food cultivated to feed a bustling population and the social and cultural use of land by the larger Hawaiian community. They would use and live off the land. Land use was ensured as long as proper respect was given to the gods and social groups performed their designated labor. Archival material depicts the land base at this time—one marked by the greatest amount of warfare in the islands—as richly fertile and expansive, thus affirming the deep structure and organization of Hawaiian *'āina*. Yet Hawaiian life was not perfect. There were limits within this organized social system. Only the *mō'ī* and *Ali'i Nui* could materially attain and control land through conquest or inheritance (especially in the case of ruling chiefs with distinguished lineage). The *maka'āinana* would be able to live on land, but never materially make claim to it.

In a non-Western culture motivated by deeply held religious and cultural practices, religiosity constituted the lived relations of Hawaiian society. It stood as the primary force in reproducing a secure, fully functioning social formation. Scholars like Elizabeth Buck highlight the difference between capitalist and noncapitalist formations; religion ideologically united an indigenous culture. She analyzes how Hawaiian religious practices "sanctified social relationships, maintained the hierarchical divisions between sacred rulers and the less-sacred ruled, and ideologically resolved structural contradictions."[24] The religious ideology of *akua* and *mana* therefore framed and motivated the social structure and the economic practices of food and resource production. Buck identifies this naturalization of power-vested relations in precontact Hawai'i as hegemonic. Such a cultural hegemony should be recognized for largely reconstituting a Hawaiian social hierarchy, even among destabilizing pressures of continual warfare among competitive *ali'i* and grievances by several *maka'āinana* for being abused by their *ali'i* or *konohiki*.[25] The hegemony of the early Hawaiian everyday would be politically transformed and historically subsumed under a larger struggle for existence at all, only when it is thrown in crisis by Western contact and the colonization of the 1700s.[26]

The Making of the Sovereign Resident: National Loyalties, Property Ownership, and "Primitivized" 'Āina Use

In the eighteenth century, European "discoverers" set out for the New World and its exploitable wealth. Sometime around 1778, secondary Western cultural contact was established through several, coaligning forms. The first contact already took place—at home—through the religious doctrine explicating the noble mission of the Christian nation and the untamed New World and its peoples who had yet to find the word of God.[27] From the initial intercultural meetings of "discoverer" and "native" on the decks, to the sexual affairs down below between Cook's men and Hawaiian men and women (which led to the spread of venereal disease and the swift collapse of the Hawaiian population), the native body called for the suspension of Western virtue for exoticized sexuality—the intriguing native male to be politically contained and the native female whose nonthreatening yet luring appeal pleasurably exceeded colonial domesticity and social conduct. Underneath the large banyan trees, American Congregationalist and French-Catholic missionaries eloquently promised physical and eternal life to the "heathenist" Hawaiians who only saw death and disease all around them. John Kelly said, "While we gazed to their heavens, they stole our land from beneath our feet."[28] These missionaries proclaimed that Jehovah or Christ could indeed save the Hawaiians from mass extinction.[29] Near the shipping docks, those points on the culturalizing maps, traders from Britain, Spain, Russia, and the United States circulated Western objects of metal, iron, guns, and ammunition to *Ali'i Nui* for Hawaiian sandalwood. On the stretches of Hawaiian land and yet cultural worlds apart from *'āina,* European and U.S. business interests and political figures questioned the Hawaiian Kingdom's strange form of governance and land tenure system, urging for the formalized institution of property rights for all residents. Through the melding of discovery, sexual desire, the transgression through Christ, trade and commerce, and formal policy, the Hawaiians would surely be (mis)recognized and reidentified.

As foreigners flocked to Hawaiian shores, King Kamehameha, a leader who has been described by historians as wise to the ways of modern nations, allowed *haoles* to live on land parcels, but through an agreement that somewhat paralleled traditional Hawaiian land tenure forms: the exchange of Western services for land use.[30] For their skilled work in circulating Western goods and practices, carpenters, shipbuilders, masons, blacksmiths, and physicians could reside in the islands and enjoy the free use of the land. Ownership or land title was never formally granted to these first lessees. Thus, the exchange of Western goods and services was absorbed into the still-predominantly noncapitalist, traditional Hawaiian formation.[31] Within the extant, ideologically bound hierarchy, Western goods represented new means to elevate one's social position and *mana*. The strange and shiny mirrors, metal pieces, nails, and iron buckets, to Hawaiians, clearly paved the divine path to power from the *akua*.

The *ali'i*, enamored with items first brought by Cook and his men, often exerted *maka'āinana* labor to cultivate sandalwood, which could then be traded for iron, guns, and fur.[32] The *maka'āinana* could not keep up with the debt demands of their *ali'i*, a debt to traders and foreign interests that could only be paid off through the surrendering of land, and this cycle took its toll.[33] This act forever changed the Hawaiian social structure. The cultural economy secured through Hawaiian religious practices and strong leadership gradually dissolved as Western goods and its exchange value dominated social relations.[34] Meanwhile, local government power amid the constant influx of *haoles* maintained the Hawaiian Kingdom, at least for a while (the number of *haole* residents exploded from a total of 5 in 1790 to 200 in 1817).[35]

After the Hawaiian islands were unified into one kingdom in 1810 by King Kamehameha, land tenure changed to ensure political stability.[36] Tactically, to retain the loyalty of those around him and establish Hawai'i as a *lāhui* capable of strong foreign relations with national powers, Kamehameha granted land parcels to lower *ali'i* and foreigners who served as political advisers.[37] These *haoles* presumed a natural right to land through which they were entitled—*before* any formal institution of Hawaiian law and *through* sovereign ideologies back at home—to pass land onto their heirs and families. This would become a prevailing mode of identity-logic throughout the 1800s, informed by the historical discourses of discovery and origins.[38]

King Kamehameha was determined to maintain the Hawaiian Kingdom in the face of great change (e.g., the arrival of *haoles*, the increasing death rate of his people). Thus, in 1814, he expelled all foreigners without land tenure, especially those who were disruptive to island life or those individuals who displayed drunkenness and corrupt influences.[39]

However, Kamehameha's unique leadership, in which he invoked modern necessities (iron, metal, guns, and ammunition) while maintaining cultural tradition, would end with his death in 1819. Hawai'i would never be the same. The Western upheaval of Hawaiian life in the 1800s, as if by colonial magic, obscured and politically transformed the traditional Hawaiian hegemonic order—with its harsh social divisions and *kapu* laws—into an oppositional flash of memory. Social differences and divine status elided, Hawaiians would struggle for a Hawaiian subjectivity in any name or title. They would fight for their *ali'i* and themselves as a threatened *lāhui*.

Immediately after his father's death, Liholiho (Kamehameha II) assumed the throne, as *haole* residents and *ali'i* continued to push for the formalization of land inheritance within Hawaiian land tenure.[40] Soon it was solidified as law. In 1825, a young Liholiho and the Council of Chiefs, heavily influenced by Britain's Lord Byron, adopted a formal policy—the Law of 1825—allowing *ali'i* to transfer retained lands (upon the king's death) to their heirs.[41] This right had *already* been ideologically assumed (and not yet formally recognized by Hawaiian leaders) ten years earlier by foreign-born residents. *Haoles* from Britain, France, Russia, and America believed they "naturally" had individual rights of property and ownership to land they occupied. In fact, even in the face of expulsion from Hawai'i, many *haoles* blatantly conducted business with one another, leasing, selling, and buying titles to land that was formally held by *ali'i*.[42] Thus, residency for Westerners ideologically exceeded mere use and leasing of land. It encompassed a superior right to the New World based on the natural order of humanity. Through the reigning mandates of their imperial homelands, *haole* (foreign) residents called on intermingling natural rights and discovery discourses together with their national identities to claim privatized rights *before, outside of,* and thereby, *over* indigenous structures.

Dating back to sixteenth-century Europe, natural rights and the doctrine of discovery constructed an unspoken racializing hierarchy of developed white nations and primitive peoples.[43] Stepping onto virgin lands in the 1700s, European Christian nations brought with them their religious virtue and "developed" forms of law and politics, which "naturally" impelled these nations to name their own supremacy over "savage tribal peoples." Written over by the laws of nature, Hawaiians were located as an unchanging, inferior "prehumanity" whose heathenist ways—the puzzling oversight of God (for how could you overlook the splendor of the Christian God?) and the lack of individuated, competitive modes of land production—proved their separation from all human groups. Natural distinctions such as these, ideologically positioned *haoles* as superior and worthy of land ownership, a privilege that would not be proffered to Hawaiians.

The material inequalities between *haoles* and Hawaiians and the glaring, intrusive presence of Westerners paradoxically conflicted with their proclaiming of Christian morality and its promised salvation: that Christ would save, liberate, and nourish all human life. This conflict was suppressed and recuperated, however, by differentiating between "humanity" and those who were "non-" or "prehuman." The Western-exclusive membership of Christianity was naturally justified as being reserved solely for "humanity": for able, civilized citizens who could live and work according to the word of God. Those without rights, privileges, and the land and wealth they afforded, were clearly and naturally "not human." Thus, while Hawaiians were indigenously installed into social positions because of religious ideology *(akua, mana),* Western contact ushered in a much larger religiosity coarticulated with brazen world imperialism, which stood as a sweeping formation that racialized and excluded natives in the same moment it created and normalized white citizen-subjects.

Living without contradiction, European settlers and American residents framed Hawaiians as "uncivilized" and "lazy," for they could not produce land and lacked any proper modes of governance that facilitated citizenship and individual labor.[44] Hawaiians, it seemed, could not sustain their society. Hiram Bingham, an American Calvinist missionary and instigator of the 1893 overthrow of the last Hawaiian monarch, Queen Lili'uokalani, harshly expressed the savage inferiority of Hawaiians in

> the appearance of destitution, degradation, and barbarism, among the chattering, and almost naked savages, whose heads and feet, and much of their sunburnt swarthy skins, were bare, was appalling. Some of our number, with gushing tears, turned away from the spectacle. Others with firmer nerve continued their gaze, but were ready to exclaim, "Can these be human beings! How dark and comfortless their state of mind and hearts! How imminent the danger to the immortal soul,

shroud in this deep pagan gloom! Can such beings be civilized? Can they be Christianized?"[45]

It was primarily within this locus—a combination of religious doctrine backed by the law of nations or the justification for New World discovery and conquest and the citizenship ideal of capitalist virtue—that the Hawaiian is excised out of temporal existence, residing only in the historical imagination as "before time" or "pre-European/before Cook time."[46]

Capitalist virtue resonated throughout Christian European nations and a similarly structured early America. It captured the ideal citizen-subject, one who lived according to a pure Christian faith of truth, community, chastity, and benevolence to others. A true citizen would pray and work and produce the land, so that the land-as-Western-capitalist-machine would always produce more goods—agricultural products and livestock—in excess of itself. This was true, right, and good; this was the Christian life. Thus, capitalist virtue inscribed a private resident subject in Hawai'i, or a self-interested subject who individually worked the land through an intimate, predestined relationship between nature and God. The principle of capitalist virtue assumes that man, a godly subject, was encouraged to exercise the interdependence of the human-land connection and actively draw out the inmost naturalness of the land. Virtue in this sense required work and ability, for land was a limited, often unmanageable, and, thus, unguaranteed resource. With the onus to prove their Christian goodness, subjects ironically set out to exert the highest form of control and dominance (termed "ultimate use") over nature.[47] Linda Parker traces the Western concept of ultimate use to European philosophical discourse and, for example, Sir Thomas More's law of nature argument: "When people holdeth a piece of ground void and vacant to no good or profitable use: Keeping others from the use and possession of it, which notwithstanding, by the law of nature, ought thereof to be nourished and relieved."[48] In the 1830s, *haole* residents pressed *ali'i* to incorporate a land law embodying this principle of ultimate use.[49] Hawaiians accordingly should receive land five times the amount they cultivated. As a result, any undeveloped land would be placed on the market.[50] This circumscribed a means of attaining a majority of Hawaiian lands while also setting into place a commercial economy based on the practice of private ownership and market competition among individual farmers. Formal modern law therefore installed a normative white citizen position while differentially marking Hawaiians as outside of Christian principles and the societal good. Their tribalistic rituals and lack of land production and economic sustenance placed them outside of legal citizenry, their identities and practices (mis)recognized by Western colonialism.

The Christianized encoding of land reproduced a different structural formation and promised that the Western land system would save and cure the inferior Hawaiians. Through capitalist virtue, Hawaiians could be remade through the promotion of Christian behavior. Land reform would create a class of independent Hawaiian farmers who could support larger families and thus reverse their massive depopulation. We were told that land would save us.

A New World order and its accompanying natural rights discourse therefore collapsed into, collided into, and racially restructured a Hawaiian social formation. After 1820, residents clamored for the necessary transition from usufruct (the granted *use* of land held in title by the *ali'i*, who could revoke land tenure at any time) to the Western ideal of fee-simple ownership (the absolute, unrestricted ownership of land). *Haoles* engaged in practices that partly dissolved the local native structure, such as intermarriage between *haole* men and Hawaiian women as well as the invocation of the doctrine of discovery and national identities.[51]

After the land inheritance mandate was approved in 1825 and Hawaiians continued to convert to Christianity, many *haole* men married Hawaiian women. Such interpersonal acts could not be separated from the Western colonialist project. They provided relatively open access to Hawaiian land through the Hawaiian women's families and their children.[52] From a structural standpoint, the apparatus of formalized marriage with foreigners undermined the traditional Hawaiian social hierarchy and threatened land retention among Hawaiians. Hawaiian women—whose dangerous sexuality both necessitated patriarchal authority in the name of a Christian God and the law (the legal sanction of Western marriage)— suddenly found themselves subordinately positioned as indigenous matrilocal power was displaced within a foreign hierarchy of white men.[53] Domesticating Western marriage between Hawaiian women and *haole* men therefore threatened the social stability found within the Hawaiian cultural hegemony.

As new marriage and love moved throughout Hawaiʻi, *haole* residency regirded itself. Private residents (British, French, and American) amplified their identity rights and privileges in Hawaiʻi by invoking the doctrine of discovery and the authority of their national homeland governments. These dominant discourses constructed a special form of residency; one in which *haole* residents could call on the law of nations, which ideologically authorized a nation's exclusive jurisdiction over new territories discovered by its representatives. Here they would claim privileged status in Hawaiʻi with complete rights, uses, and authority and compel their home governments to overrule local affairs of Hawaiian land tenure.[54] Thus, a new identity position was created, that of the *sovereign resident* who had absolute power over indigenous tenets.

Historian Linda Parker explains that in the 1830s, American ships landed at Oahu to settle foreign complaints about property rights.[55] Threats of military action by the United States loomed in the air if *aliʻi* failed to accommodate foreign demands for fee-simple ownership.[56] In 1839, a French ship *L'Artemise* docked at Honolulu to investigate the native injustices against French Catholic priests and their newly acquired Hawaiian converts. To appease the French and prevent impending attack, on behalf of the ruling monarch at the time, Kamehameha III, the *aliʻi* Kekauluohi and the governor of Oahu agreed to several demands made by French officials, one of which allowed for the exchange of land as the site for a Catholic church. In addition, Kamehameha III signed a treaty with French officials, ensuring the "protection of French residents in their 'persons and property.'"[57] Treaties between national powers and the Hawaiian monarchy (e.g., the Jones Treaty of 1826, British and French treaties) became common fare as the jurisdiction of formal Western law and policy of nation-states, or the larger colonial administration, penetrated the established Hawaiian political structure and transferred citizenry rights *only to* foreigners in the Pacific.[58] Their identities were permanently established as sovereign and formalized.

A prime example of the imposition of white patriarchal law can be found in an 1840 land claim dispute between British consul Richard Charlton and the Hawaiian government. Charlton had received a land claim and pushed for recognition of his 299-year lease title to a large land parcel.[59] But the Hawaiian government refused, reasserting the governing principle for land tenure as officially declared in the Constitution of 1840:

Kamehameha I was the founder of the kingdom, and to him belonged all the land from one end of the Islands to the other, although it was not his own private property. It belonged to the chiefs and people in common, of whom Kamehameha I was the head, and had the management of the landed property. Wherefore, there was not formerly, and is not now any person who could or can convey away the smallest portion of land without the consent of the one who had or has the direction of the kingdom.[60]

The *ali'i* argued that Charlton could formally claim a lease title to only a portion of the parcel. He argued that a Hawaiian regent granted him all of the land. On behalf of Charlton and all British subjects with vested land claims, Lord George Paulet intervened and sought military action against Hawai'i. King Kamehameha III feared the forced takeover of the kingdom and, as a result, temporarily ceded Hawai'i to Britain, hoping for a British sentiment of justice and the complete restoration of the Hawaiian Kingdom. Judicially decided within British courts, officials ruled in favor of the Hawaiian monarchy on all charges, except the Charlton land claim.[61] Although Hawaiian governance strictly forbade unapproved land exchanges, Richard Charlton's title was legally upheld through British authority, which declared at the moment of the ruling that it officially held the islands as British terrain. Thus, national/ colonial jurisdiction through forced aggression, formal policy, and imbalanced foreign relations installed sovereign residency as superior to indigenous rule via the negation of such indigenous rule. Sovereign residency also held the colonial license to realize substantially more privileges than *maka'āinana* within their own Hawaiian social order. Only the king held land title in the name of both *ali'i* and *maka'āinana*. Through this sovereign resident subject position, the *maka'āinana* were severed from the then-existing Hawaiian governmental structure and subordinately inserted into a social system based on the Western capitalist market of land and vying multinational powers. Discursively then, *haoles* assumed a built-in, normalized stance, one they had already practiced at home. And only *kānaka* (*mō'ī, Ali'i Nui, maka'āinana* together) were marked as inferior, nonindustrious inhabitants of land. Even though foreigners gained incredibly—land inheritance rights via intermarriage, the enlistment of their sovereign governments, and extremely discounted fifty-year land leases—Hawaiian leaders still refused to surrender ownership rights to their land.

Writing-Over 'Āina As a Formal (Individual) Private Right: A Legal-Economic Alliance

Ali'i submission to colonial power would be coerced through the rapid disintegration of Hawaiian land tenure from the *inside*. By the late 1800s, several *haoles* occupied influential positions within the Hawaiian government. Others established commercial outfits like plantation farms for agricultural plots and sugar.[62] These occupations would center a new cultural world for Hawai'i. In the 1900s, with the acquisition of millions of acres of Hawaiian land, these plantations prospered into commercial industries that required enormous amounts of labor (the legally disenfranchised and excluded "alien" Chinese, Japanese, Portuguese, Korean, and Filipino immigrant laborers who settled in Hawai'i), even more land, and a political structure that enabled its continued success.[63] Rapidly and deeply, Hawai'i became a forum for foreign interests, at the expense of indigenous Hawaiians.

Stuart Hall and C. Bettleheim theoretically suggest that a noncapitalist formation such as the traditional Hawaiian social order changes through a dissolution-conservation dynamic or the partial dissolving and restructuring of an indigenous structure, which eventually holds and activates, in just the right moment, conserved capitalist structural material.[64] Indeed, pressures inside Hawaiian governance—the growing economic dependence on trade and the tight-knit relation between land property and financial profit, and the increasingly invoked sovereign resident identity position—chipped away at the once-secure local native structure during Kamehameha I's rule. I stress that an indigenous and sovereign Hawaiian identity is gradually extracted by a sovereign resident position that seems more native as a citizen in its widening access to Hawaiian land entitlements and protection from national governments. Modern (British and U.S.) law, the final thread, draws together the brewing-beneath-the-surface predominant forms: an aggressive colonialist political order, capitalist relations, and racially bound citizenship. Through the codification of equalized rights to land and the formal recognition of a private resident, the law unifies the economic and political aspects of an emerging nation-state.

The coarticulated forces of formal modern law, policy, and commerce overwhelmed Hawaiian society. In 1845, pressured by influential foreigners and interested in empowering Hawaiians, Kamehameha III agreed to establish a land commission to approve privatized land claims by Hawaiians and residents. He strongly reminded all vested interests that Hawaiian land tenure would still formally guide this commission. Soon after, in 1848, the *Ka Māhele* (division) mandated the equal division of the Hawaiian Kingdom lands among the king, chiefs, government, and Hawaiian people.[65] The king claimed and divided approximately 2.5 million acres of all Hawaiian lands, 1.5 million of which were designated as the "Government Lands" of the Kingdom of Hawai'i.[66] The leftover 984,000 acres of the king's allotments were set aside as the lands of the institution of the monarchy; these were the "King's Lands" (or "Crown Lands").[67] After the king's share, the *ali'i* were assigned the remaining 1.6 million acres of the kingdom, which were privatized and awarded to 245 chiefs; only portions of these lands could be claimed by chiefs and native tenants and money payment made for titles would revert back to the government. Hawaiians were framed here as private tenants who, when occupying any of the lands allotted to the chiefs (1.6 million acres), possessed ownership rights and thus were formally obligated to individually cultivate these lands. Such a concept was strange to Hawaiians. This new structure conflicted with their *akua*-centered communal land structure based on specialized labor and reciprocity. As newly native tenants, Hawaiians could assume their rights by first applying to a land commission board for a fee-simple title claim through a historical act known as the Kuleana Act.

In the same month the Kuleana Act passed, July 1850, as pressure surmounted, the Hawaiian government granted allodial (fee-simple) ownership to foreign residents regardless of citizenship, so long as political intervention on the part of their governments was not practiced. As defined in the Kuleana Act, native tenants could be awarded fee-simple titles to individual richly fertile plots of land *(kuleanas),* which were to be taken out of the Chiefs' Lands.[68] Formally designed to provide for *maka'āinana,* the Kuleana Act minimally benefited Hawaiians. Only 26 percent (7,500 *maka'āinana* males) of the total native male population actually received claimed lands, or "only 28,600 acres (less than 1 percent of the total land)" were transferred in title to Hawaiian commoners.[69] A whopping 74 percent of native males thus remained landless.

The Kuleana Act foretold the legal future of Hawaiians: containment under the procedural hands of the law. For example, the notion of a land commission for native tenants operated under the premise that a tenant identity and land rights existed only *through* and *after* legal recognition. The act itself, while posing as an equitable procedure of law, necessitated completion in order for a Hawaiian (male) to gain the right to land. Completion seemed a difficult (and designed to be unlikely) feat, for potential tenants first had to understand English, the often ambiguous and all-too-specific letter of the law, and the complex nature of an entirely new land system through which use was reframed as an individual entitlement given certain conditions and duties. Most Hawaiians, however, did not know English nor could they take hold of these massive changes; they dismissed the Kuleana grants as a form of betrayal against their *Aliʻi Nui,* who they feared would punish them for accepting the new policy. This refusal reflected how difficult it was for Hawaiians to break from an interdependent, albeit imperfect, hegemonic order in which food and basic needs were for the most part guaranteed, to one tiered by relatively autonomous yet cooperating power outlets. Suddenly, sustenance, a responsibility that for Hawaiians called for interdependent, organized labor, was based according to the Western way: individual ability and competition. To Hawaiians, the prospects seemed dismal.[70]

Complicating the supposedly neutral procedurality of law, native applicants were required to present surveys of the land plots being claimed. However, surveys were conducted mostly by *haole* missionaries, who could read and write in English. Surveyors and census enumerators politically held the advantage of English in record keeping, which would later haunt Hawaiians in their search for seemingly accurate documents. The surveys were also expensive and reflected the dominant ultimate-use land law in which many surveyors only reported the amount of land cultivated and not the totality held.[71] Moreover, all land applications were to be filed and documented within a brief period of four years, a time substantially less than it took for Hawaiians to understand the whirlwind of legal technicalities, save enough money to pay for a survey, and find a fair surveyor for a *kuleana* plot. These pitfalls resulted in a small number of claims filed by *makaʻāinana,* the entitled beneficiaries of the act.[72] Some *makaʻāinana* surrendered their land plots to chiefs, fleeing *ʻāina* for the bustling urban life. No longer able to survive in the Western system, many Hawaiians entered the growing cities as wage laborers in a cash economy. Also, as a telling indication of the power imbalance created by this act, it is through the Kuleana Act and the for-

malization of fee-simple ownership for *haoles* that a whole island—
Ni'ihau—was purchased by a *haole*. The indigenous inhabitants of
Ni'ihau, for all of the aforementioned reasons, did not file any claims for
their land portions.[73]

This backdrop of structured disadvantage, wherein Hawaiians are always a few steps behind *haole* applicants in the land tenure process, under-
lying the supposed blank slate of process and procedure, overwrites a
kanaka identity position with a private tenant/citizen-subject, a position that historically had been practiced by *haoles* outside of and within
Hawai'i. In name, land commissions seem to assure a systematically
neutral process that equalizes all applicants. But such neutrality appears
in its true form if you look more closely at how an apparently indiscriminate, up-for-grabs private citizen position discriminates against indigenous Hawaiians via its embedded procedural mechanisms. The requirement of English as the standardized language on all certified records, the
privileging of written records over oral genealogical memory, and a presupposed capital-centered land economy dislocated Hawaiians outside
of the legal process and formal identity/rights recognition.

Upon the formal recognition of ownership rights to *all* residents,
modern law and policy officially ushered in a racially homogenous (and
soon-to-be American) citizenship and legal membership where *haole*
residents were again made native and Hawaiians rendered foreign and
racialized out of its boundaries. Modern law and governance in articulation with Christianity discursively foreshadowed yet historically preceded a science-based moral discourse that racializes Hawaiian blood and
whitens citizenship.

This critical genealogy reveals the intricate process by which an indigenous Hawaiian structure based on social stratification and a communal land system disintegrated through the vehicles of law and governance as wielded by colonial power and an emerging U.S. nation-state.
Haole residents presumed their absolute natural right to Hawai'i by
practicing their legal and citizen rights from "home." In so doing, private (white) sovereign residency was normalized while a Hawaiian subject position was racially marked and structurally excised through its
constructed difference: signs of prehuman, non-Christian ways, and the
absence of a capitalist system of land production. When foreign authorities promoted capitalist virtue and codified laws of ultimate-use, fee-
simple ownership, and equitable land commissions with open and fair

application procedures, they structurally and silently excluded Hawaiians from those very principles and rights. Ironically, through a formal recognition of ownership rights to *all* residents in the Kuleana Act, U.S. law and policy racially homogenized citizenship and legal membership to only *haole* residents. This historical move foreshadowed the pivotal moment in 1921 when blood was signified as a state technology that rendered Hawaiian identity inferior and produced an idealized (white) American citizenry.

THE HHCA: BLOODING A RACE

Historically, only *after* Hawaiians had been invisibly racialized as dark and strange and living through incomprehensible rituals and ways were they legally (mis)recognized through the discursive device of blood. Such work was articulated through the HHCA of 1921, a congressionally approved bill and the legislated origin of the heavily impacting blood quantum identifications in the name of Hawaiians. To quantum blood is to divide, assign, and regulate a factualized, known identity of parentage, of race among a social group. This quantum assignment would extend the historical writing over of the Hawaiian by Western law and policy and establish the state measuring, slicing, and surveilling of (mis)identified Hawaiians.

Blood, in this shifting historical juncture, comes to signify both an archaic, almost extinguished "prehumanity," rearticulated as a biological given and at the same time, a social indication of potential citizenship in the newfound U.S. territory. The HHCA is the generative site for racializing Hawaiians in terms of a blood economy and what largely emerges as an economy of material resources, identity positions, *and* speaking practices. As a legal-cultural production that continues to produce a Hawaiian subjectivity, the congressional hearings surrounding the HHCA—through which the merits and injustices of a bill are debated in the presence of an appointed panel of all *haole* senators—exemplifies a field of racialized discourse; that is, a historically specific formation constitutive and reflective of racialized logics, principles, and expressions that define and justify a raced identity, thus reifying it into existence.[74] As provocatively demonstrated by David Theo Goldberg, Stuart Hall, and Lisa Lowe, discourse racially produces subjects through the power-vested reproduction of logics, expressions, rhetorical claims, and systematic exclusions.[75] When backed by political governance, regulation, and the eyes of the law, this discourse more forcefully frames the kinds of cultural narratives, speaking practices, and performances of those who are suppressed.[76] I critically analyze these hearings, with the hopes of being able to examine the discursive racialization of Hawaiians and their speaking practices at that time and how it affects us in the present political moment.

The racialized discourse around the HHCA speaks to the historically specific legal exclusions of Hawaiians in relation to land. I illustrate how the HHCA identified Hawaiians and who would be authorized to speak as a Hawaiian. At the time, Hawai'i stood as an annexed territory with special-status federal jurisdiction. The territorial government oversaw impressive modes of commerce (plantations), military arsenals, and practice sites. The distinction—resident—still reflected a majority of landowning white *haoles* with more rights and land than Hawaiians. "Pure" Hawaiians drastically decreased in number from between 80,000 and 100,000 in the late 1700s to 23,000 in 1921.[77] At this historical moment, it became necessary after decades of colonially dissolving and reforming one system and conserving another now to *preserve* the economic/ national interests consolidated during the formal writing over of Hawaiian identity since the 1800s. The HHCA articulated the capitalist preservation of a preparing U.S. nation-state, rearticulating the sovereign resident position via the (white) American citizen. Separated from naturally granted citizenship and rights, indigenous Hawaiians were by degree or percentage either doomed to predestined extinction or stood as potential citizens.

Background of the HHCA

In 1898, not long after the 1893 illegal overthrow of Queen Lili'uokalani's rule, the United States held Hawai'i as a territory. This was achieved through U.S. resolution and without the consent of Hawaiian inhabitants. As such, the United States held complete authority over the island territory, and on July 9, 1921, signed into law an act "designed to rehabilitate the Native Hawaiians." The bill was created by longtime Hawaiian royalist/sovereignty leader and Hawai'i Congressional Delegate, Prince Jonah Kūhiō Kalaniana'ole who wanted to secure federal aid for his dying, landless people. Prince Kūhiō strongly believed that federal support would rekindle a spirit of Hawaiian self-sufficiency and self-determination.[78]

Before the bill's passage, the thriving sugar and ranching interests, who leased richly fertile Crown Lands (approximately 26,000 acres) for their plantations, faced a hard-hitting blow. Their lease contracts would likely be terminated. As it turned out, the official lease expiration date rolled in just as the HHCA hit the congressional floor for debate.[79] The implications were serious. All leased plantation lands could be reverted to general homesteading purposes for "Native Hawaiians." The commercial interests (C & H Sugar, Dole Pineapple) panicked. They had enjoyed years of cheap rent on the best available land.

Several commercially vested senators began to propose various resolutions that would allow sugar planters and ranchers to maintain their leaseholds. It was, after all, their money on the line. One was the House Resolution 13500 (e.g., amendment to the Organic Act, HCR 28), which united commercial venture with "federal rehabilitation" by exempting all sugar-cane lands from homesteading. Through this resolution, dominant sugar and rancher leases could continue, and Hawaiians could be "reformed" through land. The money made from the leases would be placed into a funding source that would subsidize the government administration of Hawaiian homesteads. The resolution seemed perfect; politicians and business interests in merry union.[80]

After the revised version of the HHCA was approved, about 200,000 acres of land (out of the 1.5 million acres of Government and Crown Lands) were set aside specifically for homesteading by Native Hawaiians.[81] The HHCA originally defined a " Native Hawaiian" as a descendant "of not less than one-thirty-second part of the blood of the original races which inhabited the islands at the time of their discovery by Captain Cook."[82] A later amendment further restricted the quantum to "½ part of the blood."[83]

If a Native Hawaiian qualified, he could obtain a ninety-nine-year lease for $1.00/year for residential, pastoral, and agricultural lots.[84] Ultimately, the HHCA's goal was to distribute land to qualified Hawaiians, and to create a formal commission—the Hawaiian Homes Commission, later the State Department of Hawaiian Home Lands—which would be in charge of administering the homesteads.

LEGAL MORALITY AND BLOOD TECHNOLOGY: "DYING" NAMESAKES AND "POTENTIAL CITIZENS"

Homesteading, a government-endorsed practice, continued the Western moral project; a project no longer captured in terms of Christian morality. Apparently, this time U.S. law and governance would show more of its "humanity." The nation-state reshaped itself as an allocator of federal aid designed to counteract an inherent lack in some cultural group. Specifically, it promised the "rehabilitation" of Hawaiians and, in so doing, presupposed that some natural "normal" state (whiteness) needed to be restored or at the very least, compensated. For Hawaiians, homesteading counterbalanced an absence that was naturalized as biologically and scientifically true—that they were naturally inferior and foreign to American life.

At a time when scientific rationality ruled and reproduced the modern nation, scientized instruments of classification and the modes of inquiry found in biology, natural history, and anthropology had revealed what was already there: the natural order of things and races.[85] Thus, it would seem that blood percentages merely reflected the cultural character and ability of races to survive in an American society, a reflection that could not reconcile the jarring primordialist image of Hawaiians with modern (white) citizenship. Perhaps this disassociation alone drove the grammar within the congressional hearings of the HHCA, without too obviously drawing attention to the racial selectivity of the U.S. nation and its wielded law and policy.

How does a blood technology become a part of legal-governmental discourse? It does so as unquestionable, a priori fact, for science was the new God. Blood classifications provided greater certainty and rhetorical leverage than its previous expression, the natural rights ideology. These blood identifications (e.g., pure-bloods, mixed-bloods) negatively valorize and suppress Hawaiians but in guised fashion. Blood work affords an image of unmediated, objective science and an institutionalized claim to knowledge, without indicting national power structures and its gendered and racialized particularizing of citizens. With newly afforded power, scientific classifications and descriptions, all the while invisibly operating as social-cultural productions of difference, are legally appropriated as verifying reference sources.

Discursive constructions of blood therefore fixed the nature of Hawaiians and so accounted for their diminished land holdings as compared to *haoles*. Blood and its seemingly objective markings could specify difference in the same moment it wiped away the structured dispossession of Hawaiians, a process of historical forgetting that is achieved just as a moral claim of rehabilitation emerges. By this logic, blood economizes land allotments in line with citizenship. Those of pure Hawaiian blood, undeniably the racially different, would be constructed as failing to productively use or exploit land and embody capitalist virtue. For example, on the first day of the congressional hearings, both proponents and opponents of the bill referred to pure Hawaiians as "wholly abject, thriftless, unproductive aborigines." The pure-bloods were referenced primarily in relation to their inability to hold land (e.g., Hawaiians would often abandon lands). The aftereffects of Western colonialism were reappropriated as raced effects of "those inferior Hawaiians." Historically and materially speaking, distinctions of blood came *after* the Western upheaval of Hawaiian society, but discursively functioned as always signifying "coming before."

The Myth of Extinction: Creating a "Since-Passed" Native Hawaiian Race

In line with the discourse of blood that racialized Hawaiians, the myth of extinction as discursive device articulated their inferiority as a naturally patterned demise. They would die sooner rather than later. It was again the law of nature. In the hearing testimonies, a myth of extinction helped to shape and ironically to bring about the eventual demise of pure Hawaiians. As discussed in David Theo Goldberg's work on census counts and Marie Annette Jaimes's critique of federal identification policy and Indian blood quantum, predictions of cultural extinction and depopulation work in line with economic interests but operate through the vehicle of factual probability.[86] In the officially approved write-up of the HHCA, it was estimated that the full-blood population count decreased from 142,650 in 1826 to about 22,600 in 1919 (see Figure 6).[87] Undeniably, Hawaiians had been dying in excess numbers since the late 1700s with the arrival of Cook and his men and colonial influx. In terms of population counts, the demise is represented as strikingly consistent, gradual, and not as severe considering the growing number of part Hawaiians.

I stress that while it is feasible to conclude that pure Hawaiians were dying out while mixed-bloods slightly increased in number, the representation and deployment of these figures are infused with suspicious power interests. The early missionary censuses, the first recorded population counts, are likely to be accurate estimates of Hawaiian converts only. In terms of the U.S. official census, the census enumerators, who in this context were those who spoke English and not necessarily fluent Hawaiian, recorded their own interpretations of race with no set criteria

NATIVE HAWAIIANS—A DYING RACE.

As shown by the following charts, the number of full-blooded Hawaiians in the Territory has decreased since the estimate of 1826 from 142,650 to 22,500, while the death rate has correspondingly increased until it is now greatly in excess of that of any other race inhabitating the islands:

Population—native Hawaiians.

Years.	Part Hawaiians.	Full-blooded Hawaiians.
1826, estimated by missionaries............................	....	142,650
Hawaii official census:		
1832..	....	130,313
1836..	....	108,579
1850..	....	82,203
1853..	....	71,019
1860..	....	67,084
1866..	....	58,765
1872..	2,487	49,044
1878..	3,420	44,088
1884..	4,218	40,014
1890..	6,186	34,436
1896..	8,485	31,019
United States official census:		
1900..	8,835	29,799
1910..	12,506	26,041
1919, estimated June 30....................................	16,660	22,600

Race death rate for year ending June 30, 1919.

	Death rate.
Hawaiian:	
Full-blooded	39.42
Part:	
Asiatic...	14.58
Caucasian	16.17

Figure 6. Population table, *Rehabilitation of Native Hawaiians: Report to Accompany H.R. 13500.* Sixty-sixth Congress House of Representatives, 2d sess., 1920. House Report no. 839.

for determining "pure" or "part" Hawaiian. They relied on their "common sense judgments and perceptions" of indiscriminate, socially fluctuating markers of race such as skin tone and physical appearance (e.g., body size, facial attributes).[88] These evaluative marks recorded in population counts blur the specific, fixed biological criteria distinction, if any, between what constitutes pure and part Hawaiianness, at the same time, concealing the sociohistorical constructedness around these classifications. The classifications themselves are fictions-in-process.

Accurately counting Hawaiians quickly shifted to charting their extinction cycle; then to yearly projections specifying when all Hawaiians would disappear: "It is estimated that by the year 1952, all pure Hawaiians will vanish."[89] An extinction discourse therefore positioned Hawaiians as a dying population that only the nation-state could save. Their salvation would supposedly constitute the HHCA's driving moral purpose. In a so-called moral act, the congressional senators and witnesses—with charts and counts in hand—argued that it was the government's duty to breathe life back into the Hawaiian race through homesteading. The means to do so was a federally created administrative body that would protect and serve the indigenes. This new administrative body was positioned as an official agency that efficiently and justly restored Hawaiian life on homestead lands.

But, the smooth-running administration operated through a striking irony. It structurally executed the demise of pure Hawaiians through its performative procedures. The official body developed a neutral and lengthy process of application including proof of identity claim to land. Each claim required verification, evaluation, and distribution. Such a procedure took, at the very least, anywhere from five to fifteen years, thus working in conjunction with and even exceeding the time and rate of theorized extinction. The procedural nature of the homelands administration therefore made real the possibility that most pure Hawaiians would die out before actually gaining land. True to form, approximately 30,000 Hawaiians have died while waiting for a Hawaiian homestead.[90] The myth of extinction is less a scientific projection of what will happen based on factual population counts and cycles than it is a discursive reality brought into being, perhaps more expeditiously through governmental policy and administration. I emphasize that the demise of Hawaiians in this sense is planned, sealed, and delivered via a resurfacing colonial administration.

HHCA opponents or those against the "rehabilitation" of Hawaiians have practiced other discursive moves to safeguard their own dominant subject positions through racializing Hawaiians. Their main argument is that Hawaiians were not dying out. In fact, they were increasing in terms of the part Hawaiian population. One witness, A. G. M. Robertson, a representative of the Parker Ranch on Hawai'i (a ranch that acquired a great deal of Hawaiian land through the formalization of fee-simple ownership and the Kuleana grants), differentiated between a declining sector of Hawaiians and a redeveloping one:

> Aboriginal Hawaiians of the pure blood are dying out . . . according to the census . . . in 1900 the pure Hawaiian population was nearly 30,000, while in 1919 it was . . . 22,600, a decrease of over 7,000; whereas, those

who were part Hawaiians in 1900 numbered only 7,835, and in 1919 had increased to 16,600, an increase of about 9,000, more than offsetting the decrease in the aboriginals of the pure blood, and the total increase is substantially just as much. . . . So that it can not be said, and it is not true to say, the Hawaiian race as defined in this bill is a dying race, because the figures show that it is an increasing race.[91]

Robertson repeatedly argued that though the pure-bloods were dying out, an increase in part bloods (specifically $\frac{1}{32}$ of Hawaiian blood) illustrates that a majority of the beneficiaries of the HHCA (any Hawaiian with at least $\frac{1}{32}$ blood) were growing and thriving. Thus, they would not need any form of rehabilitation. By selectively reading zero-sum population counts across equalized time frames, Robertson was attempting to exclude a large segment of potential Hawaiian beneficiaries (all nonpure Hawaiians) from land claims, which positions part Hawaiians as distinct and separate from being "Native Hawaiian." Consider Robertson's exchange with Senator Smoot:

SENATOR SMOOT: I do not see that the figures show that. On page 6 of your brief it says that the Hawaiian population in 1872 was 49,044 of the pure blood, and in 1900 the Hawaiians of unmixed race had decreased to 29,834, while the part Hawaiians had increased only from 1,487 in 1878 to 7,835 in 1900. Instead of 50,000, the total in 1872, in 1900 there is only about 37,000.

MR. ROBERTSON: Yes, Senator; I say, comparing the 1900 figures with 1919 figures, it shows an increase.

SENATOR SMOOT: No, even that shows a decrease. In 1872 there were 50,000 Hawaiians and part Hawaiians, while in 1919 there were only 39,000.

MR. ROBERTSON: I was talking about comparing the figures of 1900 with those of 1919, which show an increase.

SENATOR SMOOT: Yes of a very few, but I have no doubt in my own mind . . . the Hawaiian race is dying out.

MR. ROBERTSON: Yes; the pure-bloods . . . I do not deny that the Hawaiians of the pure blood are decreasing, but I do deny that the Hawaiians as defined in this bill are decreasing.[92]

In comparing intact categories across two frames of time, Robertson works hard to differentiate between pure Hawaiians and part Hawaiians, a differentiation serving to write out the majority of potential Hawaiian homesteaders. Eventually, the congressional representatives negotiated with Robertson and other like-minded opponents to the act to restrict further the definition of Native Hawaiian to mean "not less than ½ part of the blood." This itself unveils the blood distinction to be socially constitutive and politically motivated. For one brief memorable moment, Robertson's attempt to deny Hawaiians their own *'āina* through population counts again represents a means through policy and law to ensure U.S. control over Hawaiian lands through two conjoined paths: administratively setting into place the extinction of pure-bloods and dismissing the moral/cultural imperative to assist part Hawaiians.

Historically Outdated, Pure-Blooded Hawaiians in Modern Time

Pure-bloods who are inherently/biologically constructed never to be true citizens instead come to symbolize namesakes, or true exemplars of a nation's legal morality in assisting a dying population. The United States, no longer politically beholden to an explicit religious morality, would frame itself as the preeminent moral authority of its time, through the mechanisms of policy and law. But its morality would not be inscribed by way of the usual mythic reproduction of American opportunity and liberty. Rather, the U.S. nation recognized in part a historical injustice done to Hawaiians—the transfer of lands from Hawaiians to foreigners—without naming its own complicity in the act. By way of the HHCA, the United States emerged instead as the bearer of justice that rights a historical wrong it instituted. American justice therefore can be elevated only through a process of historically erasing earlier decades of colonialism and land dispossession.[93] Seen in this way, a legal and moral image of the nation that could save the Hawaiians is achieved through forgetting its own efforts in dispossessing them.

In the hearings, one of the senators calls attention to the hugely imbalanced materialities between Hawaiians and *haoles*:

> SENATOR NUGENT: What I had in mind was this: It was stated here at the last hearing that there were thousands of natives there that had no roof over their heads and no way of making a living except by hiring out to other people. It would seem to be a rather serious situation of affairs if one company could acquire 500,000 acres of land under those conditions.[94]

Senator Nugent begins to recognize the dire consequence of the resident-centered Kuleana Act and dominant colonial modes of land tenure. But such flashes of rethinking dominant memory are minimized through the racializing of pure Hawaiians as noncitizen-like, as marked by their low survival rate, decreasing family size, and failure to retain and productively use land. The official HHCA report concludes that "all previous systems of land distribution, when judged practically by the benefits accruing to the native Hawaiians from the operation of such systems" were "ineffective."[95] The neutralizing language of procedurality and administrative technicality effaces the nation's political acts in repressing a Hawaiian identity under that of the private resident, a discursive move that would continue to serve the U.S. nation and local State of Hawaii for years to come. As the political state is neutralized, pure Hawaiians are named and blamed in the concluding report for their material inequalities:

> Your committee thus finds that since the institution of private owner-ship of lands in Hawaii the native Hawaiians, outside of the King and the chiefs, were granted and have held but a very small portion of the lands of the Islands . . . but a great many of these lands have been lost through improvidence and inability to finance farming operations . . . The Hawaiians are not business men [sic] and have shown themselves unable to meet competitive conditions unaided. In the end the speculators are the real beneficiaries of the homestead laws.[96]

While there is an explicit understanding that Hawaiians have not received due land (granted via the Constitution of 1840 and the *Ka Māhele*), the blame would be located not in *haole* aggression and colonialism, but in the inferior blooded nature of Hawaiians themselves. This is established via a rigid pure-blood signifier, undergirded by scientific authority and which identifies pure-blooded Hawaiians as primordial noncitizens. Through the racialization of signified ambivalence, anachronistic space, and temporal difference, Hawaiians were deemed as belonging to a different time and space. Articulated as "pre-humans" in the late 1700s and 1800s, they are excised out of modern time and society and then, in the 1900s, reinserted into modern life, law, and governance in which they are further displaced via blood quantum identifications and an archaic image. As such, Hawaiians are discursively constructed as never being able to hold land or survive in a modern nation and throughout the modern era. Thus their lack is explained as a reflection of their limited racialized ability and character. Pure Hawaiians, deemed tragic in the blood, were not citizens and failed to act like citizens. But they were deemed a people—a namesake for the state—that could still be saved through national legal morality.

Native Hawaiianness As a Racial Exclusivity

With the construction of a dying or since-passed pure Hawaiian race, the formal and legal definition of "Native Hawaiian" that emanated from the HHCA was also suspect. For example, in 1921 the amendment to the HHCA defined a Native Hawaiian as a person "of not less than one-half part of the blood of the races inhabiting the Hawaiian Islands previous to 1778."[97] This is curious given that part Hawaiians, or those who were not of pure Hawaiian blood, had been around and increasing in number since 1853.[98] Meaning, that *sixty-eight years* after the birth of part Hawaiians, the congressional senators of the HHCA in 1921 still inscribed a rigid 50 percent blood requirement that most Hawaiians could never meet. If, in 1921, there were 23,723 Hawaiians of at least 50 percent Hawaiian blood and 18,027 part Hawaiians who were less than 50 percent Hawaiian blood and with the decrease in pure Hawaiians, the continual increase of part Hawaiians, and the degree of Hawaiianness becoming increasingly mixed from that point on, how in fact, could a 50 percent blood quantum mandate ever be fulfilled from 1921 on? Given this context, a Native Hawaiian identity or the mandate of 50 percent blood quantum operates like a racial exclusivity by taking on the constitution of racial purity.[99] It is a pure form of identity that most Hawaiians fail to prove as it becomes a racial tightlock, casting Hawaiians as either Native Hawaiian or non-Hawaiian. With this sense of racial purity, an identity position of Native Hawaiianness symbolizes yet again the extreme of articulated indigeneity: a historically antiquated, pure, and before-time race. In contemporary discourses, a Hawaiian identity would be signified in this way: as always racially pure and historically outdated beyond its cultural time. Any formal claim of Hawaiianness to this day is therefore judged and weighed against the racial purity/exclusivity of the 50 percent blood quantum mandate, which has permeated many social agencies created to assist Hawaiians. For instance, Hawaiian homestead applicants continually struggle with formally proving their 50 percent blood quantum. If they fail to do so, they are not formally or legally known as Hawaiian. When Hawaiians attempt to claim social services, benefits, and assistance reserved for Hawaiians from organizations like the Office of Hawaiian Affairs and the DHHL, they must meet the same 50 percent requirement. Thus, the formal Native Hawaiian identity position is held up as a present-day normative and racially exclusive mandate for all Hawaiians, which disavows a majority of the identity claims made.

Part Hawaiians As (White) Citizens

Marking Hawai'i as a territory, the United States ceded to federal control Hawai'i's Government and Crown Lands. These transferred lands were then held and controlled by a formal trust relationship. In a trust, Hawaiians became the trusts/wards/beneficiaries of the trustee. For Hawai'i, its status as a territory and the established trust relationship guaranteed federal monies and promised citizenship via incorporation into the United States through the Hawai'i Organic Act. All residents of Hawai'i, including indigenous Hawaiians, were deemed citizens of the United States with the customary rights and privileges, save voting power for the Territorial Presidential cabinet. Citizenship, however, was assigned discursively with particularized gradation to some inhabitants over others, that is, more so to *haole* residents than to Hawaiians. This "degradation" specifies a discursive mechanism tailor-made for indigenous peoples.[100] In the HHCA hearings, Hawaiians weren't quite "abstract citizens." They were identified more or less as "potential citizens." As potential citizens, Hawaiians were marked—via factual blood percentage—as more or less assimilable to a just, democratic meritocracy.

Part Hawaiians, in particular, are positioned as "potential" citizens:

> The part Hawaiian, the part Caucasian, the part Chinese, the part Portuguese are a virile, prolific, and enterprising lot of people. They have large families and they raise them—they bring them up. These part Hawaiians have had the advantage, since annexation especially of the American viewpoint and the advantage of a pretty good public school system and they are an educated people. They are not in the same class with the pure-bloods.[101]

As "virile, prolific, increasing, enterprising, intelligent people," part Hawaiians are described as not in need of rehabilitation like the "aboriginals."[102] The recombination of a population increase of part Hawaiians and the representation of "Hawaiian blood . . . as easily absorbed (a ⅛ Hawaiian looks like a white man)" unmarks Hawaiians as they are deemed "potential citizens" and the bearers of whiteness through their resemblance to white men. This identification contrasts with the hegemonic one-drop rule in racial classification of the 1900s (in which mixed-race progeny always took on the "nonwhite" label and the raced identity of the nonwhite parent).[103] In Hawai'i, where a mixed Hawaiian child is raced as either "Part Hawaiian" or "Caucasian," one drop of white blood remakes "part Hawaiian blood" into revealing degrees of American assimilability and entitlement and, ultimately, degrees of national exemption from having to distribute any land entitlements to them. Witnesses and senators generally characterize part Hawaiians as "men of education, men who have been in college and have traveled; men who are wealthy";[104] a group gendered on patriarchal grounds to have been absorbed quickly and passed the mythic tenets of American equality, freedom, and justice. The less Hawaiian one is, the more competent, capable, assimilable, and citizen-like she or he is, which in turn regirds a position of normative whiteness ironically through the articulation of a part/mixed Hawaiian identity in the HHCA hearings.[105] Part Hawaiians are citizens, yes, but potentially so. Those instances in which part Hawaiians still suffer from material inequalities (e.g., the lack of land ownership, the loss of land) question the ability of the individual in an equal meritocracy and not the racial hegemony of the United States. The whitening of Hawaiian blood thus furnishes living evidence of Hawaiian self-sufficiency (their inherent Americanization), thereby foregoing the moral and material imperative for federal aid to this sector of the population.

By contrast, today in state hearings, blood quantum and mixed-blood Hawaiianness are deployed to deny Hawaiians political voice. For example, in one case, tourism and business developers countered Hawaiian resistance to development in their traditional villages (like Miloli'i, Hawai'i). They argued that Hawaiian residents had no basis for opposition because they were merely "half-breeds" and mixed racially.[106] Thus, in one context, a mixed-blood construction promises rights, privileges, and opportunities in the name of the potentially assimilable Hawaiian citizen; and in another, it precludes part Hawaiians from claiming *any identity right to things Hawaiian* (land, cultural artifacts and sites). In the latter case, the inscription of Hawaiian blood purity (pure Hawaiianness) is delimited as the only authoritative grounds for making indigenous claims of entitlement. If restricted, though, only to those proven to be of pure blood, according to the declining state/census patterns for the Native Hawaiian population (in which the 1994 count for pure Hawaiians in Hawai'i was approximately 8,244), soon no Hawaiian will be able legally to voice an identity claim of Hawaiianness.[107] This represents an example of how legal identities ("pure-bloods" and "part-bloods") construct particular identity positions and limited speaking authority for raced groups.

Blood quantum, a hegemonic tool of classification, ultimately highlights the sheer flexibility of U.S. federal power: how the essential binaries (black-white) of race, its gradations (Native Hawaiianness as pure- or mixed-blood quantum), and the liberality of assigned whiteness can still bolster a racially homogeneous (or white) American polity; through the fixed negativity of race *and* a loosened and diluted raced identity (quantumed Native Americans, Hawaiians whose mixed blood signified potential civility and citizenry). In this light, the blood-quantumed racial characterization of Hawaiians safeguards the national capital by securing its possession of Hawaiian lands and legislatively writing out pure-bloods through administrative extinction, excluding mixed Hawaiian progeny as potential citizenry and outlining who has the discursive authority to claim Hawaiianness (which appears to be those who have already passed). All the while, the nation-state, head up high and myths in place, refashions itself as the legal-moral adjudicator of justice and rehabilitation.

According to the established legal discourse, the more "pure" a Hawaiian is (100 percent), the less she or he is a self-determined, independent American citizen with rights and privileges, while the more "mixed" a Hawaiian is (meaning less than 50 percent), the less she or he is entitled to make a cultural claim to Hawaiian land, artifacts, and practice and the more she or he (as an assimilable citizen) absolves the political state from recognizing its own colonial shadow.

The dominant-encoded signification of "citizens" and "aliens" in the HHCA Congressional Hearings, however, reveals the traces of the nation that expose the unscientifically derived, politically subjective, and conceptually open identifications of the government. This can be seen when the congressional participants worked hard to distinguish between Hawaiians, Indians, and "Orientals." Robertson adamantly rejected the argument that the HHCA was constitutional in its likeness to the Indian reservation program. He argued that

> the Hawaiians are not Indians. The status of the Hawaiians is diametrically opposed to that of the Indians on the mainland. The Indians have been regarded as aliens. They get their rights, such as they have, by treaties between them and the federal government. They have no right to vote, unless under subsequent circumstances they become naturalized. As I understand it, they are aliens and not citizens; and their inherent character is by no means that of the Hawaiians. The Indians were a roving, nomadic race of people. They did not take to civilization the way the Hawaiians did.[108]

Around this time, Native American Indians, whose history of land dispossession parallels that of the Hawaiians, had already received some land allotments through the Dawes Act while many non-Indians were granted a majority of fee-simple titles to Indian land through the General Allotment Act.[109] So it is curious that two indigenous groups, who have strong ties to the land and are similarly constructed through "barbaric prehumanity" rhetoric, are in the end identified differently from one another: Hawaiians as "citizens" and Indians as "aliens." Perhaps, the colonial fetish with a geographical paradise and the supposed inherent generosity of Hawaiian people ("Hawaiianness at heart" or normative benevolence; see chapter 1) redeems and elevates Hawaiians over Native American Indians, who are remembered as "barbaric, unassimilable" and "forever alien" savages in frequent political confrontations. Both identifications, the seemingly positive and negative, however, work in line with dominant interests. They are articulated in line with context-specific economic interests of the nation-state. A more assimilable Hawaiian race exempts the nation from assigning a relatively modest range of island land areas as available homesteads. A dangerous Indian race with land claims spanning over much of the U.S. mainland, necessitates federal governance over all regions, restricted Indian access to homesteads, and increased surveillance over Indians via the Bureau of Indian Affairs and federal control over tribal councils.

As the Hawaiians are identified as citizens, "Orientals" are racialized as "alien immigrants." Rhetorically justified through their foreign origins, "Orientals" and particularly the Japanese in Hawai'i are framed as serious economic threats to the U.S. nation in terms of their unassimilability, or rather, their wage accumulation, land acquisitions (as citizens, they could purchase land), and community growth (e.g., Japanese held a high intramarriage retention rate). The senators discussed the increase in Japanese laborers and how those born in Hawai'i had claimed citizenship and thus a right to own land. At the time, in California, there existed heated debate over a state ruling preventing any Japanese from holding lands.[110] Indeed, Lowe's analysis of the legal signification of the "alien immigrant" as sublating the contradictions between the political state (myths of liberty, justice, and equality and the regirding of a white citizenship) and the needs of capital (the need for cheap labor), can be traced throughout these HHCA hearings.[111] Several parties attempted to legally define "Orientals" and the Japanese in Hawai'i in the same manner as they had been defined on the mainland United States: as "aliens" located outside of the purview of law and rights (as illustrated in one testimony: "You can legislate against aliens and discriminate against them any way you want, but not so as to citizens").[112]

Finally, only in the opposing arguments to HHCA's rehabilitation of Hawaiians would the issue of race be explicitly addressed as a topic. According to opponents, appeals to the needs of a specific race like, for example, the HHCA, represented a class-based, unconstitutional discrimination against the very principles of American citizenship. This kind of discursive stance is used against Hawaiian sovereignty movements. Case in point, in 1994, all Hawaiians were invited to vote in a state-sponsored plebiscite, in order to determine whether or not Hawaiians wanted to have a Native Hawaiian sovereign government. A Big Island resident, Freddy Rice, "challenged the state's use of tax dollars to sponsor a vote open only to Native Hawaiians," claiming the whole issue as "racist."[113] An instance of an attack on race can be seen in the following testimony against the HHCA bill:

> Now this is admittedly a flagrant case of class legislation. No one would have the hardihood to deny that it is absolutely class legislation, drawn on what seems to me the vicious line of race. Now there is no direct provision in the Constitution that prohibits Congress from discriminating against persons because of their race, color, or previous condition of

servitude, except in relation to the right to vote; but there is an implied right not to be discriminated against because of the color of one's skin or the kind of blood in your veins.[114]

Linked to the sovereign resident and private tenant/resident positions, *haole* citizens can greatly magnify their already secure power and historically consolidated positions by invoking constitutional rights and civil liberties. We might wonder if Robertson's notion of justice—his selective interpretation and application of a constitutional right in the name of the *haole* underclass, *not to be discriminated against,* in juxtaposition with his implicit endorsement of a constitutional leeway in discriminating against other specific groups—mirrors the inner workings of the mystifying law itself. No longer solely in the discursive framework of private tenant/citizens, the U.S. governmental law and policy (mis)recognize Hawaiians through factual blood percentage, which authoritatively signifies internally divisive subject-speaking positions.

THE AFTERMATH OF HHCA

The HHCA was approved in 1921. Afterward a previously (mis)recognized Hawaiian identity was further confined at the hands of the U.S. federal government and the State of Hawaii. The definition of "Native Hawaiian" was amended from ½₂ to ½ Hawaiian blood (due to pressure from heavily vested plantation owners and ranchers). This created two distinct legal (and vernacular) identities for Hawaiians: Native Hawaiians (at least 50 percent Hawaiian blood) and Hawaiians (less than 50 percent Hawaiian blood).[115] Later, after statehood in 1959, the HHCA section 204 was amended to allow the commission to "dispose of such (homestead) lands by lease or license to the general public." Thus, non-Hawaiians could gain and lease designated Hawaiian homestead areas. Such an amendment represented a clear violation of the letter of the HHCA.[116]

Other violations became routine. For instance, former Maui mayor Elmer F. Cravalho, who is non-Hawaiian, "received 15,000 acres from the Commission in 1966 which he lease(d) for about $1.60 per acre."[117] Second, the Hawaiian Homes Commission agency administratively executed the HHCA. It was an agency supervised by the federal government, which had a formal trust obligation as trustee to Hawaiian beneficiaries or wards (meaning, the United States was held responsible for equitably distributing a portion of the ceded lands to Native Hawaiians.[118] However, this early commission carelessly and corruptly administrated the HHCA; for example, former State Representative Diana Hansen, after several complaints from Hawaiian applicants, investigated the commission's actions and found instances of applications being recklessly thrown away or misplaced without notifying the affected applicants.[119] Also, commission members allocated homesteads to their non-Hawaiian friends. When Hansen requested a listing of all the non-Hawaiian lessees, their lease-rental prices, and duration of leases, the commission declined to do so. According to Hansen's official report and journalist Susan Faludi's investigative article, the commission has consistently misappropriated and traded homestead land legally set aside for Hawaiians to business interests (e.g., development projects like the Sea Life Park in Waikiki, shopping centers, auto dealerships, hotels, multinational corporations), state outfits (e.g., airports, the University of Hawaii, waste-water treatment centers, and freeway constructions), and national needs (military bases, bombing practice sites).[120] The commission defends its actions by claiming to need revenue to fund its administrative operations and improvements made on the land (the construction of roads, utilities on undeveloped land parcels). The justification seems to be that the general revenue furnished by non-Hawaiian leases largely supports the administration of Hawaiian Home Lands.[121]

The administrative corruption continued when upon statehood in 1959, the State of Hawaii assigned the DHHL with administrative control over the homesteads and yet was still housed within the Hawaiian Homes Commission. The commission members are not elected by Hawaiians; they are all appointed by the governor. This commission, with apparently no legal accountability to Hawaiians who lack a voting say in matters of the commission, "is the specific state entity obliged to implement the fiduciary duty under the HHCA on behalf of eligible Native Hawaiians" (as ruled in *Ahuna v. Department of Hawaiian Home Lands*, 64 Haw. 237, 338).

CONCLUSION

The encroaching and surveilling nature of the modern nation-state and urbanity in identity formation must not be overlooked. These dominant structures of meaning and identification slip by "unnoticed," without drawing attention to their forceful yet somewhat guised incorporation of Western law and governance.

The writing over of Hawaiianness through law and governance historically takes time. It takes effect through the careful disintegration and restructuring of one social formation into another (a Hawaiian hegemonic society dissolved by Western imperialism) via legal land principles such as ultimate-use and individual, private land ownership. It would take the uniting of religious ideology with economic incentive (the hailed capitalist market of freedom) to produce a new hierarchy of identities: the raced Hawaiians as "prehuman, soon-to-be extinct" aborigines who are strange to modernity; the sovereign resident (the *haole*) who claims supreme authority, rights, and privileges as a native to Hawai'i, an identity position politically endorsed and recognized by national governance at home and in Hawai'i; and emerging modern legal practices like the seemingly equal land-application process, due process and procedure, and individual protection by law. As Stuart Hall theorizes, in specific contexts like Hawai'i, race and capitalist relations enable one another; they coalesce in articulation as a structure created in dominance via the sublating/reconciling power of the law with foreigners normalized into a legal system and Hawaiians violently excised.[122]

Law was magic. It could refashion itself in several guises and live in different spaces. In the 1920s, law and science conjoined into a blood technology of naming Hawaiians—an institutionalized practice of preforming "pure-blooded" Hawaiians as excessively savage, unassimilable, and racially pure, and "mixed-bloods" as "not Hawaiian at all" and "not yet a citizen" but with potential. In this way, Hawaiianness and indigenous rights are economized, regulated, and surveilled (by establishing and delimiting quantum, it can watch over what it has framed) while citizenship is normatively white. Tragically, Hawaiians are forever affected. Their communicative positions and speaking authority are determined in line with blood quantum. "Mixed-bloods" are not truly Hawaiian and thus have no identity right or claim to things Hawaiian, and the authentic "pure-blooded" Hawaiian is deemed, according to the population counts and certified records, as extinct and no more.

But, as private memories reveal, the blood could be performatively brought down. Hawaiians in Hawai'i and on the mainland engage in verbal performances that narrate how they have attempted to formally substantiate their Hawaiianness but have been denied by the state via inaccurate documents and the inconsistent assignment of race on birtu. and marriage certificates and census records. Here Hawaiians draw attention to the closed doors and preformative assumptions of legislated, administrative identity.[123] Through the rummaging of our sacred histories, we illustrate both the state gaze over our identities and a way to perform its limits. As Hawaiians begin to narrate these painful private memories of formally establishing their Hawaiianness through state definitions, the state is finally unveiled as a politically motivated and subjective identifier of race and culture and not the neutral and equitable administrator it purports to be. In the next chapter, I present my ethnographic work with Hawaiian communities, which exposes the state for its identity regulation and unjust procedurality. These performances begin to contest both the historical memory of the prehistorical Hawaiian and legal (mis)recognitions of their subjectivities. Hawaiians illustrate the resistive spirit of what seems to be a determined, racialized group, and although confined to the identity frames produced by the state, they create fissures and ruptures through private memories and performances of identity and utilize potential spaces as these open up.

3

Exposing the Racial State:
Blood Quantum and Private Memories

The lines delineate and connect at perfect points. A clean white sheet of paper, its spaces and lines uniformly sketched, reads "Check where appropriate" or "Fill in the appropriate category." Such markers, it would seem, refuse to privilege one applicant over another. Bounded categories of race and parentage and equidistant grid blocks for mapping one's genealogy promise an equitable slate of information. Ideally, the form is framed as a vehicle of neutral administration, fair procedure, equal opportunity, and nonracial criteria—that is, *if you apply*. This would be the illusion of the *form*, the last remaining trace of the state and its governmental raciality.[1] In hidden fashion, such a form "conceives, manufactures," and formalizes a specific identity position for a particular group.[2] Around (and outside of) the lines, boxes, and seemingly neutral instructions lie the muffled voices of those who *seek* to complete the form but *fail to do so*: specifically, the Hawaiians who apply for a Hawaiian homestead lease and attempt to officially prove their blood quantum to the State Department of Hawaiian Home Lands (DHHL).

In this chapter, I highlight a resonating collective experience among Hawaiians in Hawai'i and on the U.S. mainland: the dizzying maze of formally proving their Hawaiianness in terms of the designated blood quantum mandates. Such a difficult process has become an integral aspect of Hawaiians' daily lives since 1921 when the Hawaiian Homes

Commission Act (HHCA) was congressionally approved.[3] Although Hawaiians were designated a right to land through the HHCA, this particular act imposed a strict definition for a Native Hawaiian identity position. Native Hawaiianness was officially defined as any of those persons who were at least one half or 50 percent Hawaiian blood amount.

When the United States Senate Committee of Territories codified the 1921 HHCA, it predetermined Hawaiian identity, complete in name but materially unsubstantiated for those named. As a result, a government commission (Hawaiian Homes Commission) and its bureaucratic arm (the DHHL) were created while an official procedure for verifying one's blood parentage was firmly set into place. Thus, the U.S. nation-state shaped a blood quantum technology, which specifically racialized Hawaiians for years to follow. As defined by U.S. federal power and administered by the local state DHHL agency, Hawaiian identity is defined as formal (documentation of Hawaiian blood must be provided), consistent (names, dates, and race must match across time and family members), and substantiated only by written English record (and from specific agencies—State Department of Health, U.S. Census Bureau—and established churches). The mandated process for proving Hawaiian identity therefore presupposed and privileged the centrality of formal Western rationality, language standards, and social relations over the historically and culturally specific context of Hawaiians in the 1900s.

I argue that although the local State of Hawaii, which is undergirded by U.S. federal power, organizes a racial identity for Hawaiians and the process for claiming it, the undocumented private stories and "performances of proving" by Hawaiians reveal the constraints of governmental raciality and its unseen limits. Throughout a series of ethnographic interviews and oral histories, Hawaiians reenact, name, and expose the inequitable procedure of homestead application and blood verification encoded in state policy and law as itself incomplete and indeterminable. I refer to these interviews as "performances of proving" in the sense that the state and its corresponding agencies assume that Hawaiians must formally prove and establish that they are Hawaiian, based on the legal definition of 50 percent blood quantum. Thus, although my Hawaiian interviewees see themselves culturally, socially, and politically as Hawaiian "with nothing to prove to anyone," the state still requires a formal procedure of identity documentation and verification. The stories they presented to me represent narrative performances in which they remember, retell, and reconfigure such a process.

I used several broad questions during a majority of the interviews (but each interview varied depending on person and the type of relation I had with the interviewee):

- How do you define Hawaiian identity?

- How do you define blood quantum?

- How has your family talked about blood quantum?

- What is your view of blood-quantumed Hawaiian identity?

All interview excerpts are represented through a *poetic transcription approach* or a translation mode in which narratives, stories, and interview events are captured in both their *telling* and *told* forms. As such, the *telling* or the narrative event includes the sounds and sights, the nonlexical and paralinguistic expressions, voice, and social interactional moves of members' stories. The *told* refers to the recounted events and experiences. This approach represents a single interview as a narrative performance conjoined to the dynamic formations of community, history, and politics.

I present these private memory interviews through the transcription-coding format used by John Van Maanen and D. Soyini Madison.[4]

^^	higher-pitched voice
__	dramatic lowering of the voice
// //	whisper
italics	spoken with dramatically great volume and intensity
new line	a new line was started after a one- to two-second pause; a two- to three-second pause was indicated by ——
[ ]	significant *telling* information of the performance

One central theme of the life stories of Hawaiians is the difficulty of formally establishing 50 percent blood quantum according to agency guidelines and procedures, thereby making it nearly impossible for their claims to be accepted and recognized by DHHL, which is the necessary first step before the agency puts the applicant on a waiting list. Hawaiian social actors, through concrete examples and narrative excerpts from their lives, perform the inadequacy and overwritings of state definitions of Hawaiianness, revealing how its certifiable forms conceal excesses of activity, interpretation, and political interest. Their stories reveal a structured process, and they contest the notions of neutral, nonracial government rationality and fair, equitable procedure. Such performances of formally proving one's Hawaiianness conducted in the private homes of Hawaiians and in the presence of a diasporic Hawaiian ethnographer-researcher ironically stand as the necessary locus for critiquing the DHHL and State of Hawaii, especially in light of several legal cases in which Hawaiians have been denied the "right to sue" with regard to Hawaiian Home Land trust violations. For example, throughout many cases (e.g., *Keaukaha-Panaewa Community Association v. Hawaiian Homes Commission* 1978; *Keaukaha-Panaewa Community Association v. Hawaiian Homes Commission* 1984), Hawaiians' demands for the United States to sue the State of Hawaii for trust breaches have *all* been dismissed on the grounds of legal technicalities or the suing parties' failure to fulfill procedural requirements (in both cases, not being authorized to sue the state in the seat of federal power through the state).[5] Stories, then, in this context are transformed into performative political challenges, reflecting on one hand the state framing of identity and on the other its lived irregularities and abstractions. More important, these Hawaiians demonstrate the *performance* of state structure *as a mode of agency.*

Hawaiian interviewees walk us through the painful, private memories of locating identity documents. They reconcile the writing over of their names and raced identities, tragically reducing family genealogies to blood verification. Hawaiians also negotiate competing versions of their histories as told by family members versus what the formal documents reify as the concrete truth.

They [the DHHL] didn't accept what we gave.
Through all the documents we could find.
^^ *We still not on the list . . .* ^^

—Elie

Not one written record exists for my parents,
their families li dat
—————

our names just stopped . . .

—Kealoha

^^Cannot find our *koko* der.^^ [Points to a stack of papers and file folders.] We noted as *haole* in the docs.

No tell me we not kanaka.

We are. DHHL is the only who says we not . . .

—Henry

My chapter title should not be understood as emphasizing the purely state formation of private memory and experience. To some degree the state has framed these, but my essay highlights the tremendous strength and voice of Hawaiian community members who have endured and reconfigured the interlocked machinations of U.S. colonialism and local state politics with regard to identity and identification. My focus remains on their private critical memories for insight to the invisible constraints of state identification and how various social actors work within and against these structures via a range of activity: from performative struggles, private critiques, social protest, and even diasporic movements throughout the mainland.

I first ground this project in a multidisciplinary theoretical framework that includes theoretical concepts from race and ethnic studies, sociolegal studies, cultural studies, ethnography, and communication studies. Specifically, I underscore the unspoken yet dialogic relationship between the racial state, private memory, and personal narrative. I contend that the racial state and its subjectivities are not merely formal structures abstracted from our experiences; these inhabit our everyday lives through organized routines of identity regulation and surveillance (e.g., population censuses; tax forms; official registration of names, births, marriages, and deaths). It is within these identifying social relations laid down by the state that Hawaiians actively reimagine and negotiate who they are in complicated and creative ways. The experience of the *homestead process,* a coined term among Hawaiian interviewees, is resignified from a state process to a critical sense-making about their cultural authority, cultural histories, and suspicions of the state. In addition, the homestead process connotes a "real" aspect of the everyday Hawaiian experience neglected and overlooked by the state and politically explicit, pro-Hawaiian collectives and agencies (including the Office of Hawaiian Affairs and sovereignty movement groups). These everyday Hawaiians feel caught in between "the neutral" and "the political." Personal narratives and private memories, both selective articulations of life experiences and remembrances, also symbolize the interplay of dominant structures with everyday understanding and practice of those very structures. When a cultural group remembers a structure through a recurring assemblage of meanings, private memory holds the promise of becoming a charged collective history filled with ambivalences, frustrations, and social critiques.

Next I explain my methodological practice of cultural studies ethnography. The remembering—the lived pains and pleasures of Hawaiians, their tactics and strategies in applying for homesteads and combating agency demands—is captured by ethnography. Contextualized ethnography, reframed from its colonizing tradition, makes possible a resistive opening here: it recognizes and calls attention to real Hawaiian subjectivities and state injustices in identity certification. I encounter the many different processes through which interviewees examine, question, and negotiate their family histories and cultural identity, in addition to their strategies in defiance of the state.

Through ethnography, I analyze material gathered from over ninety ethnographic interviews (privatized exchanges) with Hawaiians in Hawai'i and on the continental U.S. mainland (namely, California, Arizona, Las Vegas), whose homestead claims have yet to be completed because additional proof is needed or have yet to be recognized by the DHHL. Here Hawaiians narrate the dilemma of identity absence or excess. Either they cannot locate their ancestors in formal documents or they find them reflected in multiple forms under different names. Understanding that state recognition of Hawaiianness requires certification, Hawaiians are pressured to rummage through old photographs, private genealogies, and distant memories for factual proof.

Hawaiians reveal how subjective and inconsistent the racial state's supposedly neutral and uniform procedures of identity certification truly are. For example, names in this context bear the burden of regularity and racial assignment. According to state logic, different spellings of and variations in one's name throughout official certificates and census records reflect a questionable identity, one requiring additional proof. Hawaiians also narrate how they must wrestle with inaccurate, vague, or blank descriptions of their race in forms. Many ethnically mixed Hawaiians with a Hawaiian mother and *haole* father are designated on their birth certificates as "White." Others with a Hawaiian mother and a Chinese father are identified as "Chinese." In these cases, family members struggle in substantiating any trace of Hawaiian indigeneity. Such a pattern uncovers the specific racial politics surrounding the state's formal identification practices as recorded on birth and marriage certificates and census forms.

The racial politics at work in the identity documents seem to operate through a particular articulation of race in relation to gender. The race of the male parent has long determined racial identity by the state, which rings true for many of my interviewees in which the father's race predetermined the child's racial assignment.[6] Yet, in other cases, interviewees explain how even if the mother was Chinese and the father was Hawaiian, the assignment of the child was nonetheless recorded as Chinese. Also, many mixed Hawaiian women did not formally marry the part-Hawaiian fathers of their children which means relatives are stuck trying to find any trace of their mixed father. Moreover, those with mixed Hawaiian parents and who were designated as part Hawaiian carry the burden of proving both parents' family lines of Hawaiian blood and locating enough to meet the 50 percent requirement. According to these interviewees, the accurate assignment and recording of Hawaiian identity is rare. What promises to be a consistent procedural pattern of identification through the neutral state ultimately emerges as an indeterminate, highly variable, and burdensome set of identity rules and conditions applied only to Hawaiians.

In addition, several interviewees explain how they must reconcile what they have been told about their Hawaiian family line from relatives and the conflicting version of "truth" that is presented in a sworn affidavit given by a now-deceased grandparent or relative. In the 1950s, Hawaiians who did not possess birth and marriage certificates for their parents (who were born in the 1800s) instead recorded their parentage in formal affidavits and notarized statements that were formalized by the state.[7] Once formalized, these statements would be held as the empirical truth. The racial state's norms of fixed objectivity and the authoritative positivity of formalized data disavow identity claims of Hawaiians based on *the words and memories of their own relatives.* Private stories in these instances collide against the surrounding fixed and acontextual conditions of documentation of such stories. Indeed, through their private performances and narrations of identity, Hawaiians expose and denounce the inaccuracies, overwritings, omissions, and social consequences of state identification and blood quantum.

This chapter remains close to my heart. I share the stories of many Hawaiians, including those of my own family. Specifically, I narrate the steps my family—the Halualanis—has taken in trying to verify our Hawaiian blood quantum in official documents. To this day, we have not been able to formally substantiate our Hawaiianness according to the identity requirements of the HHCA and the agency parameters of the DHHL (thus, we are not officially Hawaiian in the documents). For me, the struggle to officially establish our Hawaiian identity grates against my personal search for my deceased grandfather—John Ululani Halualani—and his mother, my great-grandmother—Eva Kahula Alohikea Halualani Kahauolopua—in the official records and state documents. I search for their names and recorded existence to shape a memory of two family members who I never knew and yet hold close; in doing so, I, like many other Hawaiians, live within the critical interface between private memories, narratives, and photographs *and* the official documents of the state to remember my grandfather and great-grandmother. We defuse the power of state identifications by narratively contextualizing and politicizing the outlined formal procedure for verifying one's Hawaiian identity.

PRIVATE MEMORIES, PERSONAL NARRATIVES, AND THE RACIAL STATE

In chapter 2, I examined how the colonial state fulfilled the task of supplanting indigenous sovereignty and instituting several technologies of rule: national policy, legal conditions, and government commissions. In the eighteenth and nineteenth centuries, colonial governance completed its work by deploying modernist and coercive modes of power as, for instance, in sovereign residency, martial law and overthrow, and land dispossession.[8] The next era, however, marked the transformation of the state into a primarily administrative and bureaucratic arm of capitalist relations and nationalist ideology. Though racialization had already been established through colonial cartography and signified ambivalence, it is during this period that the state was further intensified as a racializing vehicle. The state's purpose shifted from that of an instrumental formation to a capillary power, "meaning that it stretches, autonomically and unseen, into the very construction of its subjects, into their bodily routines and the essence of their selfhood."[9]

As a capillary power, the racial state operated through the discourses of fair, equitable procedure and neutral, bureaucratic rationality, which in turn invisibly protected capitalist and colonial relations and preserved a national order. Through administrative policies, it lay down official procedures and conditions for identification, which permeated the private, everyday experiences of social subjects. For instance, the routine mechanisms of enumeration, serialization, and identification exist via the official registration of names, births, deaths, marriages, population counts, and national origin (identity documents/cards and census records).[10] In order to be formally recognized as citizens, individuals must be registered in terms of their birth and death and identified through a numeration system. These forms then instituted a governmental surveillance over citizens by collecting data on and accounting for each person's existence and presence over time. As much as the surveillance of the state tracks citizen-subjects, it also defines and constitutes the social body politic by circumscribing racial exclusions, inclusions, and the nominal absence of white citizenship. Officially mandated processes of identification thus allow for both the constitution and containment of racial subjects in the modern era.[11]

Yet, scholars like John Comaroff, David Theo Goldberg, and Michael Omi and Howard Winant theorize the racial state, despite its increasing surveillance and bureaucratization, as both a fixed and unstable social structure, invariably tied to governance, regulation, and economic modes of power.[12] The state may organize the racial politics of social identity and everyday life but it cannot fully homogenize, determine, or suppress private practices of identity.[13] The incompleteness and instability of the racial state can be located in the private memories, performances, and personal narratives of the everyday actors who live and practice the state on a daily basis.

Private Memory

Social groups inherit and possess a collection of memories of the past. According to George Lipsitz and Lisa Lowe, memory is positioned as a resignifying practice through which traces of difficult pasts are interwoven in members' personal experiences, oral histories, and retellings of "who they are."[14] Cultural members thus occupy positions *in memory* of their historical and political exclusions by the state (legal status, citizenship and voting rights, social services and benefits, access to institutions). In this way, memory stores structural identifications of social groups as well as their active repracticing of identity.[15] Remembering, then, is far from being a passive, predetermined practice. Instead, it constitutes an active and selective process of sense-making and reconfiguring past struggles into a critically charged consciousness and collective suspicion.[16] Through collective retellings of the past, individuals remember and performatively reorganize their struggles of identity in narrative form.

Personal Narrative

Personal narratives comprise the larger ensemble of memory. Narratives represent subjective, contextualized, and relived accounts of social life.[17] An individual's story becomes meaningful through its narrative content, mode of narration, and the positionality of the storyteller in relation to the structure of relations and institutions constituting the surrounding context. One example is the state's policies, conditions, and definitions and the colonial legacy left by modern law and governance.[18] Sociolegal scholars Patricia Ewick and Susan Silbey argue that we enact injustice in our stories and everyday performances.[19] When individuals remember and retell events of injustice, they reveal specific details in relation to abstract yet lived structures. Such narratives are formed by the intersection between the generality of the structure and the particularity of experience. So, narratives as resources of identity challenge the illusion of an objective, naturalized world and the epistemological trap that narrative truths are positioned and valued equally.[20]

Storied knowledge is never neutral or innocent; rather, it is politically produced and situated within particular identity positions, yet these aspects are effaced.[21] We cannot see on the surface the inseparable connections between identity, experience, and the racial state as a larger complex of social relations and cultural processes. Through narratives, a group that has been racialized and overdetermined can contest state structures and personalize formal abstractions and exclusions that are supposed to contain them through the guise of objectivity and uniform procedurality. By exposing the state, "an individual's narrative juxtaposes private struggles with structural forces, thereby reflecting the constructed set of meanings that emerge out of and are selected from an inventory of social practices available in a delimited cultural context."[22] Pierre Bourdieu's concept of regulated improvisation can be linked to narratives of the racial state.[23] Within the matrix of shared cultural meanings shaped by the state, social actors can indeed improvise and act in un-expected and creative ways. They can refashion structured meanings to suit their own experiences, needs, and memories of the past.

Specifically, Hawaiians demonstrate the power of private memory and personal narratives in recounting and reconstituting their struggle in formally substantiating their Hawaiianness. It is through the retelling that the supposed neutrality and objectivity of the local state can be questioned as the racial state's authority is undermined and exposed as wholly unjust and hegemonic. The interviewees move one step further; they demonstrate how state classifications of identity can be brought down only through the narrative remembering of them. Through their verbal performance of private memory and personal narrative, Hawaiians re-enact and redeploy the DHHL process of identity verification and home-stead application as a narrative frame for challenging predetermined identifications by the state.

ETHNOGRAPHY AND PRIVATE EXPERIENCE

If private experience is structured by the state and reordered and re-membered by social actors, the real challenge becomes one of examining the entanglement between the racial state and its performance by social subjects. Ethnography enables the researcher as social-historical subject to engage and analyze the internally held, symbolic meanings constitut-ing experience, memory, and identity for social actors.[24] In this way, eth-nography stands as the locus for accessing private memory and narra-tives about the state process of substantiating Hawaiian identity. I use ethnography to examine the resignified performances and memories of identity by Hawaiians, or the identifying—speech acts among its mem-bers, thereby momentarily capturing the verbal and nonverbal signs, ex-pressions, and lived representations of their selves.[25] In these interviews, I probe their sense-makings, interpretations, and use of state-structured Hawaiian blood quantum.

Initially, I conducted an extensive oral history project of Hawaiian communities on the mainland exploring the identity enactments and communicative sense-makings of differently positioned diasporic Ha-waiians (featured in chapter 5). After the first twenty interviews, I no-ticed an emergent pattern: Hawaiian identity was primarily discussed in relation to the DHHL application experience and the formal verification of blood quantum. Rather than merely invoking the structural identifications of blood, they critiqued the state determination and administration of Hawaiian identity. Hawaiians questioned the delineated administrative process of recording and documenting blood quantum. Specifically, they present "frame narratives," or stories that underscore and demonstrate a particular process. The interviewees reenact the procedures required for formally substantiating their Hawaiianness for me, delineating each step of the application verification process, presenting certificates and documents to me, and reliving the frustrating experience of falling short of meeting a state-defined identity mandate. As they narrate, they call attention to invisible contextual details and political motivations of the state that surround the documents and are laden throughout the application process. I realized, then, that these frame narratives represented much more than objective recountings of an event; these performances revealed the creative agency that Hawaiians possess within delimited structural conditions. In the demonstrated link between their DHHL application experiences, the state, and their defiant claims of Hawaiianness, Hawaiians reperform state constructions to their limits as a mode of untapped agency. They continually distinguished between their own cultural authority as Hawaiians and the faulty formal-legal precedent of state blood quantum identifications. In addition, the interviewees viewed the state as an inaccurate and yet real force in their lives, one that would not disappear anytime soon. Thus, the ethnographic interviews symbolized rare opportunities for Hawaiians to disprove and challenge the state (which has become increasingly difficult in the courtroom as lawsuits issued by Hawaiian beneficiaries of the HHCA are frequently dismissed on procedural grounds).

Honing in on this significant theme, I continued to conduct more ethnographic interviews with Hawaiians in Hawai'i and their diasporic counterparts on the mainland and those who had grown up in different historical junctures (from the 1930s through the 1980s; and whose parents or grandparents grew up in the 1890s). My sample of interviewees included Hawaiians who belonged to Hawaiian civic club associations as well as those who refused to join these clubs or explicitly political sovereignty movement groups. Thus, I was able to capture the identity practices of Hawaiians in various positions; those who were actively involved in public, reformist-slanted organizations and others who kept to themselves because of their disdain for state-driven ethnic organizations and unresponsive political collectives. Unlike other analyses of Hawaiian identity, this project explores identity challenges among everyday Hawaiians who participate in and construct the political in less explicit and formal venues (e.g., civic club associations, private practice and memory, *halau,* and canoe clubs). I focused on the Hawaiian community members' performative critiques of state administrative politics, blood quantum mandates, and their narrative strategies for contesting these. My main research question was, How is blood quantum identification deployed, practiced, and remembered in the everyday lives of Hawaiians?

My interview format emerges from the ethnographic interview tradition created by James Spradley, in which grand tour questions are used to explore the relationship between experiences and blood-quantumed identity.[26] Each interview lasted about one to two hours in the home of the interviewee. Most of my interviews were attained through a personal referral system (a system that revealed identity articulations when some members described other members as engaging in similar experiences with the state DHHL process). I would note these designations and seek interviews with them. I structured each interview around broadly defined yet open-ended and semi-structured questions, which facilitated much discussion. Each interview session required a follow-up interview in which I presented my data transcriptions and preliminary analyses. Interviewees then had the opportunity to clarify, change, and elaborate on specific points. I call these sessions "member-checking" forums. Finally, each interviewee's name has been changed for privacy and confidentiality purposes; interviewees chose the name.

In their frame narratives, the interviewees repeatedly referred to "primary" and "secondary" documents for the DHHL application process, the DHHL set of instructions and official hierarchy of documents. In order to be eligible for a Hawaiian homestead lease as approved in the 1921 HHCA and be placed on the waiting list for a homestead, applicants must complete an extensive process and formally substantiate their Hawaiian blood amount. According to the DHHL application, each applicant must trace their genealogy to her or his full Hawaiian ancestor. Applicants must also follow a hierarchy of value for documents that are to be submitted. First, one should attempt to gather "primary documents" such as official birth certificates, preferably from the State Department of Health (DOH), Vital Records Section. So, primary documents are those that certify to a high degree the objective "validity" and veracity of the recorded information. The assumption is that official agencies of the state furnish "real," accurate, and verifiable identifying information. In addition, the process presupposes that each person's identity and existence must be recorded and marked. Without such a record, a person's identity is left unrecognized and presumed "nonexistent." Hawaiian applicants must provide official birth certificates for themselves, their biological father, and biological mother. If these are missing or do not clearly prove 50 percent blood quantum, then the applicant must furnish official birth certificates for the parents of their biological father and mother. Also, if the DOH does not hold a birth certificate record for a relative (or sends back a "NO RECORD" notice), then it is unlikely that an official birth certificate, particularly those from the late 1800s, will be found. (The DOH reissues birth certificates from the late 1800s and stores old, original records on microfiche.)

Without any primary documents, applicants must furnish secondary documents that verify her or his parents and grandparents' Hawaiian amount and family relation such as (respectively) certified marriage certificates, death certificates, family history charts, census records, official baptismal records from churches, official records from military services, schools, and hospitals, employment records, obituaries, and affidavits or notarized statements from family members who can verify a person's genealogy and blood line. If one primary document is found in relation to a relative, that record is held as the priority standard for judging each subsequent record presented thereafter. Also, the secondary documents, as presented in the exact order above, are counted "less" than primary documents; Hawaiians who cannot locate primary documents must therefore collect several secondary documents as proof. The same standard applies for documents with variations in names and dates; more documents need to be supplied in order to meet the inscribed burden of proof. Once applicants collect all necessary information to substantiate 50 percent Hawaiian blood, the DHHL examines each claim and the corresponding paperwork. An applicant is then notified whether or not the blood quantum requirement has been verified. If a claim is denied for failure of proof, the applicant can appeal to the DHHL and a hearing can be held to address any disagreements and inconsistencies. Those individuals whose claims are successfully completed and approved are placed on the waiting list for the next available homestead lease.[27]

PERFORMANCES OF FORMALLY PROVING HAWAIIANNESS
AND OF DISPROVING THE STATE: THE POLITICS OF
IDENTITY SURVEILLANCE AND DOCUMENTATION

All Homestead Applicants:
Please complete this formal *identity*.

Eligibility Requirements:
To be eligible to apply for a Hawaiian Home Lands homestead lot lease,
you must meet the following requirements:
- A native Hawaiian, that is, a person with at least 50 percent
  Hawaiian ancestry; **Note: Native Hawaiian qualification is
  based on biological (natural) ancestry.
- At least 18 years old

Please submit the following items to the department.
1. Application for Lease of Hawaiian Home Lands
2. Kumu Ohana Worksheet; *Note: Completed Kumu Ohana must
   be supported by documented evidence to prove at least 50 percent Hawaiian ancestry.
3. Necessary documents to prove 50 percent Hawaiian ancestry
   and at least 18 years old.

Inconclusive Documents:
Sometimes an applicant may be confused by DHHL's request for more
documentation. Usually if a request is made for more documentation, it is
because a question regarding a person's application or genealogy has
been raised. For example, the document presented may refer to the applicant as "Part Hawaiian," "Caucasian-Hawaiian," "Hawaiian-Chinese"
or "Portuguese-Hawaiian." Often an applicant will interpret statements
like this to mean the individual is 50 percent Hawaiian. In fact, because
the percentage of Hawaiian is not specified, additional documentation
will be required to identify the full-blooded Hawaiian ancestor(s).

Variation in Names or Single Names:
If a document shows a variation in names, such as the difference between a name on a birth certificate and a marriage certificate, more
documentation will be requested to explain the difference.[28]

Hawaiians engage in performances of proving their identity, all the
while unveiling how state identification erases and confounds their ge-

nealogical lineage. I present the performative and narrative challenges of Hawaiians in Hawai'i and on the mainland to structured encodings of blood quantum. In these interviews, there live several tensions. The homestead process risks racial subjection and cultural/self-surveillance by Hawaiians themselves in terms of complying with predetermined norms of identity and on the other, how stories about the process present an unfixed, valuable resource. Ironically, it is through these performances of identity that social actors can challenge and expose state injustices. Hawaiians remember and retell their private memories of identity, and differentiate between state fronts and their own lived, private truths that are not apparent in the documents. The compelling performances of proving by Hawaiians are first revealed here in the story of my family—the Halualanis—and how we had to engage in a performance of formally substantiating our Hawaiian identity; then I present excerpts from several interviews with Hawaiians with similar experiences.

Finding Grandma Eva: The Frame Narrative of the Halualanis

Equidistant lines linked together on a DHHL genealogy sheet, faded sepia photos framing family members, blood percentage calculations, and photographic glances at my fair-skinned grandfather and my great-grandmother; these images, some from the state application form to verify one's Hawaiian blood quantum and others from personal and private memories, intermix and collide together in the everyday experiences of Hawaiians. State and private images of Hawaiianness therefore flow into one another, never becoming distinct and separate. As John Comaroff argues, in many contexts such as with the Hawaiians, the state embeds itself within the everyday, private recollections of its subjects. Blood quantum, a state classification, thus frames and enters the stories, photo albums, and oral histories of Hawaiians. Likewise, historical retellings and social critiques crafted by Hawaiians spill over the seemingly neutral and objective procedures of the DHHL application process.

The indistinguishable connection between state classification and private memory is threaded through my own photo album. Frame to frame, speckled edges and faded images, old photographs remember and recapture my grandfather, John Ululani Halualani. I never knew my grandfather, who died long before I was born. I only knew of him through his images and the stories circulating around him. A half-Hawaiian and half-*haole* man, my grandfather was tall, slender, and looked more like a *haole* with his fair skin, tall forehead, and high nose (see Figure 7). My father, Ronald Alohikea Halualani, told me that his father spoke fluent Hawaiian, although his appearance would not lead people to believe so. John Ululani Halualani was featured throughout our photo album: with his beautiful wife (my grandmother), Hattie

Figure 7. John Ululani Halualani (my grandfather), 1935. Courtesy of the Halualani family.

Kuʻulei Namahoe Halualani, and their children; one with John Dunn, Alohikea (my father), and Haleloke (Caroline and Eva, the two youngest daughters, were not born yet); and the other with all five Halualani children (see Figures 8, 9, and 10). But I had always heard his name and remembered his image in relation to my family's DHHL application

Figure 8. John Ululani Halualani and Hattie Kuʻulei Namahoe Halualani (my grandmother), 1935. Courtesy of the Halualani family.

Figure 9. John Ululani Halualani with John Halualani (his oldest son), Ronald Alohikea Halualani (his youngest son; my father), and Haleloke Halualani (his daughter), 1937. Courtesy of the Halualani family.

Figure 10. The children of John Ululani Halualani and Hattie Kuʻulei Namahoe Halualani, 1946. From left in back: John and Alohikea; from left in front, Haleloke, Caroline, and Eva. Courtesy of the Halualani family.

experience. The state forms of identity had been fastening onto our private memories. With the flip of a page, the stories waned. For two different generations, they became fleeting memories. For a moment, we did the unthinkable. We forgot, becoming consumed with percentages, names, dates, locations, and interpretations. Matching, verifying, identifying the identified.

In 1996, my father had been assisting his sister, Caroline Halualani Brown, in collecting the documents necessary to substantiate their 50 percent blood quantum in order to be placed on the homestead waiting list. They had already verified 40 percent Hawaiian blood on their mother's side, the Namahoes. However, 10 percent from their father's side was still needed for official recognition by the DHHL and eligibility into the Hawaiian homestead program. Dad made several trips to Hawaiʻi to research the needed documents, and I held on to his every word throughout several interview sessions as he described the entire application process of identity, step-by-step and turn-by-turn.

Cracked papers, edges bent, identifying forms were spread out all over. Dad explained that "DHHL requires that we completely fill out this sheet." He held out a family map worksheet that featured a flowchart of lines and spaces to fill in with percentages and names (see Figure 11).

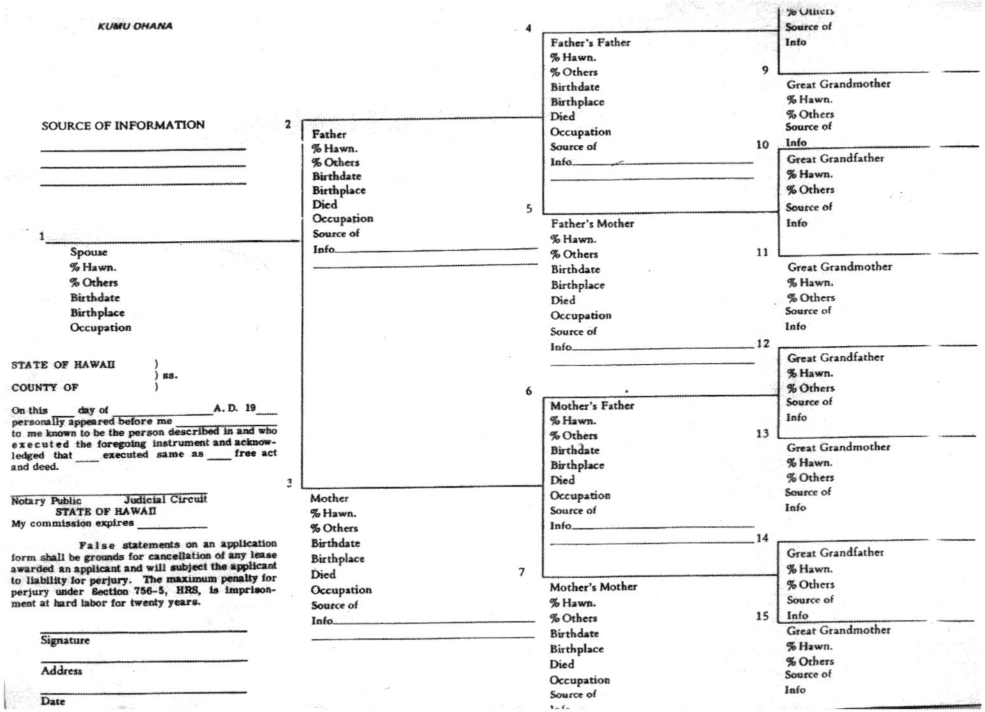

KUMU OHANA

SOURCE OF INFORMATION

1
Spouse
% Hawn.
% Others
Birthdate
Birthplace
Occupation

2
Father
% Hawn.
% Others
Birthdate
Birthplace
Died
Occupation
Source of
Info.

3
Mother
% Hawn.
% Others
Birthdate
Birthplace
Died
Occupation
Source of
Info.

4
Father's Father
% Hawn.
% Others
Birthdate
Birthplace
Died
Occupation
Source of
Info.

5
Father's Mother
% Hawn.
% Others
Birthdate
Birthplace
Died
Occupation
Source of
Info.

6
Mother's Father
% Hawn.
% Others
Birthdate
Birthplace
Died
Occupation
Source of
Info.

7
Mother's Mother
% Hawn.
% Others
Birthdate
Birthplace
Died
Occupation
Source of
...

8
% Others
Source of
Info

9
Great Grandmother
% Hawn.
% Others
Source of
Info

10
Great Grandfather
% Hawn.
% Others
Source of
Info

11
Great Grandmother
% Hawn.
% Others
Source of
Info

12
Great Grandfather
% Hawn.
% Others
Source of
Info

13
Great Grandmother
% Hawn.
% Others
Source of
Info

14
Great Grandfather
% Hawn.
% Others
Source of
Info

15
Great Grandmother
% Hawn.
% Others
Source of
Info

STATE OF HAWAII   )
) ss.
COUNTY OF   )

On this _____ day of _____ A. D. 19 ____
personally appeared before me _____
to me known to be the person described in and who
executed the foregoing instrument and acknowledged that _____ executed same as _____ free act
and deed.

Notary Public _____ Judicial Circuit
STATE OF HAWAII
My commission expires _____

    False statements on an application
form shall be grounds for cancellation of any lease
awarded an applicant and will subject the applicant
to liability for perjury. The maximum penalty for
perjury under Section 786-5, HRS, is imprisonment at hard labor for twenty years.

Signature _____
Address _____
Date _____

Figure 11. Worksheet from the Department of Hawaiian Home Lands Kumu Ohana (DHHL form B25, revised 07/96), State Department of Hawaiian Home Lands, Honolulu, Hawai'i.

This was the DHHL Kumu Ohana worksheet. Strangely though, it looked different from the genealogies I had read about—the moving tales about the origin, passion, rage, and reunion of *akua* and *aliʻi* in love and war. These would not meet the page.

Dad delineated the starting point of the DHHL application process: "Fifty percent is what is needed. My father was half Hawaiian. There is a certified 40 percent on my mother's side. We need 10 percent," he explained. The birth certificate listed my grandfather's mother's (my great grandmother's) name as Eva Kahula Alohikea but his father's name was listed as "Unknown."

To verify our Hawaiian blood, we had to substantiate that Eva Kahula Alohikea was Hawaiian. Her name emerged for me through the state identification process. I had heard brief stories about her; how neat she kept her house and how she spoiled my father and his brother, who lived next door to her. Eva Kahula Alohikea Halualani Kahauolopua was a darker woman who was pure Hawaiian. We held the personal knowledge of our family history but we could not certify it. From his binder, Dad drew out the birth certificate for my grandfather—John Ululani Halualani—which is deemed a primary identity document by the DHHL (see Figure 12). I touched the outline of his name; this image along with the photographs were the only memories I had of him. His race, though, was absent; it was not officially recorded. At this point, Dad reminded me of the state gaze over the document. In order to trace the Hawaiian percentage of my grandfather, we had to trace out his parents' line and blood quantum. We did have his name, which matched that of our family's and verified that he was born in 1903 and lived on Todd Avenue in Keaukaha, Hawaiʻi. As with my grandfather, John Ululani Halualani, I would know Grandma Eva only through the DHHL application process. She became the full-blooded Hawaiian ancestor on the Halualani line who we would need to fully trace out in order to substantiate our Hawaiianness. Dad needed official documents that strictly verified "Eva Kahula Alohikea" as being Hawaiian. The photographs we have of Grandma Eva feature a striking woman who dominates the surrounding frame (see Figures 13 and 14). I didn't know much about her, only the little I was told or what I read. In a historical book about Keaukaha, Grandma Eva, who was well known in the community, is described as a "luau caterer who held the luaus at her home with beautiful music." "Aunty Eva," as she was known to friends, "had

CERTIFICATE OF LIVE BIRTH

BOOK Maui Births (1904-09)

PAGE NO. 1 (Hana)

1. NAME OF CHILD	2. SEX
JOHN ULULANI HALUALANI	Male

3. DATE OF BIRTH

December 19, 1903

4. PLACE OF BIRTH a. City, Town or District	b. County
Kipahulu	Maui

FATHER OF CHILD

5. FULL NAME	6. RACE
Unknown	Unknown

MOTHER OF CHILD

7. FULL MAIDEN NAME	8. RACE
Eva Kahula Alohikea	Hawaiian

9. DATE RECORDED

February 1, 1904   D. P. Lawrence, Registrar

**THE ABOVE IS A TRUE COPY OF THE RECORD ON FILE IN THE
STATE OF HAWAII DEPARTMENT OF HEALTH
RESEARCH AND STATISTICS OFFICE**

September 12, 1985   *George H. Takuyama*

DATE   STATE REGISTRAR

RS-41 8/73 3M   NOTE:- *This certificate is not valid if it has been altered in any way whatsoever or if
it does not bear the raised seal of the State of Hawaii Department of Health.*
MT /sm   B8353   9/11/85

Figure 12. Birth certificate for John Ululani Halualani from the State of Hawaii
Department of Health; reissued in 1985. Courtesy of the Halualani family.

Figure 13. Eva Kahula Alohikea Halualani Kahauolopua (my father's grandmother), 1938. Courtesy of the Halualani family.

Figure 14. Eva Kahula Alohikea Halualani Kahauolopua, 1938. Courtesy of the Halualani family.

an entertaining group that entertained throughout the island and on stage at different theatres."[29] Hunched over the documents with rulers and magnifying lenses, we focused on what the documents had to say, or rather what we wanted them to say. Dad picked, probed, guessed, and speculated. Our family members were type-ridden figures and we followed them through a paper trail, that is, if they even appeared in the documents. My father requested an official birth certificate from the DOH for an Eva Kahula Alohikea, born in the year 1883. He had requested certificates for all possible names—Kahula, Alohikea, and Halualani—and for different birth years, in case the recording of her birth and identity was inaccurate. We were certain that Grandma Eva was born some time around 1883, but it wasn't so on paper. The request for her birth certificate was returned. It read, "No Record." The reply to every one of the requested names would read the same. How could that be? There was no record of Grandma Eva. Where was she?

Later, Dad discovered why we couldn't find her, or her absence, in the documents. At first, all birth records for Hana, Maui, (where my father's line originated) were destroyed in a fire. This constituted a tragic loss of certifying documents not recognized by the DHHL. Past mishaps were never compensated for by this administrative body. Instead, the hands of administration would remake them. Like neutral, blank slates, the records would be remade and redrafted by the administrative body as real. In the 1980s, the DOH reissued new birth certificates for those "Hawaiians" who could not be traced, those who could not be found and were missing. The new records, though, formally re-created and changed their existence. In addition, we discovered that there were no birth certificates issued by the state before the year of annexation.

The new retold, and the old—the census records—told too much. We still needed to locate Grandma Eva and prove that she is Eva Kahula Alohikea, the name on John Ululani Halualani's birth certificate and confirm her Hawaiian quantum. We hoped that the U.S. census records could provide the necessary information and formal data. Dad spent hours in different libraries and the State Archives in Hawai'i, and brought home copies of old census records. According to the State Archives, before 1900, Hawaiian census records (instituted as a result of *haole*-foreign insistence) existed, but were recorded in the native Hawaiian language and were difficult to translate.[30] We were left with the official census records of the United States. Beginning in 1900, after

annexation, the U.S. government conducted a census every ten years
(see Figure 15). Its categories were finite and discernible, and the names
and subjectivities bounded within its columns: the names, the relationship of each person to the head of the family, race, age, and number of
children living. I hoped that the accumulated census data would lead us
in the right direction.

Excited, I followed the lines and names, looking for her. The records
teased me. The U.S. census record of 1900 for Hana, Maui, hinted at
the presence of my Grandma Eva. She would have been about seventeen
years old at the time. There, deep within the cursive (see Figure 16), was
my family's name, Halualani. This was it at long last. Dad blurted out,
"She's not here."

Our fingers, trembling and desperate, moved from Halualani and
across. This line, bearing our name, was the male head of the household.
Possibly Eva's father. The next line down, Louisa, her mother. And
across the way, "1" is listed in the column "Mother of How Many Children." This "1" must be Eva as a child. But the next column, "Number
of Children Living" read "0." The only child died? This wasn't Eva? Our
tracking led us nowhere and everywhere at the same time.

Researching it out, we knew why. Census enumerators in Hawaiʻi
had been those who spoke pidgin English and not Hawaiian and could
write in English. They were usually either Chinese or Portuguese male
recorders. So, when each recorder went from home to home, from
Hawaiian to Hawaiian, he wrote down names as he *heard* them and not
necessarily as they were actually spelled. Family relations became a matter of guesswork and perception. If a husband and wife lived with several young children, it was assumed they were directly related. Erased
from this recorded assumption was that, in the Hawaiian family, it was
common for friends, neighbors, and distant relatives to live with one another. It was the Hawaiian way to open their homes up, especially to
those who could no longer be provided for in their original homes and
families. Family dispersal was a way to survive in poor economic times.
These details would not come from the supposedly truth-bearing cursive. They were forever disintegrated in the translation, and muddled
through the precision of an administrative census instrument.

The identity possibilities, then, became endless. Either we did not
find any trace of her or we found her in potential multiple places. Eva
might have been the ill-fated "1"; but as recorded by a Portuguese

PERSONAL DESCRIPTION

NAME	RELATION	Race	Sex	DATE OF BIRTH		Place of birth of each person and parents of each person enumerated. If born in the United States, give the state or territory. If of foreign birth, give the country.	CITIZENSHIP	Whether able to speak english: or if not, give language spoken.
Number of family, in order of visitation	Relationship of each person to the head of the family			Month Year			Year of immigration to Hawaii, or other part of United States.	
of each person whose place of abode on (date) was in this family				Age at last birthday				
Enter surname first, then the given name and middle initial, if any.				Whether single, married, widowed, or divorced			Whether naturalized or alien.	
				Number of years married				
Include every person living on (date). Omit children born since (date).				Mother of how many children				
				Number of these children living				

Figure 15. U.S. Census categories for Hawai'i in 1900.

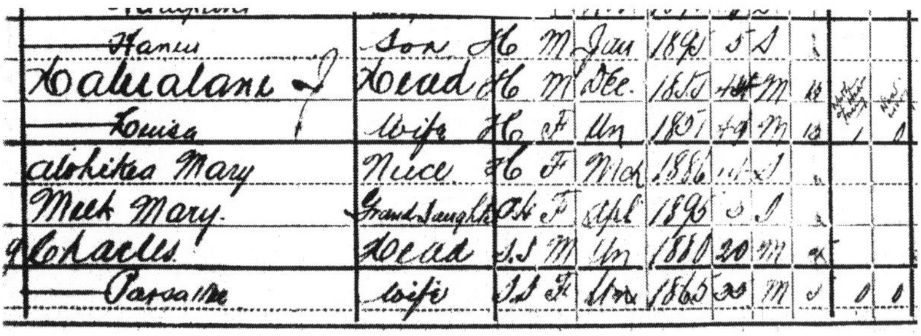

Figure 16. U.S. Census record in 1900 for Hana, Maui, volume 7, page 237. Courtesy of the Halualani family.

enumerator, the categorical distinction "Number of Children Living" could have been interpreted as "Number of Children Living *with the Family*." I shook my head. We never would know for sure.

And so we pressed on, moving wherever the print took us. To the next census page (see Figure 17). To the next scripted name—Ahulii. This was a name associated with Grandma Eva. It looked familiar. Rummaging through our files, Dad yelled, "I got it." He placed an official death certificate on the table (see Figure 18). It was for his Grandma Eva. Her father's name was recorded as Alohea Ahulii and her mother as Wahine Aea. But this was inaccurate; Dad had heard that Alohea Ahulii and Wahine Aea were Grandma Eva's grandparents. Grandma Eva was the daughter of Louisa Ahulii Alohikea and a man with the last name of Alohikea (his first name is unknown). We knew that the DHHL would not accept death certificates as primary documents in establishing Hawaiianness. They were deemed subjective assessments filled out by someone other than the deceased. For us, the certificate told us of a link—and a name that I had never held before: Ahulii.

We looked back to Ahulii on the census page. There was no trace of a seventeen-year-old female? Were these listed names Grandma Eva's relatives? Would she be living away from her parents—perhaps at an uncle's? Where is Grandma Eva?

My father tracked down yet another census record, this time ten years later. It told us even less. Dad informed me that Grandma Eva's father, Alohikea, died, and later, her mother, Louisa Ahulii Alohikea married John Halualani who adopted Grandma Eva. We were looking for Grandma Eva who would have been about twenty-seven years old and

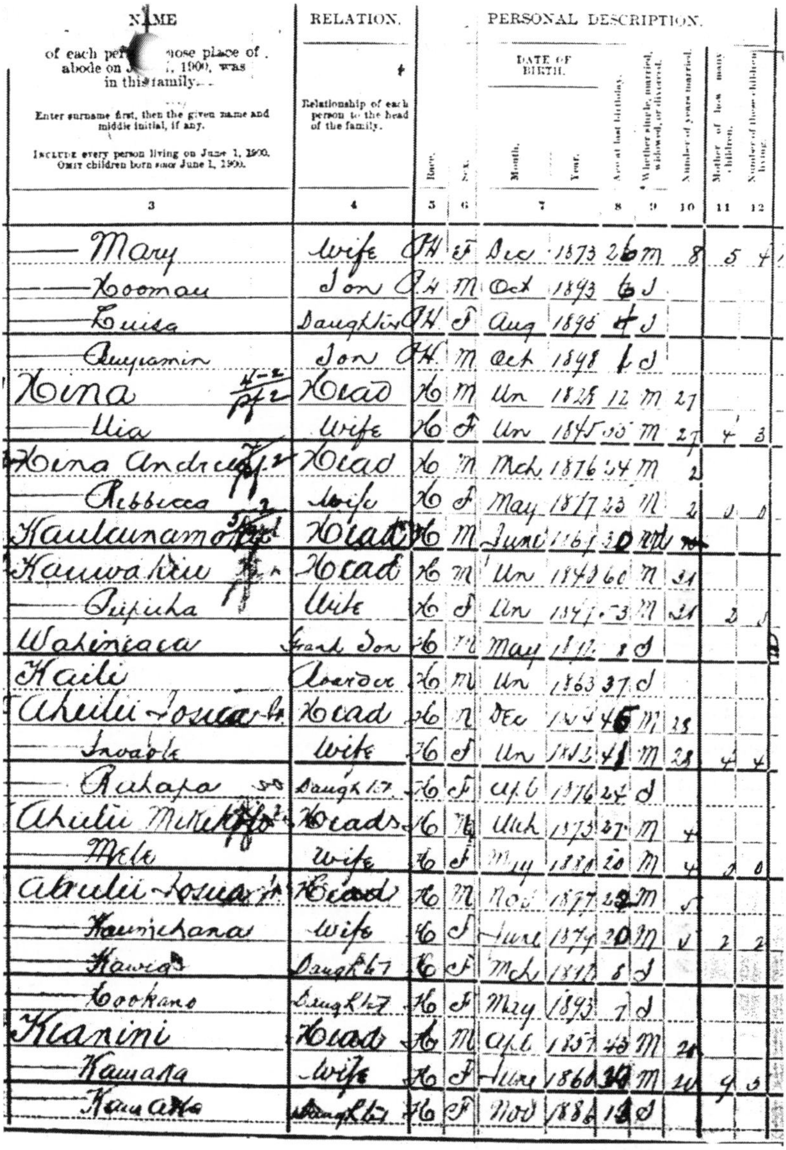

—— Mary	Wife	PH	F	Dec	1873	26	M	8	5	4	
—— Koomau	Son	PH	M	Oct	1893	6	J				
—— Luisa	Daughter	PH	F	Aug	1895	4	J				
—— Benjamin	Son	PH	M	Oct	1898	1	J				
Hina	Head	H	M	Un	1828	12	M	27			
—— Lia	Wife	H	F	Un	1845	55	M	27	4	3	
Hina Andrew	Head	H	M	Mch	1876	24	M	2			
—— Rebecca	Wife	H	F	May	1877	23	M	2	0	0	
Kaulanamoku	Head	H	M	June	1867	30	Wd				
Kauwakiu	Head	H	M	Un	1840	60	M	31			
—— Pipika	Wife	H	F	Un	1847	53	M	31	2		
Wakiniaca	Grand Son	H	M	May	1899	1	J				
Kaili	Servant	H	M	Un	1863	37	J				
Ahului Josua	Head	H	M	Dec	1854	45	M	25			
—— Snoala	Wife	H	F	Un	1853	47	M	25	4	4	
—— Rakara	Daughter	H	F	Apl	1876	24	J				
Ahului Mikek	Head	H	M	Mch	1873	27	M	4			
—— Mele	Wife	H	F	July	1880	20	M	4	0	0	
Ahului Josua	Head	H	M	Nov	1877	22	M				
—— Kaunichana	Wife	H	F	June	1879	20	M	1	2	2	
—— Kawica	Daughter	H	F	Mch	1898	8	J				
—— Cookano	Daughter	H	F	May	1893	7	J				
Keanini	Head	H	M	Apl	1857	43	M	21			
—— Kamana	Wife	H	F	June	1860	39	M	21	4	3	
—— Kau ae	Daughter	H	F	Nov	1884	15	J				

Figure 17. U.S. Census record in 1900 for Hana, Maui, volume 7, page 236.
Courtesy of the Halualani family.

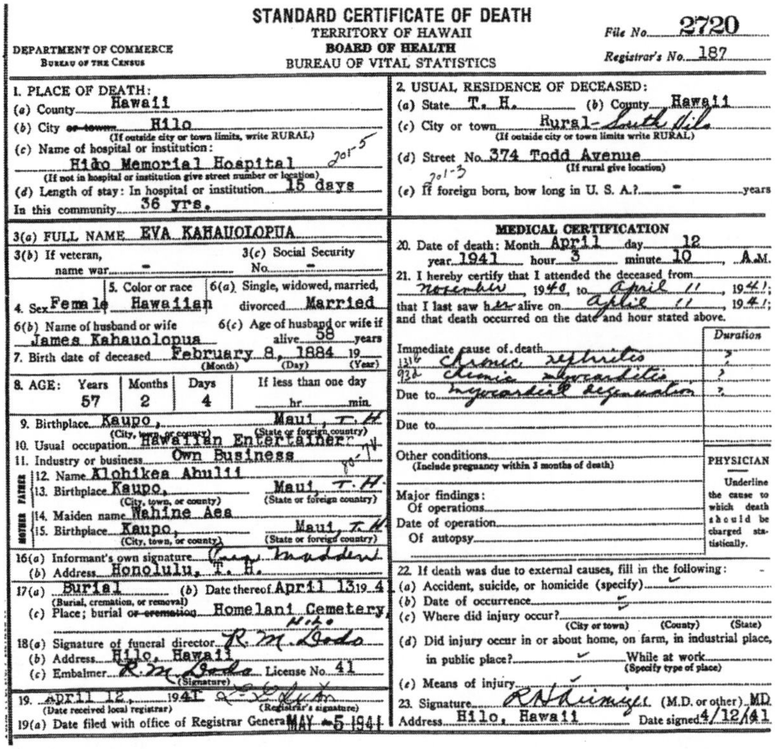
STANDARD CERTIFICATE OF DEATH
TERRITORY OF HAWAII
BOARD OF HEALTH
BUREAU OF VITAL STATISTICS
DEPARTMENT OF COMMERCE
Bureau of the Census
File No. 2720
Registrar's No. 187

1. PLACE OF DEATH:
(a) County Hawaii
(b) City Hilo
(c) Name of hospital or institution: Hilo Memorial Hospital
(d) Length of stay: In hospital or institution 15 days
In this community 36 yrs.

2. USUAL RESIDENCE OF DECEASED:
(a) State T. H. (b) County Hawaii
(c) City or town Rural- South Hilo
(d) Street No. 374 Todd Avenue
(e) If foreign born, how long in U. S. A.? - years

3(a) FULL NAME EVA KAHAUOLOPUA
3(b) If veteran, name war -
3(c) Social Security No. -
4. Sex Female
5. Color or race Hawaiian
6(a). Single, widowed, married, divorced Married
6(b) Name of husband or wife James Kahauolopua
6(c) Age of husband or wife if alive 58 years
7. Birth date of deceased February 8, 1884
8. AGE: Years 57 Months 2 Days 4
9. Birthplace Kaupo, Maui, T. H.
10. Usual occupation Hawaiian Entertainer
11. Industry or business Own Business
12. Name (Father) Alohikea Ahulii
13. Birthplace Kaupo, Maui, T. H.
14. Maiden name (Mother) Wahine Aea
15. Birthplace Kaupo, Maui, T. H.
16(a) Informant's own signature (signature)
(b) Address Honolulu, T. H.
17(a) Burial (b) Date thereof April 13 1941
(c) Place; burial Homelani Cemetery, Hilo
18(a) Signature of funeral director R. M. Dodo
(b) Address Hilo, Hawaii
(c) Embalmer R. M. Dodo License No. 41
19. April 12, 1941 (Registrar's signature)
19(a) Date filed with office of Registrar General MAY 5 1941

MEDICAL CERTIFICATION
20. Date of death: Month April day 12 year 1941 hour 3 minute 10 A.M.
21. I hereby certify that I attended the deceased from November, 1940, to April 11, 1941; that I last saw her alive on April 11, 1941; and that death occurred on the date and hour stated above.
Immediate cause of death: Chronic nephritis
Chronic myocarditis
Due to myocardial degeneration
22. If death was due to external causes, fill in the following:
23. Signature (signature) (M.D. or other) MD
Address Hilo, Hawaii Date signed 4/12/41

Figure 18. Death certificate for Grandma Eva. Courtesy of the Halualani family.

with a male child, John Ululani Halualani, who was born in 1903 (he would be about 5 years old). (Apparently, Grandma Eva had a son from a *haole* man with the last name Dunn, whom she never married and therefore, her son, John, retained the name "Halualani.") I immediately noticed my grandfather—I see his name Halualani, John, listed as "CH" (Caucasian Hawaiian) and about six years old. This is him. My eyes widened.

"John"—my grandfather—is listed as the grandson of the head of the family, Joshua Ahulii. But, where was Grandma Eva? The other women listed—among the Ahuliis and Halualanis—exceeded the possible age range for Grandma Eva. Again no trace. Nothing.

"Here is Louisa Halualani," Dad pointed out. Louisa Halualani? In the 1900 census, she was the wife of J. Halualani. But, on the 1910 census record (see Figure 19), Louisa is listed as the sister to the head—Joshua

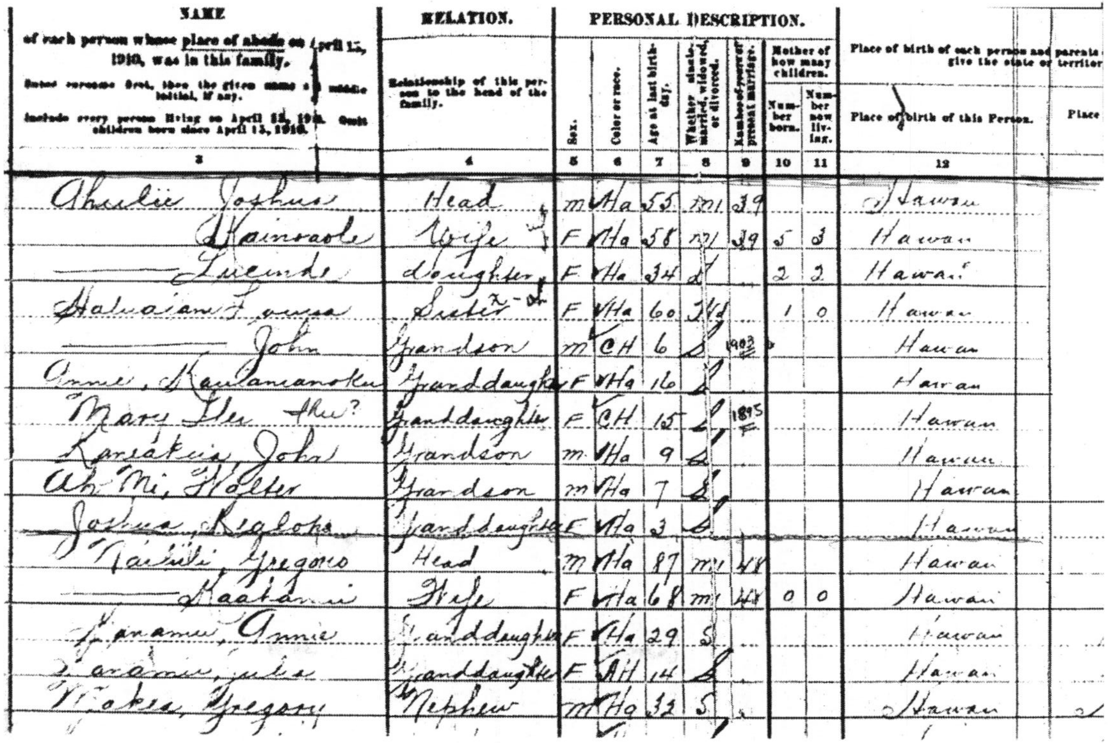

NAME of each person whose place of abode on April 15, 1910, was in this family. Enter surname first, then the given name and middle initial, if any. Include every person living on April 15, 1910. Omit children born since April 15, 1910.	RELATION. Relationship of this person to the head of the family.	Sex.	Color or race.	Age at last birthday.	Whether single, married, widowed, or divorced.	Number of years of present marriage.	Mother of how many children. Number born.	Number now living.	Place of birth of each person and parents … give the state or territory … Place of birth of this Person.	Place
3	4	5	6	7	8	9	10	11	12	
Ahulii Joshua	Head	m	Ha	55	m1	39			Hawaii	
Kainoaole	Wife	F	Ha	58	m1	39	5	3	Hawaii	
Lucinde	daughter	F	Ha	34	S		2	2	Hawaii	
Halualani Louisa	Sister-in-law	F	Ha	60	Wd		1	0	Hawaii	
John	Grandson	m	CH	6	S	1903			Hawaii	
Annie, Kaulanaokalani	Granddaughter	F	Ha	16	S				Hawaii	
Mary Lee thu?	Granddaughter	F	CH	15	S	1895			Hawaii	
Kaleakua, John	Grandson	m	Ha	9	S				Hawaii	
Ah Mi, Walter	Grandson	m	Ha	7	S				Hawaii	
Joshua, Kealoha	Granddaughter	F	Ha	3	S				Hawaii	
Kailiili, Gregorio	Head	m	Ha	87	m1	48			Hawaii	
Kaahanui	Wife	F	Ha	68	m1	48	0	0	Hawaii	
Kaaumu, Annie	Granddaughter	F	Ha	29	S				Hawaii	
Kaaumu, Julia	Granddaughter	F	AH	14	S				Hawaii	
Wohea, Gregory	Nephew	m	Ha	32	S				Hawaii	

Figure 19. U.S. Census record in 1910 for Hana, Maui, volume 7, page 92. Courtesy of the Halualani family.

Ahulii. Both are listed as speaking only Hawaiian, leaving open the possibility that the census enumerator might not have fully recorded their true relations and identities. Knowing Louisa's link would bring us closer to Grandma Eva. We found out later that at this time on the census record, Grandma Eva's mother, Louisa lived with her brother Joshua after her first husband, Alohikea, died.

The "Relation" census category bothered me. I hated the sight of it. The rule of patriarchy moved within it. Relations of the family are centrally located around the male head of the family. So the head of the family is labeled first, then his wife, children, and grandchildren. No references to indirect family relations—"Sister-in-Law," "Brother-in-Law," "Great-Grand-Nephew"—were made. The "head male of the family" centered everything—the implied domestic household and the surrounding names and identities. The difference in language further muddled the documents. The Hawaiian word *makuahine* meant "mother," "aunt," or "female cousin," while *makuakane* referred to "father," "uncle," or "male cousin." "Family Relation" would be written over by the standardized, abstracting English—in cursive, written form. It would lie and deceive.

The possibilities spun off into nowhere. John Halualani—my grandfather and the son of Grandma Eva—could have been the grandson of Louisa Halualani, who is listed as "Sister" to the Head. She was about the right age to be his grandmother—sixty years of age; and Grandma Eva's mother. But we still couldn't match John Ululani Halualani's mother—designated in Figure 13 as Eva Alohikea with any other primary documents, like the U.S. census records. Without her certified and identified presence, we could not prove her Hawaiianness and John Halualani's 50 percent blood quantum. Without these, Dad could not claim he was at least 10 percent Hawaiian blood on his father's side (to be added with another 40 percent already substantiated on his mother's side).

Our days and nights were spent guessing, theorizing, and debating. Names would fill the air, names now severed from their lives. The stories and private memories had faded away as quickly as Dad's gleam. Our home was shadowed by an altogether different presence. Some other force had been there, rummaging through our Hawaiian selves and histories.

Performances of Proving

My family's story of formally proving our Hawaiian identity underscores the structured impossibility of substantiating one's Hawaiianness. The story is the same for many other Hawaiians who have struggled to formally prove their quantum and reconcile state records with private memories.

Edith Koana, a Hawaiian woman from Kauai, shares her frame narrative about the limits of the state identification process and the privileging of a consistent, individuated, and formally documented identity. For ten years, she had been collecting and locating documents to formally prove her 50 percent blood quantum, but state documents had excised her parents out of official memory and multiplied her mothers' names and identities. She explains the process in detail:

> In my five years of application, my mama shows up ^^three times. With different names.
>
> *Different names!^^*
>
> ^^*Can you believe?^^* That means no name and no Hawaiian from her.
>
> Hawaiian Home Lands wants one name all the time.
>
> ____They [DHHL] wen' told me: Find the birth forms.
>
> My parents were both half Hawaiian, the other part *haole.*
>
> We always knew that. You know, what we were told by our family. *It's all* in my notes and files. My birth form says I am part Hawaiian.
>
> The Department of Health told me they had no record for Kahana, my mother's maiden name.
>
> ^^And it didn't hold microfilm for Kahana in 1900, her birth year. I was shocked.
>
> That means no name, no Hawaiian *from her.*
>
> *I had to look for* ^^*second-kine proof^^*—that's marriage or death certificates.
>
> Everywhere we wen look for the marriage certificate of my mother, Lei Kahana to my father, Eddy Koana.
>
> *Nothing again! Yeah!*
>
> *Blew my mind.* My parents were not in the forms. Only my birth form has their names.
>
> . . . I looked in Hawaiian records [from the Hawaiian churches]

where they lived. Nothing. They wen lose 'em. Nothing. [She shakes her head.]

^^You see,^^ it could be maybe Hawaiians never wen' follow the laws—the one say you have to record births and marriages—they didn't know or no want to live like the foreigners, or like I said, the government lost or dumped the forms. *Why else . . . Why else . . . Why so many of us* ^^cannot^^ find forms?

Someone from Hawaiian Home Lands told me, "You just need to know where to look and there it is." *Make me so mad.*

Believe me, the requirements are not as easy as it looks on paper. Forms are lost or even dumped by them.

Even the death certificate for my mother—try wait. [She runs to another room and grabs a folded paper.]

It says: Race: Part Hawaiian.

Good . . . You know, I was closer.

^^But I wen show to Home Lands^^ and they said death certificates are secondary because ^^sometimes a person who is not family fills out the information.^^

You see, my mother's death was recorded by a neighbor.

But, Home Lands, they never tell you this in the application, just when you get closer.

^^*How can a document not be proof? They [DHHL] want proof or no want proof. They say one thing and change.*^^

And then, they showed me something I didn't see. My mother's name on the death certificate is Lei Kahana [her maiden name].

^^*Why was her name Lei Kahana?*^^ The Home Land person told me, "You might need proof to show that you and your father were married or are your parents. You need 25 percent from each."

The next year, I got the U.S. census in the 1900s to find records of my mother's name and race and her parents' race. I needed records too for when I was younger. To link my mother and father as my parents. I had nothing official.

The census says my mom is Kahana and PH [part Hawaiian] when she was small. [Pulling out the form]

I saw how other family relatives who lived with my mother's family had different names—an uncle with the name Kalima, and an aunt with the name Haili.

On a chance, I applied for birth certificates under these names because in 1902, so many mistakes in the census.

^^Whose name were written down?^^

Did all of the relatives get written down? You see the kine, census takers didn't talk Hawaiian—they made guesses or asked neighbors.

It was a hit! The DOH returned with an Edith Kalima who born on the same birth date and year of my mother.

^^My mother was now a Koana, Kalima, and Kahana on three forms.^^

In the census records, when my mother was married to my father, their names are listed as Koana and PH [part Hawaiian] in one census. The next census year, my mother is Edith Koana and my father's name is put down as Kahana and as my mother's cousin.

What is going on? How can? Mama and Dad referred to each other as husband and wife and at least 50 percent each. Were my parents married? What is my mother's official name?

You talk to other people, to old kine and they say census takers would not get the names right in a household—the older male was put down as the head [of family]. They didn't talk Hawaiian and they writing the forms.

You see, back den, cousins, uncles and aunts, grandparents, kids all would live together too.

You see what I have to do—link my parents and show they are part Hawaiian. My mom's multiple names, I've got to resolve them.

How will I ever know?

[Edith placed her DHHL application on the table before me. Glancing over it, I noticed that a few spaces were filled in but most of the form remained blank.]

Edith pivots back and forth between narrating the DHHL requirements for Hawaiian identity and demonstrating the invisible, subjective limits laden throughout the seemingly neutral, objective government process of identity application. First, she draws attention to the absurdity of the identity process, or specifically how her mother is noted by three different names. Edith reveals how Hawaiian names were invariably and inconsistently recorded by either the mother's maiden name, the father's

name, or even the name of the head of household with whom the relative
was living. She raises questions about the endless identity possibilities in
a process deemed finite and objective, as illustrated in her expression of
frustration, "How will I ever know?" Throughout out her reenactment of
the application process, Edith points to the subjective perceptions and
bilingual incompetencies of state recorders and census enumerators who
documented births, marriages, and population counts for the U.S. territorial government beginning in the 1900s. Moreover, she poses questions about the effectiveness of the laws requiring the identity documentation of births, marriages, and deaths; Edith suggests that "maybe
Hawaiians never wen' follow the laws—the one say you have to record
births and marriages or . . . the government lost or dumped the forms."
Beginning in 1842, it was mandated by formal law and governance that
births, marriages, deaths, and population counts be recorded.[31] Governmental policy and legal mandates such as these operated through a discourse of neutrality and equality (meaning, individuals could supposedly
attain modern citizenship and land if only they applied to new, individuated government commissions) and yet Edith's story in the telling of
state structures and limits challenges such discursive constructions as
contradictory and incoherent. Her statements that "Home Lands, they
never tell you this in the application, just when you get closer" and "the
requirements are not as easy as it looks on paper" suggest that the very
nature of a public document is questionable. Identity requirements are
formalized under the assumption that each participant only need furnish
official evidence in an open and equitable process, yet in between the
lines of the application, these actually function with an excessive rigidi-
ty and with unspoken, hidden conditions (e.g., death certificates not
being primary proof). Names, dates, family relations, and the assignment of race must be consistent over time and documented in formal,
English-language records. Even death certificates, which are listed as secondary documents in the DHHL application, are negated because the
recorded information is too "subjective." More authority is therefore
granted to information from the actual ancestor and her or his immediate family; anyone else is unofficial and unauthorized to properly identify
the person. Thus, a regular, individuated, objective, and officially documented identity as surveilled by the state is privileged and normalized as
the formal identity necessary to claim Hawaiianness. In Edith's case, she
must explain why there are multiple names and provide additional docu-

mentation reflecting her mother as a fixed name, with 50 percent quantum, and as her own mother. Formal records work under the premise that the fixity of information is positive, objective, and real.

Edith unveils several subjective and historical conditions that surround and delegitimate her claim of Hawaiianness (for example, the difficult transition from indigenous rule to U.S. occupation and control, mistakes in census recording). The historical context of Hawai'i—the colonial incorporation of formal law and governance over the dissolved indigenous Hawaiian society—is denied by the DHHL office and must be overcome for successful completion of the application. Edith refers to the multilingual conditions of Hawai'i and the practice of Hawaiian relatives living with one another in the same household. Yet the process refuses the historical specificity of Hawai'i (and the transitional years when Hawaiians refused to participate in new governing structures and administrative procedures of identity documentation), and yet each Hawaiian applicant must confront the historical conditions that surround each document and explain why certain documents are inaccurately recorded or missing. Ironically, the blood quantum verification process itself, which seems to operate on its face through a neutral, ahistorical, and rational ideology, cannot be completed without running into the traps of historical consequence and subjective perceptions (as Edith notes of the census takers). Despite all of these subjective mishaps, the applicants today are still held to requirements for verifying Hawaiian quantum that are stringent, unrealistic, and impossible to carry out.

There also seems to be no clear distinction between private knowledge and official accounts by the state. Edith's memories—what she has always known and been told—are interwoven with her recollection and understanding of the DHHL application process. What Edith has internalized as being true and real is thrown into question by the state's official versions. Her continual exclamations of disbelief reveal the felt conflict between memory and public truth. She narrates a search common to many Hawaiians as they attempt to reconcile these two spheres and fuse what they have personally and experientially known with what is deemed empirically real. Just as Hawaiian agency seems confined, it is only within narrative performances such as Edith's that the state requirements can be problematized by retelling how she follows them and yet how she cannot fully carry them out.

Other Hawaiian interviewees presented to me stories about how the multiple names of their family members were actual misspellings recorded by non-Hawaiian-speaking registrars and census enumerators. These Hawaiians researched the names of the enumerators and several even combed thousands of census records just to pinpoint who typically served as registrars and enumerators. They discovered, as one Hawaiian woman explained, that "the recorders were all *haole* or the kine who spoke English. Chinese and Portuguese too—they would do all the writing." The racial state requires that one's existence be documented by the same name consistently over time, even though such records were noted by only English-speaking officials. Given this situation, Hawaiian applicants have found it necessary to not only locate the visible truths of state documents but also search out the invisible conditions that fully explain why they cannot find their parents or grandparents. The DHHL process is therefore deemed incomplete and indeterminable on its own terms by reperforming state requirements to their most logical endpoint.

Another applicant, Lee, also traced state identifications to their most logical conclusion or rather the logic of the state. He discovered that his grandmother was documented under two different names. During our interview session, he showed me several documents that he collected for each name. Lee commented, "My grandma—right here—is two people on paper. I can follow both directions." Puzzled, I asked what he meant. He promptly handed me two sets of papers, each representing one of the misidentified names and the false "persons" created through several documents. His grandmother was literally documented as two different people, under different names than her own, throughout a series of corresponding birth, marriage, and death certificates, and tax records and maps (each name-in-error was supported by matching documents). Strangely enough, Lee's grandmother was consistently recorded through a chain of state inconsistencies, which ultimately disallows the verification of any Hawaiian blood.

Four other Hawaiian interviewees—Harry, Elie, John, and Betty—discuss similar experiences with multiple identities of their ancestors. Elie discussed how her parents (a part-Hawaiian, part-*haole* mother and father) were never married, thus making it difficult to prove her parentage. She explained,

> Dad has two different names. Mom, . . . there is the wrong date on her birth certificate.

_____She disappears in the census_____—the ones I went for . . . I mean that's it, we don't know the exact amount of Hawaiian blood on either side.

Multiple names and identities efface Hawaiian families out of the records and place insurmountable burdens of proof on current Hawaiian generations who need to verify their Hawaiian quantum. Similar to Edith and Elie, Harry and Betty reenacted their application process by discussing line-by-line the seen and unseen in their documents. Betty boldly theorized that "they had all these names back then because they just didn't care if it was correct or not. Hawaiians were treated that way. Plus, the more Hawaiians they wrote down, the more land they would have to give up." Several interviewees shared their theories and suspicions about the state as informed by their experiences with the DHHL, and the political motive for losing documents and recording inaccurate information. Harry narrates the following:

> *Even if . . . if* everyting down is okay . . . is ^^correct,^^ DHHL and OHA li dat goin change the rules. That agency does tricks—what is first or second priority is different from one application to the next. You neva goin win with Home Lands [DHHL]. You got one challenge against Home Lands—gotta give proof or they say they goin give a hearing. You won't hear back. You cannot even get on the list or argue why you can't.

The interviews did, in fact, greatly reflect a deeply felt sentiment of suspicion toward the state (e.g., the State of Hawaii and state agencies like the DHHL and Office of Hawaiian Affairs [OHA]) in recognizing identity claims and working for the benefit of Hawaiians as a whole. Harry suggested that DHHL agency rules of application are changed on a whim and that Hawaiians are denied any means of challenging the DHHL for its failure to compensate for record inaccuracies and missing and lost documents in that hearings are never set up or are "fronts" for a forum from which to dispute the state. Likewise, legal scholars have underscored the extreme difficulty that Hawaiians face in bringing legal action against the state for Hawaiian Home Land trust violations.[32] Given this delimited political context, the performances of identity and reenactments of state mandates of identity as captured in these interviews constitute the primary locus for reinterpreting, critiquing, challenging, and disrupting the equitable, fair, and lawful face of the state. In those instances when the racial state did not produce multiple

names and identities in excess, it wouldn't provide any at all. One interviewee, Sam Kealoha, narrated his fifteen-year struggle in verifying his
Hawaiian blood and finding his mother in the documents. During our
first interview session, Sam led me to his basement. I thought he just
wanted to show me a quick photograph of a relative. Instead, he unveiled an elaborate set-up of fifteen file boxes, each with different yellow
labels: U.S. CENSUS RECORDS, BIRTH CERTIFICATES, CHURCH RECORDS,
and FAMILY NOTES. Each file had a red stick-up tab extending from it,
identifying its contents, and a chalkboard on a nearby wall featured
blood percentage calculations and genealogical diagrams in the back of
the area.

> *I spend a lot of time here, yeah? You see what I do?*
> *You can tell, huh?*
> This is what I've collected and I got most of the stuff, the kine you
> need for the required.
> ^^The missing kine I have put here.^^

Sam presented me with a shoebox of blue index cards. Each card contained a detailed explanation of why items are missing. One card read,
"Kaipo, Father born in 1885. Missing birth certificate. From early to late
1800s, certificates lost or didn't survive. Certificates reissued by the state
in the 1970s and 1980s and originals lost. State Archives." Sam had
about fifty cards like this one in his files, some citing historical dates and
corresponding laws and others listing possible explanations for inaccuracies or lost information. Another card read, "1910 missing for us, census
guys didn't go to every house in the area, seven were skipped."

> I have created my own system for backing up my claim. ^^*Right?*^^
> Fifteen years is too long.
> My father's birth certificate is missing. He's not in the census.
> Marriage certificate . . . [He grabs for a file.] Dad is put as Chinese-
> Hawaiian and mom is same way, Chinese Hawaiian. I have her birth
> certificate but nothing for her 50 percent.
> ^^Here [lifting the marriage certificate] she, my mother, right, is put
> down as Hawaiian and my father as Chinese.^^
> By . . . the Home Lands [DHHL] rule, ^^*I*^^ *have to show* that my
> mother is Hawaiian on another document and my father as Hawaiian.

Sam motions to follow him around his table, to an area covered with blown-up, magnified photocopies of census records.

> My dad's family . . . here yeah . . . is not in the census from 1890 through 1910. [He takes out a stack of my blown-up copies.] I can't find him after then.
>
> _____Up until . . . until [he takes out more papers] 1920___, my father is put as Chinese and you know, I am trying to say . . . to show he is Hawaiian.
>
> You see here . . . you see that, my dad's family lived next door to this family. I checked lots of records—tax records, maps, everything. Dad isn't in there.
>
> *I think . . . just what I think, okay?* . . . I think census guys missed families that lived way outside of city areas.

Throughout the interview, Sam's voice grew louder and he moved deftly around the table, holding out documents and blue index cards. Presented on these cards were his emergent theories about the racial state. He explained that "the state, they know Hawaiians can't show up with all the records they need. Why do you think 50 percent is the requirement? It is next to impossible to prove. All information is to be recorded more than one time by official agencies. If no can prove, the state gets the land. They have been active at making it impossible for us."

Another theory Sam suggested was that the state takes an active role in re-creating identities for Hawaiians.

> ^^You look here^^ . . . the guys whose parents, grandparents were born in the 1800s, late 1800s . . . get Department of Health birth redrafts. The agency reissued official certificates the old kine records, the kine on microfiche. They say it was for giving us more accurate dates and some for official to keep. But the reissued certificates can be inaccurate. Information was changed—the names and dates. In the time between . . . original certificates were lost or dumped.
>
> ^^So what do you get? You see where I am going?^^
>
> You get new names and dates that don't match up. Same thing with my cousin's family, they have redrafts and the names are different from what they know. But that is what they held up to.
>
> That is stamped as permanent.
>
> *They have changed who we are!*

The implication here is that in the process of organizing identity data, the racial state rewrites and re-creates formal identities for Hawaiians. Bureaucratic administrative agencies reconstruct identities by proffering new records that take on the semblance of original and permanent truths. The old can be revised and reformalized as the state both surveils and invents Hawaiianness on paper.

Through the course of his interview, Sam revealed several covert processes of the state that belie its neutral and fair administrative image. In his basement, Sam continually accounted for the information absent from state records, a process that becomes necessary and naturalized. Sam does not accept the state premise that the lack of information reflects the nonexistence of his family or Hawaiian quantum. As evident in his note-taking and file system, this interviewee actively seeks out the positivity of official and written information and is hindered at every point in the process. By challenging what is positively present in the documents and searching for explanations for what is hidden from state records, Sam therefore revises the trustworthiness of the information. What is visible and apparent is resignified as "suspicious" data, while the information that is missing and unseen gains more credibility.

Interestingly enough, Sam is a diasporic Hawaiian who has lived on the mainland since 1980. He explained that he moved away from Hawai'i after years of being denied eligibility to be placed on the waiting list.

> I tried for a long time. *A long time and you know I decided . . . that it's not going to happen.* They not going give me one homestead. Look at what I've shown you.
>
> ^^I don't need to prove who my parents are.^^
>
> And that I'm Hawaiian to DHHL. They're dirty, real corrupt, you know, the state, DHHL, OHA too.
>
> *Why stay?*
>
> ^^No more jobs, no land for Hawaiian kine.^^
>
> *I'll go back* when they confirm my quantum from the paperwork I gave them.

There exists a link, then, between Hawaiian diasporic movement and the denial of claims of Hawaiianness by the DHHL. Migration for Sam was a politicized action as he retreated from "dirty state" agencies (the DHHL and OHA). Diasporic movement symbolizes the growing re-

sentment and suspicion of Hawaiians toward the state, which is perceived as a nonresponsive, calculating, unfair, and anti-Hawaiian entity.
In fact, Sam is not the sole example; about 45 percent of the interviewees
migrated to the mainland because their claims of Hawaiian blood quantum had been denied by the DHHL (and thus they had no homestead
to live on and no incentive to stay). This pattern suggests not only that
Hawaiians are forging and circulating a suspicious and critical memory
of the state but also that Hawaiian diasporic movement, which seems
contradictory for indigenous peoples, has occurred in critical relation to
perceived state injustices and the incompleteness of the DHHL identity
process.

Sam even discussed how "sovereignty kine, they don't help us with
our documents and the homesteads. They fight for independence. But
the kine forget the real issues of homesteads and showing blood quantum. They never help us." This interview unveiled the differently positioned and often forgotten politicality of Hawaiians who do not necessarily take part in sovereignty movement groups and causes and yet who
engage in an ongoing critical consciousness against the racial state.
Everyday Hawaiians, ranging from ages thirty to seventy, like Sam differentiate themselves from both the state and the "political or sovereignty kine," critiquing the state for undermining the identity claims of
Hawaiians and reproaching the explicitly political Hawaiian groups for
their unresponsive activity on "real issues that affect Hawaiians." Thus,
performances of substantiating one's blood quantum highlight the need
for sovereignty groups to address the demands and wants of everyday
Hawaiians whose identities are continually written over by the racial
state. Until this happens, diasporic migration will increase (as the appeal
for constructing new Hawaiian communities on the mainland grows
stronger) and the larger Hawaiian public will remain polarized in the
struggle for sovereignty.

After my interview sessions with Sam, I received several phone calls
from him requesting my audiotapes of his interviews. Naturally I com-
plied with his request. One month later, Sam informed me that he had
sent multiple copies of his audiotapes to the DHHL office ("Just so
they know they no can have the last word. I am Hawaiian and their
process is wrong") and several family members in Hawai'i who are
undergoing the state process of identity. Sam now conducts informal
and unofficial homestead application workshops on the mainland to

assist other Hawaiians and their families in Hawai'i who are running into similar dead ends or the incoherencies and inaccuracies of the DHHL process. "I do this so they know they weren't wrong. The administration created a mess. I just tell 'em all the things you can't tell from the records." Sam has infused the supposedly neutral and equitable process of identity with critical reflection on the historical and political conditions surrounding Hawai'i and the identification of Hawaiians. His performances underscore the importance of diasporic movement as a critical response to the repressive state and its identity mandates and procedures.

Many other interviewees specified the arbitrary delineations of race by the state. The inaccurate and almost whimsical assignment of race or the disavowal of Hawaiianness on birth certificates magnifies the burden of proof for Hawaiians and distances them from official recognition of their identity. Lei speaks from a position shared by many Hawaiians: she is Chinese Hawaiian, an ethnic group primarily created out of the intermixing between the surplus Chinese male laborers who emigrated beginning in 1852 and worked on the plantations, and indigenous Hawaiian women. (There was a large number of these unions and marriages due to the lack of Chinese women in Hawai'i in the mid 1800s.)[33] Lei challenges the truth presented in her birth certificates and U.S. census records.

It's one of those things . . . like a mystery. My birth certificate [she and her husband pass the 1923 document to me] says that my father is Chinese.

When I saw, I thought funny you know. My father was Chinese Hawaiian, half half. His parents—his mother Hawaiian and his father Chinese. My mother same way, Chinese Hawaiian.

My father died when I was small kine. Mom told me long time ago our line was from the Lee's and Kalima's on my father's side.

She would say he was real dark but the eyes . . . the eyes were Chinese.

Mom was dark—my aunties used to say she was real Hawaiian that way.

[As Lei spoke to me, her eyes were affixed to a series of birth, marriage, and death certificates and census records.]

My parents, when they got married, on their marriage certificate, Chinese Hawaiian for both of them. They filled these out.

Mom's birth certificate, here . . . she is Chinese Hawaiian.

My father's birth certificate, he is Chinese Hawaiian.

The 1910 and 1920 census records, my father . . . you see Chinese.

In 1930, he and Mom are Chinese Hawaiian and later, in one other census, my father is Chinese and my mother is Chinese Hawaiian.

^^How come so different from each time?^^

How come my father's race on my birth certificate is Chinese, pure Chinese?

If your father or mother looked Chinese, the people would put you as Chinese, even if you have *kanaka* blood. Or you not home, they'd ask your neighbors.

Funny, yeah. Why should they put down we Hawaiians? They'd have to give us more.

If . . . for the 50 percent rule, I gotta bring in other kind records saying my parents were at least half Hawaiian each. Mom's side I got for. My father's no more and they say he is on my birth certificate as Chinese . . . I got to show more for that.

Lei contests the racial objectivity of the state in official certificates and census records. She questions the denotation of her father as Chinese when both her parents were, according to personal knowledge and several official documents—her mother's birth certificate, her parents' marriage certificate—Chinese Hawaiian. According to critical race studies scholar David Theo Goldberg, official documents like the census "purports to count without judging, to photograph without transforming . . . in the name of an objectivity that claims simply to document or to reflect."[34] However, it is precisely the work of racial constitution and racial transformation that the state brings into being through official documents and the subjective assignment of race, though such processes take place under the promise and officiality of objective counting. This is demonstrated through the arbitrary assignment of race and of Hawaiianness in Hawai'i. Goldberg also explains that typically the father's officialized race has long determined the racial assignment of a child/new citizen.[35] For example, a mixed child would be assigned the father's race. But, in Hawai'i, there exists a strange variability with regard to racial assignment. Lei's birth certificate notes her father as Chinese yet the census records list Lei's father and mother as Chinese or Chinese Hawaiian (and conspicuously not Hawaiian) over several years. The rule does not even seem to follow Goldberg's discussion of the one-drop rule or the belief and recording practice that "'black' was any person with a single drop of black blood."[36] Quite the opposite, as Lei and many other interviewees revealed, the assignment and constitution of Hawaiian blood in official documents was recorded at a minimum. In thirty interview sessions, Lei along with other Hawaiians in Hawai'i and on the mainland, narrated their family histories via their documents. A suspicious pattern of inconsistent recording emerged: children from a Chinese Hawaiian father and Chinese Hawaiian mother were recorded as "Chinese"; and children from a Chinese mother and Hawaiian father or a Hawaiian father and Chinese mother were recorded as either "Chinese," or "Chinese Hawaiian," and rarely as "Hawaiian." Individuals with parents who were either a white father and Hawaiian mother or a part white, part-Hawaiian father and mother are identified as either part Hawaiian or white. In many instances, as with Lei's father, persons with mixed Hawaiian background are assigned exclusively as the non-Hawaiian race. Lei pointed out that the census takers would judge one's racial assignment based on markers of physical appearance, which feeds into imaginings of what certain groups should look like, and guesswork in a multilingual context.

Census enumerators therefore organize the racial body politic, identifying groups based on their own "common sense judgments" and "presupposed views" of different racial groups and in the multilingual context of Hawai'i, whatever can be accessed through English, even though most of the residents spoke only their native languages (e.g., Hawaiian, Chinese, Japanese, Filipino, Korean).[37] Portuguese and Chinese census enumerators who could speak English and received recording instructions about "the races" from the state, collected information from those individuals they could understand; if they could not speak the language of the residents, as in the case of Hawaiians, subjective perceptions and notations of the "obvious" were recorded.[38] What is suspect, then, is the presiding pattern of recording mixed Hawaiians as either "Chinese," "Chinese/Part Hawaiian," or "White," at the expense of not denoting any Hawaiian blood. Lei even implies that such recording practices reveal potential political and economic motives of the state. To record less "Hawaiians" and even "Part Hawaiians," is to absolve the state from providing any valuable land and trust benefits to a racialized group. In the early 1900s, identifying mixed Hawaiians as either purely "Chinese" or "White" makes them either an unrecognized "alien" immigrant group or a white citizen, which is proof of American integration and demonstrates the social belief that Hawaiians carry specific physical markers. The recording of mixed Hawaiians as "Chinese Hawaiian" or "Part Hawaiian" limits their claims of "Hawaiianness" in the long run as the racial exclusivity signification of the 50 percent Hawaiian blood mandate becomes difficult to substantiate (especially since over time, many Chinese Hawaiians and part Hawaiians had parents who were not exactly half Chinese/White, half Hawaiian). Thus, the Hawaiian interviewees explain that they need to find more official documents to challenge the official recording of their race in primary documents. Hence, the rarely recorded Hawaiian/part Hawaiian identity is revealed only in the performances around the documents and in spite of the racial assignment from state records. Hawaiians are either reracialized into other groups (e.g., Chinese) or made into (white) abstract citizens, as Hawaiianness falls in line with its historical construction as "extinct and gone."

Lastly, the racial state not only constitutes, organizes, and fills racial categories. It transforms, fixes, and rigidifies private memory into official normative account. In the early 1950s, many Hawaiians gave sworn affidavit accounts of their family genealogies, names, dates, and the amount of Hawaiian blood held because their parents' documents were lost or never issued. These affidavits were overseen by a territorial agency akin to the DOH, under the leadership of the governor at the time. About twenty of the interviewees brought forth signed and stamped copies of notarized statements completed by their grandparents. One interviewee stated, "My grandfather, he had no certificates for his mother. So he wanted to create some official record of who she was, where she was from, and how much Hawaiian she was. But his dates and names don't match our records. And he says we are less Hawaiian than we really are." Here this interviewee points out that his relative's word differs from official records, which complicates the DHHL process for later generations as more documentation is required. For many Hawaiians, either their relatives' accounts are held as a primary yet inaccurate document or these exist in conflict with state documents. Oral private memory in the Hawaiian culture in which family histories and details were not written down is bound to shift over time as stories are circulated. However, in the case of the racial state, personal stories and memories are objectified and made permanent. The contextual specificity of personal narratives and verbal performances is therefore emptied and once private memories become normative records that undermine family stories.

It seems that the racial state has occupied several interesting positions toward the social subject and private memory; it has fused its rules, procedures, and policies of identity with private memory and narrative so that distinctions between the two become confused, and as Hawaiians explain in their performances, the state has also incorporated and remade personal stories into immovable, normative, and formalized accounts (historical snapshots) that must be disproven.

Through these private performances of identity, Hawaiians enact and narrate the limits of the racial state in formally identifying who they are. Contextual specificity becomes key to reunderstanding the (mis)recognized, quantumed Hawaiian identity, an aspect that is refused by the prevailing logic of the supposedly neutral, equitable, and rational state. Hawaiians provide what is missing in their narratives: the historical and political context surrounding the identity documentation of Hawaiians and the subjective practices embedded within the rules, conditions, and procedures of the neutral state. The structured signifiers of blood quantum that I analyzed in chapter 2 do not completely foreclose the possibilities for Hawaiian agency. Instead, in the face of such overdetermined governmental constructions, Hawaiians whose identities are surveilled, blooded, and (mis)recognized create and engage in a political determination and a sense of creativity through their narrative exposures of the racial state.

CONCLUSION

Personal narratives unfold experience . . .
Verbal performances echo . . .
Stories move, pushing beyond the confines of bounded time, space, and
   identity . . .
Private memories outlive the state . . .

The process of substantiating one's Hawaiianness—painful, shamed, and still unspoken—reveals the tragic effects of a historically extended legal (mis)recognition, how formal law and governance not only wrote over Hawaiian identities in the 1700s, but formalized into existence an identity in the (legal) making. In the pivotal moment when the United States Senate Committee on the Territories codified the Hawaiian Homes Commission Act, leasing "to Native Hawaiians the right to the use and occupancy of a tract or tracts of Hawaiian homelands" while defining "Native Hawaiian" as first "$\frac{1}{32}$ blood" to "one half part blood," it already identifies Hawaiianness, complete in name but materially "unsubstantiated" for those named. A Hawaiian must tangibly produce a formalized title (a documented identity-on-paper with material effects) through a process of filing and proving an identity claim (materially proving an identity that is presumed to be nonexistent). A Hawaiian is named, led through a maze of proving such a name, and all the while, watched over by the U.S. administrative agency and the State of Hawaii, eyes always affixed to our document faces. The State of Hawaii, protected by the armor of a purely procedural administration, continues to intervene in and control a once private practice through which Hawaiians reclaimed (and reconstituted) their *mo'olelo* and *mana*.

Administratively, the notion that all names must match and culminate into a consistently uniform (regularized) identity presupposes the centrality of dominant European forms of rationality, language standards, and social relations over a specific cultural context. Also, at its core, native women are overwritten by the patriarchal inscriptions of Hawaiian identity—the male directed family relations—and the expectation of formalized marriage (many Hawaiian women did not marry their *haole* male counterparts, even after the birth of a child.) The administrative requirement of procedurally proving one's identity, therefore, as its premise presumes that "Hawaiianness" does not yet exist and determines what it should look like in the end (e.g., verifiable matches across time, cultures, and socioeconomic conditions).

My interspersed private memory and those of many Hawaiians—painful, shamed, and still unspoken—reveal the tragic consequences of a historically extended legal mis/recognition. How formal law and governance not only wrote over Hawaiian identities in the 1700s, but formalized-into-existence a preformative, predetermined identity.

The administrative body—the DHHL—with its neutralized, uniform walls, desks, and chairs; its impersonal workers, and its machine/precision-like churning oversees a chaotic nightmare of identity documentation for Hawaiians. A procedure of proving blood quantum, through my telling, exposes the irregularities and uncontrollable subjective perceptions of race. It reveals how "formal identity is identity conceived, manufactured, and fabricated in and through forms."[39] Census records and birth certificates in the context of Hawaiians represent some of the ways in which the U.S. nation and State of Hawaii can take stock and surveil Hawaiians and reuniform them through an administration of functional/ideological social science.

The most tragic consequence of the DHHL process is the fragmenting of a Hawaiian consciousness into one obsessed with surface traces of identities at the expense of telling the stories of our genealogies, at the expense of historically relating to one's ancestors and their struggles beyond the documents. The state's surveilling gaze has become our own, imposing its watchful eyes, its administrative instruments into the sacred cultural practice of genealogies and their rich narrative forms. It does so by requiring identity verification and the public display of private genealogies. Hawaiians are thus pressured to invoke the very racial categories administered for them by the state. This necessitates blood quantum identity for attaining formal recognition and land claims. On the flip side, a necessary blood identity seems culturally authentic as Hawaiians adopt the discourse of "pure-bloods" and "mixed-bloods," and move through the proper state conditions and rules for claiming homestead land. The local state's surveilling gaze has become our own, imposing its watchful eyes, its administrative instruments into the sacred cultural practice of genealogies and their rich narrative forms.

Requiring a Hawaiian by policy and law to establish a homogenous, coherent, and consistent identity (one demanding that relatives' names and birth/marriage dates match and family relations are fully known) coincides, in my eyes, with the "tribal rolls" that have plagued Native Americans.[40] One encoding all too frequented involves recovering family genealogies mainly in terms of proving blood quantum and gaining resources (predominantly thinking of what will fulfill state requirements for blood ties). This abruptly transforms a private practice of claiming Hawaiian identity for the purposes of symbolically and publicly establishing Hawaiian sovereignty—for example, as foreign pressure increased up to 1893, when Queen Lili'uokalani's monarchical rule was illegally overthrown, Hawaiian language newspapers published genealogies so as to proclaim their title to the Kingdom and seek out new leadership—into a structurally appropriated means of racially containing Hawaiians.[41]

This appropriation pressures Hawaiians into partaking in what I call "structured genealogies" or "performances of proving." In the spirit of naming these processes, a spirit inspired by such critical works as Marie Annette Jaimes's critique of federal identification policies of blood quantum for Native American Indians and David Theo Goldberg's tracing of a principal racializing technology, the U.S. census, I expose population counts, census records, and the politics surrounding identity certification and documentation (the performativity of it all) of 50 percent Hawaiian blood quantum as politically imposed practices.[42] These are practices originating from federal and state authority and cloaked by "procedure," that stand as a built-in safeguard while claiming to proffer fairness and equality.

Genealogical practices and their cultural political force throughout Hawaiian history have been reduced to a unidimensional, state-surveilled requirement for the completion of an already predetermined legislative identity. Recently, this illustration of power reappeared in the OHA, a state agency created in 1978 to aid in the betterment of Native Hawaiians. It designed a program entitled "Operation Ohana Registry" or the agency's enrollment program, through which Hawaiians share their genealogical information and records into a larger database resource that can be used for the DHHL application process. The state thus emerges yet again as the centralized unit for publicly gathering, holding, and surveilling private family memories and histories. This rupture of Hawaiian genealogies is, among other aspects, a devastating consequence of the state appropriation of all things Hawaiian, most especially our histories and names.

Yet, according to Omi and Winant, the state cannot completely seal its ideological practices:

> The racial order is equilibrated by the state-encoded in law, organized through policy-making, and enforced by a repressive apparatus. But the equilibrium thus achieved is unstable, for the great variety of conflicting interests encapsulated in racial meanings and identities can be no more than pacified—at best—by the state.[43]

The force surrounding the state becomes destabilized and dismantled partly through the performativity of state limits—through traversing as far as one can go through designated procedures of identification policy, which will unveil the truncated paths, the closed doors, the dusty corner-options that offer possibility.[44] This is precisely my performative purpose. The representation of my Hawaiian interviewees' private performances bring into focus the constraints of governmental raciality and its limits and how its certifiable forms conceal excesses of activity, interpretation, and political interest. Performing the inadequacy and overwritings of state definitions of Hawaiianness allow us to name and expose an inequitable procedure encoded in state policy and law as itself incomplete and indeterminable. Our performances of proving ironically become the necessary means for critiquing the State of Hawaii.

Over time, as the state forms wilt, the typeset names fade, and the files crinkle, the private memories and narratives of Hawaiians will outlive the racial state and its processes. Hawaiian memory will include not only our great *akua* but also our narrative proof of being Hawaiian in the face of blood quantum technology. The racializing governmentality of the HHCA, discussed in chapter 2, is performatively challenged by everyday Hawaiians who, without legal resources and official records for support, reuse and rearticulate state constructions of identity, thereby taking them to their most illogical conclusion and locating the invisible conditions of their operation. Agency, then, for racialized groups in repressive conditions like the Hawaiians can be reinvented into a powerful force through private memories and personal narratives about the state (or using the state against itself).[45]

My family members and other Hawaiians in the DHHL process amaze me. Even though our identities are nonexistent in the documents, our blood quantum at zero for lack of certification, a homestead out of our reach, and state recognition as Hawaiians completely denied, we critically voice who we are in our narrative performances and everyday lives.

From the legal and private context to a commercially public one, "Hawaiians" would in one sense continue to be identified as primordial, "before-time" remnants of the past, but through different practices and with varied effects in the contemporary tourist popular. Tourism, a sphere combining the best of cultural and material capital, historical fantasies, popular fetishes, and performative reenactment, enters the historical imagination. These two spaces are indeed allied and conjoined, moving one into the other, with postmodern tourism infusing performative life or rather death into nativism, historical nostalgia, and the privilege of movement through Hawaiianness. Tourist structures and sites would relive the death of nativism or resurrect it, while Hawaiians would politically enliven the deathly Hawaiian spectral in such spaces. Tourism would reunite us with historical significations of Hawaiianness from the historical imagination at the same time it stretched, destabilized, fortified, and renewed forms of nativism and historical nostalgia.

4

From Queens to Calabashes:
Touring the Native

Belt fastened, hands clenched around the armrests, we were almost there. For me, it was a conflicting moment of pure ethnographic excitement and dread, the only points of focus being the steady *swoosh* of midair descent and the crazed scurry of attendants collecting cups while tossing complimentary maps to overanxious travelers. Somewhere in between the steadiness of our flight and the mayhem of arrival lived the paradoxical axes of touring native terrain. We didn't have to be on the ground to begin our travel. Travel was already moving us at home and in flight.

This movement, or the push toward understanding and traveling upon native cultural lands has compelled many: the first known explorers, missionaries, trade merchants, anthropologists and researchers, and annual vacationers. The idea is that through travel, we can explore cultural systems and different ways of relating to the social world while also managing different intercultural encounters à la temporary visitations somewhere else. At the same time, it is partly through travel and the practices of tourism that cultural systems and groups have been imagined, identified, reinvented and re-created, and reproduced over time through a set of representational and discursive practices.[1] In his riveting ethnographic analysis of the Maya culture at Chichén Itzá, for example, Quetzil E. Castañeda argues that several sociocultural entities—tourism, anthropology, Maya culture, national and business interests—negotiate how Maya culture is articulated and known.[2] Historical narratives and museum exhibits selectively incorporate particular cultural symbols and historical periods into a larger body of knowledge about a group. Maps, distributed by national structures and tourist enterprise, not only scientize the boundaries of a cultural land, but also naturalize a mode of gazing on a culture as an object of study, or a destination, and invoke elements of historical tropes and narratives about cultural groups. Tourist sites also frame social experiences and activities around a culture but through the promise of a localized, internal view, just as anthropological notes often reproduce and normalize cultural values and subjectivities already distorted and reorganized by national politics and business and commerce. Ultimately, what is produced again and again is a popular museum of culture.

In this chapter, I analyze the reinvention of Hawaiian identity through tourist practices and structures. Tourism, both as structure and site, reconfigures the range of meanings for Hawaiianness. It stands as an arena where social actors come with specific imaginary-encoded visions of cultural identities, where social interaction has previously—at home—been framed, and where interaction between the state, tourists, and Hawaiian subjects are reformed and reproduced. Tourism itself continually reshapes communication practices in the sense of how we identify Hawaiians in relation to ourselves, complicated by jolting flashes from a Hawaiian collective memory that reissues "who they are and want to be."[3]

Here, in the tourist sphere, cultural parks like Waimea Falls Park inscribe a subject position that reenacts the death of nativism while historical sites such as the Iolani Palace discursively excise nativism from modernity. Together, in cooperation and coarticulation, as you move from the Waimea Falls Park to Iolani Palace, Hawaiian nativism is signified as "this once was" to "this would never be." Practicing the demise of nativism and its incompatibility with modern time and space redeploys the before-Cook prehumanity articulation of Hawaiian identity from the sphere of historical memory. This articulation used within a global capitalist tourist context further displaces Hawaiian identity and sovereignty through the ritualized and popularized practice of the death of nativism as encouraged by tourist commerce. Different from the historical discourses I analyzed in chapter 1, these sites compel visitors to peer into and experience native life from supposedly a native Hawaiian perspective. Such a promise serves to authenticate and differentiate tourist spaces from the excessively artificial and touristy feel of other sites (e.g., the now-defunct Kodak Hula Show, Waikiki dance revues, and portable *lūʻaus*). The appeal, then, lies in the bold suggestion that modern tourism can enter and traverse an indigenous perspective, which makes the narratives circulating at Waimea Falls Park (the now gone native life) and Iolani Palace (the native monarchy that was never meant to exist) much more naturalized and disarming.

With the alliance between dominant-vested historical memory and the tourist fantasy of getting close to and yet maintaining one's safe distance from nativism, the era of tourism has dramatically changed into that of a postmodern throwback to the golden age of travel. There are historical tours of the first hotels built in Waikiki in the heyday of the 1920s and 1930s; postcards, luggage tags, advertisements, and Aloha shirts from the 1930s through the 1950s are emblazoned across tourist T-shirts and hotel displays as these become popular nostalgia kitsch and rare Hawaiiana collectibles. Thus, a new form of tourism is revealed, one that ironically relies on historical nostalgia for class-specific travel and popular consumption as a way to experience the golden and class-privileged past. Interestingly enough, in this age of tourism, the images or faces of natives are not incorporated but are articulated through other, silent signifiers: "Hawaiiana" travel kitsch and collectibles, tours of the history of tourism, and the white hula girl. The new and yet the old, postmodern discourses of travel reflect the economic subjugation of the racialized groups in Hawaiʻi, namely the Hawaiians, and highlight the necessity of native travel lands for the articulation of a white elite class.

This chapter presents my ethnographic traveling through a Hawaiian identity, one always open to others' traveling routes. I tour you, the reader, through traveling moments of my ethnographic fieldwork over the last five years in different parts of Hawaiʻi (specifically Oahu and Hawaiʻi). After much struggle then and still now, I decided to engage the structures, experiences, and consumer moments of travel through widely touted vacation packages to Hawaiʻi, for it is through the popular that representational knowledges about cultural groups and their identifications have been naturalized and immediately called forth. I take you touring through two very different and interspersed voices/ forms: an "in the moment" monograph that highlights and formatively shapes key points of analysis during the experience of touring, and a broader discussion of theoretical abstraction or the theorizing that takes place within momentary experience. I have provided a way to travel through the interplay of different levels of concrete fieldwork and theoretical abstraction, to tour through the intimate fusion of the fantastical tourist experience (to absorb the meaningful moments of travel in my monograph) and its cultural/political/economic production (the theoretical points of discussion brought to the surface) in relation to the identity construction of Hawaiianness.

I feature my travels through an "itinerary" or, as James Clifford reminds us, a concrete way of thinking about travel as an unbounded yet organized series of encounters and translations constituting different identities, power interests, cultural relations, and communicative practices.[4] Travel has always moved and reshaped itself in relation to social contextual forces and subject positions. Before, travel was the unmarked terrain of the European male elite; the boundary holders were the racialized subjects and objects of travel (the locals, natives, and immigrant labor incorporated as servants). Female travelers moved by way of their husbands' status, their names, their lineage, but always in the shadow of patriarchal movement. Today, U.S. mainlanders, foreign visitors from Japan, Korea, and Great Britain, and even diasporic Hawaiians traverse an inscribed Hawaiian identity by way of cultural museums, parks, historical sites, Polynesian revues, and tours of the first established hotels in Hawai'i. It becomes important, then, to analyze how preferred subject positions for identifying Hawaiianness are inscribed into tourist sites and practices and how these are mediated by various lived positionalities such as citizens from different nation-states and Hawaiians who were born and raised away from and yet in memory of Hawai'i.

Let me make it clear: as Dean MacCannell emphasizes, I, too, confirm that there can be no touring (with both financial and cultural economies at work) without the exploitation of indigenous peoples.[5] To argue otherwise would be to venture into the romanticized fantasy that propagates tourism—the notion that tourist experiences positively contribute to a native societies' natural character (for they can act as they truly are) and economic well-being (we pay them for what they already do). This is a historically secure relationship that visitors, ethnographers like myself, and industry workers must confront responsibly and possibly rework to a point of implosion. It is a social dilemma that, according to John and Jean Comaroff, should be used against itself via ethnography or by deploying the found paradoxes and weaknesses (and those implicit in the nature of ethnography itself—"participant observation," a splitting of objective distance and omniscient subjectivity and yet an intimacy between the knower, known, and knowledge) as productive tensions.[6]

I take up such a challenge with a heavy heart. I, in a sense, comply with the neocolonialist structures of tourism by my mere participation in the exchange of financial and cultural capital. However, it is also through an interrogation of the global popular representation of us that we can kink out and extinguish lingering colonialist forms, destroying the tracing fantasies with the pen. We can also shed light on the social practices and mighty spirit of Hawaiians in the face of entrenched global capitalism. I dare not romanticize tourism. In fact, like anthropologist Michael Taussig, I find many disturbing aspects but in the least obvious places, and more potential in the most unlikely spaces. I search for a re-signifying cultural-political Hawaiian spirit through lived practices and dialogic representations in a dangerous, neomodern context.

A METHOD FOR TOURING

An ethnographic monograph ought to structurally sign you in the thick of making you feel the momentary local experience of it all.[7] The hair-splitting relationship between empirical work and theoretical junctures in ethnography has much more to tell us about how ethnographic projects are *already* theoretically embedded.[8] Experience is therefore not inherently explanatory. Like a tourist site influx, it must be revisited time after time, at a variety of levels. This is exactly my task—to bring out more directly the theoretical connections of a traveled-upon Hawaiian identity, all the while analyzing the homogeneities, conflicts, paradoxes, and useful ruptures of these experiences. Or, in the spirit of anthropologists Jean and John Comaroff, I am compelled by "how such experiences are socially, culturally, and historically grounded" and complex in character, "with the aim of fructifying our own ways of seeing and being, of subverting our own sureties."[9]

I embrace James Clifford's theoretical and metaphorical "itinerary" device to symbolize my theoretical/methodological framework. Itineraries name, list, and organize traveling experiences.[10] Analyzing the structural and cultural production of experience through the dynamics and dialogics of ethnographic touring ultimately unbounds the itinerary as an (organized) influx process, one constituted by theoretical points that also travel and move in historically contingent ways. Together, cultural studies ethnography and articulation take me on the best kind of ride: the pursuit of a specific focus (the construction of Hawaiianness) and the unexpected thrill of not knowing what I might traverse (the representations of cultural material, the pieces of cultural memory, and the pleasure of travel itself).

An itinerary would serve me well. It would direct me into the concrete organization of identifying practices of Hawaiianness and the tourist production of specific experiences and ethnicities. At the same time, it would signal the working form of comparative knowledge embedded in my fieldwork and the "partial and composite traveling theories" around the subject positions created in the name of Hawaiians that I confront throughout my touring.[11] In Oahu and Hawai'i, through ethnography and articulation, I would tour along as a tourist, bringing along my readers and my private memories. I wouldn't explore just travel; I would also interrogate the traveling of a Hawaiian identity position itself based on the premise of traveling. For to traverse Hawai'i—its unbounded, virgin, and exotic geography—is to traverse the Hawaiian body politic, their supposed openness, generosity, and normative benevolence as a people. I would engage the much traveled "Hawaiianness at heart"–tourist subject position that could freely, repeatedly, and intensely experience the privilege of a distanced nativism and one that could flaunt the buying of location, of being Hawaiian for a stay of time and then enjoy the privileged freedom to dislocate.

The much-touted *Aloha* spirit, a tourist market ideal, echoed the explorer Cook's descriptions of the naturally "benevolent" Hawaiian people. Like the land, they were, in all senses of the word, open, free, uncontained, and new. What, then, are the significations constituting the tourist stance of "Hawaiianness at heart"? What fantasies are afforded? What of the visuality, the feelings conjured? At what price? And what identity interests of Hawaiians and tourists and their remakings are threaded through the tourist experience? What was the relationship between traveling memories and a Hawaiian collective memory that for decades had been traveled? Clifford raises these questions in the rethinking of culture as "sites of dwelling and travel"—of identity dwelling and traveling, of, specifically, a Hawaiian identity slotted for temporary, open-dwelling by tourists and travelers.[12]

Yet this space between a dwelling and travel is not so certain. You cannot exactly finger the distinction between each. In my own ethnographic work, these would shift. Between the Hawaii as the tourist field and Hawai'i as my distant home through collective memory and the identifying images of the historical imagination: field and home, one against and through the other. Like those around me, I wasn't just a "tourist" here; every ethnographer brings to bear her or his identity baggage, politicized identity positions, racialized identifications by others, and commitments to certain values and communities and the raced/classed elitism of the academy-home.[13] In terms of the "I," framing the ethnographer as a social-historical subject whose reading interrelates with that of the situated context, community, and identity is an important epistemological component of sociocritical forms of ethnography.[14] As such, I felt compelled to interrogate my positionality as a mainlander Hawaiian brought up in suburban California in relation to a Hawaiian collective memory that revolves around the struggle for self-determination and sovereignty against the historical imagining of the Hawaiian as a "savage native," and against the forced dispossession of *'āina* (land) and the blooded recognition of who we are or who we fail to be, as in the record archives. My identity position is tense at best, with pangs of guilt for not living on the homesteads or growing up on *'āina* and yet still feeling vested in the museum representations of Hawaiians and the incessant comments, presumably innocent, but deeply reflective of a naturalized racism: "Oh, you look Hawaiian," or "You must know hula," or "You're Hawaiian? I've been to Hawai'i many times." I was a painful reminder to Hawaiians of the consequences of our colonialist dispossession: the forced migration and dispersal of Hawaiians across the continent, of Hawaiian men and women who had to leave. Cutting deep, I reminded them of our forced travel from *'āina*.

Ethnographically throughout my life, I have worked hard to be "Hawaiian," going to Kamehameha exploration camps, participating in mainland Hawaiian communities, visiting Hawai'i to see family, and pursuing the academic study of Hawaiian identity. I started this project with the idea of maximizing the blurring of my identities (using the paradox of identity as an implosive force) and using my away-from-Hawai'i position to my ethnographic advantage by not taking for granted the everydayness of tourist experiences, commodities, and spectacles and even possibly identifying with a tourist position.[15] But, because the

[handwritten margin note: grappling with own identity while being a traveller]

culture being visited is my own, with my face, the surety of tourist fantasies and historical nostalgia could be more powerfully disrupted by flashes of stored collective memory and my own politicized Hawaiian identity. Working through one's complex of positionalities calls for a uniquely rich writing format for my ethnographic monograph. Dorinne Kondo explains that "such movements within and between various positionalities call for dismantling the method of detached narration through naturalized observation. Capturing the fragmented, rapidly shifting registers and modalities of the forces that shape everyday life in third time-spaces requires writing that mixes and juxtaposes genres."[16] It is through fieldwork then that I can explore my different identities and identifications as Hawaiian.

Specifically in terms of my research/method itinerary, over a period of five years (and 700 hours of fieldwork), I ethnographically toured around Oahu and Kona, Hawai'i: the airports, shops, restaurants, the top Polynesian revues, and well-attended tourist attraction sites all over the islands. Originally trained in the interpretivist/semifunctional traditions of ethnography originated by James Spradley and Dell Hymes, I grounded my work with a cultural studies emphasis on identity, power, and communicative practice.[17] Within this framework, I created my own methodological path: multiple observations at each site; several (twelve to fifteen) onsite interviews with tourists and tour guides at each place; written fieldnotes, audiotape recordings, and photographic records of each site/interview and a context-specific coding system of identity articulations based on striking themes, discursive encodings, and signification processes (signifier, signified, signified relations over time).

I set out to interrogate the following research questions: How does the tourist industry construct subject positions in the name of Hawaiians? What constitutes the production of tourist experiences and Hawaiian subjectivities? I address these questions by taking the local tours, interviewing tourists and Local and Hawaiian tour-guide workers, and absorbing the "magic of tourism."[18] Different from my past ethnographic work, I set out to absorb the in-the-moment tourist experience (to go where the momentary feel and fantastical took me) while calling attention to its structural feel. I worked hard to understand the cultural, political, and structural production of tourist experiences and commodities, tracking down the nature of Hawai'i's economy, its local division of labor and dependence on the visitor industry, and the flow of capital in, through, and out of Hawai'i to the mainland and other nations. From interviews with state officials and researchers at the Department of Business, Economic Development and Tourism (DBEDT), and local shop and restaurant merchants, from economic data sheets to annual statistical tabulations, I had to train my mind in the different terms of tourist economics, policy, and practice in order to better understand the global capitalist production of Hawaiian identities.

The structural, for me, became much more than the determined economic input/output of sites. It involved the driving incentives of a tourist industry and the practices of commodification of everything Hawaiian: from tally counts, attendance numbers, to tourist promotion discourses, state budget allocations for tourism and its operating costs, the physical setup of attractions, the encodings of Hawaiianness within sites and their narratives (which, while they are not necessarily invoked by every tourist, are structurally inscribed as dominant meanings), and the expenses incurred by differently situated tourists against the payout/income differential to Hawaiian tourist industry workers. I chose several tourist sites based on their recorded visitor attendance numbers, which were all available in my daily research at the DBEDT. I also selected sites based on the designations of the many tourists I encountered. A courtesy offered between tourists is the exchange of the "best spots to go to around the island." Together, the list of sites included the Iolani Palace, Waimea Falls Park, Polynesian Cultural Center, Aloha Tower, the untabulated Kodak Hula Show, and historical hotel tours. I also ventured into Waikiki through hotel lobbies, staged *lū'aus,* tourist-directed shops and malls (where clothing, souvenir goods, and "Hawaiiana" or Hawaiian kitsch were heavily consumed), and duty-free outlets for multinational visitors.

In touring the native, it is important to consider the larger unseen production context constituting tourism, a context embedded with theoretical issues about the flow of capital in and through Hawai'i, Hawaiian subjects, and tourist consumers. Throughout my fieldwork, it became necessary to connect the popularized fantasies and articulations of Hawaiianness with the macroproduction concerns of a tourist market and its organizing of tourists as economic units. Only in the research moment was I able to unpack how as a tourist, I was a part of a larger production cycle that always moved and operated behind the discourses, texts, significations, and visualities: from reservation to vacation package to cultural attraction participation and the consumption and collection of Hawaiian souvenirs and icons. In addition to being moving travelers, we were also resignified as a basic economic unit—the tourist, a visitor who temporarily stays at least twenty-four hours in the place visited, for a variety of purposes (leisure, business, family), and who returns the market capital through hotel stay, transportation and attraction fees, food consumption, and souvenir and clothing purchases.[19] We are reminded by John and Jean Comaroff and Michael Taussig to ethnographically read identities in context through a broad spectrum: the localized moments, the specific displays identifying and reshaping new ethnicities, the positioning of tourist spectators and the "natives/primitives" who perform themselves, and the capital flows from the mainland, into the islands, out to other nations.[20] That one slice of experience—the split second of time in a tourist space—is produced along multiple tiers: its personal, unconscious and spiritual pull of emotion and disidentification, its attractive invitation into historical nostalgia, the cultural work constituting its romanticized and pleasurable commodification, and its eliding of the cultural prostitution (the writing over of sacred indigenous rituals, icons, and subjectivities) and labor required for its reproduction.

Driven by the flexible nature of global capitalism and capital needs in excess of its own local sources at home, traveling in Hawai'i has relied on investment and tourist demand from outside nations: Japan, Hong Kong, mainland U.S., Canada, Great Britain, and Australia.[21] In fact, the majority of the guests I encountered seemed to be tourists from East Asia: Japanese and Korean visitors. The influx of different national residents to the shores of Hawai'i is demonstrative of the structured widespread fetishized appeal of a native culture and the local, oversensitive tourist economy and its concerted efforts to expand its customer base to both U.S. mainlanders and Asian travelers.

It is through the long cast of global capitalism that multinational investment and tourism have become material realities in Hawai'i.[22] After the late 1950s, as Hawai'i's visitor industry boomed, the economy could no longer rely on local sources for its capital needs. As a result, Hawai'i tourist outlets aggressively approached business interests on the U.S. mainland and other nations for investment capital; they secured funding from Canada, Britain, Australia, Hong Kong, and Japan. The structural figures are striking. As of 1994, 61 percent of the foreign-owned hotels (which is 65 percent of the total number of hotels in Hawai'i) were Japanese (national) owned, leaving the other 4.7 percent to mostly Australia and Hong Kong. Total foreign investment into Hawai'i from 1960 to 1994 was $16 billion. Of this, Japanese foreign investment is reflected as a significant influence here ($14,062,915), with Australia and Hong Kong following.[23] Japanese investment peaked in the period 1986–1991. The investment incentive was to cash in on a then-booming industry and make it easier for their business members and resident-subjects to travel and provide returns on their vested ventures (e.g., hotels, restaurants, tour groups, revues, vacation packages). The flow of capital into Hawai'i's tourist industry back out to a mainland is an ongoing, tense cycle, dependent on the changing value of money and the shifting market of capital and labor. For example, currently, because of hard economic times (the yen has depreciated), Japanese investors have been selling their interests to other national subsidiaries, and it is more difficult to assess the nature of driving capital in tourism in Hawai'i. One firm conclusion is that Hawai'i's economy has become increasingly dependent on multinational capital and visitor demand (as Japanese visitors outnumber U.S. mainland travelers three to one).

Japanese tourists have been targeted as one of tourism's main clientele. Historically, the Japanese have traveled to Hawai'i in larger numbers than U.S. mainlanders, primarily due to several factors: improvements in and expansion of Asia-Pacific air travel (and new Japan Airlines flight service from Tokyo to Kona); an established history of Japanese investment in Hawai'i's travel industry (Japanese-geared hotels, shopping outlets, transportation, group packages and tours, Polynesian revues), making Japanese travel familiar and comfortable; and the sometimes cycle of an appreciating yen (meaning, Japanese citizens could get more goods for their money). But the depreciation of the yen in the late-twentieth century has rendered Hawai'i less attractive for these tourists. Many Japanese visitors who graciously agreed to be interviewed explained how they had saved years for a vacation, but with the strengthening of the U.S. dollar against the yen, they were more likely to travel to closer locales in Asia. In their annual project plans, the state and the Hawai'i Visitors and Convention Bureau have established initiatives to more aggressively attract East Asian travelers through marketing promotions, upscale hotels and resorts, loosening airline restrictions, and instituting a visa waiver program.[24]

Japanese tourists

Hawai'i also represents a higher-classed industry that is simultaneously a raced, low-income service economy (low-paying jobs as dishwashers, chambermaids, waitstaff, bellhops, laundry workers, and retail clerk positions, justified as such for its "low-skill" tasks). As millions of dollars are allocated to tourist promotions and hotel renovations and as national residents and mainlanders come and go, Locals and Hawaiians are fixed to daily tourism jobs that provide on average less than $15,000 a year (while the average state income is $20,000), the income pattern for Hawaiians from 1989 to 1999. Most Hawaiian workers I encountered told me they worked two to three jobs to make ends meet; they claimed it was "tiring" but a "reality." Working-class Locals and immigrant Filipinas can also be located within this same material economy, often confined to poor benefits and wage output situations as the state and tourism "take them for cheap." It matters also that while Hawaiians work every day in travelers' rooms, buses, eating places, and on their tours, their historical faces as "savages" and *ali'i* are actively engaged and fetishized. Hawaiians therefore constitute the front and back of travel.[25] "In 1990, over 12 percent of Native Hawaiians lived in households with incomes less than $15,000. This group of Native Hawaiians comprised over 22 percent of all the individuals in households for the state with incomes under $15,000."[26] Hawaiians thus, are traveled and yet fail to traverse a wider variety of income levels. Most Hawaiians, roughly 60 percent, hold tourist sector–related jobs (hotel, service, restaurant, transportation), jobs that account for 25 percent of the workforce in Hawai'i and still pay less than the state average ($20,000), causing most Hawaiian tourist employees to work at least two or more jobs a little above minimum wage. As money seems to pour out of and into Hawai'i, local Hawaiians materially struggle in an industry marketed on their history, their images, and their colonialist dispossession. And yet through these real pressures, Hawaiians creatively reimagine and repractice their travel work spaces according to their lived conditions.

TOURING THE NATIVE

As the overhead fasten-your-seat-belt light flickering waned, the rows quickly dissolved single-file into the gate entryway; most of us adorned in brightly colored *Aloha* shirts (with distinct images of *'ukulele,* hula girls, and ships) and flowered hibiscus and orchid sarongs, there was no confusion or bewilderment. As tourists, we were prepared and mindful, even demanding, of what was to come. James Clifford names this preparedness a naturalized tradition, our unspoken inheritance of a colonial authority to travel other cultures with relative ease.[27] Together, we as passengers had already embarked on our journey of the native through popular fantasies of self and other (the exotic, strangely primitive cultural mass). Our ways of gazing at what stood before us, a topos about Hawai'i and Hawaiians, had already been framed in our daily lives; a localization embedded through the enticement of travel brochures, guided cues of maps, the familiar-looking airplane porthole views (akin to TV and computer screens, and other domestic products) looking down and over. It was a type of gaze that bordered on pleasurable voyeurism, panoptic knowledge, and controlling surveillance, mediated all the while by my research stares at our every move.

In line with the increasing localization of travel, tourism and its gazes are embedded in the everyday. For instance, the glance over a Hawai'i paradise is embedded in national maps, picture-framed advertisements and travel posters, television commercials (C & H Sugar, Honda) and series reruns *(Hawaii Five-0, Magnum P.I., One West Waikiki)*, and the more compact television-like views of airplane windows (akin to little windows featured on domestic appliances such as toaster ovens and microwaves). One cannot deny the constant onslaught of a traveler/gazer stance in our daily routines. Strangely and unconsciously, we are encouraged to travel imaginatively to exotic places envisioned as Hawaii and voyeuristically ogle away (a striking parallel to ethnography as well—to go elsewhere, to surveil those around you and their practices, to watch them watch you). The pleasure in this localized gaze lies in the culmination of watching at a distance, being close and yet disembedded from what is seen, and having the sense that such a look controls everyone and -thing in its frame. In this context, the illicitness of looking is absent. It seems inevitable, in fact impossible and unnatural, *not* to look at Hawai'i and its people. Thus, unseen in the displayed itinerary is the surprising localization of travel and touring in our everyday lives, in our social practices where the global production of traveling experiences is hidden from view and yet locally tangible.

The air was thick, wet, and tight. My breath clipped, I made my way to the nearest opening. I couldn't recognize anyone. All the faces looked beyond me, with leis in hand. Local family members on their lunch breaks standing behind the ropes, dressed in the typical work attire, *Aloha* shirts with slacks or *mu'umu'u* (printed cloth dresses). The rest were uniformed—Hawaiian Tours, Holiday Vacations, Aloha Travel—a scourge of wildly bright pastels tackily matched from visor to shirt to pants to name tag. Signs held up, the guides couldn't immediately identify who we were, but we knew them. We found ourselves drawn toward them.

A jarring vision—HALUALANI—on a large strip of cardboard. I rushed over in a quiet panic, hoping I could retrieve that mark of betrayal. "Halualani," asks a young dark-skinned male with glasses, walking toward me.

I smiled, "Yep." He seemed new to the job. Stacks of paper fell over my feet; he couldn't locate my travel reservations. Suddenly, his arms flew up. He only now remembered the obligatory welcome. Taking a lei from around his neck, in one fell swoop he hurled it off, firmly pressed it onto my head, and pushed me closer to him, fingertips pinching into my back, as a hesitant, upturned "Aloha" brushed across my ear. And just as I repositioned the sweet smelling lei to drape my neck, I could only see the back of him approaching the next client.

In this initial, disastrous experience of *Aloha,* I was satisfied. For the uncertainty of its telling echoed the state structurally and politically of Hawaiians in a fledgling tourist context. The colonial and commercial stretchmarks of a cultural value—"Hawaiianness at heart"—reinscribed onto Hawaiians through historical, geographic, and visual representations, reproduced, repackaged, remanufactured, and shelved again and again, were beautifully exposed. The discomfort of it all, its contrived sincerity, the awkward positioning of local tourist-industry workers, the guilt felt by the tourists in expecting greetings deemed natural to the place and people of Hawai'i and feeling disappointed when confronted with its artificial, forced nature. We silently demanded a natural *Aloha.* Above me, somewhere, the place where those before us have gone, I knew *Kanaka Maoli* were smirking.

Tourism in Hawai'i is driven by a market philosophy of *Aloha,* the seemingly internal cultural value of Hawaiians themselves as naturally benevolent, inclusive, and generous with what they have and who they are. Reproduced in popular discourse and travel promotions, the *Aloha* of Hawai'i is staged as both consumer guarantee and vacation norm. On its face, "Hawaiianness at heart," or the *Aloha* spirit would always appear to be the natural cultural character of indigenous Hawaiians while its historical-political formation and continual distortion is hidden from view.

Upon my arrival, as I feel and recognize our demand for *Aloha* and come face-to-face with its packaging, it strikes me that the manufacturing of a continually commodified *Aloha* might just bring about its own un-doing. The performed falsity of *Aloha* could eventually interrupt its glue as an aspect as natural to Hawai'i as the characteristic trade winds, wetness, and sweet smells. As discussed by Judith Butler and Dorinne Kondo, the performativity of discourse and social practices constitutes, reconstitutes, and unmasks itself at particular pressure points, as the "his-torical" and "political" changes over time.[28] So, too, as *Aloha* echoes still throughout Hawai'i, the obviousness of tourism and its plasticity, its in-flated expense, and the increasing visibility of a tourist-irreconcilable Hawaiian sovereignty (and the protests at ancient cultural sites, highway constructions, and airports) just might enclose the tourist in a face-to-face with tourism itself.

How can Hawaiians reclaim Aloha?

IOLANI PALACE AND WAIMEA FALLS PARK

On the bus, I grabbed a travel guide about Hawai'i I had purchased be-fore the trip. I had plenty of time to read about today's destination, Iolani Palace. Travel guides commodify and authorize touristic and trav-el experience, concealing their historical and social production. Nestled among a description of Cook and displays of map after map, here it was: Iolani Palace.

> Iolani Palace is the only royal palace in the USA. It was the official resi-dence of King Kalakaua and Queen Kapiolani from 1882 to 1891 and of Queen Lili'uokalani, Kalakaua's sister and successor, for two years after that. Following the overthrow of the Hawaiian kingdom in 1893, the palace became the capitol—first for the republic, then for the territory and later for the state of Hawaii.[29]

The only royal palace in the USA? In Hawai'i? A palace featuring Hawai-ian or native sovereigns? Could it possibly be? I already knew of Iolani Palace—my parents brought my brothers and I here when we were younger—but never as the only realm of royalty in the U.S. nation. Some-how it suddenly seemed different, stranger in its now-obvious regality.

This striking characteristic surely attracted loads of travelers every year; around 74,000, for instance, in 1994.[30] The man who sat next to me on the airplane told me, "I didn't know they had rulers and thrones." For most, it was a surprising combination of Hawaiian natives and European-associated royalty structures, an initial surprise that paradoxi-cally fused the age-old opposition between obscured native primi-tivism (the mysterious past) and European modernism (the stabilized, mundane present).[31] Native monarchs. Dark, sovereign rulers. Civilized natives.

A man next to me on the bus told me he had seen the palace last year when he came out with his family. "It was so beautiful. The furniture pieces were so rare. I had seen nothing like it. You could tell there was a lot of history in those halls. And the tragic ending to it all. A definite must-see," he urged. Throughout my childhood, I had fantasized about being the descendant of a famous ruler like Queen Lili'uokalani. We call this *pi'ikoi* (to claim to be of higher status and name than one is). How could you not be intrigued seeing Hawaiians as aristocratic, independent rulers, as modern-day leaders in the late 1800s? Yearning to see the royal Hawaiian way of life, many of us were fascinated. That much we had to admit. But the fascination comes from a localized place. I sought some explanation in the historical display and tour narratives, or some reconciliation of a former sovereign kingdom with the still-felt pangs of neocolonialism today—nationhood, the power of the State of Hawaii. Best of all, I wanted to see where the queen, our beloved Lili'uokalani, lived and ruled and was eventually overthrown by U.S. interests in 1893. For other visitors, it might be the same: visiting and touring in relation to a historically situated need and experience. One man I met—he was from England—reminded me of this. He explained that he toured the historic sites specifically to see the British presence in the islands. Cook he recalled as being a nationally deified symbol, but one for many British citizens who represented the failings of an empire and arrogantly proclaimed a power "over a people who were not entirely free." This is an interesting perspective that disrupts and yet does not erase a historical voyeur position. His notion of a "people" could be in reference to his particular home community, to Hawaiians as British subjects, and to the world. These localized interruptions unduly move within tourism and travel while also being pressured by a historical and capitalist legacy of travel and sold movement at the expense of Hawaiians. Travel thus represents a struggle of identifications and preferred reading positions. I pay attention to these as naturalized sets of meaning over time and outlining markers for significant identity challenges on the part of Hawaiians.

Descriptions aside, the site itself had a magnificence that one could only witness in the moment. A large gray palace structure, architecturally grand, etched with a series of large windows with wooden shutters,

tall white pillars, and the look of Hawaiian *koa* wood around the doorways. It was in a word, stunning. Gates, lush lawns, and banyan trees, pa-
vilions, and pointed arrow signs (see Figure 20). In the distance, you
could see the ongoing city life in the downtown streets.

Locals were going to work; older locals were congregating at park
benches talking story to pass the time. I was touring.

Slowly making my way through the gate, I realized I was approach-
ing its backside, and all arrows visually redirected me to an unseen front.
This was clearly not to be; a walking out of order at a historical site.
Those who passed me on the sidewalk shot me disapproving glances.
You were to begin at the front gates, enter the doors, and walk onto the
State Capitol. Or this is what seemed to be the routine touring practice,
as I studied the consistent movements of three groups of visitors moving
in this exact progression, guided by security guards and palace hosts
dressed in bright *mu'umu'u*. I decided to do the same, already feeling
anxious that I had made my first wrong turn.

"Your ticket," asked an older man in a light-blue security guard uniform. "Do you have a ticket?"

Handing it over I just then noticed its historical semblance to an
1800s dance card for one of King Kalakaua's Royal Balls, filled with the

Figure 20. Iolani Palace, Oahu, 1997. Photograph by author.

ornate magenta traces of the Kalakaua royal crown, exuding a sense of the glamorous splendor of yesterday's Hawaiian monarchs. It was as if you were entering that historical time, a narrative outcome tour guides worked hard to achieve. A fantastical outcome I enjoyed.

Adorned in a gorgeous beige Victorian hat, our guide, Miss Olea, ushered our group into the grand hallway of the palace through a narrating style of a static ethnographic present. Spread out over the porch-to-hallway space, my tour colleagues consisted of two families. The first family included one mother with her sons and their grandfather. "Oklahoma seems like another world than this," the grandfather explained. They had waited with me before the tour began. This was their first trip to Hawai'i or as he put it, "our first step to anywhere off the main continent." The distinction between a modern mainland and an isolated island was a widespread mythic invocation conducive to tourism. It made the tour sites excitingly different and strange.[32] You could suspend your thoughts into the remoteness of Hawai'i's location and, thus, its placement outside of present historical and social time.[33]

Hawai'i, always deemed as a paradise, is narratively constructed through and outside of history. Here "ancient native life" is performatively and consciously enacted for tourist exchanges, or what Dean MacCannell insightfully frames as the ritual reenacting of the death of "native primitivism."[34] To see a life since passed, pass again before your eyes. For a split second, I couldn't imagine what everyday living was like here. A tourist positionality moving from site to site, the gazed-at performative nativism *was* the imagined everyday and a natural occurrence. Here, in other words, were Hawaiians just being themselves. The grandfather, Tom, became my touring partner, asking me questions about my furious note-taking and talking with me along the way.

The second family consisted of a Korean man and woman with their daughter, who looked to be in her late twenties. Earlier, when the security guard asked for their tickets, she turned to her parents translating every word addressed to them. This would continue throughout the trip. A translation of a translation of a translation, trace after trace, resignification after resignification. At each tourist site, the translation of language, meaning, and experience poses different intercultural relations between multinational travelers and local Hawaiian tour guides such as Miss Olea at Iolani Palace. Many tourists who speak languages not addressed at tourist sites either listen to audiotape tours in their native language or rely on another person (a family member or friend who has escorted them, or a paid tour guide) who speaks the same language. At Iolani Palace, the Korean family relied on their daughter, who could move back and forth from the English tour narrations to her parents' native tongue. At the Polynesian Cultural Center, a cultural park that features the places and people of the Pacific, large tour groups of Japanese and Korean travelers often bring with them their own tour guide, who greet them at their hotels, court them on the tour buses, and walk them through the center, minimizing contact between live Hawaiian tourees at this site and most of the East Asian travelers. Even the hula demonstrations are frequently guided by Japanese, Korean, and Chinese host-escorts (hula taught in Japanese, Korean, and Mandarin Chinese). This has created a new schemata of communicative relations between tour guides, translators, and multinational tourists: translating a complex Hawaiian cultural world and subjectivity(ies) into other national languages and historically specific forms of consciousness, but still engaging face on the visual fixities of the "naked savage/prehuman."

Asian tourism

"*Hele* on." Miss Olea motioned us forward into a delicious burgundy corridor. It was the hallway. "Welcome to Iolani Palace. The king and queen have requested your presence into their home. *Alooohhaaa!* They will be down shortly to greet you. They have asked me to show you around this fine and modern-day palace."

With the delicate sway of her *muʻumuʻu,* Miss Olea took us in. The hallway was laid with thick *koa* floors, textured luxurious. A spiraling staircase stood in the middle and the ceiling disappeared in the distance. All I could see were golden embossed portraits of my monarchs atop doorways—the Great King Kamehameha I painted in his famous regal red vest (the attire he preferred to be painted in), his favorite wife, Queen Kaʻahumanu, his sons and successors, King Kamehameha II (Liholiho) and King Kamehameha III. Step after step, in line with the frames, I walked from one historical period and struggle to another, from Kamehameha IV (Alexander Liholiho), Queen Emma, Kamehameha V (Lot Kamehameha), to Lunalilo, the Kalakaua dynasty, King Kalakaua, Queen Kapiolani, and finally, the last monarch Queen Liliʻuokalani. Their distinguished looks were somber and knowing. I was losing myself in the glory of them, high above our heads.

Miss Olea broke through. "It is customary for our rulers to have their portraits displayed. As well, for other dignitaries—you will see portraits of Prince Phillipe of France, Russian kings, and other European diplomats. It was a matter of respect and proper foreign relations. Hawai'i in the late 1800s wanted the world to know it as a modern nation."

A modern nation? A historical tour of Hawai'i as a modern nation struck me as odd, in relation to flashbacks of my past summer's ethnographic touring of sites featuring "primitive and ancient Hawai'i," such as Waimea Falls Park. Waimea Falls Park in relation to Iolani Palace—the relational discourse of Hawaiian identity across two tourist attractions—piqued my interest. Two sites, which seemed to cooperate in a particular identification of Hawaiianness, one requiring a relational form of ethnographic understanding. This form would break the tourist magic of reading in determined focus, a total site in and of itself, within the time and space of a single day, separate from all others.

Here I redirect ethnography back into the objectified context, or the *very flow of tourism*—in its relations, exchanges, and connecting seams as a whole.[35] While many tourism anthropologists analyze, Dean MacCannell urges us to trace the moving nature of a tourist world, for this is its magical genius.[36] The point is not to isolate particular significations on their own terms, but to historicize and culturally connect them together into a dynamic system of social practices, gazes, and newly produced positionalities, all dependent on one another for their merging effect (the seamless continuity of meaning articulation and its unnoticed process of representation). Thus, I present a relational form of ethnographic analysis, combining how two tourist sites—Waimea Falls Park and Iolani Palace—dialogically constitute Hawaiianness that is recuperated as "before time prehumanity" through seemingly oppositional styles of communicative codes, signs, and articulations (from an ancient ruin to a modern palace).

In doing so, I pull from my observations and cooperative articulations at both these places. In both July 1997 and January 1998, I ethnographically observed Waimea Falls Park and Iolani Palace multiple times, mapping their physical spaces, attending tour after tour, and talking with tourists on site and site employees. Waimea Falls Park pulled in about 433,497 visitors in 1994, ranking sixth (out of forty-one) in attendance for tourist attractions on Oahu (Iolani Palace had a yearly attendance of 74,000 in 1994).[37]

Waimea Falls, a cultural park located on the northern side of Oahu, stands as a "a true Hawaiian paradise" where you can

> explore the grounds of an ancient temple. Learn the old Hawaiian ways. (A picture in the distance of a traditional *hale*.) Hear the legends of our ancestors [Inset profile shot of a "native male" performing a cultural ritual with two onlookers watching.]
>
> Travel into Hawaii's past. Explore our *Kauhale* (ancient living site). Experience the culture and daily activities that took place in Waimea Valley during ancient times. Learn what's authentic and what isn't.[38]

You are invited into another time-space dimension, given a chance to enter a Hawaiian world that was never more; an "ancient, authentic" living world located before our known and lived experiences. I held this memory close. The long, winding path through lush Waimea Valley spread out into reconstructed Hawaiian villages. But with no people, no sense of life in sight.

"Move a little closer. . . . Good, that's right," Miss Olea pressed. "This is the Blue Room, and his royal Majesty and her highness will be right down."

We didn't mind. The velvet walls, sinking carpet, and shaded windows contained us. The cool regality soothed us.

"Ah, *Aloha nei*, I am pleased to introduce our most prestigious King Kalakaua. Your highness."

Standing next to a table, with his back leg bent, the king looked through us. His military jacket, a dark nobility with shiny medals emblazoned all over, competed only with the glossy gold from his outer edges. The curls of his mustache seemed to touch his high neck collar. And in great fancy, I curtsied. He still looked straight ahead.

"And her highness, the great Queen Lili'uokalani." Lil'u Kamaka'aha, how I have adored you from afar. Her gown draped just right over her plump frame, sash to sash. She couldn't have been more than a few inches taller than me. Somber in expression, her eyes twinkled forward. Clip in hair, ribbons down her sleeves, she was perfect: elegant and strong. A stalwart femininity. Different from the Grecian goddesses (the historical hula models) painted on the stain-glassed doors in the hallway, they were willowy in body curve, hips extending as their long hair fell over their breasts, offering illicit peeks and pleasures as they danced with flowers. I couldn't move. Tom whispered in my ear, "How magnificent she is. Large . . . noblesse."

"The queen will now escort the most important dignitary to the Dining Room," she informed us. Tom stepped forward, on the heels of Miss Olea, taking up what he deemed as his rightful place.

I followed along. A man unlike the native in the brochure pointed me in a specific direction to where the ancient Hawaiian village stood. "Over der!"

Following a dirt path, twigs and stones, I moved from earthly corner to corner. Greeted first by a faded black rendition of Kūkā'ilimoku, the god of war, standing about three feet tall and propped on a rock. Pushed up a hill, I edged near a thatched hut, a *hale.* I was guiding myself through it in an unspoken tour, one that captured precisely the essence of a native archaism. A history that couldn't be voiced or reenacted in this site. There would be no life representative of it. It was gone (see Figure 21). The positioned tourist was to make sense of the village through its remaining tablets, its traces reinterpreted in print by archaeologists. The residual physical traces, not in glass cases this time but powerfully represented in unspoiled nature as the way it once was. I picked up a stone right before me. How was this used in this Hawaiian

Figure 21. Site of a Hawaiian cooking or eating house, Waimea Falls Park, Oahu, 1997. Photograph by author.

village centuries ago? Reeling, I wondered whose hand of my *kupuna* (elder) I was touching by extension of this native artifact. You would continue to wonder about this historical spectacle—conjecture after question to awe then puzzlement—without any evidential living testimony; a process essential to historicizing this place. As MacCannell finds, this is the display of the "primitive"/the Hawaiian "native" as an already dead form.[39] Our structured place, at this site, was to witness its demise repeatedly and thus participate in historicizing Hawaiian nativism and historically wonder and render Hawaiians as existing in "prehumanity."

A sign announced, in an untelling bold face, "*Hale Noa,* Family Sleeping House." This was the *Kauhale,* a Hawaiian living site, which consisted of several *hale* (houses), each designated a specific purpose (see Figure 22). I walked from *hale* to *hale,* the canoe house, the women's menstrual house *(Hale Pe'a).* To *Hale Mua,* where Hawaiian men once ate separately from the *wahine* (Hawaiian women). The ground, covered with an organization of scattered large rocks, some piled over others, alluded to a vision of a group of *kane* (men) huddling together on the ground in feast. Visions fed by the popular imagination of the "native" (Hawaiian men sitting around a fire speaking in native tongue).

Hawaiian as existing in prehumanity

Figure 22. *Hale* (houses) in *Kauhale* (an ancient Hawaiian living site), Waimea Falls Park, Oahu, 1997. Photograph by author.

Molten rock, cracked with whiteness, all over the ground, encasing tiny sterling forks placed perfectly at each table setting. A square table surrounded on two sides by red velvet plush backs. Along one side, centered in the middle is a tall throne chair, obviously extravagant with pointed tops peering from its back. Miss Olea explained, "King Kalakaua, the first monarch ever to circumvent the globe, knew a great deal about the political affairs around the world. When entertaining company in this dining room, the king wanted to speak to all of his guests, which is why his throne chair is in the middle."

She went on to describe the European design of the chairs, tables, and dinnerware, walking over to expose the dumbwaiters, which would "soon deliver our food." The delectable dumplings and lamb atop shining plates, the delightful clinking of crystal toasting Queen Lili'uokalani and her beautiful home.

"Ladies and Gentleman, we are so fortunate to dine here in the most European room in the palace. As you can tell, Hawai'i is not a mere small island republic; it is Hawai'i, the Nation. A Hawai'i who could in European style, house and dine you," Miss Olea fawned. She brushed across the room, extending her arms out to the fine furniture pieces— the dressers, the enclosed area for the Royal Hawaiian Band that would play our dinner music—and more frames of foreign dignitaries. Tom and I wanted to approach her every move, but the velvet rope brushing across my knee temporarily reminded us of the present moment.

"Let us move on to the other rooms . . ." past the porcelain sinks, the wooden toilets with the hanging handle, its dazzling marble fixtures, the spacious closets, all richly cased in *koa*. Under the amazingly sophisticated ceiling carvings. Through the dirt channels, to the imagined animal pens, to the confined *Hale 'Āina*, the women's eating house, where dried leaves blanketed the ground. A narrow space for *wahine* to convene, sharing breadfruit, poi, and other foods designated for Hawaiian women. As the trade winds echoed behind me in the valley bottom, I imagined the cultural activity once held here: the noise-uttering animals behind me, the lines of categorized social activity in two separate *hale*—poised now as an exercise of social power, a sanctification of the male element over the dangerously potent Hawaiian woman. Separate stone-lined spaces amassed under three large banyan trees—*this once was.*

Constructed doorways, an opening to chandeliers and the first electricity fixtures on a palace grounds, from the king's inkwells to parchment paper, with a banyan tree sliding near its shutters. [Closed shutter folds in the queen's Imprisonment Room—*this would never be.*]

A wet air filled her room. It was draped in complete darkness, a scorn discernible only by a tiny hospital bed, an end table with adjoining chair, and her piano.

"A most tragic room, the Imprisonment Room. The Hawaiian monarchs were convicted of treason in 1893 when they tried to write a better constitution for the Hawaiian people and this is where the queen was imprisoned for eight months as Hawai'i became a republic, then a territory, and today, a state."

I was impressed with her detailed narration of the 1893 overthrow of Queen Lili'uokalani. The constitution, a silent but swift entrance of military troops and the illegal seizing of the kingdom (at the palace site) by a group of *haole* conspirators.

"Imagine two guards outside. And your queen without any visitors, or contact with the outside world. Not even newspapers. She would never be the same. . . . A tragedy indeed. *Auwe!*" She would write her music and her memoir, gifts we Hawaiians would forever cherish, in the name of framing her imprisonment as a modern tragedy.

Taken together, Waimea Falls Park's old cultural world in before-time, with its remaining stones and natural traces of a place and people gone, articulates a Hawaiian native subject in relation to a modern, Europeanized Iolani Palace tour and its housed fetishes with Western-influenced, modern-day (and now antique) carvings, architectural pieces, banisters, and sterling door locks. In Waimea Falls Park, the positioned tourist can imagine historically the Hawaiian native—its unabashedly vulgar, next-to-nature existence, in its former environment; a highly organized dwelling but strange in logic and still mysterious in practice, for all that is left are the few physical remnants in hand and at our feet. It becomes then a spectral mystery—a "magic" we performatively constitute—as question-asker, actor, and audience-consumer.[40] This was the "hook" of postmodern tourism; to occupy finally that over-imagined space outside history. To live there for just a little while. To wonder and speculate. In this space, the popular tourist imagination, the "native" visited upon is still male, dark, and incomprehensible, with no voices present to explain or disconfirm the popular fantasy. No, as structured tourists, "we" are invited to witness through our wondering that he is surely dead; nativism is gone, and "we" are all still here.

Unsettling the comfort a bit, Iolani Palace locates the Hawaiian native, its king and queen, in modernity, in modern, moving time.[41] *Ahhhh,* the pull of now witnessing the Other in our own civilized, current existence, our world made familiar. The queen, the racialized traces of her hair, like mine, thick and wavy, her nose and eyes, she is now robed in a silk gown made in Europe. Feathers, ribbons, ruffles, the works. But these somehow don't suit her; she still appears out of place and strange in this scene. From room to room, every trinket, every furniture piece signifies a progressive civility, a future-minded manner of living, a "native nation" adopting the advances of the Western world. Indeed, we can't move beyond this point: the resituating of the "native" into modernity. We fuss over the physical items we find throughout the palace, emphasizing their sheer rarity, calling them antiques, the last vestiges of a modern native situation and ultimately, a modern wrong. Tom and his daughter would repeatedly compare the present material traces in the palace with its displayed pictures from the 1800s, calling attention to any missing items and rationalizing their absence. "I don't think they knew how rare these items were; how unique their door locks were even for the time." A cultural competency afforded only to neo-modern subjects.

The ideal tourist is consumed with a particular type of fetish, not about the modern aristocratic world (a world present yet distant). More disconcerting rather is the uncanny insertion of the still-primordially conceived native in what is deemed and structured as "our world." The popular imagination cannot do this reconciling. The reader is encouraged to obsess with someone else (a stranger) being framed in "our house."

At the tour's end, after the fantastical absorbing of luxurious modernity, through the Imprisonment Room back out to the front porch, you understand once again the Hawaiian native, particularly the Hawaiian woman (namely the queen) as modern in dress and manner but eternally native in fate. She, lacking in nature, would never survive the modern American nation. Her overthrow considered to be less an illegal injustice that unveils the larger unspoken colonial shadow than the historical employment of a modern-day tragedy.[42] It becomes a fated, natural occurrence experienced by a cultural group that should never have existed beyond its own time/space. To the popular imagination, they could never change their ways; two completely different worlds-in-collision; this was never meant to be. Ironically, in a tourist space, in which a critical history has potential to be popularly reproduced and exchanged, the narrativity takes you through the queen's Imprisonment Room without visiting upon the invisible movements of *haole* interests and conspirators, without focusing on the bullying pressures of the overthrow. Perhaps, then, as expounded by MacCannell, this was the very magic of global tourism: the romantic eliding of cultural politics into coherent, comforting historical tales; the neatly fused identity articulation of the much-desired primitivism and modernism (native monarchies) to signify the same native in that stubborn telos—the unthreatening "vision of History as an epic passage from past to present."[43] She, the queen, would always mark the demise of the Hawaiian Kingdom; the overthrow of the indigenous by an evolutionary modernity (and not the American nation). Through her, Hawaiians would be feminized as an archaic, "unfitting" nativism, outfitted in European clothes and replaced into modern life while tailored to tribalistic character.[44]

These thoughts—the coproduction of such a Hawaiianness as always native and tragically unmodern—enrapt me. Step to step to step to sidewalk, I could still hear Tom and his family asking Miss Olea questions about the rare porcelain vases in the Grand Ballroom—the lingering traces of a modern wrong. The rest of us dispersed out toward the space across from us, the State Capitol, which ironically stands next door to the Iolani Palace, leaving with a complacent sadness. Strolling from the past site of a modern tragedy to the halls of the state, the formal arena of justice.

PRIVATIZED STORIES OF THE SPECTRAL: THE UNDOCUMENTED TOUR

From the Iolani Palace (and its relation to Waimea Falls Park), I followed the site narrative order practiced by all those around me, walking after a family as they moved toward the capitol. We stopped at this next site: *"Ua Mau Ke Ea O Ka Aina I Ka Pono"* (loosely translated, "The Life of the Land is Perpetuated in Righteousness." Underneath, a heraldic shield covering the Hawaiian flag, held on one side by a bronzed King Kamehameha I, cloak and helmet signaling to curious eyes. On the other, it is the goddess of liberty, a laurel wreath crowning her presence over the glorious phoenix below her feet).

The Great Kamehameha and Liberty, they would never face each

other. A forced union-in-contention. Imprinted on a hanging enlarge-
ment of the state motto, which would greet you at the capitol. Built in
1969, what once stood as a modern, futuristic architectural structure (a
building in the form of a volcano, with no dome-center) needed a face-
lift, its walls tattered, its paint cracking off. The mosaic tiles at the center, the deepest ocean blue faded in reflection of the overpowering sun-
light. While regressing, the capitol and most other state buildings
worked hard to carry on the imagistic representation of its neighboring
tourist sites: the volcano, necessary palm trees, simulated oceans and
waters, and the official memory proclaiming, flaunting "Hawaiianness
at heart" in our faces.

At the State Capitol, icons abound: the state motto and references to
the state *Aloha* spirit. Upon annexation, the state reinscribed the Hawaiian royal coat of arms, originally designed by King Kalakaua; the crest
included two male *ali'i* surrounded by monarchical vestiges, crowns, the
Hawaiian Kingdom flag, and *kahili* (feathered adornments), Lady Liberty and the starred "red, white, and blue." The state also officialized "Hawaiianness at heart" or normative benevolence into policy. Hawai'i's
statute on official emblems and symbols reads:

> "Aloha Spirit" is the coordination of mind and heart within each per-
> son. . . . Each person must think and emote good feelings to others. In
> the contemplation and presence of the life force, "Aloha," the following
> unuhi laula loa may be used:
>> "Akahai," meaning kindness to be expressed with tenderness;
>> "Lokahi," meaning unity, to be expressed with harmony;
>> "Aluolu," meaning agreeable, to be expressed with pleasantness;
>> "Haahaa," meaning humility, to be expressed with modesty;
>> "Ahonui," meaning patience, to be expressed with perseverance.
>
> These are traits of character that express the charm, warmth and sin-
> cerity of Hawaii's people. It was the working philosophy of native
> Hawaiians and was presented as a gift to the people of Hawaii. . . .
> "Aloha" means mutual regard and affection and extends warmth in car-
> ing with no obligation in return. "Aloha" is the essence of relationships
> in which each person is important to every other person for collective
> existence.[45]

Orderly citizen conduct and the structured-into-being selflessness of Hawaiians is inscribed through official memory, the appropriation of indige-

nous symbols and the distortion of a Hawaiian philosophy/practice—*Aloha*—embedded in a stratified Hawaiian society.

I covered every detail of the place, peering up and down, to meet an Asian boy in a dark navy uniform. He, covered with badges, a yellow-gold kerchief snugly scraping his neck, directed us.

"Aloha, ma'am. You like one tour?"

I paused. He couldn't have been more than twelve years old, a boy scout who had already collected about eight other onlookers. They awaited my response.

"Free, you know. And I goin' take you places no one dare go. Beeeeleeeevvee me. Guaranteed," he jabbed me. Leading all of us down a stairwell, Eddy Liu conducted State Capitol tours every weekend for his service badge. He was as skilled as any guide with the threaded-in jokes and stories. He pulled us through the visibly typical: the official meeting rooms and corridors, the podiums and platforms, the legislative convening places. But we weren't touring the official activity of the site. Eddy had one focus in mind: the "after hours," the unexplainable, the dark and mysterious. A ghost tour, of all things. No politicians' names were recited, he didn't even detail the history of the capitol's development. Eddy had other stories for us.

Whispering and motioning us into a huddle, "Late at night, it is believed pleny security guards hear voices in dis hallway" (Eddy waves down to a vacant corridor; you could only see shadows at its end). "They moan. And moan. So loud, you know, for a while the guards refused to come down and lock up."

Fetization of culture

Eddy, a skilled performer, slowly slid his hand against the walls.

"They say it was the pain of it all; about the fate of Hawai'i. Spirits of the *ali'i* who would stroll over from the palace. They are here." Similar and so different from what we did.

"Has anyone seen them?" one woman in front of me queried.

"Yes, ma'am. Many sightings have been reported. Tons. Even tourists. A visiting couple wanted to take pictures late one night. Of the statues and the motto. But before they could set their flash, the man saw the image of an older woman in a *mu'umu'u.* No one knows if she spoke to them or if she took them. They can't remember the encounter. They were found by the security guards, crouched in fear up against the brush on the side of the capitol."

At this point in the story, we ascended back up to the main court. He

How can you change Hawaiian tourism to make it less problematic w/o causing people to lose jobs?

pointed in a direction facing Iolani Palace to a statue (see Figure 23). I walked closer to it, the queen, in marble this time, older and knowing. Her hair pinned up, a sash crossed her gown, and she extended sweet-smelling leis, while holding on to stone tablets. Peering closer, these were the Constitution and her famous "Aloha Oe" song composition (the music she wrote during her imprisonment). She gazed at the motto, her back toward her former home.

"The couple said this was the woman they met. Queen Lili'uokalani. Her statue was placed here in 1982. In between the palace and the capitol. Many say that sometimes, at night, the queen moves in circles."

I stepped back noting the dented and eroded concrete blocks surrounding her. She was anxious, restless, a spirit no longer contained in her room. While appraisers obsessed over her trinkets in the palace, she overtook the urban and state elements herself. I smiled; we all steered clear of the statue, refusing to touch her. Anguished and restless Hawaiian spirits are referred to throughout my tour: the overthrown queen, pained at the tragic fate of her people, circling near the contested Iolani Palace, the arrogance of the state near her home, flaunting its motto, its *Aloha* spirit in her face. *Auwe!* The discursive figure of Queen Lili'uokalani roaming at night, discontented with the historical, poses a

Figure 23. Statue of Queen Lili'uokalani between Iolani Palace and the State Capitol, 1997. Photograph by author.

significant challenge to the matter-of-fact, uncritical narration of the 1893 overthrow; a modern but naturalized tragedy. Eddy made sure we knew that "she would take you."

Eddy kept pulling out surprises, story after story, most of them he heard from other Locals and Hawaiians. He told one story about a sighting by a little girl who was playing in the basement, the place we started our tour. She waited for her mother, a legislative aide, to finish a late night's work. Ready to go, the aide searched for her daughter, who she found dazed in a corner, bouncing a ball toward an empty space before her. Led out to the street, the little girl jumped up, "Mommy, Mommy, that's my friend." She spoke of a woman playing with her all night long, pointing to the queen. My tour colleagues gasped in delight, a fright we enjoyed about the spectral we dare not believe in and one we would never doubt.

Eddy rambled off stories about the Father Damien statue (Father Damien, the much-loved French Catholic missionary who comforted the Hawaiian lepers in Kalaupapa, Moloka'i), how he circled the centered blue tiles. I could see it: the spectral meeting of the queen, Father Damien, and from across the street, King Kamehameha (his statue faces Iolani Palace) (see Figure 24). Our tour guide described stories he heard

Stories by Eddie

Figure 24. Statue of King Kamehameha behind Iolani Palace and the State Capitol, 1997. Photograph by author.

from friends and family about how King Kamehameha would step off his statue pulpit and wander the city streets late at night, around the capitol, and on the palace grounds. You should never look his way if you see his image, Eddy warned us. These spirits, they would wander together, night march, and encircle Hawaiʻi. They might befriend you, or take you, any one of you: Local, Hawaiian, tourist.

I had many unofficial tours like this. In unofficial and informal spaces, I was told that "they, the Hawaiian spirits could take you." Through narratives of the spectral, Local and Hawaiian tour guides participate in circulating the social belief that angry and restless Hawaiian spirits roam now exoticized touristic sites (which were once their homes): Iolani Palace, Bishop Museum, the State Capitol, and cultural parks. These stories feature details of Hawaiian spirits roaming in angst and horror over their land. As I visited the Bishop Museum, I followed a group of visitors that was led on both a formal tour of the museum displays and an informal ghost tour of the site by a Hawaiian tour guide. "The janitors have said that an older woman sits on this bench or in that carriage over there at closing time. She looks tired and saddened." He continued, "She misses the Hawaiʻi she has known before." As this tour guide's stories filled the air, we all walked silently. Could it be that when the flashing touristic light shows and venues close for the night, the Hawaiian spirits emerge, walking aimlessly throughout a new, commercialized home? Narratives such as these were contained within a touring framework while also serving as a form of sublated critique against tourism itself. This was a way in which Hawaiian tour guides could survive within and yet still be critical of a tourist economy that provides financial sustenance at the expense of exploiting and overwriting Hawaiian identity. Whether real or not, the stories of the spectral symbolize the social circulation of an embodied hostility toward the deeply saturated and globalized tourist context.

In another example, I encountered a Hawaiian tour guide and shuttle driver and a mini ghost tour when I first arrived at the Honolulu Airport.

"No more too much bags, ma'am?" asked a tall man who opened up a white van door. His name, Henry—a Hawaiian, it seemed, whose large frame was negotiated with a beaming smile, soft blue *Aloha* shirt, and white pants.

"No, this is it," I returned.

Henry apparently approved, nodding. "Smart, eh, more room for stuff goin take home."

The other tour guide members were already in the van. I was holding them up. One woman sighed, signaling her impatience at again having to wait for her vacation to begin. Luggage in tow, I turned around, smiling at the other passengers. No one smiled back. We didn't talk; our eyes were focused on the road ahead. Anxious to engage. Closed off to relating to each other as tourists in tow. We weren't supposed to encounter one another; only the "natives" and "native land."

SLAMMM!!!! "Ok, folks, *Aloooohhhaaaa*. My name is Henry and I will be taking you to your hotels." He takes our "hotel orders": "Halualani to Moana View, Wilsons to Outrigger West, Eidua to Queen Kapiolani." Pulling the car toward the freeway, Henry began his unexpected tour with his deep yet soothing voice.

"Anybody been here before? Well, you know then that Hawai'i is pretty small compared to the mainland. But so much to do and lots to eat."

touristy ride

All of us chuckled. The ice had been broken.

"*Poi*, you betta get da *poi*. It is a purple-looking paste that is for us, what your potatoes and brown rice are. *Poi* is our starch staple and Hawaiians from long ago would get it from the *kalo* plant and pound the root. There should be some at your *lū'au*." The two women in the back crouched forward.

"You also should try our *haupia*—a coconut milk dessert—so *ONOOO! Ono* means 'delicious.' And other specialties will soon fill your stomachs." The van shifted toward the outer left lane; Henry wasn't phased.

"At the *lū'aus* or dinners, you will see our beautiful and graceful hula dancers. Hula is our version of storytelling—there is a certain language of movements, meanings, and expressions. This is what are known for. And don't be hard on yourself, when you try, it is not as easy as it looks. I still can't do it." Again the van filled with laughter; we were finally relaxed. Lounging back in our bench seats, holding on to his every word, yearning for his light humor, his comforting cultural knowledge, the way he easily and sincerely accepted us.

Hula

Throughout the drive, I was drawn to Henry. In the midst of a traffic craze in downtown Honolulu Henry calmly and cooly offered a temporally bounded performance.[46] He would reproduce the fetishized travel system of signs from home, but with a stylized panache. A year ago, it was different. At home, in front of my computer, I had spurned Hawaiian tourist industry workers like Henry and their submissions to a swarming, unforgiving economic structure. But now, it wasn't so clear anymore, I envied him, his negotiations managing economic and cultural realities, welcoming guests to Hawai'i, and infusing a potentially jolting layer of questions and native mysteries, of disquieted Hawaiian specters, to a tourist experience. Henry moved beyond being just a "cultural broker" providing necessary social information.

He would graciously initiate us into our traveling positions while also holding something back; Henry wouldn't give it all away. Just enough to greet us, to welcome me, to make you feel natural to Hawai'i and strange and forbidden to island life and its fierce, wandering spirits.

Through the light-hearted lessons of "Hawaiian words" you need to know to survive—*kane* (men) and *wahine* (women), no walk in da wrong restroom; to get around the islands, *mauka* or "mountainside," *ewa* or "beachside"—he weaved in tales about the Hawaiian gods and spirits. "Pele no visit this island too much; but she does appear on roads as either an old woman or a young girl, asking for a ride and, royal figures, please submit to her every demand. Do as you are told. Her wrath is not easy to take, her blessing protection for life."

He knew what he was doing. Every word crafted, deliberate. And spoken before, yet still laced with a fresh and clear sincerity, convincing us of this was our own tailor-made presentation. Jokes patterned with the best of ghost stories.

"You see da road over der. Take you right up to da Pali mountain pass where King Kamehameha the Great, our first leader, fought and won the battle unifying all of the islands into a kingdom. No go over der at night. No have pork when you drive up der, your car will be mysteriously stopped. No be big, no challenge them like most visitors, you might be sorry," in his deep husky voice. "One friend of mine wen go up der one night. He wen tol me he saw an *'oi'o*, a procession of da kine, ghosts. Some say there are nightmarchers, spirits of the dead who come back to walk der sacred places or go take a dying relative to the *'aumakua* [Hawaiian/family spirit] world. My friend was on da road, and den Kamehameha the Great and his men, he wen see 'em marching on the highway. In faded form. And he hide; da buggah wen hide; if you discovered by a nightmarcher, they take you, boy. So, folks, always watch da road. Go where it's safe."

The *haole* couple next to me nervously chuckled. An understated fright. The rest of us, though, were intrigued. Yet we preferred *not* to probe further about these tales; perhaps we didn't want to know more than we had to. I had heard them before from my family. They would tell me how Hawaiian spirits always roamed *'āina*: Pele, the queen, the *ali'i*, King Kamehameha and his nightmarchers, most of whom were *ali'i*, "they would never ever rest. Always yield to their power. They'll take you," an uncle once told me. The nightmarchers would walk through you, "they would take you," unless one of your ancestors or family spirits steps up and begs for your sparing.

At every turn, I continued to encounter informal and undocumented tours of the spectral. At a cultural park, a Hawaiian tour guide detailed ghost sightings at the park. She led a few of us to the sighting locations and explained that "we think the ones who come are chiefs, they are described as wearing only what the chiefs wear. They walk all over and have even approached those who wander around the park late at night. Ever since this park opened for business, it's been like this." She made connections between the spirits that supposedly appear in the park and the popular appeal of the park to tourists. "We think they no like all kine people come into their space." The visitors around me gasped with shock. What do these stories of the spectral mean within a set of tourist/travel-encoded significations of Hawaiian identity?

In the face of an overwhelming sense of despair surrounding the rampant commercialization of Hawaiian identity, Hawaiians actively participate in acts of storytelling about the unseen and the spectral that grate against the grain of the tourist commercial enterprise and the presumption of native openness and sharing. The spectral and ghostly, or the Hawaiian spirit world, emerged fantastically throughout my tourism fieldwork; it constituted a lived social relation for Locals and Hawaiians (thereby rendering it culturally "real"). Throughout my tours and travels in Hawai'i, several Local and Hawaiian tour guides circulated narratives about fierce, restless spirits who roamed late at night at historical and tourist sites: the Bishop Museum, Iolani Palace, the State Capitol, the Pali Highway, and more. They were mysterious and wrathful. You did not know the will of their ways. But you instinctively understood their demand for cultural respect and authenticity of tradition. Thus, it would be through the unseen and the invisible that an antagonistic, uncertain, and yet authentic Hawaiian spirit is kept alive in narrative form and practice. The expressions "They will take you" and "Do as you're told" reposition the visitor as strange, unwanted, and in danger, an identity position very much in contrast with the mass "*Aloha*ness" pervading Hawai'i.

The summer camps, books, oral histories, the *halau* (hula instruction), and my relatives, through all I had heard (as both warning and private memory) of the Hawaiian *akua* and their power. The ones you couldn't see. The Pali Highway as a passage for the kings and royal courts. As a passage for our deceased family ancestors who would march this site one day to come for us Hawaiians. I remembered the large rock formation located on the Pali, the *ipu-o-Lono,* which is a *mo'o wahine,* or a lizard woman, with supernatural powers. The warning about carrying pork in the car over the Pali—this would attract hungry, dangerous spirits and Pele would strike you for it, for bringing to her side of the mountain a form of her tempestuous lover, the pig-god, Kamapua'a (half man, half pig) whom she violently loved and fought. She wouldn't have that. She'd take you.

I have been assured that being Hawaiian might save me from these spirits; they are "your elders," one aunty reminded me. "Respect them and they will know a Hawaiian from the rest." That I would be protected from the spirits at the volcano parks, on the Pali, and anywhere else. But no one was certain. It seemed as if "anyone could be taken."

In these tours, I was captivated also by the narrative inclusion of a tourist: how either an unknowing or unbelieving tourist faced a Hawaiian spirit, the former being completely naive about the exploitation of tourism and the other a skeptic, scoffing at such folklore and defiantly challenging Pele and the gods at the Pali. The notion that a tourist can actually see Hawaiian spirits is an important discursive shift in this context. Before it was believed that only Hawaiians could see their faces, while today, it would seem that the spirits are seething about the postmodern age of tourism and thus making their furious presence known to foreigners. Their rage recuperates a past but still vibrant Hawaiian ghostly subjectivity, filled with wrath, might, and vengeful power. The lost, warring, and confrontational image of the Hawaiian therefore manifests itself only at night in the most haunted of places. Today's Hawaiians are promised immunity from spectral harm. But in some stories, this was not necessarily the case. If a Hawaiian failed to respect the spirit world, the toll exacted on her or him was unimaginable. As a subtext, then, the Hawaiian who has modernized her- or himself out of existence would surely be taken. While Michael Taussig alludes to "spirits" as a so-

cial practice of both a collective memory and the state, the Hawaiian
spectral significantly clashes with tourist discourses and sites, thus making its communicative reproduction a promising space for a challenging
Hawaiian subjectivity.[47]

[Throughout my fieldwork, I was impressed with Native Hawaiian
tour guides and their realness. In interviews, tour guides (Henry, Miss
Olea, Frank) were candid about their history of touree labor in a perva-
sive tourist structure.] They emphasized the necessity of the industry for
jobs and at the same time, understood the tourist objectification of their
culture. A way for them to mediate the capitalist paradox of raced labor,
tourism, and exploitation was through their touree performances. In
their roles, they would selectively incorporate specific historical narratives and cultural concepts. One touree explained, "You do have this
job. But how you choose to go about it makes a difference." Their selections or tailored negotiations reveal their own complex schemata for
moving between a "duty to inform and relax visitors" with jokes and stories and "cuing" them to authentic aspects of Hawai'i and Hawaiianness, with "facts" and "historical fables." Each performance is sincerely
crafted, deliberate, revealing only what is necessary for that travel moment. I was struck by one guide's explanation: "You can't possibly tell
the tourists everything. And you really shouldn't anyways. There should
always be something untouched at the end of the day." These tailored
forms of knowledge (in terms of the amount and type of information)
proffered to tourists reflect the context-specific, pressured, and creative
practices among indigenous tour guides. Thus, there exists great potential in the daily strategies of tour workers, who "won't give everything
up," especially in contexts where the direct parodying, stereotyping, and
burlesque performances of "tourists," as found by D. Evans-Pritchard, is
not feasible or desirable.[48]

[The Hawaiian spectral, full of critical potential to rupture sweeping
tourist discourses, is, unfortunately, being commodified and politically
defused.] It has entered the tourist popular as "kitsch." At night, there are
highly priced ghost tours on which you visit the Pali, the *heiau,* the capitol, and near Iolani Palace. Recently, mainstream books about Hawaiian
ghost stories have been top sellers in the islands (to Locals and tourists).[49] Useful communicative forms that might reshape a cultural subjectivity usually experience a short lifespan, as the popular penchant for
fetishizing fast approaches.

THE NEW MARKETPLACE OF "OLD"

There was no set time or place. It was everywhere. Without schedules or lines, space and time would lovingly embrace each other, a union between everything and nothing: pure magic. Our movements, organized, orderly, and ritualistic, were framed within the other part of tourism; its unstructured but far-reaching, clinching world, without formalized conventions, admission prices, or live tourees, yet filled with illicit propositions, trademark promises, and obsessive pleasures. Remember, "it was free to look." "You could always wander while waiting for your tour to begin." But "we" as tourists had been touring all along and didn't even know it. Before us was a popularized tour often taken for granted as innocent leisure and as an extension of an activity encouraged at home.

In scattered fashion, there was a New World Order to the cultural souvenirs and products on the shelf. Like the older couple in front of me, fawning over which image to take home. It would either be a tiki, encased in a painted plastic lava rock, which had that worn historical look, or the statue, carved out of monkeypod wood, both useful for a bookshelf back home. They didn't check the price stickers underneath or the place of production (whether it was Hong Kong, Thailand, Malaysia, or Hawai'i). The decision, they said, rested on "what was more characteristic of Hawai'i." It would eventually be the famous tiki with green plastic rhinestone eyes for $4.95, small enough to fit on their key chain. Critical and cultural studies scholars have focused on this intersection between identity and the New World Order worlds of production, regulation, and consumption and its changing nature of cultural identities, the confrontation of communicative meanings and signs, and the flow of social relations and knowledges. Specifically, anthropologists John and Jean Comaroff and Rosemary Coombe encourage us to engage these newly shifting contexts and the flow of people, information, capital, goods, and services, breaking free from the monolithic search for imaginary "traditional societies."[50] Comaroff and Comaroff explain:

> Such systems only seem impersonal and unethnographic to those who would separate the subjective from the objective world, claiming the former for anthropology while leaving the latter to global theories. In fact, systems appear impersonal, and holistic analyses stultifying, only when we exclude from them all room for human maneuver, for ambiva-

lence and historical indeterminacy—when we fail to acknowledge that meaning is always, to some extent, arbitrary and diffuse, that social life everywhere rests on the imperfect ability to reduce ambiguity and concentrate power.[51]

Tracking social meanings and practices through national and international marketplaces, diasporic formations, development banks, and tourist flows therefore yields great insight as to how identity positions for raced/gendered/sexed consumers and cultural groups are reconfigured.

I recognized these trinkets on the shelf much differently (see Figure 25). The tiki was a rendition of Kūkāʻilimoku, the famed God of War and Snatcher of Land. Its sculpted face was the same: an elongated helmet fin-top with large dark eyes blazing through the plastic and a gaping mouth. Kukaʻilimoku is the Hawaiian symbol for political confrontation. It is an honored icon of political rallying and the same image-mask (originally made of feathers, human hair, and canine teeth) given to King Kamehameha I by Kalaniopuʻu, chief of Hawaiʻi as a symbol of great *mana* (spiritual power) and one Kamehameha always took with him in battle. In 1782, when Kamehameha fought against another chief and his supporters, his priest raised the Kūkāʻilimoku statue and directed its power against the enemies, its look destroying everything in sight. During such conquests, it is said the statue Kūkāʻilimoku let out horrible screams and a piercing rage. Kū was, according to Hawaiian Studies scholar Liliʻkala Kameʻeleihiwa, "the *Akua* whose nature was erect, sharp, and thrusting"—"he," a male generating power, was fearless, powerful, and sacred.[52] A quieted sacredness that now resided in the pockets of a pleasantly consuming couple—compact, politically neutralized, and romanticized as kitschy totemism in a new marketplace.

The tiki was lined up next to its other face, another Kukaʻilimoku statue, stout, widened, and with teeth snarling outward. Down and to the right was its carrier, a foot-long glossy King Kamehameha the Great, blankly looking up at me, his muscular build perfectly defined, his *aliʻi* cape pushed back by a miniature replica of Kūkāʻilimoku. He held Kū tightly near his plastic heart, awaiting another political conquest, one that he would—at this site for $9.95—always lose.

Another shelf good is the *ipu*-gourd helmet-mask, or a miniature replica of a tiny helmet with circular apertures cut for eyes and nose, a

Figure 25. Shelved King Kamehameha I, Hawaiian warriors, Kū (god of war), and Hawaiian tikis, warriors, and hula girls. Waikiki store, Oahu, 1998. Photograph by author.

raised feather top, and strips of *kapa* hanging from its bottom (see Figure 26). Speculation still circulates about the function of this mask. This we do know. These masks were spotted during the time of Cook's arrival. His ship artist John Webber painted its only sighting as an image of a double-hulled canoe paddled by masked wearers. These masks were never seen again. Some argue that the paddlers are priests of Kū, the element of War and Struggle, (and the mask as that of Kū) and were therefore forbidden to show their faces during the *Makahiki,* or the Celebration of Lono, the god of peace and fertility (the same god Hawaiians believed appeared in the flesh form of Captain Cook).[53] Another theory, posited by Donald Kilolani Mitchell, is that these were the priests of Lono, for they were carrying a pig sacrifice, a tribute always given to Lono, who could assume the shape of a pig.[54]

Taken either way, the mass reproduction of large and mini-helmets in Waikiki stores and the international marketplace revalues Hawaiianness. The tourist circulating of the mask as symbolic, again, of Kū, serves further to contain and write the Hawaiian warrior symbol out of existence. As it enters the popular consciousness (and dangles from car mirrors and homes away from Hawai'i), its politicality does not simply fall to the wayside (in a process of historically forgetting the energy and

Figure 26. Miniature replicas of the *ipu*-gourd helmet-mask. Kona, Hawai'i, 1999. Photograph by author.

power ascribed to the symbol and the Hawaiian belief that it would spiritually/materially work for its people). Rather, it is resignified as a forgotten relic of the past that could now be collected and managed. Structurally, from a tourist-consumer standpoint, the exhibition of cultural goods is pleasurable and harmless—"it's just a souvenir." Exhibitional displays for a Hawaiian context, however, performatively constitute its larger material and spiritual being. Thus, the shelving of Hawaiian political icons conjures a real violence to our spirit, our cultural world, and our historical selves.

Politically charged cultural symbols like Kū, Kamehameha the Great, and the helmet were always in stock, reentering the process of commodification and a war over the sign.[55] From the canoes from which bloody wars were waged between chiefs (all before Cook's arrival) to the establishment of the Hawaiian Kingdom under King Kamehameha (at a time when struggles over political power were commonplace) and finally to today's bustling, sedated Waikiki mecca of cultural goods, something had gone terribly wrong. The Hawaiian sacred, our cultural material for political challenge and confrontation, had been revalued in postcapitalist terms as a "native bygone." As a dead form, it embodied a Hawaiian exotic strangeness for visitors, a strangeness easily replaced by other tikis, hula girls, and statues.

The most sacred of Hawaiian symbols that pre-dated Cook's arrival is massively reproduced, mostly in the Philippines and Malaysia and locally shelved in Hawai'i, as the historical-spatial boundaries between culture and commerce, sacred iconography and money, aesthetics and economy, are "confused."[56] The buying couple selected the "most Hawaiian-looking" souvenir to evidence their trip; indeed they were right about its Hawaiianness. But, in a deeply situated context, the plastic Kuka'ilimoku couldn't be severed from its confrontational spirit of Hawaiianness, an image in dialectical opposition with "Hawaiianness at heart," or normative benevolence. In the moneyed exchange, however, the translation had been lost and drained. There would be no circulation of signified knowledge about Kū and his role in the Hawaiian everyday, its source of strength, a reminder of social and political uncertainty. They wouldn't know how each year, after the *Makahiki* was celebrated, Kū and War took over. "Just as Lono nourishe[d], Kū destroy[ed]."[57] A dualistic world forever changed by Westerners, missionaries, and capitalists, all preserving and distorting the memory of Lono (accentuating the peace and generosity as necessarily Hawaiian) while stamping out the spirit of Kū. Kamehameha and his icons of Kū would be, as commodities, abstracted from the historical context and valued for exhibition, and prized in terms of the ceremonial value of a curiously antiquated Hawaiian royalty (a pleasure about savage queens and kings similar to the modern us) and as an eliding, the totemism of nativeness in general. Commodities of Hawai'i could do this. They could fetishize a specific Hawaiian sociality—the aristocrat-like *ali'i* (the selling of the King Kamehameha icon everywhere—on label tops of breads, cigarettes, chocolate candies, books, *Aloha* shirts, statues, candies, and as the official trademark of the Hawai'i Tourist Bureau itself, appearing on a white flag sign in front of each tourist site)—*and* universalize "nativism," fusing the prehistoric savage, the *maka'āinana,* and the *ali'i* as "undeniably Hawaiian." Historically specific cultural icons and figures, known to Hawaiians, are transformed into mass-produced commodity markings of "prehistory" and "presociety" as we know it; their ferality domesticated through open capitalist exchange and the indiscriminate tastes of consumption.

In this same space, the looseness of confusion between culture and commerce has been productive in other ways. My brothers and I and today's Hawaiian youth buy graphic-designed T-shirts of Kamehameha, Hawaiian chiefs, and warriors with religious helmet-masks (known either as the masks of Kū or Lono), with "Hawaiian Warrior" or "Year of the Hawaiian" in large print. These cotton images, sold in local stores, the Waikiki district, and swap meets, represent Kamehameha in spectacular poses. He is much larger in stature and muscle-bound, towering over the length of the shirt, and with spear in hand.[58] No longer does Kamehameha look up at a promising consumer, he sternly peers down, possibly at the hordes of spectators, his changed *'āina*. We Hawaiians gaze at him watching over Hawai'i. His larger presence intimates, though, that we are being watched by him right now. Sometimes, he appears atop modern cities, in urban Honolulu, on beachfronts, he appears to be "any time." On these items, he is therefore ours (ours as *Kanaka Maoli*): powerful, uncompromising, still unknown, and of today. Contemporary Hawaiians can hold close these popularized visions of Kamehameha, an icon seemingly from their own time, as they learn of his history and spirit in class, at *halau,* and from their families. Or the T-shirt vision might impel a yearning to know more. And as yet another possibility: the image has reinvigorated several Hawaiian rap music groups who don similar warrior images or *Kū'ē* (Fight!) expressions on their album covers and through historically detailed songs about Hawaiian sovereignty, the overthrow, and homesteads. This symbolic war being waged over reexperiencing the Hawaiian spirit might just save the shelved Kū and Kamehameha. They would be reunited in the bloodiest battle of all: a contest over Hawaiian identity itself. This is not to argue that fight motifs within the popular are necessarily resistive for Hawaiians. The reemergence of a symbol and its visual contestation, however, does indicate a type of brewing activity within Hawaiian collective memory; that historical distinctions are being made (between the real Kamehameha and Warrior and their artifices) and particular images are being reexperienced in relation to current political struggles.[59]

Everywhere else, throughout the rows, there are no specifically Hawaiian images—no Hawaiians, (the *wahine* and *kane* on *'āina*), none of their crafts—the *koa* bowls, *kapa* cloth, patterns, and woven hats— none, not a trace. For it is the case nowadays that you no longer need the native to have nativism.

A tall, strangely slender woman pointed me toward a separate arena; an adjoined market center with several headlined specialties: "Antiques," "Collectibles," "History," and "Hawaiiana." The woman, sleek and long, her hair in a bob with a band across her forehead, she was a cut-up straight out of the 1920s. Her modified "grass" skirt with her top adorned by leis— around her neck, her wrists, and her head as bands. She peers toward us with a horizon in the background (see Figure 27). The pleasures of male-others while also suppressing the unseen "native," her presence unquestioned and woman is the "Modern-Day Hula Girl" and "*Ukulele* Lady." She isn't Native Hawaiian but wears Hawaiian markings and sits on Waikiki Beach. She, a white mainlander, is therefore a Hawaiian by way of travel and class privilege. But, in the creation of new local positionalities, her figure is a replaced tourist fantasy of white bourgeois patriarchy. Patriarchy would have its exotic nude Hawaiian women *and* the modestly pleasing modern-day white hula girl. She would attend to the popular seemingly natural. The modern-day white hula girl signifies a class distinction and white male fantasy while also implicitly and explicitly problematizing the occupation and reconstruction of a native space with very different cultural images and meanings. Thus, the dilemma is two-fold. On one hand, the white hula girl is reshaping and resignifying a native hula image,

[handwritten marginalia: "How can you 'be' Hawaiian through class privilege"]

[handwritten marginalia: "Is it possible to just adopt their identities?"]

infusing the image with false and empty images of a traditional cultural practice that expresses Hawaiian identity and sovereignty. This image is both replacing and displacing a native female subjectivity with a racialized and class-based distinction. White women could become hula girls by way of sovereign residency, colonial privilege, and class distinction. By entering

Figure 27. Modern *'ukulele* girl. From Brown 1982, page 60. Courtesy of the DeSoto Brown Collection.

such a space, the native dancer identity becomes abstracted and universalized for access by all via travel and class privilege.

On the other hand, the white hula girl is objectified within her own racial and gender hierarchy at home; she becomes the somewhat exotic and yet within-class/race female of desire within a white male fantasy. The modern-day hula girl is positioned as part of a distinctive social class that can pass through all others, but as one contained underneath a male power that cannot be seen but does the viewing.

In addition to being the modern-day hula girl, the white female is also represented as the visitor to the islands throughout travel discourses. She is captured as part of the wealthy elite class who can travel to Hawai'i. After the Great Depression of the 1930s, when the wealthy elite struggled to maintain their class distinctions, travel discourses often signified "travel" itself as "class distinction."[60] White women are seen dancing arm in arm with their male counterparts and being served by both native males and females. Thus, explicit images of native females were literally absent from many of these travel discourses for these were replaced/displaced by white female images signaling both privilege and different gender/racial/class hierarchies. One could argue that perhaps this was a positive move given the contemporary context in which Hawaiian women have become cheaply commodified as exotic and sexual spectacles (hula-girl icon in movies, television shows, and as souvenirs). I am interested, however, in how these white hula-girl images contributed to the contemporary images of the darker and nude hula girls. White female images and class-based travel discourses universalized nativism (while also positioning white females in an inferiorized native position) and created a cultural memory of the hula girl to be consumed and imitated for later decades. The Hawaiian hula girl from the 1920s and 1930s were far too strange and dark for the consuming traveler while the modern-day hula girl was "just woman enough" to be native. White female iconography via the native woman is therefore used to signify class distinction and capitalist desires.

No product shelves in sight, the modern-day hula girl was encased next to "Matson History" in this place: Matson was the first commercial shipping line to transport tourists to Hawai'i (which took about five to six days each way for a then-whopping price of $80 to $1,200). Only the elite could afford such a luxury. There stood before me a life-size replica of a Matson Ship (see Figure 28). I touched its shiny white posts and as-

Figure 28. Nostalgic display of Matson Shipping Line: Matson Ship Deck. Maritime Museum, 1999, Honolulu, Oahu. Photograph by author.

cended onto its sloped deck. I looked through its portholes. There lay glass-framed Matson Travel Brochures, ragged ticket stubs, faded passenger lists, luggage tags, old advertisements, and on-board menus (see Figure 29). Delicately placed, their detailed titles read:

> Hawaii Inclusive Tours for
> Matson Line and American Railway Express Co.
> Very Rare
> Mauna Galleries, Hilo, Hawai'i. $50–100

Each piece naturalized and nostalgic. You could even move from port-hole to porthole, enter your room accommodations, via an old black-and-white picture of the ship rooms enlarged in the case (see Figure 30). Two steps away, you enter the ship's grand ballroom, with (white) male travelers donned in tuxedos and the women in gowns (see Figure 31). The class details of chandeliers, sparkling crystal, and champagne hold-ers fill the case. Back on deck, in yet another case, a game of shuffle-board awaits you as travel posters fill the walls and one magnified image of a *haole* couple playing deck games of shuffleboard is captured under-neath the following text: "Matson's Passenger Lines . . . almost half a century of elegance at sea" (see Figure 32).

Figure 29. "Matson history": nostalgic commodities of Matson Shipping Line (travel pouches, ticket stubs, and luggage tags). Matson Ship Deck, Maritime Museum, 1999, Honolulu, Oahu. Photograph by author.

Figure 30. Nostalgic display of Matson Shipping Line: guest room. Maritime Museum, 1999, Honolulu, Oahu. Photograph by author.

Figure 31. Nostalgic display of Matson Shipping Line: grand ballroom. Maritime Museum, 1999, Honolulu, Oahu. Photograph by author.

Figure 32. Nostalgic display of Matson Shipping Line: ship deck and shuffleboard. Maritime Museum, 1999, Honolulu, Oahu. Photograph by author.

In the late 1800s to early 1900s, tourism was already being normalized within Hawai'i. Steamer ships were built to transport visitors to Hawai'i. By 1898, tourism had allowed for two thousand visitors per year to enter the islands and Hawai'i had already been annexed as a territory of the United States. At this time, U.S. mainlanders had money to spend on travel and leisure. Also, in this decade, many Americans were enjoying an era of unregulated capitalism before the income tax mandate had been established and thus, Americans were "amassing large fortunes to afford long expensive vacations."[61] Luxury ocean liners and hotels quickly developed for Hawai'i and the wealthy elite traveled to Hawai'i for weeks at a time.[62] At its end, the tourist position could reimagine the golden age of travel (the 1920s to 1930s), the *Lurline* ship in the distance, direct from Los Angeles, awaited by anxious "natives" in their canoes, hula girls holding out their leis and bosoms, and *ali'i* and warriors, with their capes in midair, raising their arms in greeting. Travelers would descend to a deck filled with lei girls (the male traveler, with luggage, would be "lei"ed by a "native" woman), hula dancers, and the Royal Hawaiian Band. You could feel the *Aloha*. The smiling "natives." The distinction of the modern traveler and signs of a new local-class elite: the men's tailored suits and tuxedos, the women's crimped bobs hidden under hats, their gowns and sleek gloves, by day lounging on the Waikiki beach shore, and by night swooning in the moonlight, her gown hem gracefully sliding near his feet.

Other glass cases and a live tour await you. Propped up by a glass stand is a "Moana Hotel" key, labeled as one from the 1920s; next to it, old baggage tags and hotel brochures from The Royal Hawaiian and the Moana hotels, and the first postcards for their first tourists.

Moana Hotel Luggage Label, c. 1920s
Rare; Crisp Folding; Original Color
Aloha Galleries, Hilo, Hawai'i
$50–100

The hotel's first guests—their pictures—centered on the shelf; their signatures in the reservation book laminated for all to see. The name Moana belonged to a white mainlander baby girl born to a couple who first honeymooned at the Moana, her portrait elegantly framed. Snapshots of military men and the first business travelers shower an entryway. A card near a door reads: "Imagine turning back the hands of time.

[margin annotations: "Normalization & History of Hawaiian tourism"; "Aloha"]

Leaving your cares behind for the grandeur of a more elegant era. Discovering the legendary Aloha of the 'First Lady of Waikiki.' Only one hotel in paradise offers such timeless allure . . . the Sheraton Moana Surfrider."

Entering, a live man greeted me, "Welcome to the Moana Historical Remembrance Tour!" For the next two hours, he would reveal the latest practice of tourism: the historicizing of tourism itself into Hawaiian history. The sentimental memorializing of the Moana, one of the first tourist hotels in Waikiki, as a seamless, essential part of Hawai'i and its *Aloha* people. From the exhibit on the Early Hawaiians, with artist drawings of *heiau* (ritual and temple grounds; burial sites) and religious symbols to its natural, historical successor comes the development of Waikiki and the age of travel (see Figure 33).

It was as naturally inscribed as placing one foot in front of the other, absorbing tourism as the glorious past. From early photographs of the newly built Moana, to its guests sipping drinks on the veranda in their wool bathing suits, to the postcapitalist corporate buyout of Waikiki and the ongoing renovations. We moved on from the glass cases; now we were in awe of the "Old Wing," the oldest part of the hotel, the banyan tree outside the hotel, now a historical landmark. Similar to Iolani Palace, we fussed over the architectural detail with the guide providing handouts about the physical features of this historic site: the archways, the colonial roof, the woods, the open-air observatory, the palladian windows, and the veranda. I slipped into a crickety, paint-chipped rocking chair on the original hotel veranda. I was immersed and tempted by a golden history. A history of travel, a history of Waikiki, the history of Hawai'i. The tourist-subject position invokes not only tourism as natural history, but also the incorporated aesthetics of history—the glass cases, the framed souvenirs, all labeled with dates, the included historical tidbits, the black-and-white photographs—remind us that the golden age was indeed the nostalgic past.[63] It was no longer today.[64] It had slipped by like a trade wind. Thus, making its return a grand fantasy (wouldn't it be grand to have the golden age of travel back?): to unlock the precious cases, freeing the glamour and prestige of travel, tourism, hotel culture, and Waikiki, warding off the gaudy, cheap, and artificial nature of postmodern tourism.[65] To be amid elegant gowns and nightclubs and fanciful dining; to be the new local class elite, where tourism was again about status and prestige and not exploitation and

Figure 33. Historicizing tourism displays. Historical tour of Sheraton Moana, Waikiki, 1999. Photograph by author.

falsities (see Figure 34). To the emerging tourist identity position, tourism had to stop being so obvious (the vacation packages, the transported *lūʻau,* the emphasis on budget pricing, the staged savagery), and the new discourses of tourism seemed to promise an authentic turn to its histori-

Figure 34. The image of the golden age of travel. From Brown 1982, page 115. Courtesy of the DeSoto Brown Collection.

cal roots. In Waimea Falls Park and the Iolani Palace, tourists are marked with the stigma of tourism. Here in this marketplace space, with its glossy posters and trinkets, that stigma is transformed into an honorable distinction.

The communicative resignifying of travel and tourism as history draws from a representational taxonomy merging historical valorization and commodification (i.e., the more historical, the greater the value) into a commodified history. Hawai'i is ladened throughout with shops, centers, fairs, and exhibit halls (in Waikiki and in gift shops at each tourist site) featuring rare memories of tourism: travel ads, brochures, posters, luggage tags, music books, postcards, old *Aloha* shirts, and hula-girl figurines that swivel on your car dashboard. Each "Hawaiiana" artifact is first dated to establish the basis of its semiotic value: How nostalgic is it and from which era? The more reflective of the golden age of travel, the higher the value. Its origin explained: Where did it come from? The hotels, shipping lines, or Hawai'i Visitor's Bureau? If the originating structure no longer exists, the commodities become "rarities" or "originals" valued in the hundreds to thousands of dollars. In such cases, the material condition is meticulously described: the folds, tears, missing pages, fading of color print with "mint condition" items more highly valued. Thus, they become "antiques" and "collectibles," and constitute a new postcapitalist tourist industry of an appropriated "Hawaiiana."

At its historical beginnings, "Hawaiiana" named the local "Native Hawaiian" range of crafts and handiwork—the *lauhala* mats, the *koa* bowls and jewelry, the leis, and *ipus*—that emerged out of the Hawaiian Renaissance in the 1970s, a time when Hawaiian communities would protest their inequalities and highlight its indigenous and modern-adapted practices (hula, chanting, music) and craftwork (the canoes, quilts, *lauhala* mats, leis, calling attention to the skill and art involved in their making).[66] Native Hawaiian themes and practices smoothly transition as if by magic into "objects produced and designed for the tourist industry in the islands during the period from the turn of the century to the post war years when jet travel changed the islands and its way of life forever." This stands as a redefinition of today's Hawaiiana by collector Mark Blackburn.[67] Side by side, Kū, King Kamehameha, and the 1920s love-lorn modern couple in the Waikiki moonlight are stitched together as "Hawaiiana" (as the Hawaiian Historical). This is a discursive suturing that sublates its original function as a politically conscientized practice. Framing early Hawaiian society in the same breath as the development of tourism, they were deemed complementary and continuous.

This unification would be possible through the production of "'the historical' as an abstract system of equivalences."[68] The image of history, its significance and moving nature, is extracted from the everyday and restaged and visually preserved in specific coded sites. Preserved images—the ancient "native," the Matson ship, the first Waikiki hotel—are abstracted and smoothed over as "the historical." An encoded collection of equivalences, "purged of difference, it has become a unifying spectacle, the settling of all disputes."[69] The new "Hawaiiana," with tourism as its center, is recoded as the reconciler of Western colonization, the mediator after the U.S. overthrow. It could cure, cleanse, and bring the positioned tourist and "native" peacefully and pleasurably together.

"Hawaiiana's" historical texture also relies on the conflation of everything Hawaiian as a matter of place. In chapter 1, I discussed how the placing of Hawaiianness is achieved through "the culturalization of the natural and the naturalization of the cultural" or the rewriting of Hawaiianness via the geographic Hawai'i as essentially open, inviting, and generous. So placed, Hawai'i is vested with global capitalist venture and a sensitive tourist economy, regirded through historical abstraction. "Precontact" Hawai'i (kings, queens, and calabashes), Western history (Cook, moral missionaries, and the United States), and modern economic systems (trade, finance, corporate capitalism, tourism) are blurred together in a progressive timelessness.[70]

While collectors buy the originals of this timelessness, the structured tourist could own a slice too, although through a newly installed high-class hierarchy. Aggressively marketed and mass-produced, the images of nostalgic tourism are pasted everywhere, popularized at each Waikiki corner and fetishized for their glamour: on affordable T-shirts, *Aloha* shirts, *mu'umu'u*, postcards (the first set of postcards from Hawai'i's old days are reprinted and sold at sites for $2.00 each), computer mouse pads, mugs and plateware, and posters. Nostalgia is everywhere. In the Waikiki Duty-Free Shop, multinational visitors carefully choose from a large section of "Vintage Hawaiiana" where bright *Aloha* shirts are marked by decade ("1950s," "1960s," "1970s") with prices starting at $800. Hula dolls and hula "nodder" figurines (produced in Japan and plastered in Paris) for $200–$300 (see Figures 35 and 36). Hawaiian

Figure 35. Hawaiiana: tourism as nativizing. Waikiki shop, Oahu, 1998. Photograph by author.

Figure 36. Tourist kitsch. Waikiki shop, Oahu, 1998. Photograph by author.

sheet music written by *haole* songwriters about Hawaiians—"Honolulu Eyes," "I Lost My Heart in Honolulu," "A Little Rendezvous in Honolulu," and "Sweet Leilani." Hula lamps on hula-girl stands. Postcards and old plane tickets. Everything shelved and on sale, carnival Hawaiian novelties at your fingertips. The tourist position could take home a piece of yesterday, something native, and a travel-class badge of honor. In this way, we seek to become a part of the golden age of travel, not tourism.

Tourism has encased/framed/museumed itself as naturalized history, as "Hawaiiana," so who needs the native anymore? The signs of Hawai'i moved on without him, and at the expense of her. Her swiveling hips, almond eyes, and brown body. Through the abstraction of her, tourism established itself as native to the islands. A nativizing raced and classed travel; the restoration of a new (but inherited) class elite. Imagined tourists who had been there and always would be. Dominant structures wouldn't even need maps anymore, signaling to Denis Wood that maps' "culturalization of the natural and naturalization of the cultural" would now operate through tourism, which has become its own agent and practice, easily eliding its own colonizing of a cultural people and their subjectivities.[71]

CONCLUSION

Tourism and its representational practices, in addition to structured tourist roles and ironically my own ethnographic fieldwork, have all coarticulated and imagined Hawaiianness as specifically native and severed from modern time. My travel encounter with the Hawaiian subject (my own face), however, began long before my arrival in Hawai'i. It is this way for most of us as Hawaiian tourists. Framed tourists stroll the historical imagination, the displayed native, fierce, irrational "male," ready to strike at any moment. And while "he" is made strange to us, his home is made familiar through the inscribed gaze of maps, televisual representations, and travel images. Hawai'i, his home and ours, its savage gone, its beauty preserved, and its runways open for all.

The naturalization of travel here to Hawai'i marks the greatest feat of global capitalism. As both structure and practice, it had placed Hawaiians in the same moment it freed modern subjects. Social actors could move and travel. They would be organized and solicited by historical and political structures to occupy a native position everywhere and everyplace. The ideal tourist could move from site to site. And indigenous natives would be its object. Dialectically rereading tourist sites, the encoded traveler/tourist position could experience a Hawaiian already gone (Waimea Falls Park) and revisit how native queens and kings could never live in modernity (Iolani Palace) (with the overthrow matter-of-factly narrated as "sad, but inevitable"). Thus, the signified Hawaiian identities throughout tourist structures are seductively implicated through compelling narratives, engaging tours, and performances of the "dead" into fantastical castings of prehumanity or premodernity. Hawaiian identity therefore becomes a reconstructed ethnicity narrowly confined to a cultural industry banking on the exotic and spectacled.[72] The tourist position is encouraged to know Hawaiian culture primarily through its death—through what it could not be.

[margin note: Commodif. of Hawaiian identity]

But, in the movement of it all, postcapitalist tourism would reveal itself. I and other tourists would feel distant from one another, alienated and isolated, dissatisfied with our free-flowing venture. I never saw or spoke to the same person twice, a point also mentioned by the tourists I interviewed. The fantastical contact with native images was therefore fleeting, as many, on the airplane, in the bus, and at the sites, stared *Aloha*'s emptiness in the face. We called on our localized identities and politicalities partly to refuse tourism's callings.

In my fieldwork, I realized and identified with the complexities of the tourist. It is no longer the case or might never have been that a tourist is easily duped into native fantasies or spectacled native performances. While she or he is greatly pressured by travel images and structural tendencies to read Hawaiianness in a particular way and materially sustains a larger economic and hegemonic structure, today's tourist has changed from MacCannell's time, where the search was solely for "primitive authenticity."[73] Travelers now seek out its postauthentic resignification as intriguing, vivaciously performative, and less obvious. Yes, tourism would be where we as social-historical subjects satiate our modern thirst for a new form of authenticity, an authenticity still ideally judged against our imaginary relation to it and against the gaudy plasticity of tourism. Tourists demand the best performances of the real thing—asking performers to be creative, without taking the tourist for a fool—to watch the most subtly exaggerated verisimilitudes of postprimitive native acts possible in a changing world.[74] At the same time nevertheless implicated into the manufactured appeal of difference as a response to a suppressive whiteness, national community, and secular faith. The shift in popular

[margin note: tourists no longer "duped" into native fantasies]

taste, therefore, reflects a changing tourist subjectivity. Such a subjectivity might eventually grow weary of the different nativisms featured at sites and in revues. Or it may already have and we, MacCannell and I, have not been able to understand the complex relations between tourist structures and the ways in which social subjects (Locals, Hawaiians, tourists from differently situated communities) live out the conditions of their framed experiences.

My positionality through this touring—the difficult translation of "I," "we," and "us"—speaks to the torsions of a social-historical subject through naturalized historical and structural legacies. Economically, I join other tourists in being surveilled and invited, treated as a visitor. As a mainland Hawaiian, I have always been fascinated with the fantastical nature of kings, queens, and nativisms. When I was younger, these representations resonated with me differently as close semblances of a Hawaiianness that I had to work to know. But while I momentarily enjoy what I study, I am not fully hailed into the representations before me. As a Hawaiian who has grown into her critical consciousness about the representation of Hawaiians, perhaps, I feel more conviction in clarifying what seems to be the structural tendencies of tourism (the ideal tourist positionality) and what belongs to the Hawaiian popular (without revealing too much of the latter). Only after engaging private memories and oral histories of Hawaiian community members both in Hawai'i and on the mainland has this kind of clarity enabled me to reread tourist structures. This is a consciousness practiced and performed by Hawaiians and various compassionate social agents, but difficult to uncover. This is not to say that a clarity objectively exists. It is socially and politically formed through my lived conditions; a clarity that represents more an identity practice of reading the different constructions of Hawaiianness in different conjunctures and places and a rereading that indicates my informing, changing, and in-contest subjectivity of Hawaiianness.

Ironically and perhaps by Hawaiian destiny, Local and Hawaiian tour-guide discourses about the Hawaiian spirit world offered the greatest challenge to tourist structures. In an industry dependent on the visually visible, narratives and significations of the mysterious unseen would alone construct a Hawaiian subject who was restless, confrontational, and not with *Aloha*. The Palace Queen whose story is toured as an empty, mere nodding to the past, without a colonialist confession, justly roams and confronts those who have strolled through her room. "They will take you" refers to more than just reproduced narratives. It speaks to a historically engrained/politically situated consciousness communicatively lived as "real" by those who must every day face a readjusting tourist world. The dominant encodings of travel as practice are only ensured in framing Hawaiian private memory, while Hawaiians communicatively reshape their subjectivities, agency, and faces by rewriting "Hawaiianness at heart" and "tourism" itself as remembrances of their authenticity and speaking authority.

The signifying practices of tourism undoubtedly reinvent and reimagine culture in a variety of contexts. The question then becomes one of specifying the processes and conditions of meaning that restructure a culture, its formative values and behaviors leading to the disintegration of a group's political agency, and our knowledges about who Others are in relation to us. To what extent might we be studying cultural practices structured and organized by tourism and the age of discovery and travel? How might we be theorizing cultural contact based on state-structured formations and distortions of cultural identities? And if so, how can we conceptualize and analyze cultural contact as a closely regulated and managed body of knowledge between sociocultural entities like tourism, national and business interests, researchers, and cultural members themselves? "Hawaiianness at heart" or what I term the normative benevolence of Hawaiians and its suspicious public heightening during the age of discovery brings to mind significant questions about the necessary and complicitous role of tourism, the state, and ethnographic research in imagining and reifying objects of culture. A focus on the interworkings of these forces and others (religion, international relations, and regional politics) on the development of culture might just lead us to the nexus of critical insight on analyzing the formation of cultural subjectivity over time and making sense of identity articulations that seem to be on its surface convincingly real, empirically practiced, and commonly understood.

The construction of "normative benevolence" has become popularized over time into a reconfigured articulation of "Hawaiianness at heart" and the famous *Aloha* spirit. Travel discourses and popular discourses (commercials, televisual and filmic texts, T-shirts, and souvenir items) feature the unconditional love and naturalized benevolence of Hawaiians, while excising out any references or symbols to the earlier Hawaiian identity aspects based on war and political confrontation. The continual focus on *Aloha* and "Hawaiianness at heart" deepens the liberalization of nativism and the reification of Hawaiian sharing and communion, which grates against the demands of sovereignty and land activists.

Artist Eugene Savage unmasks a reconfigured Hawaiianness in his murals, which were used for menu covers in 1948 on the Matson company, the first major passenger shipping line, as well as early *Aloha* attire. Today Savage's images have reemerged in what is now a popularized craze of Hawaiiana kitsch or a series of nostalgic goods such as old postcards, travel posters, advertisements, hula-girl images, *Aloha* shirts, and tiki icons. It is a common sight to see high school youth in California, New York, and Japan wearing *Aloha* shirts and Hawaiiana images (the whitened hula girl) and historic images that romanticize the golden age of tourism (1910–1950). These images are deemed as "Hawaiiana" or coming from a period of the 1960s and 1970s when a Hawaiian renaissance emerged with a renewal of traditional dances, song, language, and crafts/icons, but most are pulled from tourist manufacturers and interests promoting travel to Hawai'i. It is curious how everything from Hawai'i—a tiki key chain and hula-girl lamp—is deemed naturally and indigenously Hawaiian, a move inherited from the discourse that displaces sovereign nativism and ethnic distinction. These reproductions of Hawaiian culture and identity appeal to ethnic/cultural traditions and images while radically transforming them in line with an expansive nativism.

In a different place and moment, the tourist spectacles and discourses from this chapter and the blood references from chapter 3 emerge in diasporic Hawaiian community and memory, taking on politically charged meanings. No longer a blood technology in service to the state, blood speech within Hawaiian community represents a resignified means to both challenge external (mis)recognitions of who they are and reestablish their own natural cultural authority as Hawaiians. Likewise, commercial tourist spectacles are featured in mainland Hawaiian festivals and symbolize an adjusted practice for incorporating diasporic youth into private Hawaiian memory. Blood, along with the tourist popular, becomes a creative identity form for diasporic Hawaiians whose subject positions are overdetermined by historical memory, Western law and governance, the racial state, and tourism, and thus serve as more powerful vehicles through which they can rearticulate their Hawaiianness within such conditions.

5

Little Bit Blood, Heart, and Spectacle: Practicing Hawaiian Memory and Community in the Diaspora

At first glance, it seemed as if I never left. Tourism was still here. Chain separators and camera flashes. Posters of natives and hula dancers splashing over the banisters. The stage, lit with bright bulbs, *ti* leaves, and flowers, held up the host, a smooth-voiced dark man in *Aloha* attire, who, extending his arms and heart, beckoned us into his cultural world. Behind him were two female dance troupes in Hollywood splendor: one in cellophane grass skirts and the other in skimpy Tahitian dress—bright cotton bikini tops, long grass skirts, towering headdresses, and grass hand instruments. The Hawaiian dancers gracefully swept from side to side, as the Tahitians accentuated their hip swings with each drum bonging. Our host blared into the microphone, "Ladies and Gentlemen, this is Polynesia!" The drum rolls, and the audience gasps in delight.

Adrienne Kaeppler describes such a sight as "airport art," or the spectacled cultural representations of "native" cultures that tourists first meet
upon their arrival.[1] At the flight gates and baggage claim areas, the love-
ly hula hands and friendly sways of female native dancers invite travelers
into the romantic illusion of tourism's naturalness, into the notion that
Hawai'i is open, unexplored, and free terrain. But this specific display of
airport art does not take place near the flight runways, Waikiki, or even
in Hawai'i. It resides on the mainland at a *Hawaiian community event*:

our annual festival celebrating Hawaiian culture. More intensely now, this airport art poses a jarring dilemma given both its new context and larger dominant-framing as for-profit exploitation of the other. Could it be that tourism's image of the native really does speak to Hawaiians?

To most, the answer might seem obvious. Hawaiians everywhere are indeed the postprimitive, exoticized, and willing performers Dean MacCannell describes, or as I concluded in chapter 1, it is their cultural nature.[2] Yes, it seemed that tourism was truly about and for them. Thus, one's first critical instinct might be to brand this mainland Hawaiian performance as an extension of touring of the native (see chapter 4), as an indication that Hawaiian communities themselves reproduce (and comply with) tourism's dominant authentic identity encodings of the sexually charged hula girl and the happily greeting native king or tourist entertainer. Or worse, they directly and unequivocally valorize such commercialized images as truthful and real. As their own faces.

However, as suggested by the Popular Memory Group, Richard Johnson, and Anne McClintock, we are impelled to rethink identity positions as structurally framed *and yet* not fully foreclosed. Johnson insightfully deepens the analysis by posing the question, What are the different ways in which subjective (identity) forms are inhabited?[4] He highlights how identities constitute and frame social subjects, who are "contradictory, in process, fragmented, and produced," and who, within a determined range of meanings and options, can actively repractice and reimagine identity encodings in their everyday lives.[5] Thus, the everyday communicative practices of identity—via community performances, oral histories and narratives, and private memories—contain more than meets the eye. These identity practices reveal how a nativized, racialized, and (mis)recognized cultural group still reassembles who they are in complicated and creative ways, although not always oppositionally.

In this chapter, we come full circle to the identity significations of the historical imagination from chapter 1 (the "soft and savage" Hawaiian), chapter 4's tourist spectacles (the exoticized Hawaiian hula girl and premodern Hawaiian kings and queens), and the sphere of law and governance (the "pure blood" and "mixed blood") from chapters 2 and 3, but from a different vantage point. Here I am concerned with witnessing how Hawaiianness or nativism is collectively remembered and resignified in the everyday lives of Hawaiian community members. The everyday marks the locus whereby dominant identifications of Hawaiianness are reconfigured and managed so as to speak to Hawaiians' experiences, needs, and memories of the past.

I focus on a community of diasporic Hawaiians who moved from Hawai'i to the continental U.S. mainland as early as the 1930s. Hawaiians represent a cultural group rarely considered to move between two nations: an American one borne of U.S. colonialism and a sovereign nation, the historically remembered independent Hawaiian Kingdom prior to 1893. As Hawai'i increasingly becomes the site of global access, belonging, and consumption, Hawaiians who have limited access to land and economic opportunities have left their homeland and settled as far away as Europe, Japan, Mexico, and the United States. These diasporic movements of Hawaiians are due in large part to the concentration of globalized power and corporate colonialism *back at home*, or within the small space of Hawai'i and the resulting dispossession of Hawaiians. In doing so, Hawaiians have also reconfigured the nature of their identity across the globe in such a way that a connection with the 'āina of Hawai'i can be maintained and a claim of indigeneity can be preserved. Hawaiian diasporic movement, which itself seems to contradict the notion of indigenous peoples, or those who are rooted in one's ancestral land, is therefore transformed in the context of globalization into a culturally authentic act. Diasporic Hawaiian community members refuse the delineated oppositions of "rootedness" and "displacement" and "indigenous Hawaiian on the land" and "American citizen away from home" in their speech acts of identity.[6]

I stand in awe of the critical identity practices moving within a diasporic mainland Hawaiian community, the Aloha Club.[7] The Aloha Club, with membership open to genealogically defined Hawaiians and "Hawaiians at heart" (those who have lived in, traveled through, and explored Hawai'i), ironically reinvokes tourist spectacles in the staging of its authenticity as a significant cultural community in the expansive mainland. Staging itself as a burgeoning, exotically/racially different, and yet inclusive community speaks to several needs of mainland Hawaiians. Spectacled displays of Hawaiianness stem from the community's need for dominant recognition from the general mainland public. This becomes a means to strategically carve a unique, appealing image—a presence—in the more explicitly whitened mainland center.

Ironically, staged authenticity also becomes a privatized communicative form for addressing diasporic mainland Hawaiians who do not identify with their Hawaiian culture or who have never been to Hawai'i. Here tourist spectacles help to reconstruct and reincorporate cultural members born and raised in different and conflicting social locations (e.g., those who are mainland-born, brought up in upper socioeconomic classes, and those of mixed backgrounds) into a Hawaiian community that privately practices the language, traditions, and spirit of Hawaiians. Paradoxically, tourist constructions of Hawaiianness—the new, or the dances resembling Hollywood revues and blurred-in Tahitian numbers, the hotel image of the hula girls, and the staged dramas highlighting royalty figures as mere ceremonial symbols of "prehumanity" and "premodernity"—are redeployed and reinserted into the diasporic Hawaiian community so as to authenticate mainland Hawaiian identities.

Hawaiian community members also performatively practice *pi'ikoi*, or claiming to be of a higher rank than he or she is. We work hard to assert our genealogical links to Hawaiian royalty: either that of Queen Lili'uokalani or King Kamehameha, two of Hawai'i's most hailed monarchs. Such a practice symbolizes an effort and desire to gain a cultural power and status that are absent from our lives. We strive to actualize a power position that becomes cultural currency only within a larger Hawaiian community, as Western tourism degrades Hawaiian monarchy as a fetishized tragic nativism that could never be. *Pi'ikoi* emerges as a politicized means to claim more Hawaiianness or a cultural authenticity long denied to diasporic Hawaiians. Specifically, by establishing oneself in the name of a royal blood line, Hawaiians seek to exercise a valuable yet differently positioned indigenous Hawaiian speaking authority, one that is largely denied in the state process of identification and in the courtroom and one that is inexorably linked to a historical memory and without geographic specificity.

Mainland Hawaiians remember and make public their individual performances of proving blood quantum (see my own family's performance of proving, chapter 3). Their acts of remembering call attention to the state's overwriting of their names and historical selves. The remembering—the lived pains and pleasures of Hawaiians, their tactics and strategies in establishing their identities—is captured by ethnography. Ethnography, reframed from its colonizing tradition, makes possible a resistive opening here: it enables the publication of real Hawaiian subjectivities and state injustices (or the suspicious nature of state administrations such as the DHHL, Hawaiian Homes Commission, and

DOH, in identity certification). It presents, in blatant form, an active Hawaiian subjectivity and a wrongful, villainous state. At the same time, my cultural studies ethnography risks additionally surveilling and disciplining our private *moʻolelo* (histories) and names by unveiling deep cultural wounds, secret family names, and still-in-use-micropractices for proving quantum.

Finally, while they unveil the repressive nature of state blood technology, mainland Hawaiians also performatively invoke both blood and heart in their social practices. Blood reenters the Hawaiian vernacular as a resignified communication practice and a form of speech that performatively verifies Hawaiianness. Through a discourse of blood, Hawaiians invoke the naturalization of blood to claim exclusive authority and authenticity as true Hawaiians. They write themselves back into indigenous authority through the scientific reification of blood and its undisputed realness. Deeply held within the private memory of *Kanaka Maoli* (indigenous Hawaiians), blood quantum invocations culturally work as historical recollections of being denied indigenous recognition (and sovereignty) and serve as departure points from the sweeping, nondiscriminating identity sentiment, "Hawaiianness at heart," in addition to illustrating in part the unquestionable discursive influence of the racial order encoded by policy and law.

But, blood work via discourse continues to quantify identity on the mainland Hawaiian community, this time, by ushering in an internal hierarchy of Hawaiianness. "Pure-bloods" are discursively framed as the original experts on Hawaiian tradition, a tradition once practiced with a sincerity now lost in a modern world. They hold the cultural power, they are the last links to the indigenous. Separate yet connected are the "mixed-bloods" or *hapas* (originally meaning "part"; part Hawaiian) and later generations of Hawaiians (born from the 1950s on), who serve as living reminders of modernity's sweep over the Hawaiian culture. "Mixed-bloods" and later Hawaiian generations are deemed Hawaiian but with a different connotation. As modern subjects who are products of foreign contact with Hawaiians and born of a different world, they enact a much different Hawaiian culture than yesterday. As one member puts it, "the language is different, their dances are too modern, and even when they act 'real Hawaiian-kine,' is still different-kine." The notion that mixed and contemporary Hawaiians practice a different Hawaiianness highlights a critical consciousness among Hawaiians that key *mixed bloods*

elements of cultural practice historically have been rendered foreign, modernized, Americanized, and stamped out. And though power divisions arise between "pure-bloods" and earlier Hawaiian generations and modern-day Hawaiians, this economy of speaking positions works to sanctify particular cultural practices and historical moments. They remember and embody their own historical gallery, all the while exposing the intrusion of Western colonialism.

In articulation with blood is the heart. Yet another identity rung within the Aloha Club is "Hawaiian at heart," or those who share an interest in Hawaiian culture or who have traveled and lived in Hawai'i. A "Hawaiian at heart" identity position is invoked among mainland Hawaiians as a localized adjustment to a different social fabric of the mainland. It works on one level as a form of public outreach through which community membership boundaries are adapted, and yet, internally, it remains within a differentiating hierarchy of Hawaiian identity. Genealogically linked Hawaiians use a blood speech to differentiate between Hawaiians and those who are here in the heart. Throughout private memory interviews, several members cast "Hawaiians at heart" as friends but not "true/authentic *kānaka.*" They explain that Hawaiian culture can be shared but the *koko* (blood), as performed through speech and its reproduced natural image, isolates out the true cultural subjects. Such a complex schemata of identification illustrates the powerful influence of dominant identity encodings as represented in naturalized Hawaiian normative benevolence (chapter 1) and the racializing HHCA hearings and their redeployment in community practice (chapter 2). Within the diasporic Hawaiian identity position, uniquely situated on the mainland, "individuals and collectivities struggle and remember and, in that difficult remembering, imagine and practice both subject and community differently."[8]

CULTURAL STUDIES ETHNOGRAPHY, IDENTITY PRACTICES, AND PRIVATE MEMORIES: A LIFE PRACTICE

If indeed identity practices are embedded in everyday living and community life stands as an arena "through which social difference is both invented and performed," the real challenge lies in unpacking the lived relations between dominant structures (and memories) of identification, public discourses, and the more privatized sense-makings and productions of self.[9] Several cultural studies, ethnography, and performance narrative scholars lend their insights, methodological perspectives, and case studies to the cause.[10] Together, these theoretical contributions constitute not only a means of tracing the sociohistorical production(s) of identity across several levels but also a practice through which we, as researchers, can probe scholarly questions with deep integrity, commitment, and caring for a particular community greater than ourselves. It is the outlining of a life practice.

In the face of the postmodern age and the shifting nature of identity and identity politics, we have increasingly watched over the relationship between social community and cultural-political identity. Benedict Anderson theorizes the nation as an imagined community, imagined creatively and historically.[11] Community, therefore, becomes more than just an embodied space. It is a historically specific "system of cultural representation whereby people come to imagine a shared experience of identification with" those to whom they are in some way historically, politically, and culturally connected.[12]

But, this system, which often deceives us by appearing as a fixed, unitary group structure, holds and activates a hierarchy of meanings, memories, and social subjects. The Popular Memory Group, led by Richard Johnson, traces such a dialogic structure.[13] They argue that communities re-create dominant historical memories, or the formal constructions of cultural histories and subjectivities found in state forms (e.g., museums, "History" textbooks, national commemorative discourse, administrative and legal documents). In social life, community members make different sense of the formal past by selectively remembering, forgetting, and rearticulating images, histories, and narratives of who they are, thereby constructing private memories. Without the authoritative pen and the recognition of history proper, we, as social readers, rely instead on what is already within our reach: a generative "materials memory" of life moments, pains, joys, displacements, and structural pressures experienced by a racialized, gendered, and overwritten cultural group. But just as a romanticized nostalgia creeps in, as we lean toward championing social communities over specific fields of power relations, the Popular Memory Group's theory goes a step further: "Private memories cannot in concrete studies be readily unscrambled from the effects of dominant historical discourses. It is often these that supply the very terms by which a private history is thought through."[14]

A community member's story, a community performance, or a

[margin handwriting: How should we study/teach history? in a way that is truthful]

distinctive speech act is, in some way, interrelated with dominant-framed identity logics (e.g., colonial discourse, the state, Western religion, law and governance, the national/state economy).[15] To analyze these inter-relationships as cultural productions of identity and complex hierarchies of significance and power is to, at long last, take seriously the social actor/subject who is produced and productive in different moments, spaces, and relations. Taking seriously the concrete everyday—as conse-quential, structured by specific modes of power, and infused with some degree of social agency—is long overdue. In the past, we have mostly cast privatized communities as populist heroes inherently resistive to any so-cial order *or* as absent fictions that, in the end, are hegemonically locked into serving the nation-state.[16] Private memories, with their paradoxes, conflicts, ironies, driving needs, and pleasures, cannot possibly breathe in these academic headlocks. According to the Popular Memory Group, "Really to respect them [social actors] is to take them as the basis for larg-er understandings, for the progressive deepening of knowledge and for active political intervention."[17] This respect for both community and the possibilities of identity is our gain as we notice the conditions, structures, and processes that have formed unconsciously lived experience and how social actors actively move within and reassemble identifying social rela-tions. It is our gift, toward recognizing cultural groups whose most trans-formative work lies in the unseen nexus between an overwhelming ideo-logical structure and a seemingly obvious daily practice or personal story.

In this chapter, I feel it is imperative to relationally understand identi-ty, from its forces of production to its reproduced form in community life. With a broadened, localized focus, I look to a specific community and their subjective practices of responding to, reenacting, restructuring, and reinvoking identities made for and about them. Community life, how-ever, proffers different lived forms, many of which are not apprehendable.

Cultural studies and feminist ethnographers delineate several kinds of practices that churn identity and are possible to engage. For example, D. Soyini Madison and Tamar Katriel highlight personal narratives as spaces where identities are performed, addressed, and in dialogue with "the cultural, geopolitical, and economic circumstances" touching their lives.[18] By narrating their lives, (mis)recognized social members can retell the identity constructions through which they have been narrated. These individual stories spill over with rich theoretical insight. Com-munity members' remembrances, though captured through individuated interviews, reveal the presence of pluralized subjects who achieve their identities as extensions of a historically and locationally bound collective. No longer a single subject, the pluralized community subject, according to Anne McClintock, "cannot be heard outside its relation to communities."[19] The community member can only be viewed through a network of relationships spread out across time, space, and power dimensions (e.g., historical moment, class, racialized classification, gender, regional origin, and sexuality). The network itself is overlaid with structural and institutional forms of power (governmental discourse, legal identifications, economically driven difference), making even oral histories never safe in the comfort of privacy. Also never safe is the recording of personal narratives and oral histories. Within this practice brews a struggle between the ideal of cultural mimesis (where the political is concealed via nostalgic sentiment), researcher authority, and the member's experiential voice. The narrative unsteadiness of oral histories and ethnographic interviews is where we might be able to catch live identity forms and their momentary ruptures and contradictions.

Identity practices also move in the forms of popular literature and media, social protest, and community events and performances in addition to speech acts, or how stories and experiences are communicatively signified, arranged, and expressed.[20] These are spaces where social actors represent and reimagine the relations between themselves and the real conditions of their existence: where they have been identified and implicated and where they continue to act and struggle. All of these significantly live within a historically specific, diasporic mainland Hawaiian community, which struggles in the face of the most overwhelming structures to reorganize their displaced and dispersed identities.

Methodological Framework: Radical and Relational Contextualism

All along, throughout the collection of chapters, I have been tracing Hawaiian identity in terms of community via dialogic memory. In chapter 1's historical imagination, historical retellings from Hawaiian leaders, sovereignty movement groups, and everyday Hawaiians have cued me toward the dominant "native" articulations of migrations, maps, and racialized fantasies. In chapter 2 and 3's legal arena, Hawaiians' private testimonies about their unacknowledged identities, signaled the stately nature of blood. In chapter 4's arena of tourism, you could hear Hawaiian voices muffled under the consumer commotion and mythical capital of native sites. Hawaiians via the tactical Hawaiian tour guide and the unseen spectral, told of an unfulfilled and violently suppressed way of life. It was not completely extinguished (for nightfall reawakened Hawaiian forms and figures that would never die), just swept aside and dispersed by the Western world and the presiding American nation-state. Hawaiians were here all along. However, I have lingered over the dominant constructions of Hawaiian identity, obsessing over every move and moment that touches our lives. Up until the moment I realized that power, practice, and identity mean nothing without appreciating the ways in which Hawaiian community members, in varied social locations, maneuver within conditions not of their own making.

 The Aloha Club is just one grounded example of Hawaiians who shift and make do with the identities proffered *for* them and *in their name*.[21] Here I share a few real and lived moments of Hawaiian identity from a diasporic Hawaiian community group—the Aloha Club—better known as a social outlet for Hawaiians and Locals. The Aloha Club makes up a growing network of Hawaiian civic clubs on the mainland (spanning from California to Washington, from New York to Texas). These social outlets began after World War II, a time when Hawaiian men enlisted in military service for material gain from the GI Bill's promise of technical training and a college education. These Hawaiian men were stationed on the mainland and eventually settled into new mainland homes. On the mainland, most Hawaiian men and some Hawaiian women intermarried, continued their education into graduate and professional schools, and experienced a socioeconomic status difficult to attain back at home (on *'āina*). I focus here on these Hawaiians— my father and Aloha Club community members, among many others— whose travel movements were in response to the historical and legal overwriting of Hawaiian identity and blooded obstacles to obtaining land, benefits, and sustenance. I remember and honor these Hawaiians.

Exploring Hawaiian Diasporic Communities

I have lived within the Aloha Club for eight years, regularly attending meetings, dancing at our functions, and working at the community events (e.g., the festival booths, the kitchen lines for our *lū'au*). I had done the same everywhere else I lived: as a part of a Hawaiian civic club and Hawai'i college clubs in Sacramento, California, and Arizona during my college and graduate school years. This was the usual routine for other mainland-situated Hawaiians, who join clubs through which the Hawaiian culture (via *lū'au,* language acts, and dancing) is recognized and practiced. And this was the driving force behind the Aloha Club. Meetings are held every month, and two major community events displaying the Hawaiian culture are sponsored each year. At the core of these practices is a need to belong to and continually bring into being a larger cultural community where difference is a binding and marketable tie, where localized and staged connections somewhere else (that is, on the mainland) mediate the cultural and geographic displacement of many Hawaiians from their homeland.

Ironically, difference in the Aloha Club is revised and negotiated in that membership as a Hawaiian is redrawn to include more than those who are racially, legally, and genealogically defined as Hawaiians. This mainland community espouses an inclusive motto: "You can be da kine Hawaiian and da kine Hawaiian at heart." For instance, several community texts and interactional sequences reproduce membership qualifications as either being "of Hawaiian ancestry, or hav[ing] lived in the islands, or hav[ing] a serious interest in some aspect of the culture." A Hawaiian is therefore either a genealogical member, a sovereign resident, a Local, or a museum-framed traveler or tourist. Thus, the Hawaiian community in the name of the Aloha Club resembles a multicultural, racially mixed grouping. At any meeting or event, "pleny" more *haoles* and Locals seem to make up the community than "Hawaiian essential-looking" members. However, in this context, such multiculturalism is named and remembered as Hawaiian; as a social formation driven by an ideologically created benevolence and sense of equality ascribed as being naturally native and Hawaiian. Dominant multiculturalism, or an official state-endorsed discourse that universalizes and codifies the social body as an abstract and equalized citizenry makes its way into a localized setting. It operates through the "integration of differences as cultural equivalents abstracted from the histories of racial inequality unresolved in the economic and political domains."[22] Ironically, Hawaiians' specific displacement and dispersal and the core reason why they have settled on the mainland are neatly elided under the rubric of group and intercultural relations.

Yet we cannot foreclose the possibility that somewhere within Hawaiians' everyday use of "Hawaiian at heart" relations lies a mindful cultural agency. That "Hawaiianness at heart" holds more than one would at first suspect. Hawaiian historians suggest that friendly social relations on the part of the Hawaiian were politically strategic—that is, Hawaiians were overly generous to foreigners so as to gain their Western goods and thus, new forms of *mana* and greater political status.[23] This strategic mode of living partly represents Hawaiians mimicking a colonial economy, and an appropriation in that Hawaiians incorporated Western items and trade practices into their own culturally framed hierarchy.[24] If Hawaiian subjectivity moves somewhere within a contact based on its presumed benevolence, its traces need to be carefully unpacked from the foremost image of the ever-natural "friendly native" and nativized harmonious relations. The Aloha Club's expansive identity therefore poses a challenging notion: How might varied yet seemingly unified and harmonious Hawaiian identity distinctions be practiced in the everyday? And specifically what political effects do these serve, meet, and transform?

The historical, legal, and economic displacement and dispersal of Hawaiian identity across the mainland and the culturalization of the natural Hawai'i as open, inviting, and inclusive—as "Hawaiian at heart" in a community formation—makes for a thought-provoking engagement with identity. Throughout seven years of fieldwork (approximately 650 hours of participant observation, interviewing, and oral histories), I engaged the varied practicing of identity and the mainland inflecting of dominant-framed subject positions. As for my ethnographic practice, I've come a long way, falling back on my now all-too-natural methodological training in the rigid empirical traditions of Dell Hymes and James Spradley as well as incorporating perhaps the most exciting feminist and cultural studies sociopolitical ethnographic work to date.[25] I invoke its close attention to empirical detail laden through community practices, or identifying-rituals and events and speech acts among its members, thereby momentarily capturing the verbal and nonverbal signs, expressions, and lived representations of our selves.[26] I also draw upon its thematic focus, highlighting recurring themes and sequential patterns among the communicative significations of Hawaiianness in my fieldwork (via speaking practices, everyday and staged performances, and visual and rhetorical encodings found in community newsletters and event advertisements). But where the lines are deceptively clear between a blind empiricism and a political positionality, feminist, cultural studies, and critical ethnographers and anthropologists unveil the identity muddle for what it really is and uncover the social-historical construction(s) of cultural identity, lived community consciousness, ethnographic practice, and ethnographer.[27] These rich, historically specific constructions would surely exceed and spill over the abstract theoretical boundaries of objectivist cultural sociology, racial essence, or cultural ritual. Thus, I would let them breathe in contextual motion. Historically and politically specific forms of cultural analysis save ethnography from its own limitations—from its abridged interrogation of complexly articulated subject positions, subjectivities, and political agency, and its own dominant authority in speaking for cultural subjects and relegating them yet again to the oppositional confines of savage exoticism versus neomodern development.[28] In my interview work, I interwove a historical specificity, a moving politics, and ethnographic practice in order to analyze more insightfully the following research questions:

- How do Hawaiian community members practice identity and dominant identifications?

- How do Hawaiians reassemble identity in their everyday lives? How is a subject position constituting "Hawaiianness at heart" performed and invoked?

- How is a subject position of Hawaiianness articulated away from the place of Hawai'i?

- What are the political consequences of these subject formations for the diasporic Hawaiian community on the mainland?

- How might my identity position as a mainland Hawaiian and researcher be articulated in relation to community members?

In addition, my opened and contextualized study of lived Hawaiian community also relied on a relational form of identity analysis.[29] Through this relational form I engage the differences, oppositions, likenesses, cooperating, and paradoxical articulations of Hawaiianness in relation to one another and across a variety of power spheres, namely "History Proper," the geographic, the tourist industry, and law and governance. This analysis enabled me to explore critically how such articulations, whether relations, oppositions, or historicized separations, historically and politically come into being. Thus, this community analysis, which I originally wrote in 1997, looks much different than its first version.[30] The relational focus of this analysis on the articulation(s) of Hawaiian identity positions has captured what was missing from my early analysis of the Aloha Club's cultural practices. I had analyzed these practices in isolation from their conjoined historical representation, legal encoding, and tourist framing, from the structures and significations of identification that constituted and produced them. Walking through the historical imagination, tourist sites, and the courtroom significantly unpacked how Hawaiianness is inhabited and practiced in the everyday. Without this extended look, I would never have been able to witness the sophisticated inflections and compromises of Hawaiian identity among community members.

My fieldwork extends from August 1993 to January 2000, including participant observations made during community meetings, public events, and interactions (privatized exchanges). It also encompasses more than one hundred interviews (and about ninety oral histories) with various community members in which I probed the communicative practicing of Hawaiianness via private histories of their own lives, narrated retellings of Hawaiian history and politics, and individuated outlooks on Hawaiian identity and community.[31] Like Bette Kauffman, I politically infused my ethnographic study, selecting interviewees based on their self representation of Hawaiianness (their proclamations of being Native Hawaiian and/or "Hawaiian at heart") and their structural identifications as Hawaiians (by legislative mandates defining Native Hawaiian by blood, by historical imagery of early "dark" native settlers, and by the mass-produced, racialization of Hawaiians as savages and smiling dancers).[32] I spoke with and observed community members whose perceived or ascribed identity locations traversed a range: genealogically Hawaiian, "Hawaiian at heart," mainland Hawaiians who have never been home or who have merely "visited Hawai'i like a tourist" (as one interviewee described himself), and Local Hawaiians who recently moved to the mainland.[33] My goal was not to reproduce the lofty notion of ideal representativeness or to satisfy some contrived point of validity, but rather to understand how social members are placed in relation to their perceived and/or ascribed representativeness and how they articulate their identities in relation to the perceived or ascribed identity position they seem to represent.[34]

Many of these interviews coalesced with an oral history project that I started in 1993. For a long while, I have been interested in preserving and uncovering the private memories of Hawaiians, particularly mainland Hawaiians, through oral histories. My interest first developed in

[handwritten margin note, left side: "Clark's test doll"]

[handwritten note, bottom: "other people have the affect to imprint identity onto you"]

learning about my own family's stories and experiences and then transitioned into a fascination with the histories of Hawaiians who had migrated from *'āina*. As it turns out, most of the mainland community members I interviewed fit a consistent profile. They were mostly Hawaiian men, now around sixty-five to seventy years of age, who came from the first Hawaiian homestead areas, served in the U.S. military, filed a land claim that was in some way denied by the DHHL, and thus, settled on the mainland for more "economic security and freedom." So, analyzing mainland Hawaiian identity practices proves to be a compelling relational point of identifications and identity encodings; a point where the constructions of Hawaiianness from the historical gallery, colonial and state administrations, and tourist arena meet and confront one another and take daily form.

HAWAIIANS IN THE DIASPORA: PRACTICING HAWAIIANNESS

Historical Moves

Jon, an eighteen-year-old Hawaiian male born and raised in Las Vegas, Nevada, has never been to Hawai'i:

> In hula practice, my teacher told of our past. That for centuries we lived in an ordered society, ruled by *ali'i* and then it changed as more and more outsiders came. The sovereign period had ended with the overthrow of the kingdom of 1893. Which is how I am here today. The Hawaiian people left home when their home changed . . . to Oregon, Washington, California, New York, and Nevada.

The specific Hawaiian diaspora is best understood within a reiterated historical contextualization (discussed in chapters 1 and 2). The year 1778 marked the moment in which Westernization dramatically altered the Hawaiian culture.[35] Up until 1778, Hawai'i had been a self-sustaining and organized society and an independent kingdom, but after, struggles over political governance, sovereignty, and native and land rights dominated for the next few centuries.[36] Settlers from countries such as Britain, Russia, France, Spain, and America came to the islands and demanded naturalized land rights.[37] These foreigners were "sovereign residents," in that through the reigning mandates of their imperial homelands, they called on intermingling natural rights and discovery discourses together with their national identities to claim privatized rights *before, outside of,* and thereby *over* indigenous structures. Rapidly, native belonging and residency in Hawai'i lost its ethnic distinction and began to liberally include all residents. British and later U.S. colonial forces restructured Hawaiian society from a stratified cultural system to a capitalist market-driven society in which land is a commodity and a natural right for all productive citizens (which did not include Hawaiians). More and more outsiders and external business interests flocked to Hawai'i as U.S. colonialism overthrew the independent Hawaiian Kingdom in 1893. Hawaiians lost any cultural right to land they had previously held, and over the next fifty years, a plantation economy, exporting sugar and pineapple, burgeoned. By 1941—World War II—Hawai'i's economic focus had shifted to the visitor industry and military defense. Large sections of land were appropriated and seized for tourist development and the construction of military bases.[38] Over time, tourism became the economic mainstay of the islands, presenting a dilemma for Hawaiians who were pressured to take jobs that commodified and exoticized their culture. Travelers from all over the world visited Hawai'i, some even buying property for permanent vacation homes.[39] Global capitalism permeated the islands and cultivated a dependency on multinational investment and tourism.

"Home" for Hawaiians became a concentrated site of colonial and globalized interests. In response, according to Jean Barman and J. Kēhaulani Kauanui, there were three waves of Hawaiian out-migration.[40] The first wave occurred during and after World War II: facing a paucity of jobs and scarcity of available land (most of the Hawaiian land at that time was reserved for U.S. military purposes), many Hawaiian men joined the U.S. military, at a rate "double the national average."[41] Hawaiian men could gain more materially through military service and the GI Bill's promise of technical training and college education in return for a minimum of three years' active duty. But most of these men were shipped to the mainland (and stationed in both the Northwest and the South) and never returned to Hawai'i; those who did return to Hawai'i had difficulty finding jobs.[42] In the wake of the HHCA with its 50 percent blood quantum mandate and the challenges in securing a Hawaiian homestead, it was economically better to stay away from home. Hawaiian women also sought out schooling opportunities on the mainland, but their migration outward was much more constrained than that of their male counterparts. Instead, marriage to *haoles* and mainlanders ensured many Hawaiian women a different life and class existence. Hawaiians moved to British Columbia, Mexico, Europe, and the continental U.S. mainland (California, Oregon, Washington, New York, Texas, Arizona, and Nevada, respectively in terms of population size).[43]

The second wave occurred in the 1970s as multinational and foreign investment in the tourist industry gained momentum and the state agency—the DHHL—failed to equitably distribute homestead lands to "proven" Hawaiians (many died while on the waiting list for land). Hawaiians struggled in locating jobs and attaining homestead lands *at home*. In the 1990s, the third wave of diasporic migration by Hawaiians occurred, in response to several intensifying pressures: the soaring cost of living, the limited supply of low-wage jobs, and the rising price of homes. In addition, state agencies—the OHA and DHHL—had for too long failed to furnish Hawaiians with cultural entitlements and land rights.[44] Homestead claims made by Hawaiians were denied, stalled, or not recognized. When Hawaiians took legal action in the state courts, their challenges were quelled under the guise of legal technicalities. Only the U.S. government could sue the State of Hawaii for homeland trust violations. Hawaiians dispersed to other spaces away from Hawai'i to realize a stable or at least a better economic living and to retreat from the ineffective and unjust local government and its state agencies. As of today, there are approximately 72,272 Hawaiians living "off-island" on the continental U.S. mainland in comparison to 138,742 Hawaiians living in Hawai'i.[45] Diasporic Hawaiian communities have settled in northern and southern California, Washington, Colorado, Florida, Arizona, Illinois, New York, Nevada, Texas, Utah, Oregon, and Virginia.[46]

These diasporic Hawaiians have been branded by their local Hawaiian counterparts as the "upper class" or "wannabe Americans" who have integrated into white mainland society.[47] This necessary connection between living on the land and cultural authenticity belies the complex cultural meanings surrounding diasporic movement and moving cultures. As reflected in Jon's comment, Hawaiians have incorporated their diasporic movement into their historical memory, framing it as both an externally induced pressure by colonialism and global capitalism and a necessary cultural adjustment for survival as Hawaiians. In their speaking practices, "off-island" Hawaiians describe themselves as "traditional" counterparts of their community and their mainland positionalities as distinctively Hawaiian.[48] One woman, Mary, a Hawaiian woman who moved to San Francisco in 1950 describes her "traditional" background.

Looked down upon to live on the mainland.

Back then, *not too* many jobs, you know? Hotels had some [jobs] but so many of us want them.

_____Hawai'i had changed._____

^^From baby time, my neighborhood—all Hawaiian, *you know*? They wen talk Hawaiian too . . .^^

_____When I turned 18, *haole* and locals all over. Some friends' houses were bought by stores and owners. You'd see barbed wire around property. Pleny military all over. All over.

My parents wen told me of what it [Hawai'i] used to be. Hawaiian land for Hawaiians. *Hawaiian old ways.*

All that wen change.

I was 18 when my father told me that maybe better if I left [Hawai'i]. He knew the future. Moving might give me more and let me be. (Interview 42)

Mary, who was born in the early 1920s, shared her lived experience in Hawai'i, a reality marked by significant changes: the eradication of spoken Hawaiian in communities, the loss of traditional all-Hawaiian communities, and the presence of economic business development and the increasing militarization of the time. She explained how she moved away and its cultural function.

I danced but all the hotels *wen* fill. So a friend wen tell me about a dance revue in the mainland. In San Francisco. I went. Why not?

My parents told me it was good.

I went in _____ . . . 1951, 19 . . . 50_____.

^^I danced for a hotel for five years.^^

My mother moved out [to the mainland] when dad died. I bought a home and we stayed. I could take care of her on the mainland. If I stayed in [Hawai'i], we'd get no benefits, no home.

I lived here like a Hawaiian, with *'ohana* and a home. (Interview 31)

In the context of colonial and globalizing effects at home—that appropriation of land, the shortage of jobs, and the increasing presence of outsiders—a "traditional" standpoint suddenly changes. "Tradition" dialectically shifts as "home" becomes the center of modern business development and foreign control. Clearly, a traditional life is no longer possible at home. Mary associates "home" in Hawai'i as being newly foreign, resignifying out-migration and resettlement in this context as practices that connote true Hawaiian identity, meaning practices that provide a self-sufficient and family-oriented living.

Similarly, Hale, another diasporic interviewee, framed her resettlement in Las Vegas, Nevada, as a cultural adjustment.

Yes—we adjusted. You had to. In the 1970s and maybe '80s, other *kānaka* had at least two part-time jobs. To even get by, that's what you'd have to do.

Can you believe? Two jobs?

I worked for Hilton for six years. I got laid off and worked at my uncle's garage for two years.

^^You can't control the market. It's all up to the market. Before, my parents never had to worry so much about the market.^^

I . . . applied for a homestead land and my brothers had already.

Two years wen by and I did not have some documents of proof. That's OHA and the Department of Hawaiian Home Lands—real bad.

They no give to us, they no give to the Hawaiians.

My mom couldn't get a homestead either.

How can? How can everybody get land but Hawaiians who no can prove quantum dis or dat?

I can't live like my grandparents—on their homestead. The old way.

The mainland was an adjustment. Moving, I mean. It's a Hawaiian adjustment. You could live there on your own terms. Your own. To me, Hawai'i wasn't for Hawaiians anymore.

^^They [friends] told me to come back. Before I lose touch.^^

I kept saying . . . *it's not about me as more* American or *haole*. It's about being more Hawaiian. (Interview 10)

When asked about her Hawaiian identity, Hale focuses on her move from an economically strapped and restrictive Hawai'i. The statement "Hawai'i wasn't for Hawaiians anymore" reveals her view that the combined forces of colonialism and globalization had dissolved an original cultural site. With the felt threats of globalization, diasporic movement for Hale represents a means to preserve a cultural spirit suppressed at home; the movement away from Hawai'i becomes a necessary adjustment to a seemingly indiscriminate capital market and the unjust withholding of Hawaiian homestead land from Hawaiians. Hale sees her actions as being Hawaiian (and not "American" or *haole*) and in contradistinction from the contemporary and "foreign" shifts at home. Also, note the way in which Hale refers to the state agencies—Office of Hawaiian Affairs and the Department of Hawaiian Home Lands—as "bad" and unfair. Many Hawaiians perceive the state that way: encroaching upon their native entitlements of land and benefits. Given the struggle between Hawaiians and these state agencies, diasporic movement away from Hawai'i can also be considered a political act of identity and a means to separate oneself from unjust and "real non-Hawaiian" interests.

In most of my interviews, when I asked about the nature of Hawaiian identity and experience, Hawaiians emphasized the topic of out-migration and characterized it as a Hawaiian act. Such an act is Hawaiian in a very different way from past identity claims that highlight rootedness and indigeneity. At the very moment contemporary colonial and globalizing structures take hold of Hawai'i, culture, all the while appearing fixed and stable, transforms into a larger dialectic of indigenous memories, modernized Hawaiian cultural practices (e.g., the tending of land by Hawaiians incorporating Western ways, the incorporation of new costumes and dances to the *hula* over time in response to new religion and tourist consumption), and modern forms of governance, labor, and living. This dialectic holds new points of meaning as traditional Hawaiian life takes on two different forms: living on a homestead and, if that's not possible, which happened most of the time, moving away to new spaces. Globalization thus changes the conditions of culture and the means (the forms) through which we can enact and practice culture amid different circumstances.

As a globalized "home" becomes foreign and strange and out-migration becomes more "traditional," the diasporic experiences of Hawaiians may involve more than progressive adaptation and integration. Different from intercultural theories about cultural adaptation, diasporic Hawaiians may be aiming for more than integration into the mainland social hierarchy and achieving socioeconomic stability. Rather, as revealed in their comments, Mary, Hale, and other "off-island" Hawaiians emphasize their main goal to reconstruct Hawaiian community differently from what Hawai'i has become in new urban and rural spaces. Reconstruction, for Hawaiians, entails establishing a community network of Hawaiians in particular regions, maintaining an interregional connection with other Hawaiian communities in the United States and preserving a solid link to Hawaiians back in Hawai'i. In this case, adaptation takes on a dynamic form in that cultural identity is reorganized along contemporary changes. Being Hawaiian in the diaspora involves dynamically reshaping "what it means to be Hawaiian" in a new context with a symbolic concept of *ʻāina* (living on the land), different forms of cultural capital, and diverse non-Hawaiian ethnic groups (in northern California, for example, Hawaiians have lived near and among Latino, Pacific Islander, Vietnamese, and Anglo-American populations). Such reconstruction of culture refuses the age-old opposition between originating culture and Americanization and requires a creative reimagining of culture in new forms and a dynamic remembrance of the cultural past.

In Hawaiian community meetings in northern California and Las Vegas, Nevada, I frequently heard community members narrate tales of Hawaiian history to children of the diaspora, most of whom had never been to Hawaiʻi. The narrative included three main themes: a discussion of the early Hawaiian Kingdom with "sovereign rulers" like King Kamehameha and Queen Liliʻuokalani; a tracing of the U.S. overthrow in 1893, which revolves around the story of Hawaiʻi's last monarch, Queen Liliʻuokalani; and the "search" for another "home." Community members did not emphasize the replacement of their homeland but instead discussed how they are newly creating and extending it in different contexts. "Home" stands as a relational discourse stretched across an interregional network of Hawaiians. It involves remembering the past and discursively incorporating and making sense of the presence of diasporic Hawaiians. One member explained to an audience of children how their community came to be in Las Vegas, Nevada.

> Many came to Hawaiʻi from all over. There were so many people and not enough space or land to go around, especially to Hawaiians. A new government came to be with no sovereign rulers. Like the ones before. And so it happened that Hawaiians . . . our relatives . . . traveled to every port and town and took what they knew. There they did look for new jobs and somewhere . . . somewhere new to create a home . . . to create a community for us to live. (Note set 19, page 10)

The seamless inclusion of diasporic movement as an act of community is not characterized as a form of exile or temporary refuge. In fact, most of these Hawaiians do not return home to live and many do not desire to do so. Diasporic movement is framed as a direct result of the foreign

changes and colonialism in the islands as well as a cultural adjustment.
Jon explains that

> my life here is directly linked to the period of the overthrow.
>
> ^^If that did not happen, I wouldn't be here. No mainland Hawaiian would be here if that did not happen.^^
>
> The time had changed so much
>
> . . . that Hawaiian survival depended on going to the mainland. Spreading our seeds. You could see that here, California, lots there, Washington, all over. The community spread cuz they had to. (Interview 8)

What is most interesting about Jon's comments is that it is the identity articulation of an eighteen-year-old Hawaiian who has not been raised in Hawai'i or even visited there. Instead, Jon is enculturated into a diasporic Hawaiian memory that *remembers* mainland settlement as both a result of colonialism and globalization (with the overthrow directly creating a mainland Hawaiian community) and a survival tactic of Hawaiians to preserve and re-create community. In his narration, Jon shares how diasporic movement became a way to preserve a Hawaiian identity. Diasporic Hawaiians of all ages have fused together historical events, foreign influences, and their settlement on the mainland. The children of diaspora present interesting possibilities for how cultural memory and identity are dynamically constructed beyond and yet in remembrance of Hawai'i.

Spectacling and Staging Hawaiian Community

Every year, the Aloha Club kicks off two major events open to the public; one displaying the arts, crafts, and dances of Hawai'i and Polynesia and the other a representing of a Hawaiian *lū'au*. The first event, the "Pacific Festival," features a dance revue about Hawai'i. As the main event, the dance show invokes both the fetishized images of Hawaiian royalty and tourism's exotic female Hawaiian dancers. Every year, a Hawaiian royal procession begins the dance show. Two females dressed in *mu'umu'u* and carrying *kahili* (feather stands symbolizing the presence of royalty), escort a chief donned in a simulated red woolen cape and an elongated red-lined chief helmet atop his head. The beautiful bright yellow *kahili* is draped over the king's frame. Our master of ceremonies exclaims, "Welcome to Hawai'i. A place of kings and queens and famous leaders!" The unnamed king walks across the stage and peers down at the first two rows of *keiki* (children) from the community. They giggle in amazement and nod their heads.

The host continues. "The king presides over all the islands bringing peace and love with him." Then, from behind, two groups of female dancers enter center stage. They swivel out toward the edge of the stage as the king and his escorts fade behind a taupe curtain. In one quick moment, as royalty is introduced and the face of Hawaiian peace and love is featured, Pacific dance emerges. Several dark-haired women adorned in requisite grass skirts and white cotton-gathered tops move in fast pace to the crooning accompanied by a string guitar and *'ukulele.* They combine various hula forms traditionally held separate—*hula kahiko* (ancient hula pre-dating Cook's arrival) with its traditional gestures for sun, sky, wind, mountain, love, and water and *hapa haole hula* (a contemporary form introduced by early tourist and commercial interests) with band accompaniment, English-style structure and lyrics, and Western-driven topics (monogamous heterosexual love and travel).[49] Renditions of *hapa haole* music—"Blue Hawaii" and "My Little Grass Shack in Kealakekua, Hawaii"—written by white American male composers to suit an orchestra band and a fast-moving, heavily bodied hula, filled the air. The dancers, a core group of community mothers and daughters, annually performed this show. They even traveled to local schools and civic clubs interested in Hawaiian entertainment.

Just as my toe finds the music's rhythm, the second group of dancers suddenly break into the well-known Tahitian hip number. With the drums clocking, Tahitian dancers with high headdresses, bikini tops, and grass skirts shimmy all over the stage, bodily belting their hips. They were not introduced as Tahitian. To the audience, this is still Hawai'i or Polynesia, the same difference. A generalized nativism steadily circulates within the mainland Hawaiian community.

Strangely, this community display reminds me of the once-famous touristy Kodak Hula Show in Waikiki, Oahu. Indeed, the Aloha Club reproduced this very same tourist spectacle—the purely ceremonial placing of Hawaiian royalty as peaceful leaders ushering in Hawaiian celebration and dance while the female native dancers' bodies are sexualized and commodified for popular consumption and the political and cultural power of hula dance forms severely condensed.[50] The dance forms, both Hawaiian and Tahitian, are presumed to be authentic, but they are actually new. These displays were restructured by foreign contact, religious tightholds, and tourist demand for the exotic and inserted back into the Hawaiian culture as authentic or "Hawaiiana."[51]

But, authenticity works differently here. Behind the scenes, the Pacific Festival planning committee, along with the *Kumu hula* (hula teacher), design and stage these annual spectacles. One year, I was asked to serve on the committee and subsequently, I, along with another member, pushed the community to present a different, less touristy dance revue. An onslaught of opposition emerged both on the planning committee and among the larger community populace. One long-time member argued, "This [revue] is what the general public comes for. We need to give them what they want." The club president, Dan, quieted our suggestion, citing the large turnout numbers to the festival (approximately 25,000 each year and increasing) and explained that "the show promotes the kind of community image and visibility we want. It took awhile to establish the Aloha Club out here." He retold the community's modest beginnings. In 1968, there were only ten Hawaiians who had established themselves on the mainland and yearned for a community outlet. At the beginning, Dan said, "no one knew we was out here." Leila also pointed out that "the show pulls in the bigwigs. The buying public. No can change." Community members therefore practiced and guarded spectacled images as identifying factors: material traces that could bring about public recognition as Hawaiians away from home.

Thus, a tourist-impelled spectacle practiced by a mainland Hawaiian community is understood both as a staged form and a meaningful practice. In several interviews, members referred to the festival dance numbers as "showy shows." Yet, in the next breath, they described the numbers as "real faces of traditional hula"; a hula they claimed looks different only because of Westernized changes over the years. The distinctions—"real" and "false," "front" (artificial fronts) and "back" (authentic sites), and "staged" and "lived"—used for Hawaiian cultural practices melt into one another, revealing how these distinctions are not determined in the mere staging of Hawaiianness as exotic, fetishized, and sexualized. They are decided in the moment of its contextually specific use-value for mainlander Hawaiians. Tourist spectacles constituted an attractive public face for the Aloha Club. Their memorable exoticized difference drew on the mainland general audience and distinguished the community through the reproduction of familiar "native" images from global tourism and filmic and televisual imperialism of Hawai'i and its people (*From Here to Eternity, Hawaii Five-0,* and *Magnum P.I.*). Through dance spectacles, the Aloha Club could be, according to club founder Bill, recognized as a "real community."

Such realness ironically relied on and necessitated the mass reproduction of commodified Hawaiianness; dominant recognition by a mainland center and its public demanded a self-spectacling and the practicing of a "reconstructed ethnicity." According to Dean MacCannell, "reconstructed ethnicity" is the "maintenance and preservation of ethnic forms for the entertainment of ethnically different others."[52] This form becomes a useful practicing of "their former colorful ways both as commodities to be bought and sold, and as rhetorical weaponry . . . ; suddenly it is not just ethnicity anymore, but it is understood as rhetoric, as symbolic expression with a purpose or a use-value in a larger system."[53] For the Aloha Club community, capitalizing on a reconstructed Hawaiianness or a commodified nativism involves more than material gain. It allows for mainland recognition of a displaced, diasporic Hawaiian community. It feeds an insecure yet proud group's need for public attention and acknowledgment, a need in active response to a popular assumption that Hawaiian or native identity is inexorably bound to the specific geographic and to the islands. We face the culturalization of the natural—the culturalization of the Hawaiian through the seemingly real geographic—and it is this signifying process that locks indigenous Hawaiians into the place of Hawai'i, a place that specifically reproduces a native subject position as open, inviting, and with *Aloha*. And yet a subject position generally tied to the state, as Hawaiian becomes an identity claim based on geographic occupation in terms of residency and travel. The state abstracts and freely distributes Hawaiianness to all while also confining the racialized group of Hawaiians to blooded identity measures, limited benefits, the disavowal of native self-determination, and the State of Hawaii (as their freedom to move, travel, and settle somewhere else, unlike tourists, is discouraged in that homestead lands and benefits for Hawaiians can only be received upon proof of permanent residency in Hawai'i). Through the popularized remembrances of Hawai'i, the Aloha Club seeks to establish its Hawaiian presence on the mainland ironically by reusing tourist constructions that have historically fixed the Hawaiian to Hawai'i. As Leila pointed out, "The show lets people know we are here." The most commodified images proffer a still-exoticized uniqueness for the Hawaiian community. Through these, they can gain the visibility and stand-out identity that distinguishes them within the mainland social fabric. It is a difference actively pursued, as the most racially Hawaiian-looking dancers are purposefully positioned front and center and are selected to escort and usher in local politicians and officials to our community functions. For two years, I was asked to seat the invited county and state officials at our festival dance revue. Bill explained that I "look like one real Hawaiian" and would be "perfect." When pressed about the specific nature of this essentialized look, he described my "wavy hair and pressed nose" as distinctively Hawaiian, aspects that, when interacting with other cultural groups (Filipinos, Samoans, Chinese), are claimed as their faces as well. Perhaps, again ironically, tourist spectacles provide the mainland Hawaiian community with a particularized yet restructured identity-face that is denied back at home where the State of Hawaii's citizen, resident, and tourist identity positions prevail.

Spectacles of Hawaiianness create even more cultural capital for mainland Hawaiians. They reintegrate a differently located Hawaiianness—those who are mainland born—into a Hawaiian community. Leila, for example, described how important the dance revues were for her children, two of whom participated in the Pacific Festival's dance number.

LEILA: They're [her daughters, Maita and Kiana] not from Hawai'i.
 Born and raised in Colorado, then to here.
 ^^Since around that time, I was 'fraid they'd never grow up knowing what it's like to be Hawaiian.^^
RONA: ^^To be Hawaiian?^^
LEILA: *Oh yes.* To learn our *'olelo* [language]. How we came to be. ^^From Maui to here.^^ If not, I was afraid they would lose their culture. (Interview 4)

Leila continued to explain how her experiences in Maui distantly affect her children; this alone saddened her. They had no knowledge of their family's life in Hawai'i. They were not familiar with their practices at the *lū'au* or in dance, until they watched the festival's shimmying dancers.

^^Sure they have me.^^ No guarantees but. There's no exposure to the lifestyle and how they [Hawaiians] lived. For them made no difference.
 My daughters only became interested in being Hawaiian when they

were small, they would watch those festival dance shows over and over. *Never tired about it.*—[She sighs] They wanted to dance just like them.—
   To be up there on stage.
   Next day, we was at the *halau* place. *Just li' dat.* (Interview 4)

The dance revues therefore serve as critical impetuses for mainland Hawaiian youth to become more involved in cultivating and practicing their own Hawaiianness by joining hula schools. The public attention and the deemed centering of such spectacles piqued the interest of Leila's daughters in Hawaiian culture; something she suggests did not previously exist. Leila's persistent concern for the differences in social location between her and her daughters (her local Hawai'i background and their mainland roots) and their "loss of Hawaiian culture" subsides only through the enticement of the Pacific Festival's popular dance spectacles.

Leila's daughter Maita, an eighteen-year-old college student, elaborated on the value of the dance shows to her.

Pacific Festival brought my sister and I into the *halau*. I wouldn't have joined otherwise.
   Cuz it's so scary. You don't know anyone. You don't know how to do it [dance hula].
   The dances are hard. Oh, ^^the *Kuma hulas* are strict, too.^^
   I'm glad I did it though.
   Each year, we went to watch [the festival revue]. All the women were in sync and they could move. *That's what I really liked.* The quick-moving dances are my favorite.
   The audience gets totally behind it. Moving with the music and cheering them. From then, I wanted to do it too and become more active in the club.
   Before . . . I never cared really. (Interview 17)

The dance revues trigger a curiosity and fascination with a Hawaiianness that seemed so distant to Maita and her sister. For mainland Hawaiian youth, the relation between their experiences and tourist displays of Hawaiianness is loosened and disorganized. These members often first learn about their Hawaiian identity from public images and displays (television images, travel magazines, and mainland community stagings) and not from privatized practice. The entryway into their

Hawaiianness is therefore established through publicized dance revues, and only after this point do they come in contact with privatized Hawaiian beliefs and practices. Maita explained how the festival dance showings opened her eyes to both hula instruction and historical narrations of indigenous Hawaiians.

> RONA: What do you do at hula practice?
> MAITA: You always run through dance drills and practice the dances you gotta do. Sometimes though you practice speaking Hawaiian with a partner. Or you learn how to make the traditional skirts and costumes.
>
> *That shocked me.* ^^The first three classes Lori [her sister] and I had, we didn't dance.
>
> I thought as soon as you walk through the door, you get to learn the hip moves or the *ipu* dance. Unhuh.
>
> No, they made us go to the library. I had to look up what history books had to say about Hawaiians.
>
> We didn't find much. *Kumu* taught us that our history is oral and by movement.
>
> . . . The next couple of sessions, you had to learn basic Hawaiian language elements. If you don't practice, *Kumu* no let you dance. You get the whole thing.

Thus, although a trendy, popularized image of nativism impels mainland Hawaiians to participate in identity practices (dance) in the first place, the public front (festival shows) eventually transitions into private memory (*halau* practices of history and language) through which young members are reincorporated into a new and strange Hawaiianness. Touristic showiness and the popularizing of the Hawaiian speaks then to distantly involved mainland Hawaiian youth, placing them in closer contact with their own Hawaiianness. Through a public face—a staging—differently situated Hawaiians can both practice and reshape identity according to their sociohistorical circumstances and locations.

Another member, John, a fifteen-year-old male dancer praises the Aloha Club for bringing Hawai'i to him.

> JOHN: Everyone asks if I'm from Hawai'i. ^^You get that?^^
> RONA: All the time.
> JOHN: I'm Hawaiian but I wasn't born there. I haven't even been there.
> RONA: Ever?

JOHN: Nope. Maybe later on I will. Now I get it all from the club.
   The people . . . they teach about *'ohana* [family]. The functions show us ol' kine dances, ^^all the past Hawaiians.^^
      . . . No difference. I know it as who I am today.
      No different from a local Hawaiian . . . like Dad.
      Dad and I, we end up the same. (Interview 12)

When John refers to sameness (that he, a mainland Hawaiian who has never been to the place of Hawai'i, and his father, a Maui native, are the "same kine" Hawaiian), he seems to be discussing a true, authentic form of Hawaiianness, an identity position he feels should not be compromised or subordinated under a more meaningful or Hawai'i-centered Hawaiianness. His verbal performance of his sameness helps to authenticate his mainland identity to that of one at home in Hawai'i, challenging the notion on the part of both dominant society and Hawaiian sovereignty activists that a Hawaiian should remain on the *'āina*. They should live as nativized citizens to dominant society and as a politically and spiritually infused *Kanaka Maoli* to sovereignty activists. John narrates how the Aloha Club community continually circulates Hawaiianness through collective rituals (the gathering of families, *lū'au*, language school) and community functions (where Hawaiian games, dances, and stories are reenacted). Community life—either here (on the mainland) or there (in Hawai'i)—unduly reinscribes real practices.

And so it just might be that a lived Hawaiianness can traverse geography. That is, Hawaiians can be who they are in multiple spaces and sites, replacing their identities in varied positionalities (Hawaiians born and raised on the mainland, Hawaiians who have never been to Hawai'i). Thus, reconstructed Hawaiianness and even one publicly shaped through touristlike spectacles (ceremonial narratives about unnamed royalty and foreign structured dances) stand as identity productions that do great cultural work. The productivity of such community reimaginings (the redeployment of even the most gaudy and popular forms from an exploitative tourist arena) might be Dean MacCannell's greatest oversight.[54] Practicing the travel popular of Hawaiianness has something to offer community members. It speaks to their need for authenticity in relation to home (Hawai'i) and at the same time authenticates their own identities as Hawaiians. Indeed, while the Aloha Club's identity constructions and images are differently arranged and performed than what might appear in local Hawai'i, their reconstructions—to them—are the same. Traveling spectacles provide new and adapted points of identification for differently situated Hawaiians. These spectacles, according to another parent, "keep the youth's interest." They couldn't be reached any other way. Hawai'i was a distant place etched on their screens and in their magazines and socially, anything Hawaiian was a novelty and not an everyday practice. Our youth—our future—surprisingly become familiarized with cultural practice through the tourist popular. The brighter the lights, the better, the faster the dance styles, the more appeal there is, and the flashier the community show, the more attention is inflected to such cultural displays.[55] Displays that would later lead them—quietly and offstage—to private identity practices reserved for the sanctity of concealed and much-guarded locations (*halau* practice, which is reserved solely for members). The Aloha Club maximizes images of Hawai'i and Hawaiians to better address mainlander Hawaiians, using what is available and what at first glance does not seem useful to draw their members into their Hawaiianness. But, MacCannell's oversight that reconstructed ethnicity forms too often exploit the displayed natives is the risk we take in the Aloha Club. In the Pacific Festival and community dance revues, we risk further reifying the popularized images of romantic travel and the normatively benevolent Hawaiian, holding close privatized identity practices made possible only through such public faces. Dominant recognition might be ours at the expense of fixing nativism in alignment with racialized travel fantasies. But, in the end, the Aloha Club trusts who they are and without hesitation rely on the privatized cultural knowledges of parents and *Kumu hula* in reaching a Hawaiianness displaced in pressure from forces such as the state and the national economy.

Sovereign Relations

In new spaces, diasporic Hawaiians continually negotiate the oppositional construction of "on-island" authenticity and "off-island" assimilation. These Hawaiians reimagine their unique relation to the homeland and to one another as Hawaiians. One interviewee, Moana, professed her family's link to King Kamehameha. "The King Kamehameha?" I asked in disbelief. She nodded. "*The King Kamehameha.* Our great leader." She didn't stop there. She showed me old photographs, paintings, journal entries (written in Hawaiian), and name listings. These would establish her professed linkage to Hawaiian royalty, to the Great King Kamehameha I. Her shaking finger traced for me her mother and father and then her father's great-great-grandfather, who could be connected to the royal court of the early 1800s, a time when Kamehameha I had risen to power.

> No [his name] was the second cousin to King Kamehameha I. ^^Through this line.^^ [She pointed to an archival graph of the Kamehameha line reproduced in several Hawaiian history books.]
>
> We are told he worked under him. Like a server. A carrier. (Interview 17)

I encountered these kinds of claims quite frequently in the interviews. Diasporic community members would share their tragic performances of proving and intersperse stories of their family relations to Hawaiian royalty, particularly to King Kamehameha and Queen Liliʻuokalani. After thirty or so oral histories, it dawned on me that this was the raw material of identity resignifications. We were deep in *piʻikoi*, the practice of "claiming to be of higher rank than one is," to claim to be something one is not.[56] I had heard the word before. Relatives would say, "No make *piʻikoi*. Tell them who you are, be true" or "No make high nose or *piʻikoi*." Hawaiians were typically told not to act or talk out of their own cultural place and location; speak one's true status and name. But I had done it before. I had claimed to be a close relative of the great Queen Liliʻuokalani. I would tell my friends that I was of Hawaiian royalty. Some say there is a book alleged to list every family line related to the Kalakaua (Queen Liliʻuokalani's) dynasty. In high school and college, I told everyone, "My name is in these pages."

Moana shared every genealogical table and faded photo she could find to talk about her family and their royal blood. She had no concrete proof King Kamehameha I was her descendant. In fact, the dates of the designated server in Kamehameha I's court did not coincide with the estimated time of Kamehameha I's existence. It did not matter, for her practicing of *piʻikoi* represented a significant identity encoding for today's Hawaiians. Through historical retellings, Moana could authenticate and sanctify both her personal experience and individual voice as a Hawaiian on the mainland. She, a woman who was forced to move to the mainland with her son when her homestead loan fell through, longed for a time, as she put it, "when being Hawaiian was a real high honor . . . ^^When you neva show nutin.^^ You had the land and your family. And the *ali'i* wen watch over you. The high times of Hawaiians." Moana's seemingly nostalgic longing stems from the historically specific overthrow and land dispossession of *Kanaka Maoli,* from the time of the Hawaiian Kingdom when the *ali'i* ruled over the *maka'āinana* to the Western writing over of their names and lands. This communication practice of identity, *pi'ikoi,* spread throughout diasporic Hawaiian communities as a practice in response to both a threatened and dispossessed historical memory by colonialism and neocolonial globalization *and* the marginalizing perception of "off-island" Hawaiians as "absentee" or less-Hawaiian cultural members. We remembered and redrew our family lines to sovereign monarchs who represented the authentic Hawaiian traditions and spirit. We would work hard to connect our lives with since-passed historical moments of the Hawaiian Kingdom. In this practice, Hawaiians continually refer to the historical past of Hawai'i as originating, but they also use it as a dynamic link that exceeds specific genealogies and bloodlines and geographic place. Such references are not merely nostalgic remembrances or romanticizing "museum-like" moves used to appropriate a foregone cultural past. "Time" and "history" are instead resignified not in terms of the past but in context of the present. Speaking of the past, which is always a resignified construction, fulfills a cultural function in response to the present. Linking one's identity to that of the sovereign monarchs enables diasporic Hawaiians to authenticate their identity claim as a Hawaiian and to claim a political power and independence that is deemed as suppressed by globalizing forces, state agencies, and foreign control of Hawai'i.

Pi'ikoi thus works to reestablish the political prestige and power stripped away from Western colonialism. It, in this community context, did not work to increase just an individual's name and reputation. It was practiced to narratively re-create an entire Hawaiian *lāhui* and an era in which their subjectivity was preserved and protected. It also created a means to authenticate their mainland positionalities via relations to historical figures. Moana highlights the glossing over of the Hawaiian hegemony of Kamehameha I's time. She describes her descendant as a royal servant under the king, which wouldn't make him a blood relative (royal lines presided over court servants and the commoners). It becomes an interesting narrative strategy that speaks to the current political and diasporic conditions of Hawaiians. Western colonialism surely helped to obfuscate the rigid social divisions in the traditional Hawaiian hegemony; after Cook's arrival, all Hawaiians—across the hierarchy range—fought for their existence as a Hawaiian nation, as traditional divisions politically collapsed. So, as Hawaiians struggled for a space in which to exist at all, Hawaiian royals were politically transformed into cultural heroes and brave warriors fighting for all Hawaiians. In this vein Moana identifies her descendant as Kamehameha's server. His descendancy is not a matter of blood or genealogy; rather it refers to his historical placing and situatedness. Moana's great-great-great-grandfather is signified as a relative to Kamehameha by virtue of historical moment; she could connect him to his time and his sovereign monarchy. She has authenticated her family line and magnified her cultural voice as descendant of Kamehameha's time. It was a time when Hawaiianness was an already assumed honor and when it already held cultural capital. And it was a historical time when the connection would never be denied. Significantly, these *pi'ikoi* appeals refuse a geographic specificity of Hawaiianness in that the genealogical and blood connections provide mainland Hawaiians with a sense of cultural permanency and interiority. Connecting a sovereign ruler in terms of genealogy naturalizes a Hawaiian identity in new spaces.

In another interview, a "mixed Hawaiian," Ken, from the Big Island who now lives in northern California, practices *pi'ikoi* in relation to Queen Lili'uokalani. Here Ken and I *pi'ikoi* each other, competing for Hawaiian political status in a time and space where Hawaiianness carries a heavy burden of proof.

KEN: Hawaiian Homes threw away our applications. You know the forms?

Oh we fo grumble at them. Again we wen back. *Two months.*

Two months and den say we need other forms.

^^You see, Rona^^ we had down Loilea for our great-grandma's name. She wen back long you know. Over to Lili'uokalani's cousin.

RONA: Queen Lili'uokalani?

KEN: Yes. ^^Queen Lili'uokalani.^^ She was us. Oh, excuse, we one of her.

RONA: How do you know?

KEN: In the archives have two parched registers of land allotments. One has Loilea down. And we wen show DHHL. They didn't accept. Said we back to square one.

^^But I know. Royalty li dat neva give that much land to just anybody?

RONA: Sometimes they did.

KEN: No, you tink! Dat much only go to one *reeeellaatiiive.* It's there. Trust me. We a noble line. Always belonged to Hawaiian church. Sang and dance just li her [Lili'uokalani's] family.

RONA: We're supposedly related to her too.

KEN: Oh yeah. How?

RONA: Our names. [Gave him our names.]

KEN: Neva heard of dem. You see, Rona, her line is well known. Like mine. Loilea—that's known around Hawai'i and the land register. That's proof. (Interview 68)

Ken and I mildly rally as to who is more closely related to the famous queen. In the act of articulating a blood relation to Queen Lili'uokalani, he authenticates his own experience by claiming that his family had always practiced Hawaiian tradition much like Lili'uokalani. The queen was known for resisting American attempts to destroy traditional Hawaiian practices (like *lū'au,* dance, and language). By linking himself to her line, historical moment, and traditions, Ken authenticates his Hawaiianness in his new locale. He later explained, "Hey, I no look like one. You look through my line, no doubt." Half "Hawaiian" and half English, Ken's *pi'ikoi* narratively brings into being an original Hawaiianness physically absent and state-denied by the DHHL at "home." What is concealed and unrecognized in the state of their blood could be recreated as authentic Hawaiianness and Hawaiian sovereignty and pride through *pi'ikoi.* Ken and other Hawaiians on the mainland engage in *pi'ikoi* in order to authenticate their mainland identities and experiences and to remember a historical past and sovereign period that traverses geographic boundaries in identifying who they are. Through diasporic community life and collective memory, mainland Hawaiians can aspire to be as they once were and still are: concealed in the blood.

Performing Blood Authority

Koko embeds the community vernacular in the Aloha Club in sophisticated and creative ways. I was stunned at how deep a blooded communication practice identified and reimagined the Hawaiian voice. At first, I rationalized the blood references as dominant metaphors, thus revealing how the state once again overdetermined Hawaiian community. After a series of ethnographic interviews and oral histories, I knew more: <u>blood talk carried a resonating force within Hawaiians' everyday practices</u>:

> ^^It's got to be in the blood.^^ [Folds one leg over the other; he falls back into the chair.]
>
> My brothers, sister, and I all at least 75 percent Hawaiian. With what we know now. <u>Being Hawaiian is about a blood tie</u>. What we share, the legacies . . . *It's got to be.* (Harry, a Chinese-Hawaiian contractor in Northern California. Interview 4a)

> //No, it [blood quanta] is accurate. Prince Jonah Kuhio knew what he was doing.// [She smiles, pausing for a moment.]
>
> You see, da kine 100 percent are the old-timers, *they* live Hawaiian style—speak ol' Hawaiian, fishing village, go Hawaiian church. Things like dis.
>
> You mixed kine—50 percent—are more Americanized, parents married all kine, no dance and live how was early day. (Elia, a seventy-year-old Hawaiian woman from Kauai now living in the Southwest. Interview 7a)

It was not enough just to note blood. I needed to situate blood in relation to the specific context historically and legally framing Hawaiianness. As I uncovered blood work in community practice, I also began analyzing the Hawaiian Homes Commission hearings of 1920. As one member emphasized, "Hawaiian Homes—that's where *koko* began."

Rigid definitions of Hawaiian identity centered on the scientific verifiability of blood and its unquestioned nature in addition to the state's supposedly neutral procedures in proving, presenting, and certifying one's blood quantum and thus, one's Hawaiianness. Their performances in the archives and their own family albums problematized the professed certainty of the state and scientized blood technologies. Just as Hawaiians hit the state limits of documenting their identities, they created new ones, redrawing identity links to Hawaiian royalty and the historical periods they represented. However, blood proves to be more flexible and in-movement than state science's matching/nonmatching criteria. Blood can be performed to its endmost state point and can be resignified through the Hawaiian community vernacular.

Here the discursive objectification of Hawaiian blooded identities is

Blood = power

reproduced throughout the Hawaiian vernacular, and for many, this alone seems to illustrate the truthfulness of factual parentage to indigenous Hawaiian identity—that the blood preceded the political conditions framed through blood (e.g., distribution of land and social services, sovereignty claims) and constituted the most appropriate criteria for the HHCA. But, how is an identity definition created in conditions of dominance—legislated blood quantum—used and practiced within Hawaiian community vernacular? And what might this mean for a Hawaiian subjectivity that resides somewhere between being either fully overdetermined by the law or resignifiable through the law?

Traces of Blood

Hawaiian community members practice blood talk in their daily lives by invoking blood as real, as here and now. They refer to blood as coming first and as being a priori. For example, in a Hawaiian community press release in response to new blood quantum mandates hitting the floor in the State Capitol Mililani Trask explains that "all the statistics demonstrate that Native Hawaiians of 50 percent blood and more have the greatest need for housing, for food, for assistance; they suffer from the highest suicide rate, post- and prenatal losses, drug use, and incarceration. It would serve our population well to make sure that those persons receive the benefits first."[57] Steve, a mainland Hawaiian, refers to blood and the state of Hawaiians.

> [Scooping the food, Steve continues to look down at his plate.] In fact, I saw a TV special and we're going to go extinct of pure Hawaiians in about another 100 years.
>
> Because of intermarriage.
>
> ^^But to me, on the health side, intermarriage is good for us. It strengthens our bloodline. In the past we used to marry to keep our bloodline, but it weakened it, the bloodline. But to me intermarriage is the best thing that ever happened to Hawaiians.^^
>
> There'll never be a nation of pure Hawaiians anymore or a nation of totally only Hawaiians.
>
> We're too intermingled with non-Hawaiians. [Pause.]
>
> In fact, there's no place except homestead lands, where you will find pure or completely only Hawaiians. ___So what do you do?___ (Interview 2)

negative stats about blood... why proud?

Lei, a mixed Japanese, Chinese, Hawaiian woman and an Aloha Club member, addresses blood as a contemporary issue:

> [She is a bit distracted. We are passing out event flyers at the Pacific Festival. She vacillates between passing out flyers, touching my arm, pointing her finger, and motioning me to listen to her.] *Percentage tells* you that pure bloods are having more difficulties than mixed-bloods. *I personally agree.*
>
> *They . . . pure bloods . . . have* a hard time fitting in a Western life-style. They need the land more than us. They should get *'āina* before any of us. No one wants to admit that, but that is the truth.
>
> We just have to face the odds. . . . That's what I say. (Interview 17)

Throughout variously situated positions, Hawaiians practice—through speech—blood as real to their lives. Each of these examples reproduces a sequence in which blood is deemed by communicative signification as a reflector of material conditions and resources, material and cultural experiences, and in most cases, suffering. Blood is presupposed and practiced as always coming first and long before their act of talking about it (before their at-the-moment speech act narratively performing blood). Thus, through talk, blood is naturalized and reified into existence, a naturalization afforded by communication practice. The repeated performativity of blood as always "coming before" is enabled and made more powerful through the naturalized language and imagery discursively created around blood (through formal policy, identity certification for health care, and the rhetoric of science). Consequently, the performative speech of blood allows for its verifiability and symbolically makes it real among Hawaiians.

Based on a Foucauldian perspective, Judith Butler recognizes the power structures constituting discursive objects but grounds such a critique in the performativity of it all. The performative act of a blooded Hawaiianness "brings into being or enacts that which it names, and so marks the constitutive or productive power of discourse."[58] Simultaneously though, somewhere within the moving performativity of discourse, through its necessary repetitive nature and coding, the agency of resignifying originally dominant terms and subject positions, of remaking seemingly locked-in subject positions, becomes possible. Blood could be performed and it could give them more—in excess of state limits.

(Mis)recognition of Blood

In the same breath, as they communicatively make blood real, many community members also emphasize its arbitrary nature. They individually bemoan the difficulties in proving quantum and challenging the widely interpreted public records, documents, and census reports. One member, Bob, pulls from his own ill-fated performance of proving.

> RONA: Hawaiians ^^are^^?
> BOB: The ^^real,^^ first settlers in the islands.
> Descendants of descendants of the originals.
> Me^^? No more. Not really. [He laughs softly.] Not one written record exists for my parents, their families, my cousins li that. Believe me, Rona, it's a long story. A big mess, really. You wouldn't believe.
> We tried to match a name of ours—^^Lahua^^—with my name—^^Keoni.^^
> *You cannot find.* It's registered as *Lahia* and DHHL won't have it. [Sighing.] _____On so many forms like this, with lots of families, the names are all misspelled or missing._____
> Percentage amounts too; like with us, one says we about 75 percent, another only *50 percent,* and one I just found about 32 percent.
> It's all up in the air. And it has a lot to do with the scriptors of the census process. Scribes?
> Everybody wen' talk different. (Interview 48)

[Handwritten marginal note: "Who to trust?" with an arrow]

In this and several other private memory interviews, Hawaiians expose the state identification process as skewed and the census records as wholly inaccurate. Bob and others bemoan the state of blood and strongly emphasize that there is something about the formalized blood technology (via administration and procedurality) that is not verifiably accurate.

Economy of Cultural and Speaking Practices

It appears then that if the *koko* is deemed real and yet its accurate recording flawed, then who should emerge as the only true authorities or cultural experts in recognizing Hawaiianness but Hawaiians themselves? In community vernacular, Hawaiians narratively and performatively emerge as the sole cultural authorities of who they are. Matt and Tricia, for example, establish the true criteria for Hawaiianness:

> RONA: Last time, you talked about "definite ways to tell one *kanaka*"?
> MATT: [Nodding head.] Yeah, I . . . I think of it one of two ways.

You can point to *kanaka,* you *know* who is, where they are from, how much they are, how they grew up. ^^We knew plenty da kine pure.^^ You knew, by their last names, where they wen grow up.

Like which side of the street they wen live. You know how traditional the family was. At parties, you knew who danced, who sang ol kine, wen prepare Hawaiian style *imu* [underground oven].

It's all the old timers who *make* [died] by now. Today is real different, too much blending of local and Hawaiian style, not real old style, not like the pure kine *kanaka.*

Koko can't be seen or made. . . . It's who you are.

How you carry the culture.

TRICIA: Ehh. [Shaking head; she reaches over behind her.]

Pleny more not pure, I come from a line ^^originally Hawaiian.^^ And we lived on homestead, Waianae side, Mama raised us a Hawaiian way.

^^You know all kine?^^

We wen talk Hawaiian in da house, outside no more. You not allowed. Da bradas at school wen keep you in line. Oder kine, today kids, mixed Hawaiians lived different, little bit Chinese, Japanese.

Little bit here, der. Dissolved. More mixed.

Cheryl dem [her grandniece's family], they're half Portuguese, one quarta Chinese, one quarta Hawaiian, they no understood the difference. They grew up on da Mainland, their mama was from here, they joined clubs like dis, more Hawaiian style but not da same as us.

They speak and think differently. For themselves, not for da group. With one different heart.

Cheryl did teach dem Hawaiian I taught her. So our world may be returning but ^^again still different.^^

^^*Haoles,* not da rest aren't Hawaiian. Just not naturally.^^ In time, they open their ways to living, . . . thinking like one *kanaka.* Pleny marry Hawaiians and that's how. (Interview 15)

In this rich excerpt, Hawaiians themselves are deemed the experts in recognizing those who are truly Hawaiian. The authority of blood and the distinction of blood purity are associated with particular names, traditional cultural practices (*lū'au* and language practices), and community spaces, or those who practiced particular traditions and lived in designated areas are identified as the "most" or "pure" Hawaiian. This interview is laden with references to a complex internal hierarchy of Hawaiianness and authenticity. Those who enact specific practices (eating, dancing, speaking Hawaiian in a certain way) and are originally from (born and raised in) Hawai'i are <u>real</u> and <u>original Hawaiian</u> and likely to be <u>pure</u>. Thus, <u>mainland Hawaiian identities continue</u> to be inferiorized within the <u>Aloha Club and the Hawaiian vernacular.</u> Matt and Tricia conjoin mainland Hawaiian identities with those of mixed blood and you get the sense that these members are conceptualized as being "different kine Hawaiians." They are perceived not only as acting differently than the sanctified, originally Hawaiian *kupuna,* but also internally as being of "different kine blood." A generational hierarchy therefore takes form. Older generations more connected—in time and space—to old Hawai'i and its traditions are again exalted and made culturally nostalgic through the scientific and historical authority of blood, while <u>mixed and main-land Hawaiians represent the effects of modernity and foreign contact</u> (their diminished blood substance captures them as lesser than "real" Hawaiians). They, to many older community members, are reminders of a tragically changing Hawaiianness, a reminder of foreign intrusion into their once-pure culture. Resulting from this hierarchy is an internal economy of cultural and speaking practices among Hawaiians. To be of a certain time, place, and through specific practices is to be able to truly speak as a pure Native Hawaiian; to belong to the mainland, several blood natures, and the modern aftermath upon which Hawaiian life is to be mixed, to be less, and if part European heritage, to be named "more *haole.*" At the same time, both are connected through Hawaiian collective memory yet situated differently by way of historical and political moment, and both are within the framings of Hawaiianness.

In contrast, Matt and Tricia briefly refer to those standing outside of such delineated identifications. This is not to say, according to Tricia, that "da rest aren't Hawaiian," just not by way of the *koko.* Tricia explains, "^^*Haoles,* not da rest aren't Hawaiian. Just not naturally.^^ In time, they open their ways to living, . . . thinking like one *kanaka.* Pleny marry Hawaiians and that's how." She presents a complex sequence of identity, one involving blood and heart. While blood economizes identity and speaking practices internally among "pure" Hawaiian elders and their "mixed" youth, in the public outside sphere blood isolates out Hawaiians in general. It is a strange moment when the naturalized image of blood reifies their cultural authority as Hawaiian over any claims by genealogically "outside" *haoles* and Locals. Unseen and unproven yet spoken and performed blood makes the difference; it makes Hawaiians naturally Hawaiian. It establishes indigenous rights to an identity historically and legally written over as U.S. citizen, wards of the state, and the people of *Aloha*.

"Hawaiianness at heart" is therefore an identity distinction granted to outsiders in the Aloha Club without the natural authority its genealogically bound members hold. "Hawaiians at heart" are not originally Hawaiian then; they are friends who gradually learn the practices of the Hawaiian community. They are also those non-Hawaiian (genealogically speaking) spouses who married many Hawaiian men and women in the islands and on the mainland. Thus, "Hawaiianness at heart" within the Aloha Club serves an essential role. It involves Hawaiians' mainland friends and more of the mainland social fabric into a largely unrecognized mainland Hawaiian community. Most importantly, it responds to a particular social relation historically and structurally framed by the state's misrecognition of Hawaiians and their economic-pressured migration away from *'āina*: the increasing rates of inter-marriage between Hawaiian men and women with *haoles*, Locals, and mainlanders (Asian Pacific Americans, Latino/as, Blacks).

Bill, an officer of the Aloha Club, described "Hawaiianness at heart" as speaking to the "non-Hawaiian mothers and fathers of our Hawaiian youth. They still part of Hawaiians but in a different way." This social relation is an adaptation to a changing Hawaiian community and a growing mixed Hawaiian progeny. Surely, they couldn't exclude the changing Hawaiian family (as Lei, a member, explained, "A non-Hawaiian mother loves her Hawaiian child just as a Hawaiian mother does. She is not Hawaiian but becomes more so through her child"). The mixed Hawaiians are therefore quite critical. They create a mediating link between an outside foreign relation and a "pure" and historically original Hawaiian identity position. Through the mixed bloods, new types of social relations with *haoles*, Locals, and mainlanders could be shaped as Hawaiianness is pressured to re-create itself somewhere within their articulations of historical nostalgia. Heart, therefore, represents an amazing identity practice. It embodies the spirit of a racialized group actively exerting its own identity authority at the same time that it includes variously positioned outsiders (defined by blood) on different terms and through an internal hierarchy. Such a schemata captures a community strategy tailor-made for a particular historical and political moment (the now burgeoning growth of mixed Hawaiians, increased migration of Hawaiians to the mainland, and further state repression as blood quantum mandates are both rigidified and liberalized).

One of our community's *kupuna*, Moana, performs her blood authority and recirculates the hierarchy of authenticity. She narrates:

> I am half Chinese, half Hawaiian. Our mama was *hanai* [adopted] by a Chinese family, so really we might even be more Hawaiian dan Chinese. ^^Some say almost pure Hawaiian.^^
>
> *They say* we wen come from one traditional, very Hawaiian line. They say we were famous weavers.
>
> So many like dis are gone or have really paid. We're a forgotten people.
>
> No land . . .
>
> For history's sake, we da links.
>
> And now . . . so much of what used to be is all *pau* [finished] no more. Every ting we do is modern. The *hula*, . . . our music, and even Hawaiian with the *keiki* [children]. Every ting is much different den before. (Interview 6)

Moana emphasizes the purity (and thus original Hawaiianness) of her line. She speaks as a pure Hawaiian who lived in the presence of a more authentic and true Hawaiian life and slightly degrades today's modern practices. From her voice, it seemed it could never be the way it once was. Moana's references to a bygone past and a dead Hawaiian life operate differently than the similar encoded forms within the tourist sites of Waimea Falls Park and Iolani Palace. Not only are they spoken from different power positions, one is strengthened through the image of death (the tourist arena sells the fantasy of living a dead culture; that is the thrill) and the other through the image of living. Within the Aloha Club, Moana narrates herself and others as living links—as surviving witnesses of a Hawaiianness since past. As living links, she and other Hawaiians remain as the last vestiges of a now-discursively sacred Hawaiianness. She holds the cultural knowledge, experience, and blood missing from her modern counterparts. Thus, she communicatively authenticates her experience and authority as a Hawaiian. Images of a bygone, dead past sanctify then the only living trace left from that time: herself—Moana.

Writing In and Writing Out

As Judith Butler theorized, the performativity of discourse houses its own becoming and undoing, its own actions-in-process.[59] Such is the case for Hawaiians whose subjectivity is *layered* with a resiliently dangerous dominant framework of blood authority and a community's deployment of blood as a means to write themselves back into indigenous authority through the scientific reification of blood (and its undisputed, naturalized circulation today). In a private memory interview with Aloha Club member John, he explains what a Hawaiian is not:

> JOHN: You ^^cannot^^ just *be* from Hawai'i.
> Living there for years.
> Living on state land.
> I mean that's fine, but . . . *it is about* originally being Hawaiian and how much you are. ^^Myself,^^ I am half Hawaiian, half *haole*. The Hawaiian blood part distinguishes you, what you can genealogically trace as living proof.
>
> I see too many . . . they say they Hawaiian cuz live there. And that is just not true.
>
> At one point, can tel' by home. Or by church, . . . the religion one went to. After years, so many missionaries and visitors stayed here and we let them.
>
> Now, today, the only way you can know if da guy next to you is Hawaiian, is by blood amount . . . ^^you know, the *koko*.^^ [He stops for a minute or so.]
>
> RONA: How can you tell blood amount?
>
> JOHN: ^^How can you tell? Come on, Rona.^^ [He laughs heartily, pausing afterward.]
>
> You know, everyone goin' know their blood amount. You have to these days. Survival.
>
> When the state makes you keep your records straight, I mean all the families do the research.
>
> So, like my *'ohana*, we goin papers proving 50 percent and I can tell otherwise. Goin with . . . records, certificates, maps . . . _____tell you the amount._____
>
> By the way people look, how they are. I knew you one—your features, Halualani come on, one rare name li dat. Pleny rest have real old

[handwritten annotation: Who's to say?]

names—Niihau . . . those you can tell, you know roughly how Hawaiian the family is.

Aala [another member in the group] she lighter, but her nose, her
eyes. Very much like Hawaiians.

^^Hawaiians about what is here [pounds on chest].^^

Anyone can act like one *kanaka*—right, you could fish like one,
weave,

dance the most difficult hula, know the '*olelo*.

The Aloha Club, plenty *haole*, guys from Hawai'i, act like *kanaka*,
but no more the blood.

^^So cannot truly be.^^

But it is our way to still share what we can. (Interview 10)

John, formerly a Hawaiian homesteader, goes on to describe the oppressive sociopolitical conditions of Hawai'i, rapid business development on
Hawaiian lands, and the ongoing dispossession of Hawaiians. He makes
reference to the constructs of blood percentages as metaphors, expressions, and performative utterances, only, however, in defining who is
not Hawaiian. A grammar of terms originally created formally to identify Hawaiians is reperformed by community members to culturally reclaim their own Hawaiianness and deny the equality claims of "Hawaiianness at heart," or of being originally Hawaiian through emotional
identification, residency, and colonialist benefiting. John is quick to
mention instances of "false" Hawaiianness and curiously, he uses blood
quantum to expose its falsity. The performativity of his speech grows increasingly complex as he speaks of Hawaiianness as originally fixed, as a
priori, and culturally first.

At the outset, John argues that blood amount isolates out the true
Hawaiians from the false ones (the state residents and Locals who claim
to be Hawaiian). He historically specifies how the recognition of Hawaiianness changed as a result of foreign contact, Western religion, and tourism. Thus, in the end, only blood amount stands out as the real identifying factor. Although blood amount is described as encompassing names,
certificates, and racial (physical) essence, John implicitly delimits these as
belonging to a particular group—Hawaiians, a group that he claims is
not enacted, it just is. For acting like a Hawaiian (dancing, speaking the
language, and creating Hawaiiana) does not necessarily make a Hawaiian. Rather, John suggests that acting like a Hawaiian is easily taken up,

learned, and routinized. Cultural enactment in this sense is deceptive. Identity actions can indeed deceive us as Hawaiianness takes more than performance. It is clear from John's earlier comments that it takes the naturalized authority of blood, which he performs and brings about through speech and strengthens through the scientific image and rhetorical leverage of blood. Thus, I find that John and several other members ironically represent identity recognition as stemming from blood substance and not through recognizable actions. Blood is however performatively constituted through a speech act. Thus, through a surrounding discourse of blood, Hawaiians like John seem to invoke the naturalization of blood as a vehicle of their unquestionable authority and authenticity as Hawaiians. He reuses state-originated blood quanta to redefine who is not Hawaiian against a public sentiment of claiming everyone is.

The community vernacular reveals a performativity of identity that politically uses the scientific realism of a blood representation. Critical studies scholar Dorinne Kondo explains that "'realism' itself must be problematized and opened to the play of historically and culturally specific power relations. The speaker's position, the intended audience, the stakes, and the larger discursive fields of history and power through which meanings are constituted are not mere 'contexts' that nuance an essentialized meaning; rather, these are essential in determining the political weight of any narrative strategy."[60]

Thus, as the sociopolitical context reproduces and widely distributes a Hawaiian identity claim to state residents and visiting tourists and Hawaiian politics still faces a readjusting state, the Hawaiian vernacular relies on a scientific classification for its presumed authority and discursive leverage to make real a more exclusive and privatized Hawaiian identity and salvage and fortify their own cultural voice and authority. Ironically, the down side of this performative remaking lies in its many risks: the continued naturalization of blood parentage and the *repetition* of the dominant discursive structure established through formal policy and law; the delimiting of Hawaiianness as warranting material resources and inherently political stances, which can further divide Hawaiians as a whole. However, blooded speaking practices found in the Aloha Club are more likely to outlast the state system of regulating and surveilling Hawaiian blood quantum, thus ensuring re-created Hawaiianness its authority for some time, perhaps even beyond the life of the state itself.

In this way, Hawaiian members will continue to authorize their names, experiences, and identities in relation to the signifying power of blood. Resituating blood quantum as a layered performativity filled with dominant encodings and challenging reconstitutions suggests that a Hawaiian social subject can reemerge quite differently from its installment in the most repressive governmental structure.

CONCLUSION

At last, on these pages, we meet and know a Hawaiianness culturally embodied, practiced, and with lived meaning. A Hawaiianness that refuses to be imprisoned in the historical wax museum of culture. It is a Hawaiian community that no longer needs the public formality of quotation marks. In this chapter, we engaged a lived mainland Hawaiian community, the Aloha Club, which practices Hawaiianness—not within their own terms, but within their own specific locations and collective memories.

The Aloha Club remembers their displacement by the colonial state (the federal governmental power and its administrative arm, the localized State of Hawaii) in terms of the mass production of a Hawaiianness through the state and the tourist arena and their specific confinement to state agencies. On the mainland, economic and material pressures are mitigated by a wider range and availability of jobs and, in some areas, a more manageable cost of living. And if they could not regain their *'āina,* the mainland offered some economic solace. However, the identity needs of Hawaiians are not confined to being only of a material or socioeconomic nature; they relate to a historical memory of agency, freedom, and pride. The Aloha Club members yearned for a community visibility in their newly situated space. They wanted to be remembered and recognized by all before them. Such mainland recognition could be tied both to an externally structured need for dominant approval and a realistic aspect of a community that wanted to integrate their members into the mainland social fabric (where social benefits, contextualized local service, and more funding could be secured). By forging their own unique exotic difference on the mainland, the community guarantees a sense of security and attention paid for mainland Hawaiians, done surprisingly through the tourist popular. Flashy dance spectacles and community shows exoticize the mainland Hawaiian community, establishing an appealing and nonthreatening connection to the general public. In this way, they publicize their existence and secure much-needed local populace support.

Just as it seemed as if we sold a part of ourselves in these dance spectacles, the practice of identity reveals its dynamic, moving form. The mainland community whose Hawaiian youth relate differently to their Hawaiianness are reintegrated into privatized memory only through the tourist popular. It becomes their point of identification—the remaining connection for a Hawai'i that seems far away in both time and space. Dance spectacles and Hollywood-ized shows featuring Hawaiian kings and queens and exotic dancers capture the attention of Hawaiian youth who at first simply want to take part in a public display. The public tourist images of the Hawaiian thus usher mainland Hawaiians into private *halau* whereby they learn, behind closed doors with no secrets revealed, the language and historical meanings of their culture. Only through the public are today's Hawaiians entering the private, and suddenly tourist encodings seem productive as well as dangerously produced. This community has therefore made the most of its racialized difference in a new geographic location and its popularized images, which have made their way into the hearts and minds of society. They have made do with stagings and frontings to relate to differently located Hawaiians.

Historical memory calls for a reimagining of our relations to one another as Hawaiians. Through *pi'ikoi,* community members aspire to be the Hawaiians they once were: sovereign, proud, authentic. They revel in re-creating their identity connections to royal figures and their resignified historical moments of Hawaiian glory. In this practice, they momentarily shatter state and public suspicion of their indigenous, sovereign selves.

Hawaiians—whose identity is concealed in the blood and exalted through *pi'ikoi*—rework blood classifications and definitions to address their felt needs for cultural authority and voice. The scientized image of blood and its rhetorical potency as already real offers a powerful communicative practice. Practicing blood speech reauthorizes Hawaiians as the true cultural subjects, the indisputable indigenous originators of Hawaiianness. They alone are originally Hawaiian. The performativity of the social subject through discourse and the enduring spirit of private collective memory save Hawaiians from the stately nature of blood. Reperforming blood work both names them as the natural cultural authorities at the same time that it reveals the state as an encroaching administrative force demanding formal proof of blood. For Hawaiians, the proof is the blood, their unquestioned, internal nature as Hawaiians.

Internally, blood talk sanctifies older, Hawai'i-born, and "pure" generations (those defined as practicing particular traditions) and inferiorizes diasporic mainland and mixed generations. Divisions exist here, especially among local and mainland Hawaiians. Mixed mainlanders are denoted as too modern, but parents and *kupuna* communicatively practice these distinctions as indications of an injustice done to all Hawaiians. The presence of mixed and mainland Hawaiians represents a foreign-induced pressure on Hawaiians, pushing them away from *'āina* and one another. This hierarchy then stands as a subdued cultural critique of Western modernity.

There is much to learn about this diasporic community's hierarchy of membership. The Aloha Club's specific practice of "Hawaiian at heart" is different than how we have seen it. It does not assume a free-flowing equality and reciprocity between a native and outsider. Claiming to be Hawaiian even by heart is not a natural identity guarantee. Instead, the Hawaiian community distinguishes between those who are culturally and historically Hawaiian via blood and, within this, who is more or less so. The heart symbolizes an identity position created for non-Hawaiian spouses (and mothers and fathers of mixed Hawaiian children) and community friends. Heart makes them part of a Hawaiian community as a social adaptation and not as a naturalized identity distinction. The Aloha Club demonstrates the strength of a living Hawaiian people to "make do" and make the most of their current sociohistorical locations.[61] This strength is reflective of a community that does not feel it gives anything up by including, in racial terms, non-Hawaiians. Indeed, this community practices and names its authority and locates a place for others within their own privatized yet adapted framings.

Yet there still remains a debate over the authenticity and political effectivity of diasporic Hawaiian communities like the Aloha Club and their impact on Hawaiian cultural politics. Specifically, material consequences exist for those homelands that desperately need the numbers of their cultural members-in-residence at home to secure federal aid, support, voting power, and land allotments. Hawai'i is the key example here. I have highlighted how important diasporic Hawaiian identities and communities are as well as understanding the tensions that pervade the debate over sovereignty and indigeneity. Some believe that for sovereignty to be achieved, Hawai'i needs the return of its diasporic Hawaiians. Politicians cannot understand how indigenous Hawaiians can exist "off-island" in the larger struggle for sovereignty. These tensions are very real and only time will tell how diasporic Hawaiian communities might contribute to and reframe the sovereignty debate and maintain the new community spaces they created long ago. Many diasporic Hawaiians I interviewed feel strongly that sovereignty has become a co-opted state exercise, and they expressed great resentment against the larger sovereignty movement. Many of the interviewees see themselves creating their own community space off-island. However, focusing on diasporic Hawaiians risks politically defusing the fights back home over who has native rights and belonging; it risks perpetuating the popularized perception that Hawaiians have given up their rights to native entitlements. How, then, could geographic specificity and cultural identity be reframed as a dynamic bounded by historical memory and political specificity so that diasporic Hawaiians can claim their movements are linked to colonialism and serve as a contemporary means to survive until native rights are restored or extended across geographic boundaries?

No chapter in a book can ever capture the Aloha Club and other diasporic Hawaiian communities.[62] Members embody a community that practices, remembers, and reorganizes who they are and who they want to be. These lived identities compel me more than their identifications. These Hawaiians use what they can, when they can, and with a strong mindful sense of a collective spirit. They are incredibly creative in that they have more distant connections to a cultural agency historically centered on 'āina or Hawai'i and thus more to lose. Their unique Hawaiian practices store identity possibilities for an impending future in which the state regirds more power and Hawaiians are continually denied homesteads, benefits, legal agency, and the right to claim themselves as indigenous. We can look to Hawaiian community in the diaspora for contextualized practices through which we can strongly emerge in a now postcapitalist world and reimagine our self-determination as Hawaiians.

Afterword
Identity Legacies and Challenges

Throughout this book, I have traced the legacy of identity articulations created in the name of Hawaiians. I theorize the legacy of identity as a vested collection of signified meanings, subject positions, and discourses that come to represent a group over time. Such a collection is constituted both by largely overdetermined meanings from social structures and historical moments and those identity challenges issued by the designated group, as in their public and private remakings of identity. However, dominant meanings and a group's identity remakings are often combined, fused, and made similar in discursive appearance and form while operating quite differently in function and in the name of a specific power interest. So what appears to be a form of native essentialism, or the uncritical acceptance of a dominant signification by a group, or even the "truthfulness" of a dominant identity position to an indigenous community, may not be necessarily so. Identity significations are overlaid with one another so much that the key question becomes not what meanings are produced and used but *how* these meanings are practiced in relation to the larger structural conditions and political forces. Moreover, the historicization of specific power interests (the colonial and racial state, law and governance, Western capitalism, tourist economic incentive) preserves and reproduces some identity positions over others and overdetermines entire contexts, particularly those effaced by centuries of colonialism and extended neocolonialism. It is important to recognize that somewhere between poststructuralism and structuralism the signifier-signified relationship, while inherently unnecessary, can potentially become necessary or tightly fused meanings over time given a series of particular historical events, the far-reaching stretch of colonization and dispossession, and the naturalization of social structures that have overdetermined the formal and material aspects of a group's social experience.[1] The challenge for critical and cultural studies scholars is therefore to trace, analyze, and critique identity forms in constant relation with the constitutive set of historical moments, the political stakes at hand, and the range of political options afforded to the group in order to ferret out different kinds of political practice and contestation (for example, negotiation, covert subversion or hidden micropractices, the reenactment of dominant forms to the endmost limits, and explicit resistance).

This challenge leaves us with the theoretical conceptualization of identity as a moving and politicized dialectic between lingering historical moments, material structures, and everyday cultural practices. Such a dialectic is stable, firmly established, and at the same time, subtly changing in practice and political activity. Hawaiians, a cultural group long considered to be marginalized in their own homeland in terms of their sovereign status, land, and material opportunities, have not been fully viewed within this dialectic. Rather, the academic focus on Hawaiian identity has largely been placed on the formal structures that subjugate Hawaiians: the federal and local government's failure to recognize Hawai'i as an independent political nation, the fight for Hawaiian sovereignty, and the legal battles for the restoration of Hawaiian land.[2] Thus, the political options proffered to Hawaiians seem limited and bleak and their existence forced into compliance. However, focusing solely on these important formal structures without a dialectical reading of such structures in relation to the everyday cultural practices of Hawaiians (especially those practices that are not deemed explicitly political, such as narrative performances or diasporic movement) has been a major oversight. We have for too long discounted the popular and everyday aspects of Hawaiian identity, namely their private performances, oral histories, deployments of popular culture, and reassembled identity forms practiced in the diaspora. Within these forgotten spaces, Hawaiians have reused, reassembled, and redeployed the overdetermined encodings of the native—blood as authenticity and tourist spectacles—in ways that are not possible in formal arenas. They have lived and contested the forces that be within conditions not of their own making, which has demanded a keen sense of resourcefulness. The context of Hawaiian identity therefore highlights theoretically the type of cultural spirit and social resistance on the part of an indigenous group that can occur within an overdetermined context.

However, the articulations within a legacy of identity can also be reactivated and suppress other meanings in particular political moments. At this writing, the articulations of blood and a nativism defined out of existence have solidly recombined and rigidified into a dominant assemblage of meaning that has further restrained the political and legal voice of Hawaiians. In the cases of the 1996 Hawaiian Vote and the most recent *Rice v. Cayetano* in which the court ruled in favor of Freddy Rice that the Hawaiians-only voting procedure in the Office of Hawaiian Affairs, a state agency created for Hawaiians, is unconstitutional because it excludes others on the basis of race, it seems that any claim to prerequisite Hawaiian blood is immediately deemed a form of racial exclusion. Thus, blood takes on the semblance of race while its racialization over time is never brought to the surface. The historically antiquated nativism operates in full effect in that the native is considered a relic of the past. Modernity and the era of civil rights have come into being primarily through the coarticulation of an extinct native and a blood quantum vehicle that distinguishes Hawaiians by way of specifying necessary procedures for documenting their identities and at the same time, denies any historical contextualization or acknowledgment of a dispossessed indigenous group whose cultural entitlements are stripped. The uneven constructions of race in Hawai'i have naturalized and installed the color-blind ideal of white citizenship and a multiculturalist hegemony that invisibly place Hawaiians at a disadvantage and then justifies such actions as adhering to the fairness and equality of legal doctrine. State programs designated to assist Hawaiians stand in jeopardy in the wake of the *Rice v. Cayetano* case as Hawaiian communities must now be extremely self-conscious about how their identity, whether by historical consequence, blood quantum, or geographic residency, is articulated within official statutes, program missions, and membership clauses. Under the jurisdiction of the local state of Hawai'i, Hawaiians will always be recognized first and foremost as citizens. The real struggle, then, lies in the Hawaiian community's efforts to gain federal recognition of the special political and independent status of the Hawaiian people and their attempts in locating the most optimal path toward reconfiguring or rewriting citizenship so that it refers to Hawaiian identity as historically a form of sovereign nativism.

With approximately one-third of the total Hawaiian population residing on the continental U.S. mainland, Hawaiians must now look to the Hawaiian diaspora for the emerging set of diasporic politics surrounding Hawaiian identity and diasporic communities' resignified constructions of dominant articulations.[3] The age-old conceptualizations that residency in Hawai'i denotes authentic Hawaiianness, and migration and settlement on the mainland suggest one is a *haole*—of a higher economic class and wanting to be completely assimilated—need to be dismantled. The Hawaiian diaspora is a vibrant locus of dynamic cultural practices and reassembled identity articulations that extract once overdetermined meanings and make them new. In addition, the history of the Hawaiian diaspora, one believed to be simultaneously created with the modern nation of Hawai'i, reveals that diasporic movement can serve as a political practice against the racial state.[4] With the political now appearing in new form, Hawaiian communities in Hawai'i have much to gain culturally and politically by acknowledging and including diasporic networks in the struggle for sovereign rights; for example, diasporic Hawaiians have mobilized in formal groups for sovereignty, incorporated diasporic movement into their collective memory as responses to a changing and unjust system back at "home," referred to the creation of a new home until the sovereign status of Hawai'i can be restored, and created a growing generation of mainland Hawaiian youth who invoke their Hawaiian identity differently from those at home. Most importantly, diasporic Hawaiians bemoan the DHHL's process of verifying one's Hawaiianness and they recombine blood articulations with authentic claims of membership and loosen geographically specific prerequisites of membership. Such practices carry great political advantage and at the same time risk being conflated with dominant constructions of blood and citizenship. The Hawaiian diaspora should be remembered and included in the larger political struggle for Hawaiians, for this is where untapped strategic resources of identity and a solid cultural spirit live. Indeed, the future for Hawaiians, whether in the diaspora, blood, or a tourist-referenced nativism, is filled with unexpected possibilities across social structures, political losses, and entrenched conditions and this would be the workings of the legacy and spirit of identity.

Notes

INTRODUCTION

1. This image stems from the famous "The Death of Cook" tale, as captured in John Webber's well-known portrait, *The Death of Captain Cook (Death of a God)*, Ka'awaloa, Kealakekua, Hawai'i, February 14, 1779.

2. Grant and Ogawa 1993, 146–48.

3. Okamura 1996, 2–4.

4. Lind 1980, 90.

5. Grant and Ogawa 1993, 149–50; Ogawa 1981, 7.

6. Grant and Ogawa 1993, 146–48.

7. Hawaiian Homes Commission Act (HHCA) 1921, 2(201), 7.

8. Apoliona 1993; Nakao 1993; Na Maka O Ka 'Āina 1993; Nakashima 1996. See, for example, newspaper and magazine articles on Hawaiian sovereignty and land issues such as Faludi 1991; Fullard-Leo 1993; Goldberg 1996; Hale 1993; Nakao 1993; Nakashima 1996; and Novak 1989.

9. Office of Hawaiian Affairs 1996; "Native Hawaiian Population Shows Steady Annual Growth" 2000.

10. Throughout the book, I capitalize the word *Local* in order to acknowledge the significant identities of settled peoples who emigrated to Hawai'i in the mid- to late 1800s (the Chinese, Japanese, Portuguese, Filipino/as, Koreans, Puerto Ricans, Blacks, Samoans, and Tongans) (Buck 1993; Dudley and Agard 1993; Okamura 1994).

11. Dudley and Agard 1993; Hasager and Friedman 1994; Hawaiian Voices on Sovereignty 1993; Kame'eleihiwa 1992; Linnekin 1985, 1990a, 1990b; Parker

1989; Sahlins 1981, 1995; H. Trask 1993a. Since this writing, however, new perspectives on Hawaiian identity are emerging. See the work of J. Kēhaulani Kauanui (1999), Houston Wood (1999), and Rob Wilson (2000). Kauanui is one of the first scholars to theorize about diasporic Hawaiian subjectivity (or "off-island" subjectivity). See also Han and Kauanui 1993 and Hall and Kauanui 1996 for analyses of identity in terms of politics, gender, and sexuality. Eric Yamamoto (1999) has conducted an extensive legal analysis of Hawaiian sovereignty claims, identity, and the sociolegal relations between Locals and Native Hawaiians.

12. Such a critique can be made of those scholars involved in the poststructuralist movement: Derrida 1976, 1978; Foucault 1978, 1979; Lacan 1975a, 1975b, 1977a, 1977b; Kristeva 1977; and Barthes 1974, 1983.

13. See Hall 1983, 1986b for thorough discussions of the tensions between poststructuralism and cultural studies.

14. Hall 1980b, 1983.

15. Grossberg 1996a, 155.

16. Grossberg 1996a, 156.

17. Grossberg 1996a, 155.

18. Grossberg 1996a; Hall 1980a, 1980b, 1983; Lowe 1996; McClintock 1995.

19. Marx 1973.

20. Hall 1980a, 1980b, 1989, 1992; Lowe 1996.

21. Hall 1996, 5–6.

22. Hall 1996, 6.

23. Fiske 1987; Grossberg 1997; Hall 1979, 1980a, 1980b, 1991, 1996; Lowe 1996; Storey 1996.

24. Gramsci 1971; Hall 1980a, 1980b, 1996.

25. Grossberg 1997; Hall 1996; Lavie and Swedenburg 1996.

26. Laclau 1977; Laclau and Mouffe 1985; Hall 1979, 1980a.

27. Hall 1996.

28. Hall 1980a, 1986b, 1996.

29. Grossberg 1992, 54.

30. Hall 1979, 1980a, 1980b, 1996.

31. Mouffe 1981, 7.

I. ABSTRACT NATIVISM AND THE HISTORICAL IMAGINATION

1. For key discussions on historical memory, see Lipsitz 1990; Lowe 1996; Zerubavel 1995.

2. See Popular Memory Group 1982.

3. The first two excerpts derive from a series of ethnographic interviews I conducted in 1997 with Hawaiian community members, Locals, and *haoles* who consider themselves "native" to Hawai'i.

4. *Haole* is a Hawaiian term originally meaning "foreigner." Through vernacular discourse, it has come to mean "white," "Caucasian," American or En-

glish person (Pukui and Elbert 1986). The term *haole* is also significantly different from a Local identity position (see Okamura 1994 and Yamamoto 1979).

5. Local identity is based on more than geographic residency. This identity form is specific to Hawai'i's unique social history, which is characterized by a group of indigenous Hawaiian inhabitants and later, several waves of immigrant groups who were brought into Hawai'i by dominant *haole*/U.S. business interests as the surplus laborers on the sugar plantations in the mid-1800s. (The Hawaiians, who were still reeling from the disintegration of their traditional land system, refused to work on the plantations.) See Buck 1993; Lowe 1996; Okamura 1994; Okihiro 1991; Yamamoto 1979 for the Local history of Hawai'i.

6. Yamamoto 1979; Ogawa 1981; Okamura 1994.

7. Generally, many Asian "Locals," the Japanese and Chinese in particular, emerged as the middle class in Hawai'i in the 1960s and 1970s, occupying top government positions, attaining access to education, and establishing professional careers as doctors and teachers (Buck 1993; Fujikane 1994; Okamura 1994).

8. Fujikane 1994.

9. Sumida 1991, xv.

10. According to Cooper and Daws (1985) and Yamamoto (1999), Locals have been historically subjugated to colonialist structures of oppression (e.g., the *haole* oligarchy of the late 1800s and early 1900s and the principles of private property development and state citizenship and civil rights). Yet, these Locals later invoked these very structures to increase their mobility, which in effect disadvantaged other groups, namely Hawaiians.

11. Ma 1999.

12. Ma 1999, A36.

13. See Yamamoto 1999 for an analysis of the tuition waiver controversy.

14. Ma 1999, A36.

15. Goldberg 1996.

16. Tom 1996.

17. Goldberg 1996; Ozawa 1996.

18. In 1996, fifth-generation Hawai'i resident Harold "Freddy" Rice filed a suit in the U.S. District Court against the State of Hawaii for the "unconstitutional" nature of the Office of Hawaiian Affairs (OHA) voting procedures. The OHA, a state program created in 1978 to assist with the needs of Native Hawaiians, have in the past designated voting rights for the nine OHA trustees to Hawaiians only. Rice filed several lawsuits, claiming the procedure violated the 14th and 15th Amendments, "which established the 'one-person, one-vote' principle barring the government from denying the right to vote 'on account of race, color, or previous condition of servitude'" (Donnelly and Young-Oda, 2000, 2). In October 1999, the United States Supreme Court voted in favor of Rice's claim of OHA's illegal procedures based upon race and issued an order to

open up OHA elections to both Hawaiians and non-Hawaiians. See Donnelly and Young-Oda 2000, "Hawaiians-Only Programs at Risk" 2000, and Yaukey 2000 for a legal analysis of the precedented *Rice v. Cayetano.*

19. Buck 1993.

20. Kameʻeleihiwa 1992.

21. Wood 1992.

22. Anderson 1983.

23. Fabian 1983; Goldberg 1993; McClintock 1995; Wood 1992.

24. Goldberg 1993.

25. Comaroff and Comaroff 1992.

26. Cook 1784, vol. 2. The map, although sketched sometime between 1778 and 1779, was printed four years after Cook's ships arrived home. It was printed in Cook's *Voyage* (1784).

27. Cook 1784.

28. McClintock 1995.

29. McClintock 1995.

30. Pratt 1992, 204.

31. See Fitzpatrick 1986 for evidence of colonial maps.

32. Duncan and Ley 1993.

33. Fabian 1983; McClintock 1995.

34. McClintock 1995.

35. See White 1980.

36. Personal photo collection of Bishop Museum display.

37. Kilolani Mitchell 1982.

38. Kilolani Mitchell 1982, 11.

39. Kuykendall 1938.

40. Kuykendall 1938, 3.

41. Kuykendall 1938, 3.

42. Daws 1968; Day 1955.

43. Daws 1968, xii–xiii.

44. Day 1955, 4.

45. Fabian 1983.

46. McGrane 1989, 94.

47. Kuykendall 1938, 3.

48. Duncan 1993; Fabian 1983.

49. Comaroff 1998.

50. Goldberg 1996; Tom 1996.

51. Waihee 1993, B3.

52. Hee 1993.

53. Mullins 1978, 63.

54. See Fujikane 1994.

55. Halualani 1998.

56. Duncan and Ley 1993; Wood 1992.

57. Duncan and Ley 1993; Wood 1992.

58. Duncan and Ley 1993.

59. Harley 1988, 278.

60. Daws 1968; Day 1955.

61. Kuykendall 1938, 2–3.

62. Kuykendall 1938, 3.

63. Kuykendall 1938, 4.

64. Cook and King 1785, vol. 2, 57.

65. Kuykendall 1938, 1953.

66. Wood 1992.

67. Wood 1992, 79.

68. Wood 1992, 79.

69. Kameʻeleihiwa 1992; Malo 1951.

70. Interview 2.

71. Interview 18.

72. Kameʻeleihiwa 1992; H. Trask 1993a; Interviews 4, 7, 9.

73. Kameʻeleihiwa 1992.

74. Kameʻeleihiwa 1992; Malo 1951.

75. Sahlins 1985.

76. Malo 1951.

77. Interview 4.

78. Kuykendall 1938, 13.

79. Kuykendall 1938, 13.

80. Cook and King 1785, vol. 2.

81. Daws 1968, 3.

82. Cook and King 1785, vol. 2.

83. Cook and King 1785, vol. 2.

84. Fitzpatrick 1986.

85. See the debates between Sahlins and Obeyesekere in Sahlins 1995 and Obeyesekere 1992.

86. Daws 1968, 2.

87. McClintock 1995.

88. Sahlins 1981, 1985, 1995; McClintock 1995.

89. Comaroff and Comaroff 1992; Comaroff 1998.

90. Comaroff 1998.

91. See MacKenzie 1991.

2. RACIALIZED NATIVES AND WHITE CITIZENSHIP

1. See McClintock 1995; Yamamoto 1999; and Matsuda 1996.

2. See Committee on the Territories 1920.

3. *Rehabilitation of Native Hawaiians* 1920; Act of July 9, 1921; HHCA 1985, 1989 supp.

4. HHCA 1921, 1A(1101); 2(201), 7.

5. See Goldberg 1993 and Hall 1979.

6. According to the Office of Hawaiian Affairs *Native Hawaiian Data Book* (1996), the birth of part Hawaiians began in 1853. Specifically, at this time, there were 70,036 pure Hawaiians and 983 part Hawaiians.

7. The localized State of Hawaii took over the administrative and enforcement role of the U.S. federal government in terms of overseeing the HHCA and the Native Hawaiian trust situation upon its annexation in 1959.

8. See Kameʻeleihiwa 1992; MacKenzie 1991; Parker 1989.

9. Hall 1979, 326.

10. Lowe 1996.

11. ʻIʻi 1959; Malo 1951; Kamakau 1961; Kameʻeleihiwa 1992; Pukui, Haertig, and Lee 1972.

12. Kameʻeleihiwa 1992; Kelly 1984; MacKenzie 1991; Parker 1989.

13. As discussed later in this chapter, David Stannard's (1989) arguments are key to demonstrating the devastating population collapse of the *lāhui*. In other historical accounts (e.g., Daws 1968; Day 1955; Kuykendall 1938, 1967), the politics of population counts is made known as either an extremely low 1778 population estimate or an inflated total for Hawaiians in the mid-1800s, thus attempting to guise the Western-influenced decimation of a native people.

14. Kameʻeleihiwa 1992; MacKenzie 1991; Malo 1951; Parker 1989.

15. Kameʻeleihiwa 1992; MacKenzie 1991; Parker 1989.

16. Kameʻeleihiwa 1992, 41; Barrere 1969.

17. Linnekin and Poyer 1990.

18. See Kamakau 1961 and Malo 1951 for examples of these traditional texts.

19. Kameʻeleihiwa 1992; Barrere 1969.

20. Kameʻeleihiwa 1992.

21. Parker 1989.

22. David Malo (1951) calls attention to the hard, oppressing existence of many *makaʻāinana,* subjected to the demands of the chief (87).

23. Kameʻeleihiwa 1992; MacKenzie 1991; Parker 1989.

24. Buck 1993, 26.

25. Kameʻeleihiwa 1992; Malo 1951.

26. Mercer 1994.

27. Kameʻeleihiwa 1992; Parker 1989.

28. Scholar John Kelly quoted in Kameʻeleihiwa 1994, 108.

29. Kameʻeleihiwa 1992; Parker 1989.

30. Kameʻeleihiwa 1992; Parker 1989.

31. This represents a point that Sahlins 1981, 1985, 1995 persistently argues.

32. Buck 1993; Kameʻelehiwa 1992; Sahlins 1981, 1985, 1995.

33. Buck 1993; Parker 1989.

34. Buck 1993; Kameʻeleihiwa 1992.

35. Vancouver 1798, 122; Kotzebue 1967, 2: 333; Parker 1989.

36. Kameʻeleihiwa 1992; MacKenzie 1991; Malo 1951; Parker 1989.

37. Kameʻeleihiwa 1992.

38. Such a logic—in readapted form—would push well into the modern/postmodern age of tourism through Hawaiʻi, as discussed in chapter 4.

39. MacKenzie 1991; Parker 1989.

40. Kameʻeleihiwa 1992; MacKenzie 1991; Parker 1989.

41. Kameʻeleihiwa 1992; MacKenzie 1991; Parker 1989.

42. Kotzebue 1821, 1: 333; Parker 1989.

43. Goldberg 1993; Hall 1979; Kameʻeleihiwa 1992; McClintock 1995; Parker 1989.

44. Kameʻeleihiwa 1992; MacKenzie 1991; Parker 1989; H. Trask 1991.

45. Bingham 1847, 81.

46. Duncan 1993; Duncan and Ley 1993; Fabian 1983.

47. Parker 1989; More 1516.

48. More 1516; Parker 1989, 3.

49. As discussed in MacKenzie 1991 and Parker 1989, indigenous Hawaiian practices of tending the land were dramatically different from Western practices encoded in formal law. Unlike ultimate use, Hawaiians would often let land lay fallow for a long period of time, which would allow for the accumulation and storing of rich nutrients and increased arability. To *haoles,* such a practice was unproductive; for *kānaka,* it was *pono* (right) for *ʻāina* to be blessed, favored, and granted.

50. Parker 1989; *Polynesian,* July 8, 1848.

51. See Hall 1979.

52. Parker 1989.

53. Culturally, the Hawaiian woman lived as powerful female *akua* like Pele, and strong political leaders such as Kaʻahumanu (who broke the eating taboos forbidding men and women to eat together) and Kinau. I stress that Hawaiian women have resisted this positioning; they have channeled their political power into hula, chanting, genealogies, and language reclamation projects and most impressively, rising as the most vehement and confrontational leaders of the Hawaiian sovereignty movement (See Jaimes Guerrero 1997; Kameʻeleihiwa 1992; H. Trask 1993a; M. Trask 1992, 1993).

54. Parker 1989.

55. Parker 1989.

56. Kameʻeleihiwa 1992; MacKenzie 1991; Parker 1989.

57. Parker 1989, 100.

58. Kameʻeleihiwa 1992; MacKenzie 1991; Parker 1989.

59. Parker 1989.

60. Thurston 1904; also reprinted in MacKenzie 1991, 5.

61. Parker 1989.

62. Parker 1989.

63. Buck 1993; Cooper and Daws 1985; Parker 1989; Yamamoto 1979; Ogawa 1981; Okamura 1994.

64. Hall 1979; Bettleheim 1972.

65. The *Ka Māhele* event is referred to by most sources as the "Great *Māhele*." Tragically, it wreaked havoc on the Hawaiian people by dividing the Hawaiian Kingdom, as noted by Davianna Pōmaika'i McGregor.

66. *Revised Laws* 1925, 2152–2176; also in MacKenzie 1991, 7; Parker 1989; Kelly 1956.

67. Kame'eleihiwa 1992; MacKenzie 1991; Parker 1989; Kelly 1956.

68. Kame'eleihiwa 1992; MacKenzie 1991; Parker 1989; Kelly 1956.

69. A total of 8,205 awards were given by the land commission. According to Bishop Museum anthropologist Marion Kelly, out of these 8,205 awardees, "200 were foreigner, 560 were chiefs, and 7500 were *maka'āinana*" (lecture on April 22, 1982; cited in MacKenzie 1991, 22). See also MacKenzie 1991, 8; Marion Kelly cited in Levy 1975, 856.

70. MacKenzie 1991; Parker 1989; Kelly 1956.

71. MacKenzie 1991; Parker 1989; Kelly 1956.

72. MacKenzie 1991; Parker 1989; Levy 1975.

73. Parker 1989.

74. Goldberg 1993.

75. Goldberg 1993; Hall 1979; Lowe 1996.

76. Yamamoto, Haia, and Kalama 1994.

77. MacKenzie 1991; Parker 1989.

78. Act of July 9, 1921; HHCA 1985, 1989 supp.

79. MacKenzie 1991; Parker 1989; Vause 1962; Dinell, Doi, Horwitz, Meriwether, and Spitz 1964.

80. Murakami 1991.

81. Murakami 1991.

82. *Rehabilitation of Native Hawaiians* 1920, 8.

83. Committee on the Territories 1920: 201(a), 7.

84. Murakami 1991.

85. Goldberg 1993.

86. D. Goldberg 1997; Jaimes 1992.

87. *Rehabilitation of Native Hawaiians* 1920, 2, population table.

88. D. Goldberg 1997, 38.

89. This is an example of an imaginary statement that could follow the logic of counting Hawaiians.

90. MacKenzie 1991; Murakami 1991; Parker 1989.

91. *Rehabilitation of Native Hawaiians* 1920, 14.

92. *Rehabilitation of Native Hawaiians* 1920, 14–15.

93. Goldberg 1993; Lowe 1996.

94. *Rehabilitation of Native Hawaiians* 1920, 8.

95. *Rehabilitation of Native Hawaiians* 1920, 5.

96. *Rehabilitation of Native Hawaiians* 1920, 6.

97. HHCA 1921, 2(201), 7.

98. Office of Hawaiian Affairs 1996, 4.

99. D. Goldberg 1997, chapter 4.

100. D. Goldberg 1997.

101. *Rehabilitation of Native Hawaiians* 1920, 15.

102. *Rehabilitation of Native Hawaiians* 1920, 15.

103. A similar discursive construction of whitened nativism was articulated for and in the name of Native American Indians (Parker 1989; D. Goldberg 1997).

104. *Rehabilitation of Native Hawaiians* 1920, 15.

105. It is interesting that the assignment of potential citizenship also seems to apply to *haole* Hawaiians and Chinese Hawaiians. Asians, as Lisa Lowe explains, were constructed as foreign, noncitizens in many modern discourses; yet in this discourse, the mixture of Chinese and Hawaiian is largely framed as being "part Hawaiian." Of course, the modern state reconciles such a contradiction by excising "Asians" from citizenship and signifying Chinese Hawaiians as non-Hawaiians, or *even more* of those who could be exempt from homestead land gain for Hawaiians. The Asian aspect of identity is written over and defined against indigeneity. Thus, a Chinese Hawaiian identity seems to symbolize less Hawaiian and thus more like a citizen as a non-Hawaiian.

106. Elkholm-Friedman and Friedman 1994.

107. Office of Hawaiian Affairs 1996.

108. *Rehabilitation of Native Hawaiians* 1920, 30.

109. Parker 1989.

110. *Rehabilitation of Native Hawaiians* 1920, 34.

111. Lowe 1996.

112. *Rehabilitation of Native Hawaiians* 1920, 34–35.

113. "73 Percent" 1996.

114. *Rehabilitation of Native Hawaiians* 1920, 34.

115. MacKenzie 1991; Murakami 1991; Parker 1989; H. Trask 1993c; Vause 1962.

116. Hansen 1971.

117. Hansen 1971, 6.

118. Murakami 1991.

119. Hansen 1971.

120. Hansen 1971; Faludi 1991.

121. Hansen 1971.

122. Hall 1979; Lowe 1996.

123. The performative nature of discourse is discussed by Butler (1990, 1995).

3. EXPOSING THE RACIAL STATE

1. See D. Goldberg 1997.

2. D. Goldberg 1997.

3. Hearings before the Committee on Territories, United States Senate 1921.

4. Van Maanen 1988; Madison 1993.

5. In the courtroom, Hawaiians are denied the "standing to sue" on the grounds that the beneficiaries of a trust cannot sue the state through the federal agency power given that the HHCA became a state act upon admission of Hawai'i into the United States.

6. D. Goldberg 1997.

7. I noticed that several interviewees (including members of my family), possessed sworn affidavits from past relatives. Hawaiians filed sworn affidavits in the 1950s because they either did not possess primary documents for their parents and or the documents were never issued.

8. See Comaroff 1998; Goldberg 1993; McClintock 1995.

9. Comaroff 1998, 12.

10. Comaroff 1998.

11. Comaroff 1998.

12. Comaroff 1998; D. Goldberg 1997; Omi and Winant 1994.

13. Comaroff 1998.

14. Lipsitz 1990; Lowe 1996.

15. Popular Memory Group 1982; Johnson 1986–87.

16. Johnson 1986–87.

17. Langellier 1989.

18. Mumby 1993; Reissman 1987.

19. Ewick and Silbey 1995.

20. Delgado 1989; Matsuda 1987.

21. Mumby 1993; Ewick and Silbey 1995.

22. Ewick and Silbey 1995; Engel and Munger 1996.

23. Bourdieu 1977; Ewick and Silbey 1995.

24. Hymes 1962, 1972; Johnson 1986–87; Spradley 1979.

25. Bauman 1977, 1986; Hymes 1962 (1973).

26. Spradley 1979.

27. The priority of documents is listed in the *Loa'a Ka 'Aina Ho'opulapula*—"Directions for Applying for Hawaiian Home Lands," 1998.

28. This set of instructions comes directly from the *State of Hawaii, Department of Hawaiian Home Lands, Application for Lease of Hawaiian Home Lands*. I was able to retrieve the full set of administrative documents required of Hawaiians to be granted a land lease—that is, the actual application: *Loa'a Ka 'Aina Ho'opulapula*—"Directions for Applying for Hawaiian Home Lands."

29. Akoi 1989.

30. Hawaii State Archives, *Census Collection 1840–1896.*

31. Hawaii State Archives, *Census Collection 1840–1896.*

32. MacKenzie 1991; Yamamoto, Haia, and Kalama 1994.

33. Mullins 1978.

34. D. Goldberg 1997, 34.

35. D. Goldberg 1997.

36. Davis 1991, 5; D. Goldberg 1997.

37. D. Goldberg 1997, 38.

38. D. Goldberg 1997; Hawaii State Archives, *Census Collection 1840–1896.*

39. D. Goldberg 1997, 31.

40. Jaimes 1992; I can only theoretically suggest the presence of tribal roles for Hawaiians, meaning I do not have concrete, written proof of these master references. Instead, I make this allegation based on the living proof of private testimonies by Hawaiians. It is rumored that a master file of names and dates of Hawaiian family information exists at the DOH. All Hawaiians' applications for land leases must match this list. To fail to do so, is not only to fail to gain access to land once used by all Hawaiians, but to be denied state recognition as a Hawaiian.

41. Kameʻeleihiwa 1992.

42. D. Goldberg 1997; Jaimes 1992; Jaimes Guerrero 1997.

43. Omi and Winant 1994, 53–55.

44. Butler 1995; Kondo 1996.

45. As yet another form of agency, many Hawaiian interviewees suggested to me that I send forth my collected interview performances to the DHHL so that the racial state can be cited for past violations and forced to restructure their formal process of identity. Some decided to send their own tapes and transcripts to state agencies as "proof" of their Hawaiian quantum.

4. FROM QUEENS TO CALABASHES

1. Castañeda 1996; Rosaldo 1993.

2. Castañeda 1996.

3. Hall 1980a; Slack 1996.

4. Clifford 1997a.

5. MacCannell 1992a.

6. Comaroff and Comaroff 1992.

7. Taussig 1997.

8. See Comaroff and Comaroff 1992; Conquergood 1991, 1992; Johnson 1986–87; Katriel 1997; Madison 1993; Visweswaran 1988.

9. Comaroff and Comaroff 1992, 9.

10. Clifford 1997a.

11. John 1996.

12. Clifford 1997a.

13. Comaroff and Comaroff 1992; Conquergood 1991, 1992; Katriel 1997; Kondo 1996; Lavie and Swedenburg 1996; Madison 1993; Rosaldo 1993.

14. See, for example, Comaroff and Comaroff 1992; Conquergood 1991, 1992; Katriel 1997; Kondo 1996; Lavie and Swedenburg 1996; Madison 1993; Rosaldo 1993; Visweswaran 1988.

15. Comaroff and Comaroff 1992.

16. Kondo 1996, 21

17. Spradley 1979; Hymes 1975.

18. Taussig 1997.

19. Interview with the State of Hawaii, Department of Business, Economic Development and Tourism (DBEDT) 1997; Hitch 1992; Inskeep 1991.

20. Comaroff and Comaroff 1992; Taussig 1997.

21. State of Hawaii, DBEDT 1996a; Hitch 1992; Inskeep 1991.

22. Hitch 1992.

23. Data in this paragraph are derived from the State of Hawaii, DBEDT 1995.

24. Data in this paragraph are derived from the State of Hawaii, DBEDT 1997; Inskeep 1991; Hitch 1992; State of Hawaii, DBEDT 1995, 1996a, 1996b.

25. MacCannell 1973.

26. Office of Hawaiian Affairs 1996, 484.

27. Clifford 1997b.

28. Butler 1995; Kondo 1996.

29. Tregaskis 1996, 150.

30. State of Hawaii, DBEDT 1995.

31. Comaroff and Comaroff 1992.

32. Fujikane 1994; MacCannell 1992a.

33. Fabian 1983.

34. MacCannell 1992b.

35. Comaroff and Comaroff 1992.

36. MacCannell 1989, 1992a.

37. State of Hawaii, DBEDT 1995.

38. This text is taken from a 1997 Waimea Falls Park brochure.

39. MacCannell 1992b.

40. Taussig 1997.

41. Fabian 1983; MacCannell 1992a.

42. White 1980.

43. MacCannell 1992b; Comaroff and Comaroff 1992, 4.

44. This theme of gendered and racialized nativism fits my chapter title. In my analysis, Hawaiian culture is imagined through queens and calabashes. Stanley Porteus's (1945) title *Calabashes and Kings: An Introduction to Hawaii* captures beautifully the coarticulated productions of Hawaiians as either bound to a "civilized" monarchical social structure or a primitive preworld of naked

savages, irrational impulses, and archaic artifacts. I modified his title for this chapter (from "Kings" to "Queens") to highlight how an engendered element of Hawaiian society—the power of female political leaders within a Hawaiian structure—is domesticated in travel via a historically established traveler/tourist fetish for the native woman's positioning in foreign cultures (Clifford 1997a).

45. Hawaii Statutes 1997.

46. Katriel 1997; MacCannell 1989.

47. Taussig 1997.

48. Evans-Pritchard 1989.

49. See Carroll 1996; Grant 1996. Grant also teaches a course on ghost stories at the local community college.

50. Comaroff and Comaroff 1992; Coombe 1993, 1995a, 1995b.

51. Comaroff and Comaroff 1992, 11.

52. Kameʻeleihiwa 1992, 324.

53. Kane 1991.

54. Kilolani Mitchell 1992.

55. Coombe 1993, 1995a, 1995b; McClintock 1995.

56. Lukács 1977; McClintock 1995.

57. Kameʻeleihiwa 1992.

58. See Jocelyn Linnekin's (1997) critical analysis of local Hawaiian T-shirts and the reconstruction of ethnicity and cultural agency.

59. Coombe 1995a, 1995b.

60. See James Clifford's (1997b) discussion of travel discourses and subject positions and the reconstruction of culture. See Desmond 1999.

61. Hitch 1992, 67.

62. Hitch 1992.

63. Duncan 1993.

64. Fabian 1983.

65. MacCannell 1992a, 1992b.

66. Dudley and Agard 1993; Kilolani Mitchell 1982; Buck 1993.

67. Blackburn 1996.

68. Bommes and Wright 1982.

69. Bommes and Wright 1982, 290.

70. Popular Memory Group 1982.

71. MacCannell 1992b.

72. MacCannell 1984, 1989.

73. Bruner 1996.

74. MacCannell 1984, 1989, 1992b.

5. LITTLE BIT BLOOD, HEART, AND SPECTACLE

1. Kaeppler 1973.

2. MacCannell 1992a, 1992b.

3. Popular Memory Group 1982; Johnson 1986–87; McClintock 1995.

4. Johnson 1986–87, 5.

5. Johnson 1986–87, 69.

6. Clifford 1997b.

7. In order to protect the privacy of the featured diasporic mainland Hawaiian community, all names and identifying features have been modified. Names of community members and events have been changed as well.

8. Lowe 1996, 3.

9. Anderson 1983.

10. Anderson 1983; Johnson 1986–87; Katriel 1997; McClintock 1995; Popular Memory Group 1982; Madison 1993.

11. Anderson 1983.

12. Anderson 1983, 10.

13. Popular Memory Group 1982.

14. Popular Memory Group 1982, 211.

15. Johnson 1986–87; Lowe 1996; McClintock 1995; Popular Memory Group 1982.

16. Fiske 1987, 1989a, 1989b, 1993; Hartley 1988; Young 1990.

17. Popular Memory Group 1982, 240.

18. Madison 1993, 216; Katriel 1997.

19. McClintock 1995, 326.

20. Lipsitz 1990; Lowe 1996; Katriel 1997; Zerubavel 1995; Bauman 1971, 1977; Briggs 1988; Conquergood 1991, 1992; Katriel 1997.

21. de Certeau 1984.

22. Lowe 1996, 30; see Goldberg 1994; Gordon and Newfield 1996.

23. Kameʻeleihiwa 1992; Malo 1951; Sahlins 1985; H. Trask 1993a.

24. See McClintock 1995.

25. Hymes 1962, 1972; Spradley 1979; Behar and Gordon 1995; Comaroff and Comaroff 1992; Kauffman 1992; Madison 1993; McClintock 1995; Popular Memory Group 1982.

26. Hymes 1962, 1972; Spradley 1979.

27. Bauman 1977, 1986; Behar and Gordon 1995; Comaroff and Comaroff 1992; Kauffman 1992; Madison 1993; McClintock 1995; Popular Memory Group 1982.

28. Comaroff and Comaroff 1992; Popular Memory Group 1982.

29. See Comaroff and Comaroff 1992, and McClintock 1995.

30. Halualani 1997.

31. My interview format emerges from the Spradley (1979) ethnographic interview tradition, in which "grand tour" questions were used to explore the most salient aspects of Hawaiian identity and the Aloha Club community. Please see chapter 3 for interview approach and transcription coding legend. Specific queries were used to probe unspoken issues of Hawaiianness, or identi-

ty aspects of historical representations, tourism, and law and governance that were not initially introduced by interviewees, but still spoke to them in some unconscious and unnoticed way. It is worth noting that the oral histories I conducted with members worked a bit differently than the interview situations. The oral histories usually focused on the member's *'ohana* and not necessarily on community practices and rituals.

32. Kauffman 1992.

33. See Fujikane 1994.

34. Popular Memory Group 1982.

35. 'I'i 1959; Kame'eleihiwa 1992; MacKenzie 1991; Malo 1951.

36. 'I'i 1959; Kame'eleihiwa 1992; MacKenzie 1991; Malo 1951.

37. MacKenzie 1991.

38. 'I'i 1959; Kame'eleihiwa 1992; MacKenzie 1991; Malo 1951.

39. Hitch 1992; State of Hawaii, DBEDT 1995, 1996a, 1996b.

40. See Barman 1995; Kauanui 1999; Wright 1983 for summaries and theoretical analyses of diasporic migration. J. Kēhaulani Kauanui, in particular, is one of the few scholars who has focused on "off-island" subjectivity and underscored the reconfiguration of Hawaiian identity in the diaspora.

41. Wright 1983, 18.

42. Barman 1995; Wright 1979, 1983.

43. Office of Hawaiian Affairs 1996.

44. I have traced this tentative genealogy of the Hawaiian diaspora by using key sources (Barman 1995; Kauanui 1999; Wright 1979, 1983) and oral history interviews.

45. Kauanui 1999; Office of Hawaiian Affairs 1996.

46. Office of Hawaiian Affairs 1996.

47. See Fernandez 1993.

48. Kauanui 1999.

49. See Buck 1993.

50. Buck 1993.

51. Buck 1993.

52. MacCannell 1984, 385.

53. MacCannell 1984, 385.

54. MacCannell 1984.

55. Buck 1993.

56. Pukui and Elbert 1986, 327.

57. Mililani Trask, unpublished paper, year unspecified.

58. Butler 1995, 134.

59. Butler 1995.

60. Kondo 1996, 109.

61. de Certeau 1984.

62. I am currently writing a book manuscript that traces the history of the

Hawaiian diaspora from the 1800s to now. I examine the nature of the different diasporic Hawaiian communities and their uniquely reconfigured identities on the continental U.S. mainland (Oregon, Las Vegas, California, Texas, Arizona, Colorado, Washington, New York, and Florida).

AFTERWORD

1. Marx 1973.

2. See Dudley and Agard 1993; Hasager and Friedman 1994; Hawaiian Voices on Sovereignty 1993; Kameʻeleihiwa 1992; Linnekin 1985, 1990a, 1990b; Parker 1989; Sahlins 1981, 1995; H. Trask 1993a.

3. "Native Hawaiian Population Shows Steady Annual Growth" 2000.

4. As early as the late 1700s, Hawaiians had left Hawaiʻi for better economic opportunities that could not be achieved in the then newly installed Western-based capitalist economy and as an exercise of their political identities, meaning, many Hawaiians foresaw the dissolution of the native monarchy and Hawaiian way of life and fled to Europe, Mexico, and the continental U.S. mainland (Barman 1995) in the 1700s and 1800s. In a new book manuscript I am writing that focuses on the history of the Hawaiian diaspora throughout the United States, I contend that the Hawaiian diaspora came into being in the same time frame as the modern colonial U.S. nation-state did. As a result, the Hawaiian diaspora becomes incorporated into the Hawaiian historical memory, which authenticates diasporic members who can argue that "movement" has been a longtime Hawaiian act in the past.

Bibliography

Act of July 9, 1921, Pub. L. no. 34, ch. 42-203, 207, 208, 42 stat. 108.

Akoi, Rhea. 1989. *Kuu Home I Keaukaha.* Published as a Keaukaha 65th Anniversary Celebration Project, Hui Hoʻomau O Keaukaha Panaewa.

Althusser, Louis. 1971. *Lenin and Philosophy and Other Essays.* London: New Left Books.

Anderson, Benedict. 1983. *Imagined Communities.* London: Verso.

Apoliona, S. Haunani. 1993. "E Mau Ana Ka Haʻaheo (ʻHe Hawaiʻi Au Mau A Mauʻ)." In *He Alo A He Alo: Face to Face,* edited by Hawaiian Voices on Sovereignty. Honolulu: Hawaiʻi Area Office of the American Friends Service Committee.

Barman, Jean. 1995. "New Land, New Lives: Hawaiian Settlement in British Colombia." *The Hawaiian Journal of History* 29: 1–32.

Barrere, Dorothy B. 1969. *The Kumuhonua Legends: A Study of Late 19th Century Hawaiian Stories of Creation and Origins.* Pacific Anthropological Records no. 3. Honolulu: Bishop Museum Press.

Barthes, Roland. 1974. *S/Z.* New York: Hill and Wang.

———. 1983. *The Fashion System.* New York: Hill and Wang.

Baudrillard, Jean L. 1981. *For a Critique of the Political Economy of the Sign,* translated by C. Levin. St. Louis: Telos Press.

Bauman, Richard. 1971. *Story, Performance, and Events: Contextual Studies of Oral Narrative.* Cambridge, UK: Cambridge University Press.

———. 1977. *Verbal Art as Performance.* Prospect Heights, IL: Waveland Press.

———. 1986. *Story, Performance, and Event: Contextual Studies of Oral Narrative.* Cambridge, UK: Cambridge University Press.

Beckwith, Martha Warren. 1970. *Hawaiian Mythology.* Honolulu: University of Hawaii Press.

Behar, Ruth, and Deborah Gordon. 1995. *Women Writing Culture.* Berkeley: University of California Press.

Bettleheim, C. 1972. "Theoretical Comments." In *Unequal Exchange,* edited by A. Emmanuel. London: New Left Books.

Bingham, Hiram. 1847. *Residence of Twenty-one Years in the Sandwich Islands; or the Civil, Religious, and Political History of Those Islands.* Hartford, CT: Hezekiah Huntington.

———. 1898. *The Annexation of Hawaii: A Right and a Duty.* Concord, NH: Rumford Press.

Blackburn, Mark. 1996. *Hawaiiana: The Best of Hawaiian Design (with values).* Atglen, PA: Schiffer Publishing Ltd.

Bommes, M, and P. Wright. 1982. "'Charms of Residence': The Public and the Past." In *Making Histories: Studies in History-Writing and Politics,* edited by R. Johnson, G. McLennan, B. Schwarz, and D. Sutton, 253–302. London: Hutchinson and the Centre for Contemporary Cultural Studies, University of Birmingham.

Bourdieu, Pierre. 1977. *Outline of a Theory of Practice.* Cambridge, UK: Cambridge University Press.

Brettell, C. B. 1986. "Introduction: Travel Literature, Ethnography, and Ethnohistory." *Ethnohistory* 33(2): 127–38.

Briggs, Charles. 1988. *Competence in Performance: The Creativity of Tradition in Mexicano Verbal Art.* Philadelphia: University of Pennsylvania Press.

Brown, DeSoto. 1982. *Hawaii Recalls: Selling Romance to America, Nostalgic Images of the Hawaiian Islands: 1910–1950.* Honolulu: Editions Limited.

Bruner, Edward. 1996. "Tourism in the Balinese Borderzone." In *Displacement, Diaspora, and Geographies of Identity,* edited by S. Lavie and T. Swedenburg, 157–80. Durham: Duke University Press.

Buck, Elizabeth. 1993. *Paradise Remade: The Politics of Culture and History in Hawai'i.* Philadelphia: Temple University Press.

Budnick, Richard. 1992. *Stolen Kingdom: An American Conspiracy.* Honolulu: Aloha Press.

Butler, Judith. 1990. *Gender Trouble: Feminism and the Subversion of Identity.* New York: Routledge.

———. 1995. "For a Careful Reading." In *Feminist Contentions,* edited by S. Benhabib, J. Butler, D. Cornell, and N. Fraser, 127–44. New York: Routledge.

Carroll, Rick. 1996. *Chicken Skin: True Spooky Stories of Hawai'i.* Honolulu: Bess Press.

Castañeda, Quetzil E. 1996. *In the Museum of Maya Culture: Touring Chichén Itzà*. Minneapolis: University of Minnesota Press.

Clifford, James. 1988. *The Predicament of Culture: Twentieth-Century Ethnography, Literature, and Art*. Cambridge, MA: Harvard University Press.

————. 1997a. *Routes: Travel and Translation in the Late Twentieth Century*. Cambridge, MA: Harvard University Press.

————. 1997b. "Traveling Cultures." In *Routes: Travel and Translation in the Late Twentieth Century*, edited by J. Clifford, 17–46. Cambridge, MA: Harvard University Press.

————. 1997c. "Spatial Practices: Fieldwork, Travel, and the Disciplining of Anthropology." In *Routes: Travel and Translation in the Late Twentieth Century*, edited by J. Clifford, 52–91. Cambridge, MA: Harvard University Press.

Comaroff, John. L. 1998. *Reflections on the Colonial State, In South Africa and Elsewhere: Factions, Fragments, Facts and Fictions*. ABF Working Paper 9712. Chicago: University of Chicago, American Bar Foundation.

Comaroff, John, and Jean Comaroff. 1992. "Ethnography and the Historical Imagination." In *Ethnography and the Historical Imagination*, edited by John Comaroff and Jean Comaroff, 3–48. Boulder, CO: Westview Press.

Committee on the Territories. 1920. *Hawaiian Homes Commission Act: Hearings on H.R. 13500*. Sixty-sixth Congress, 3d sess.

Conquergood, Dwight. 1991. "Rethinking Ethnography: Towards a Critical Cultural Politics." *Communication Monographs* 58 (June): 179–94.

————. 1992. "Ethnography, Rhetoric, and Performance." *Quarterly Journal of Speech* 78(1): 80–97.

Cook, James. 1784. *A Voyage to the Pacific Ocean. Undertaken by the Command of His Majesty, for Making Discoveries in the Northern Hemisphere, Performed under the Directions of Captains Cook, Clerke and Gore . . . 1776, 1777, 1778, 1779, and 1780*. 3 vols. Dublin: Chamberlain et al. Maps are reproduced from a London edition of the same year (published by W. and A. Strachan for G. Nicol and T. Cadell).

Cook, James, and James King. 1785. *A Voyage to the Pacific Ocean. Undertaken by the Command of His Majesty, for Making Discoveries in the Northern Hemisphere, Performed under the Directions of Captains Cook, Clerke and Gore . . . 1776, 1777, 1778, 1779, and 1780*, vol. 2. 2nd ed. (published by W. and A. Strachan for G. Nicol and T. Cadell).

Coombe, Rosemary J. 1993. "The Properties of Culture and the Politics of Possessing Identity: Native Claims in the Cultural Appropriation Controversy." *Canadian Journal of Law and Jurisprudence* 6(2): 249–85.

————. 1995a. "Marking Difference in American Commerce: Trademarks and Alterity at Century's Ends." *Canadian Journal of Law and Society* 10: 119–28.

————. 1995b. "The Cultural Life of Things: Anthropological Approaches to Law and Society in Conditions of Globalization." *The American University Journal of International Law and Policy* 10: 791–835.

Cooper, George, and Gavin Daws. 1985. *Land and Power in Hawaii*. Honolulu: Benchmark Books.

Davis, F. James. 1991. *Who Is Black? One Nation's Definition*. University Park, PA: Pennsylvania State University Press.

Daws, Gavan. 1968. *Shoal of Time: A History of the Hawaiian Islands*. Honolulu: University of Hawaii Press.

Day, A. Grove. 1955. *Hawaii and Its People*. New York: Meredith Press.

de Certeau, Michel. 1984. *The Practice of Everyday Life*. Berkeley: University of California Press.

Delgado, Richard. 1989. "Legal Storytelling: Storytelling for Oppositionists and Others: A Plea for Narrative." *Michigan Law Review* 87: 2411–37.

Derrida, Jacques. 1976. *Of Grammatology*. Baltimore, MD: The Johns Hopkins University Press.

————. 1976 (reprint 1986). "Structure, Sign and Play in the Discourse of the Human Sciences." In *Critical Theory since 1965,* edited by H. Adams and L. Searle. Miami: University Presses of Florida.

————. 1978 (reprint 1986). "Differance." In *Critical Theory since 1965,* edited by H. Adams and L. Searle. Miami: University Presses of Florida.

————. 1978. *Writing and Difference*. Chicago: University of Chicago Press.

Desmond, Jane C. 1999. *Staging Tourism: Bodies on Display from Waikiki to Sea World*. Chicago: University of Chicago Press.

Dinell, Tom, Herman S. Doi, Robert H. Horwitz, Michael A. Meriwether, and Allan A. Spitz. 1964. *The Hawaiian Homes Program: 1920–1963, A Concluding Report*. Report 1, Legislative Reference Bureau. Honolulu: University of Hawaii.

Donnelly, Christine, and Lucy Young-Oda. 2000 (March 20). "In Wake of *Rice v. Cayetano,* What Happens Now?" *Honolulu Star-Bulletin,* 1–4.

Dudley, Michael Keoni, and Keoni Kealoha Agard. 1993. *A Call for Hawaiian Sovereignty*. Honolulu: Na Kane O Ka Malo Press.

Duncan, James. 1993. "Sites of Representation: Place, Time, and the Discourse of the Other." In *Place/Culture/Representation,* edited by J. Duncan and D. Ley, 39–56. Routledge: London.

Duncan, James, and David Ley. 1993. "Introduction: Representing the Place of Culture." In *Place/Culture/Representation,* edited by James Duncan and David Ley, 1–21. London: Routledge.

Elkholm-Friedman, Kasja, and Jonathan Friedman. 1994. "Big Business in Small Places." In *Hawai'i: Return to Nationhood,* edited by U. Hasager and J. Friedman, 222–53. IWIGIA (International Work Group for Indigenous Affairs) Document 75. Copenhagen: Nordisk Bogproduktion.

Engel, David M., and M. Munger. 1996. "Rights, Remembrance, and the Reconciliation of Difference." *Law and Society* 3: 7–53.

Evans-Pritchard, D. 1989. "How 'They' See 'Us': Native American Images of Tourists." *Annals of Tourism Research* 16: 89–103.

Ewick, Patricia, and Susan S. Silbey. 1995. "Subversive Stories and Hegemonic Tales: Toward a Sociology of Narrative." *Law and Society Review* 29(2): 197–229.

Fabian, Johannes. 1983. *Time and the Other: How Anthropology Makes Its Object.* New York: Columbia University Press.

Faludi, Susan C. 1991 (September 9). "Broken Promise: How Everyone Got Hawaiians' Homelands Except the Hawaiians." *The Wall Street Journal* 49, A1–A8.

Fanon, Frantz. 1968. *Black Skin, White Masks.* Trans. Charles Lam Markham. London: Paladin.

Fernandez, Y. 1993 (August 29). "Mainland Hawaiians: Out of Sight and Out of Rights." *Honolulu Advertiser,* A1, A6.

Fine, Elizabeth, and Jane Speer. 1985. "Tour Guide Performances as Sight Sacralization." *Annals of Tourism Research* 12: 73–98.

———. 1992. *Performance, Culture, and Identity.* New York: Praeger.

Fiske, John. 1987. *Television Culture.* London: Methuen.

———. 1989a. *Understanding Popular Culture.* Boston: Unwin Hyman.

———. 1989b. *Reading the Popular.* Boston: Unwin Hyman.

———. 1993. *Power Plays, Power Works.* New York and London: Verso.

Fitzpatrick, Gary L. 1986. *The Early Mapping of Hawai'i.* Honolulu: Editions Limited.

Foucault, Michel. 1978. *The History of Sexuality.* New York: Pantheon.

———. 1979. *Discipline and Punishment: Birth of the Prison.* New York: Vintage Books.

Fuchs, Lawrence. 1961. *Hawai'i Pono: A Social History.* New York: Harcourt, Brace and World.

Fujikane, Candace. 1994. "Between Nationalisms: Hawaii's Local Nation and Its Troubled Racial Paradise." *Critical Mass: A Journal of Asian American Cultural Criticism* 1(2): 23–57.

Fullard-Leo, Betty. 1993. "The Movement for Hawaiian Independence." *Aloha* 16: 18–25.

Glauberman, S. 1993. "Onipa'a Rites Kindle Warmth and Bitterness." *Honolulu Advertiser,* A1–A6.

Goldberg, Carey. 1996 (July 23). "Native Hawaiians Vote in Ethnic Referendum." *The New York Times,* 1–3.

Goldberg, David Theo. 1993. *Racist Culture: Philosophy and the Politics of Meaning.* Oxford: Blackwell.

———. 1994. *Multiculturalism: A Critical Reader.* Oxford: Blackwell.

———. 1997. "Taking Stock: Counting by Race." In *Racial Subjects: Writing on Race in America,* edited by D. T. Goldberg, 27–58. New York: Routledge.

Gordon, Avery F., and Christopher Newfield. 1996. *Mapping Multiculturalism.* Minneapolis: University of Minnesota Press.

Gramsci, Antonio. 1971. *Selections From the Prison Notebooks,* edited and translated by Q. Hoare and J. Nowell Smith. New York: International Publishers.

Grant, G., and D. Ogawa. 1993. "Living Proof: Is Hawai'i the Answer?" In *The Annals of the American Academy of Political and Social Science (Interminority Affairs in the U.S.: Pluralism at the Crossroads),* edited by P. I. Rose, 137–54.

Grant, Glen. 1996. *Obake Files: Ghostly Encounters in Supernatural Hawai'i.* Honolulu: Mutual Publishing.

Grossberg, Lawrence. 1992. *We Gotta Get Out of This Place: Popular Conservatism and Postmodern Culture.* New York: Routledge.

———. 1996a. "History, Politics and Postmodernism: Stuart Hall and Cultural Studies." In *Stuart Hall: Critical Dialogues in Cultural Studies,* edited by D. Morley and K. Chen, 151–73. London: Routledge.

———. 1996b. "Identity and Cultural Studies: Is That All There Is?" In *Questions of Cultural Identity,* edited by S. Hall and P. du Gay, 87–107. London: Sage.

———. 1997. *Bringing It All Back Home: Essays on Cultural Studies.* Durham: Duke University Press.

Hale, S. 1993 (March 24). "Aloha No More: Native Hawaiians Plead Their Case in San Francisco." *San Francisco Weekly,* 10.

Hall, Lisa Kahaleole Chang, and J. Kēhaulani Kauanui. 1996. "Same Sex Sexuality in Pacific Literature." In *Asian American Sexualities,* edited by R. Leong, 113–18. New York and London: Routledge.

Hall, Stuart. 1977. "Rethinking the Base and Superstructure Metaphor." In *Papers on Class, Hegemony, and Party,* edited by J. Bloomfield, 43–72. London: Lawrence and Wishart.

———. 1979. "Race, Articulation and Societies Structured in Dominance." In UNESCO, *Sociological Theories: Race and Colonialism,* 305–45. Paris: UNESCO.

———. 1980a. "Encoding, Decoding." In *Culture, Media, Language,* edited by S. Hall, D. Hobson, A. Lowe, and P. Willis, 128–39. London: Hutchinson.

———. 1980b. "Cultural Studies: Two Paradigms." *Media, Culture, and Society* 2(1): 57–72.

———. 1983. "The Problem of Ideology: Marxism without Guarantees." In *Marx 100 Years On,* edited by B. Matthers, 57–85. London: Lawrence and Wishart.

———. 1985. "Signification, Representation, Ideology: Althusser and the Post-structuralist Debates." *Critical Studies in Mass Communication* 2(2): 91–114.

———. 1986a. "Gramsci's Relevance for the Study of Race and Ethnicity." *Journal of Communication Inquiry* 10(2): 5–27.

———. 1986b. "On Postmodernism and Articulation: An Interview with Stuart Hall." *Journal of Communication Inquiry* 10(2): 45–60.

———. 1989. "Ideology and Communication Theory." In *Rethinking Communication, 1, Paradigm Issues,* edited by B. Dervin, L. Grossberg, B. J. O-Keefe, and E. Wartella, 40–52. Newbury Park, CA: Sage.

———. 1991. "The Local and the Global: Globalization and Ethnicity." In *Culture, Globalization, and the World-System,* edited by A. King, 19–40. Binghamton: Department of Art and Art History, State University of New York.

———. 1992. "Cultural Studies and Its Theoretical Legacies." In *Cultural Studies,* edited by L. Grossberg, C. Nelson, and P. Treichler, 277–94. New York: Routledge.

———. 1996. "Introduction: Who Needs 'Identity'?" In *Questions of Cultural Identity,* edited by S. Hall and P. du Gay, 1–17. London: Sage.

Halualani, Rona Tamiko. 1997. "Centrality and Intersectionality: Mapping the "Space"/"Place" of Hawaiian Community." Paper presented at the annual meeting of the National Communication Association, Chicago, IL.

———. 1998. *Communicatively Signifying Identity Positions by, for, and in the Name of Hawaiians: A Cultural Studies Project.* Unpublished doctoral dissertation. Phoenix, Arizona State University.

Han, Ju Hui "Judy," and J. Kēhaulani Kauanui. 1993. "'Asian Pacific Islander': Issues of Representation and Responsibility." *Asian American Women's Journal: Moving the Mountains* 1: 24–25.

Hansen, Diana. 1971. *The Homestead Papers: A Critical Analysis of the Management of the Department of Hawaiian Home Lands.* Honolulu: State of Hawaii.

Harley, J. B. 1988. "Maps, Knowledge, and Power." In *The Iconography of Landscape: Essays on the Symbolic Representation, Design and Use of Past Environments,* edited by D. Cosgrove and S. Daniels. Cambridge, UK: Cambridge University Press.

Hartley, John. 1988. "The Real World of Audiences." *Critical Studies in Mass Communication* 12: 234–38.

Hasager, Ulla, and Jonathan Friedman. 1994. *Hawai'i: Return to Nationhood.* IWIGIA (International Work Group for Indigenous Affairs) Document 75. Copenhagen: Nordisk Bogproduktion.

Hawaii State Archives. *Census Collection, 1840–1896.* Honolulu, Hawai'i.

Hawaii Statutes. 1997. Chapter 5, sections 5–7.5.

Hawaiian Homes Commission Act. 1921. Title 1A.

———. 1921. Title 2, section 201, line 7.

———. 1985, 1989 Supp. 42 Stat. 108, reprinted in 1 *Haw. Rev. Stat.* 167-205.

"Hawaiians-Only Programs at Risk." 2000 (March 1). *San Mateo County Times,* 2.

Hawaiian Sovereignty Elections Council. 1996 (October 16). *Current Update and Alert Bulletin,* 1–5.

Hawaiian Voices on Sovereignty. 1993. *He Alo A He Alo: Face to Face.* Honolulu: Hawai'i Area Office of the American Friends Service Committee.

Hearings before the Committee on Territories. United States Senate. 1921. Sixty-sixth Congress, 3d sess. on H.R. 13500. *A Bill to Amend an "Act to Provide a Government for the Territory of Hawaii." Approved April 30, 1900, as Amended to Establish an Hawaiian Homes Commission, and for Other Purposes.* Washington, DC: GPO.

Hee, Clayton. 1993 (January 17). "Sovereignty: Out of Pride, Not Prejudice." *Honolulu Advertiser,* B1.

Hitch, Thomas. 1992. *Islands in Transition: The Past, Present, and Future of Hawai'i's Economy.* Honolulu: First Hawaiian Bank.

Hymes, Dell. 1962 (1973). "The Ethnography of Speaking." In *Anthropology and Human Behavior,* edited by T. Gladwin and W. C. Sturtevant, 13–53. Washington, DC: Anthropological Society of Washington.

———. 1972. "Models of the Interaction of Language and Social Life." In *Directions in Sociolinguistics: The Ethnography of Communication,* edited by J. Gumpert, 35–71. New York: Holt, Rinehart and Winston.

———. 1975. *Foundations in Sociolinguistics: An Ethnographic Approach.* Philadelphia: University of Pennsylvania Press.

———. 1981. *"In Vain I Tried to Tell You": Essays in Native American Ethnopoetics.* Philadelphia: University of Pennsylvania Press.

'I'i, John Papa. 1959. *Fragments of Hawaiian History,* translated by Mary Kawena Pukui. Honolulu: Bishop Museum Press.

Inskeep, Edward. 1991. *Tourism Planning.* New York: Van Nostrom Reinhold.

Jaimes, Marie Annette. 1992. "Federal Indian Identification Policy: A Usurpation of Indigenous Sovereignty in North America." In *The State of Native America: Genocide, Colonization, and Resistance,* edited by M. A. Jaimes, 123–38. Boston: South End Press.

Jaimes Guerrero, Maria Anna. 1997. "Civil Rights versus Sovereignty: Native American Women in Life and Land Struggles." In *Feminist Genealogies, Colonial Legacies, and Democractic Futures,* edited by E. Jacqui Alexander and C. Mohanty, 103–21. New York: Routledge.

John, M. E. 1996. *Discrepant Dislocations: Feminism, Theory, and Postcolonial Histories.* Berkeley: University of California Press.

Johnson, Richard. 1986–87. "What Is Cultural Studies Anyway?" *Social Text* 16: 38–80.

Kaeppler, Adrienne. 1973. "Polynesian Dance As 'Airplane Art.'" *Dance Research Journal* 8: 71–85.

———. 1992. "*Ali'i and Maka'āinana*: The Representation of Hawaiians in

Museums at Home and Abroad." In *Museums and Communities: The Politics of Public Culture,* edited by I. Karp, C. Mullen Kreamer, and S. D. Lavine, 458–75. Washington, DC: Smithsonian Institution Press.

Kamakau, Samuel M. 1961. *Ruling Chiefs of Hawai'i.* Honolulu: Kamehameha Schools.

Kame'eleihiwa, Lilikalā. 1992. *Native Land and Foreign Desires: Pehea La E Pono Ai?* Honolulu: Bishop Museum Press.

———. 1994. "The Role of American Missionaries in the 1893 Overthrow of the Hawaiian Government: Historical Events, 1820–1893." In *Hawai'i: Return to Nationhood,* edited by U. Hasager, and J. Friedman, 106–19. IWIGIA (International Work Group for Indigenous Affairs) Document 75. Copenhagen: Nordisk Bogproduktion.

Kane, Herb K. 1991. *Voyagers.* Bellevue, WA: Whalesong.

Katriel, Tamar. 1997. *Performing the Past: A Study by Israeli Settlement Museums.* Mahwah, NJ: Lawrence Erlbaum Associates.

Kauanui, J. Kēhaulani. 1999. "Off-Island Hawaiians 'Making' Ourselves at 'Home': A [Gendered] Contradiction in Terms?" *Women's Studies International Forum* 21(6): 681–93.

Kauffman, Bette J. 1992. "Feminist Facts: Interview Strategies and Political Subjects in Ethnography." *Communication Theory* 2: 187–206.

Keaukaha-Panaewa Community Association v. Hawaiian Homes Commission, 588 F.2d 1216 (9th Cir. 1978).

Keaukaha-Panaewa Community Association v. Hawaiian Homes Commission, 739 F.2d 1467 (9th Cir. 1984).

Kelly, Marion. 1956. *Changes in Land Tenure in Hawaii, 1778–1859.* Unpublished master's thesis, University of Hawaii.

———. 1984. Statement. *Hearings on the Report of the Native Hawaiians Study Commission before the Senate Committee on Energy and Natural Resources,* Ninety-Eighth Congress, Second Session 104.

Kilolani Mitchell, Donald D. 1992. *Resource Units in Hawaiian Culture.* Honolulu: Kamehameha Schools Press.

Kondo, Dorrine. 1996. "The Narrative Production of 'Home,' Community, and Political Identity in Asian American Theater." In *Displacement, Diaspora, and Geographies of Identity,* edited by Smadar Lavie and Ted Swedenburg, 97–117. Durham: Duke University Press.

Kotzebue, Otto von. 1821 (1967). *A Voyage of Discovery into the South Sea and Bering's Straits, for the Purpose of Exploring a North-East Passage, Undertaken in the Years 1815–1818.* 3 vols. London: Reprint ed. in 2 vols.

Kristeva, Julia. 1977. *Polylogue.* Paris: Editions du Seuil.

Kuykendall, Ralph S. 1938. *The Hawaiian Kingdom, 1778–1854: Foundation and Transformation.* Honolulu: University of Hawaii.

———. 1953. *The Hawaiian Kingdom, 1854–1874: Twenty Critical Years.* Honolulu: University of Hawaii Press.

————. 1967. *The Hawaiian Kingdom, 1874–1893: The Kalakaua Dynasty.* Honolulu: University of Hawaii Press.

Kuykendall, Ralph S., and A. G. Day. 1961. *Hawaii: A History: From Polynesian Kingdom to American State.* Englewood Cliffs, NJ: Prentice-Hall.

Lacan, Jacques. 1975a. "Seminar XX." In *Feminine Sexuality: Jacques Lacan and the Ecole Freudienne,* edited by J. Mitchell and J. Rose. New York: W. W. Norton.

————. 1975b (reprint 1986). "The Mirror Stage." In *Critical Theory since 1965,* edited by H. Adams and L. Searle. Miami: University Presses of Florida.

————. 1977a (reprint 1986). "The Agency of the Letter in the Unconscious or Reason Since Freud." In *Critical Theory since 1965,* edited by H. Adams and L. Searle. Miami: University Presses of Florida.

————. 1977b. *Ecrits: A Selection.* New York: W. W. Norton.

Laclau, Ernesto. 1977. *Politics and Ideology in Marxist Theory.* London: New Left Books.

Laclau, Ernesto, and Chantal Mouffe. 1985. *Hegemony and Socialist Strategy: Towards a Radical Democratic Politics,* trans. W. Moore and P. Cammack. London: Verso.

Langellier, Kristen M. 1989. "Personal Narratives: Perspectives on Theory and Research." *Text and Performance Quarterly* 9: 243–76.

Lavie, Smadar, and Ted Swedenburg. 1996. "Introduction: Displacement, Diaspora, and Geographies of Identity." In *Displacement, Diaspora, and Geographies of Identity,* edited by S. Lavie and T. Swedenburg. Durham: Duke University Press.

Levy, Neil M. 1975 (July). "Native Hawaiian Land Rights." *California Law Review* 63(4): 848–85.

Lind, Andrew William, 1980. *Hawaii's People.* Honolulu: University Press of Hawaii.

Linnekin, Jocelyn. 1985. *Children of the Land: Exchange and Status in a Hawaiian Community.* New Brunswick, NJ: Rutgers University Press.

————. 1990a. *Sacred Queens and Women of Consequence: Rank, Gender, and Colonialism in the Hawaiian Islands.* Ann Arbor: University of Michigan Press.

————. 1990b. "The Politics of Culture in the Pacific." In *Cultural Identity and Ethnicity in the Pacific,* edited by J. Linnekin and L. Poyer, 149–73. Honolulu: University of Hawaii Press.

————. 1991 (Spring). "Text Bites and the R-Word: The Politics of Representing Scholarship." *Contemporary Pacific* 3(1): 172–77.

————. 1997. "Consuming Cultures: Tourism and the Commoditization of Cultural Identity in the Island Pacific." In *Tourism, Ethnicity, and the State in Asian and Pacific Societies,* edited by M. Picard and R. E. Wood, 215–50. Honolulu: University of Hawaii Press.

Linnekin, Jocelyn, and Lin Poyer. 1990. *Cultural Identity and Ethnicity in the Pacific.* Honolulu: University of Hawaii Press.

Lipsitz, George. 1990. *Time Passages: Collective Memory and American Popular Culture.* Minneapolis: University of Minnesota Press.

Lowe, Lisa. 1996. "Immigration, Citizenship, Racialization: Asian American Critique." In *Immigrant Acts: On Asian American Cultural Politics,* edited by L. Lowe, 1–36. Durham: Duke University Press.

Lukács, Georg. 1977. "Realism in the Balance." In *Aesthetics and Politics,* edited by E. Bloch et al., 28–59. London: New Left Books.

Ma, Kenneth. 1999 (April 30). "Controversial Bill to Waive Natives' Tuition Moves Through Hawaiian Legislature." *The Chronicle of Higher Education,* A36.

MacCannell, Dean. 1973. "Staged Authenticity: On Arrangements of Social Space in Tourist Settings." *American Journal of Sociology* 79(3): 589–603.

———. 1984. "Reconstructed Ethnicity: Tourism and Cultural Identity in Third World Communities." *Annals of Tourism Research* 11: 375–91.

———. 1989. *The Tourist: A New Theory of the Leisure Class.* New York: Schocken Books.

———. 1992a. *Empty Meeting Grounds: The Tourist Papers.* London: Routledge.

———. 1992b. "Ex-Primitive and Postmodern: Cannibalism Today." In *Empty Meeting Grounds: The Tourist Papers,* edited by Dean MacCannell, 18–73. London: Routledge.

MacKenzie, Melody Kapilialoha. 1991. *Native Hawaiian Rights Handbook.* Honolulu: Native Hawaiian Legal Corporation and Office of Hawaiian Affairs.

———. 1993 (February). "1893–1993: Overthrow, Annexation, and Sovereignty." *Hawaii Bar Journal*: 8–11.

Madison, D. Soyini. 1993. "That Was My Occupation: Oral Narrative, Performance, and Black Feminist Thought." *Text and Performance Quarterly* 13(3): 213–32.

Malo, David. 1951. *Hawaiian Antiquities,* translated by Dr. Nathaniel B. Emerson in 1898. Honolulu: Bishop Museum Press.

Marx, Karl. 1973. *Grundrisse,* translated by Martin Nicolaus. New York: Penguin.

Matsuda, Mari. 1987. "Looking to the Bottom: Critical Legal Studies and Reparations." *Harvard Civil Rights-Civil Liberties Law Review* 22: 300–26.

———. 1996. *Where Is Your Body?: And Other Essays on Race, Gender, and the Law.* Boston: Beacon Press.

McClintock, Anne. 1995. *Imperial Leather: Race, Gender and Sexuality in the Colonial Context.* New York: Routledge.

McGrane, B. 1989. *Beyond Anthropology: Society and the Other.* New York: Columbia University Press.

Mercer, Kobena. 1994. "'1968': Periodizing Politics and Identity." In *Welcome to the Jungle: New Positions in Black Cultural Studies,* edited by K. Mercer, 287–308. New York: Routledge.

More, Sir Thomas. 1516. *Utopia.* London: M. P.

Mouffe, Chantal. 1981. "Hegemony and Ideology in Gramsci." In *Culture, Ideology and Social Process,* edited by T. Bennett, G. Martin, C. Mercer, and J. Woolacott. London: Open University.

Mullins, Joseph G. 1978. *Hawaiian Journey.* Honolulu: Mutual Publishing Company.

Mumby, Dennis. 1993. *Narrative and Social Control.* Thousand Oaks, CA: Sage.

Murakami, Alan. 1991. "The Hawaiian Homes Commission Act." In *Native Hawaiian Rights Handbook,* edited by M. MacKenzie, 43–76. Honolulu: Native Hawaiian Legal Corporation and Office of Hawaiian Affairs.

Nakao, Annie. 1993 (June 20). "Sovereign Sisters." *San Francisco Examiner,* 12–17.

Nakashima, E. 1996 (August 27). "Native Hawaiians Consider Asking for Their Islands Back: 100-Year-Old Cause Spurs Sovereignty Vote." *Washington Post,* A01.

Na Maka O Ka ʻĀina. 1993. *Act of War* [film]. Honolulu: Na Maka O Ka ʻĀina.

"Native Hawaiian Population Shows Steady Annual Growth." 2000 (March 20). *Honolulu Star Bulletin* (Special Project), 4.

Native Hawaiian Study Commission Report. 1983 (June 23). *Report on the Culture, Needs, and Concerns of Native Hawaiians,* vol. 11. Honolulu: Native Hawaiian Study Commission.

Novak, V. 1989. "Hawaiʻi's Dirty Secret." *Common Cause* (November/December): 11–16.

Obeyesekere, Gannath. 1992. *The Apotheosis of Captain Cook: European Mythmaking in the Pacific.* Princeton, NJ: Princeton University Press.

Office of Hawaiian Affairs. 1996. *Native Hawaiian Data Book.* Honolulu: Office of Hawaiian Affairs Research Study.

Ogawa, D. M. 1981. "Dialogue: What Is Local?" *Hawaiʻi Committee for the Humanities News* 2(1): 1, 7.

Okamura, Jonathan Y. 1994. "Why There Are No Asian Americans in Hawaiʻi: The Continuing Significance of Local Identity." *Social Process in Hawaiʻi* 35: 161–78.

———. 1996. "The Illusion of Paradise: Privileging Multiculturalism in Hawaiʻi." In *Making Majorities: Comparing the Nation in Japan, China, Korea, Fiji, Malaysia, Turkey, and the United States,* edited by D. C. Gladney, 1–30. Palo Alto, CA: Stanford University Press.

Okihiro, Gary Y. 1991. *Cane Fires: The Anti-Japanese Movement in Hawaii, 1865–1945.* Philadelphia: Temple University Press.

Omi, Michael, and Howard Winant. 1994. "The Racial State." In *Racial Formation in the United States: From the 1960s to the 1990s,* edited by Michael Omi and Howard Winant, 77–91. New York: Routledge.

Ozawa, Ryan K. 1996 (September 9). "Sovereignty Vote Result Delayed." *The Net of Light: Hawai'i News*, 1–2.

Parker, Linda S. 1989. *Native American Estate: The Struggle over Indian and Hawaiian Lands*. Honolulu: University of Hawaii Press.

Polynesian newspaper. 1848 (July 8). Honolulu, Hawai'i.

Popular Memory Group. 1982. "Popular Memory: Theory, Politics, Method." In *Making Histories: Studies in History-Writing and Politics*, edited by R. Johnson, G. McLennan, B. Schwarz, and D. Sutton, 205–52. London: Hutchinson.

Porteus, Stanley. 1945. *Calabashes and Kings: An Introduction to Hawaii*. Palo Alto, CA: Pacific Books.

Pratt, Mary Louise. 1992. *Imperial Eyes: Travel Writing and Transculturation*. New York: Routledge.

Pukui, Mary Kawena, and S. H. Elbert. 1986. *Hawaiian Dictionary*. Honolulu: University of Hawaii Press.

Pukui, Mary Kawena, E. W. Haertig, and Catherine A. Lee. 1972. *Nana I Ke Kumu (Look to the Source)*. Honolulu: Hui Hanai.

Rehabilitation of Native Hawaiians: Report to Accompany H.R. 13500. 1920. Sixty-sixth Congress House of Representatives, 2d sess. House Report no. 839.

Reissman, Catherine. 1987. "When Gender Is Not Enough: Women Interviewing Women." *Gender and Society* 2(1): 172–207.

Revised Laws of Hawaii. 1925.

Rosaldo, Renato. 1993. *Culture and Truth: The Remaking of Social Analysis*. Boston: Beacon Press.

Sahlins, Marshall. 1981. *Historical Metaphors and Mythical Realities: Structure in the Early History of the Sandwich Islands Kingdom*. Ann Arbor: University of Michigan Press.

———. 1985. *Islands of History*. Chicago: University of Chicago Press.

———. 1995. *How "Natives" Think: about Captain Cook, for Example*. Chicago: University of Chicago Press.

Saussure, Ferdinand de. 1966. *Course in General Linguistics*. New York: McGraw Hill.

"73 Percent Say Yes to Hawaiian Sovereignty: Supporters Say the Plebiscite Is an Important Step toward a Native Hawaiian Government." 1996 (September 12). *Honolulu Star-Bulletin*, A1.

Slack, Jennifer Daryl. 1996. "The Theory and Method of Articulation in Cultural Studies." In *Stuart Hall: Critical Dialogues in Cultural Studies*, edited by D. Morley and K. H. Chen, 112–27. London: Routledge.

Spradley, James P. 1979. *The Ethnographic Interview*. Fort Worth: Harcourt Brace Jovanovich College Publishers.

Stannard, David E. 1989. *Before the Horror: The Population of Hawai'i on the Eve of Western Contact*. Honolulu: Social Science Research Institute, University of Hawaii.

State of Hawaii, Department of Business, Economic Development and Tourism (DBEDT). 1995. *The State of Hawaii Data Book 1995: A Statistical Abstract.* Honolulu: DBEDT.

———. 1996a (First Quarter). *Hawaii Tourism in Transition: A Quarterly Report from the Department of Business, Economic Development, and Tourism.* Honolulu: DBEDT.

———. 1996b (First Quarter). *The Economic Impact of Tourism in Hawaii: A Quarterly Report from the Department of Business, Economic Development, and Tourism.* Honolulu: DBEDT.

Storey, John. 1996. *What Is Cultural Studies: A Reader.* London: Arnold.

Sumida, Stephen. 1991. *And the View from the Shore: Literary Traditions of Hawai'i.* Seattle: University of Washington Press.

Taussig, Michael. 1997. *The Magic of the State.* New York: Routledge.

Terdiman, R. 1985. "Deconstructing Memory: On Representing the Past and Theorizing Culture in France since the Revolution." *Diacritics* 15: 14, 19.

Thompson, E. P. 1963. *The Making of the English Working Class.* New York: Vintage.

Thurston, Lorrin. 1904. *The Fundamental Law of Hawaii 3.* Honolulu: Bryman.

Tom, J. 1996 (July 19). "Lawsuit Won't Stop Plebiscite, Council Says." *Honolulu Star Bulletin,* A2.

Trask, Haunani Kay. 1991. "Natives and Anthropologists: The Colonial Struggle." *Contemporary Pacific* 3.1 (Spring): 159–67.

———, (ed.). 1993a. *From a Native Daughter: Colonialism and Sovereignty in Hawai'i.* Monroe, ME: Common Courage Press.

———. 1993b. "Coalitions between Natives and Non-Natives." In *From a Native Daughter: Colonialism and Sovereignty in Hawai'i,* edited by H. K. Trask. Monroe, ME: Common Courage Press.

———. 1993c. "Neocolonialism and Indigenous Structures." In *From a Native Daughter: Colonialism and Sovereignty in Hawai'i,* edited by H. K. Trask, 131–43. Monroe, ME: Common Courage Press.

———. 1994. "*Kupa'a 'Aina*: Native Hawaiian Nationalism in Hawai'i." In *Hawai'i: Return to Nationhood,* edited by U. Hasager and J. Friedman, 15–33. IWIGIA (International Work Group for Indigenous Affairs) Document 75. Copenhagen: Nordisk Bogproduktion.

Trask, Mililani B. 1992. "The Blood Quantum Issue." Ka Lāhui Hawai'i. Unpublished paper.

———. 1993. "An Interview with Mililani Trask." In *He Alo A He Alo—Hawaiian Voices on Sovereignty: Face to Face,* edited by Hawaiian Voices on Sovereignty, 113–24. Honolulu: Hawai'i Area Office of the American Friends Service Committee.

Tregaskis, Moana. 1996. *Hawai'i.* Oakland, CA: Fodor's.

Vancouver, C. G. 1798. *A Voyage of Discovery to the North Pacific Ocean and*

Round the World . . . in the Years 1790, 1791, 1792, 1793, 1794, and 1795. 3 vols. London.

Van Maanen, John. 1988. *Tales of the Field: On Writing Ethnography.* Chicago: University of Chicago Press.

Vause, Marilyn M. 1962. *The Hawaiian Homes Commission Act, History and Analysis.* Unpublished master's thesis, University of Hawaii.

Visweswaran, Kamala. 1988. "Defining Feminist Ethnography." *Inscriptions: Feminism and the Critique of Colonial Discourse* 3–4: 26–44.

Waihee, John. 1993 (January 17). "Sovereignty." Honolulu Advertiser, B1.

"What Inheritance for Hawaiians?" 1997 (May). *Ka Wai Ola O OHA* 14(5): 5.

White, Hayden. 1980. "The Value of Narrativity in the Representation of Reality." *Critical Inquiry* 7: 5–27.

Williams, R. 1966. *Culture and Society 1780–1950.* London: Penguin. First published in 1958.

———. 1975. *The Long Revolution.* London: Penguin. First published in 1961.

Wilson, Robert. 2000. *Reimagining the American Pacific.* Durham: Duke University Press.

Wood, Denis. 1992. *The Power of Maps.* New York: Guilford Press.

Wood, Houston. 1999. *Displacing Natives: The Rhetorical Production of Hawai'i.* Lanham, MD: Rowman and Littlefield Publishers.

Wright, Paul. 1979. *Residents Leave Paradise: A Study of Outmigration from Hawaii to the Mainland.* Unpublished doctoral dissertation. Honolulu, University of Hawaii.

———. 1983. "Ethnic Difference in the Outmigration of Local Born Residents from Hawaii." *Social Processes in Hawaii* 30: 731.

Yamamoto, Eric. 1979. "The Significance of Local." *Social Process in Hawaii* 27: 101–15.

———. 1999. *Interracial Justice: Conflict and Reconciliation in Post-Civil Rights America.* New York: New York University Press.

Yamamoto, Eric. K., Moses Haia, and Denise Kalama. 1994. "Courts and the Cultural Performance: Native Hawaiians' Uncertain Federal and State Law Rights to Sue." *University of Hawaii Law Review* 16(1): 1–83.

Yaukey, John. 2000 (February 24). "Hawaiians Lose Key Policymaking Right." *Honolulu Advertiser,* 1–5.

Young, Iris Marion. 1990. "The Ideal of Community and the Politics of Difference." In *Feminism/Postmodernism,* edited by L. J. Nicholson, 300–23. New York: Routledge.

Zerubavel, Y. 1995. *Recovered Roots: Collective Memory and the Making of Israeli National Tradition.* Chicago: University of Chicago Press.

Index

Rona Tamiko Halualani is assistant professor of communication studies at San José State University. Her research focuses on cultural identity, intercultural communication contact and race relations, cultural studies ethnography and speaking practices, diasporic formation and politics, and transnational circuits of capital and globalization.